This new book explains all you need to know about industrial psychology to help you in your business or industry. The author shows how to handle personnel selection and placement problems, plus the newer areas of man-machine systems and motivation research. The treatment of industrial psychology is organized around three parties to industrial activity: workers, managers, and consumers.

Industrial Psychology

THE IRWIN SERIES IN MANAGEMENT

Consulting Editor JOHN F. MEE *Indiana University*

BOWMAN & FETTER (Editors) *Analyses of Industrial Operations*

MOORE *Manufacturing Management* Third Edition

NIEBEL *Motion and Time Study* Third Edition

ROSCOE *Organization for Production* Third Edition

JUCIUS *Personnel Management* Fifth Edition

CRUICKSHANK & DAVIS *Cases in Management* Third Edition

FILIPETTI *Industrial Management in Transition* Revised Edition

SPRIEGEL & MYERS (Editors) *The Writings of the Gilbreths*

TERRY *Principles of Management* Third Edition

VORIS *Production Control: Text and Cases* Revised Edition

SIMONDS & GRIMALDI *Safety Management: Accident Cost and Control*

JONES *Executive Decision Making* Revised Edition

NIEBEL & BALDWIN *Designing for Production* Revised Edition

PATTON & LITTLEFIELD *Job Evaluation: Text and Cases* Revised Edition

SHULL & DELBECQ (Editors) *Selected Readings in Management: Extensions and Modification* Second Series

BRENNAN *Wage Administration: Plans, Practices, and Principles* Revised Edition

LAITALA *Engineering and Organization*

JUCIUS & SCHLENDER *Elements of Managerial Action*

HANEY *Communication: Patterns and Incidents*

JOHNSON *Personnel and Industrial Relations*

DEPHILLIPS, BERLINER, & CRIBBIN *Management of Training Programs*

MORRIS *Engineering Economy: The Analysis of Management Decisions*

THAYER *Administrative Communication*

ROSCOE *Project Economy*

EELLS & WALTON *Conceptual Foundations of Business*

HOUSTON *Manager Development: Principles and Perspectives*

SEIMER *Cases in Industrial Management*

REED *Plant Layout: Factors, Principles, and Techniques*

AMMER *Materials Management*

BROOM *Production Management*

SCOTT *Human Relations in Management: A Behavioral Science Approach*

SIEGEL *Industrial Psychology*

TIMMS *The Production Function in Business: Fundamentals and Analysis for Management*

NADLER *Work Design*

INDUSTRIAL PSYCHOLOGY

Laurence Siegel, Ph.D.

Professor of Psychology

Director, Institutional Research Service

Miami University

1962

RICHARD D. IRWIN, INC.

HOMEWOOD, ILLINOIS

To CORKY,
CARRIE,
and JACK

Preface

This book is intended primarily for students enrolled in courses variously designated *Business Psychology* or *Industrial Psychology*. I am hopeful also that it will prove useful to persons functioning in the field as personnel managers, training directors, etc. My intention has been to provide an overview of industrial psychology broadly conceived. Instead of restricting the scope to personnel problems or management problems, I have organized the content about the three major parties to industrial activity: workers, managers, and consumers.

A background in Introductory Psychology will probably prove helpful to the reader but is not indispensable. While preparing the manuscript I have attempted to keep in mind the kind of student likely to enroll in the course. For a few students, this course will be a first contact with an offering in psychology; most will have had a prior course in Introductory Psychology. It has been my experience that both groups benefit when certain "bridges" between the content regarded as *general* psychology and that as *industrial* psychology are provided.

Such bridges appear at various points in the text: the viewpoint and methods of present-day psychology are presented in the first chapters; certain principles of measurement are discussed in the chapter on testing; pertinent concepts of learning are presented in the training chapter; a discussion of motivation precedes the chapters dealing with job satisfaction and morale. These bridges are relatively brief and are not intended to duplicate the content of an Introductory Psychology course. Rather, they were designed to facilitate the transition from discussions of behavior in general to a discussion of industrial behavior.

I have had the frustrating feeling as teacher and author that the arbitrary compartmentalization of knowledge into topics or chapters is too often reflected in a genuine compartmentalization by the student. He sometimes considers a topic as if it were a discrete element unrelated to what has preceded it, what will follow it, or to any macrocosmic view of the subject. Therefore, I have introduced him in the first chapter to an overview of the book and to the S–I–R concept as an organizing notion. I return to the latter often and deliberately throughout the succeeding chapters.

You will observe that I have departed from the procedure followed by the journals of the American Psychological Association whereby references are ordinarily keyed by the investigator's name. This departure was born of the conviction that professional publication practices are not always suitable for textbooks. In an attempt to provide the student with a smooth flow of content, I have followed the general practice of minimizing the use of investigator's names in the body of the text. This practice has been extended to the reference notations which are keyed by footnote superscript rather than by author's name.

I am under no delusion that this book will satisfy all psychologists with respect to breadth of coverage, depth of treatment or topical emphasis. The instructor will sometimes undoubtedly wish I had expanded the treatment of this issue and reduced the treatment of that issue, included this topic and excluded that one. However, I hopefully anticipate that the book will contribute effectively to the instructional partnership formed by teacher and author. A textbook, after all, is not a course. It may serve as the skeleton for a course and even provide some of the muscle for it; but the life blood of a subject is infused into it by the teacher.

I am indebted to many more persons than can be listed here for assistance in preparing and revising the original manuscript. Several students exposed to preliminary versions have made valuable suggestions. Likewise a number of friends have read and commented upon individual chapters.

I must acknowledge particularly the contributions made by a few persons who have generously invested a tremendous amount of time and effort during the manuscript's preparation:

Mrs. Mary Kay Casebere's assistance while typing the manuscript was considerable. She called to my attention certain matters of style, and constantly monitored format and internal consistency.

Dr. Lila Corkland Siegel has had to fill the doubly difficult role of critical reader for the entire manuscript, for which she is qualified by training, and ego-supporter in the face of her own critique as well as that offered by others, for which she is qualified by her marriage to me. I am grateful to her beyond words on both counts.

Dr. Douglas H. Fryer started reviewing the manuscript but passed away before he could finish. His contribution was tangible for the chapters he read, and one of the spirit for the chapters he did not get to see. My experiences as his student remain forever with me.

The manuscript, or a large portion of it, was read and evaluated by Dr. John F. Mee, Indiana University; Dr. St. Clair A. Switzer, Miami University; Professor Marvin D. Dunnette, University of Minnesota; and Professor A. C. MacKinney, Iowa State University.

All of these persons made thought-provoking comments and all will recognize, in the finished work, some evidence that certain of their suggestions were implemented. However I hasten to add that, in the final analysis, the responsibility for the book as you see it is mine.

LAURENCE SIEGEL

March, 1962
Oxford, Ohio

Foreword to the Student

You are undoubtedly approaching this subject matter with certain expectations. Perhaps you plan a career in sales and would like to learn about the "psychologist's-eye view" of the potential purchaser of soap or diesel equipment or breadboxes. You may be planning a career in industrial management and seeking "rules" for increasing production without increasing costs. Or you may anticipate some kind of work in the broad area of personnel and would like, therefore, to learn something about "getting along with people." Maybe you haven't yet decided upon a vocation and anticipate that this book will familiarize you with career opportunities and offer guidance that may be of assistance in making your occupational choice. In view of the disparity in expectations of individual readers, it will be useful at the outset to clarify the objectives of this book and to provide an overview of its contents.

Let us begin with two basic premises. In the first place, psychology is concerned with the behavior of organisms. Secondly, these organisms are systematically studied by psychologists using techniques that are *scientific* in the same sense that techniques of investigation in physics or chemistry are scientific. Organisms are, to be sure, extremely complicated. Unlike atoms of hydrogen, people are not identical to each other. There is considerable variation in behavior from person to person, and the behavior of a single individual may vary from one occasion to another. The unique individuality and personal dignity of every human being is prized above all else in a democratic society. People are not like interchangeable units on a piece of mechanical equipment. The fact that organisms, and most particularly human beings, are complex and variable does not, however, imply that psychology must perforce be unscientific. The essence of science is not *what* it studies but the *methods* by which it studies.

If psychology is the scientific study of behavior, industrial psychology is simply the scientific study of behavior as it occurs in business and industry. We may conveniently class the behaving organisms in this setting into three groups: workers, management, and consumers. This classification does not imply that each of these groups is homogeneous. Workers differ, for example, with respect to occupational level, age, sex, personal aspirations, physical health, home environment, and many other factors. Management and consumers may be similarly classified into subgroups that are psychologically important. This broad classification, *workers, management, consumers,* forms the backbone of the organization of the book.

You will undoubtedly be somewhat disappointed by the exclusion of certain topics and perhaps you will be surprised by the inclusion of certain others. You may be dismayed by the fact that nowhere in the book is there a list of "rules" for getting along with people or for impressing a recruitment interviewer. It is important to recognize at the outset that the book focuses upon human relationships in business and industry and not upon oversimplified prescriptions for particular sets of circumstances.

You will encounter discussions of technique from time to time in your reading. You will, for example, learn something about the procedures involved in the construction of psychological tests, development of attitude surveys, and the conduct of market research. These techniques are not described for the purpose of training you to do the work of an industrial psychologist. Rather they are presented because of the conviction that the proper interpretation of research findings is dependent upon an understanding of the ways in which research is conducted. A degree of familiarity with the techniques employed by the industrial psychologist will better enable you to evaluate the worth of his contribution to industry and will highlight both the specific areas in which extensive knowledge is now available and the areas in which present knowledge is, at best, incomplete.

L. S.

Table of Contents

III. WORKER EFFICIENCY

I.

Introduction

1. *Scope of Industrial Psychology*
2. *How the Industrial Psychologist Works*

The psychologist working in an industrial setting may find himself called upon, in the course of a single day, to administer tests, confer with supervisors, attend a training conference, design an experiment to test the effectiveness of a new advertising campaign, perform the statistical analysis of questionnaire data from a morale survey, and counsel an employee who is experiencing some kind of personal difficulty. This list of functions is by no means exhaustive; it represents just a sample of the industrial psychologist's sphere of activity.

The chapters in this section are designed to provide a base for subsequent discussions. These chapters will introduce you to the field of industrial psychology by indicating something of the scope of psychological services available to business and industry, the training and employment of industrial psychologists, and the research methods employed by them. In short, the two chapters which ensue focus upon what the industrial psychologist does and how he goes about doing it.

Scope of Industrial Psychology

1
A conceptualization about the role of the psychologist in business and industry presupposes some knowledge of the activities of psychologists in general. Regardless of his sphere of operation, be it a clinic, school, research organization, government agency, or industry, the psychologist represents a scientific discipline. Thus, it is to the broad problem of defining the subject matter of psychology that we will first address ourselves.

THE SUBJECT MATTER OF PSYCHOLOGY

Misconceptions about psychologists and the phenomena they study are still quite prevalent even among otherwise well-informed persons. These misconceptions take several different forms. A few persons, for example, still regard psychologists with what amounts almost to reverent mysticism. They may be afraid to look the psychologist in the eye for fear that they will fall under the spell of some mysterious power emanating from his eyes. They may be convinced that he can "read" their thoughts even before these thoughts are uttered. The psychologist is, to these people, a combination of demigod and seer. He is almost like the image of the all-powerful, all-knowing visitor from another planet conjured up by an imaginative science fiction writer. Fortunately, such a naive conception about psychologists is relatively rare.

However, at the other extreme, a sizable number of persons regard psychology with disdain and its practitioner as a fraud. "Psychology" is, for them, a fancy way of spelling "common sense." For justification of their point of view, they point to the endless series of "psychological" articles appearing in newspapers, magazines, and Sunday supplements offering prescriptions for child care, advice to the lovelorn and helpful hints for happy homes. One writer maintains that children must never be spanked because in so doing the parent descends to the child's level; another maintains that spanking itself may be beneficial because it establishes the parent as an authoritarian figure. Ima Dudd advises her female readers to take an active interest in their husbands' activities and hobbies in order to better experience "togetherness"; Ura Fule, on the other hand, advises wives not to pry into their husbands' activities lest the husband resent the invasion of his sense of privacy. The more he reads such articles, the more confused the reader becomes until he is forced to conclude that it's all just so much hogwash. The problem arises, of course, because most of these articles are based upon idle speculation rather than upon scientific evidence. They are, in most cases, written by professional writers capitalizing upon man's desire to understand himself.

Conceptions about psychology held by most of the public fall within the vast middle ground between these two extreme viewpoints. Most persons feel that psychology involves something more than common sense, although they are not always quite certain what psychologists do. Such persons have a rather hazy notion that psychologists study "mental functions" like intelligence, thinking, and attitudes.

Although fundamentally correct, this notion is a gross oversimplification of the psychologist's activities. We must recognize at the outset that such an important psychological concept as "attitude" is not directly observable. A person's attitudes cannot be seen or bottled for laboratory analysis. They are not immediately apparent to anyone else, even though this someone else may be a psychologist.

We become aware of the existence and operation of such factors by inference. We judge from something a person does or says that he feels and thinks in certain ways. Thus, when dealing with psychological phenomena, we must begin with something observable. However, even when our observations are carefully made we may arrive at a number of alternative inferences or explanations, each of which seems reasonable or tenable. These in turn must be further studied in order to reject all but the most promising of them. The psychologist's orientation throughout the process of observation, inference, and subsequent test of the inference, is one of rigorous scientific verification.

To illustrate, an industrial psychologist might hypothesize from an employee's record of abnormal absence from work that he may be dissatisfied with the job for some reason, or that he may be experiencing personal difficulties in his home environment, or that the work itself may be either too demanding or too unstimulating for his intellectual abilities. This by no means exhausts the list of possible explanations, but it will serve for the present illustration. These hypotheses, once made, would have to be examined and sifted until the most likely ones are isolated for the particular case in question, and remedial steps would follow.

The observable factor studied by the psychologist in the instance noted above is the employee's *behavior*. First, attention is focused upon this particular employee because of undesirable industrial behavior: that is, high rate of absence and sickness reports. The psychologist formulates possible explanations and verifies or discards each by noting other behavioral indices. The suspicion of a discrepancy between level of ability and level of required job performance may be checked by administering intelligence and aptitude tests. Such tests provide a sample of the employee's behavior in a controlled setting designed to determine the level of his abilities. The employee may be interviewed and his responses evaluated with respect to job attitudes and personal adjustment. Supervisors or fellow workers may be called upon to record their observations of the employee's behavior on the job.

Human behavior was not always perceived as the key to understanding psychological processes. Historically, there were many byways in the development of a scientific understanding of psychological phenomena. Unfortunately, remnants of these *pseudo*psychological approaches still persist to a certain extent.

Pseudopsychology

One of the erroneous approaches to understanding man's behavior, *Physiognomy*, maintained that character was revealed through physical signs. People with large ears were "generous" and persons with receding chins were "submissive." Generalizations like these were based upon casual observations of specific individuals with large ears who were indeed generous and of individuals with receding chins who were rather submissive. It has undoubtedly occurred to you that the error involved in drawing such gross generalizations is that they are based upon an inadequate sampling of observations. A careful compilation of personal characteristics of large-eared people would reveal that a few are indeed very generous. But about an equal number would be classified as truly miserly and most would fall somewhere between these two extremes. The same general distribution of personal characteristics may be offered in refutation of every relationship between physical and personal characteristics hypothesized by physiognomists.

Do not, however, be too hasty in discarding psysiognomy as something that belongs entirely to the past. Even at present, people who are reasonably sophisticated fall prey to this kind of erroneous thinking. Have you ever heard or read a reference to the "criminal type"? Of course you have! An imaginative newspaper reporter may employ such adjectives as "shifty-eyed," "heavy-browed," and "snarling" when describing the physical appearance of a captured criminal, implying that he fits the typical picture of a "mad-dog killer." The truth of the matter is that even trained criminologists cannot correctly distinguish between criminals and noncriminals with greater than chance accuracy simply from looking at photographs.

Let us bring the matter of physiognomy a little closer to home. Imagine yourself about to be interviewed for a job. What advice have you heard regarding your behavior during such an interview? Probably the one "rule" for interview behavior more often stated than any other is to look the interviewer squarely in the eye. Many employers still subscribe to the unfounded belief than an honest person with nothing to hide will not avoid visual contact. And untrained interviewers may reject a thoroughly qualified applicant simply because the interviewee finds it difficult to look directly at the interviewer. The use of this as a sign that the applicant is untrustworthy is not good psychology. It is not even good common sense! It is, rather, a remnant of the past—a holdover—of physiognomic thinking. Consequently, it is possible, without any qualms, to offer a bit of advice to the many trustworthy and honest persons who find it difficult to stare at an interviewer's eyes. If you feel that this will prejudice him against hiring you, and if you still want the job, stare at the bridge of his nose. He will never know the difference!

We have dwelled upon physiognomy at some length because it persists in so many forms yet today. There are many other pseudo-psychologies based upon a presumed relationship between personal characteristics and some kind of physical sign. Palmistry, for example, is based upon the rationale that both character and future events are somehow revealed by the lines in the palm. Phrenology assumes that personal characteristics are related to protrusions on the skull. And there are still some businessmen who will not make a vital decision without consulting their astrologer to find out whether the stars and planets are in a "favorable" position.

Emergence of Scientific Psychology

The fact that relics of the past in the form of pseudopsychologies still influence activities and ways of thinking today is not at all surprising when one considers the comparative newness of psychology as a scientific discipline.

Man has, to be sure, speculated about phenomena of a psychological nature for a long, long time. One can almost imagine Eve selecting from her wardrobe of fig leaves the ones she calculated to make the most favorable impression upon Adam. A *scientific* approach as opposed to a speculative approach, however, awaited a definition of psychological phenomena in terms that were amenable to observation and experimentation. The key to the development of a scientific body of information in the area was the realization that the only phenomenon that could be directly studied was behavior. And this delineation of the subject matter of psychology as "the study of behavior" is generally identified with the establishment of the first laboratory for the study of psychological phenomena by Wilhelm Wundt in 1879.

Psychologists in the early twentieth century adopted a systematic approach to understanding behavior. Instead of correlating external signs with character traits, the early scientific psychologists studied the responses made by organisms to particular environmental conditions. The basic approach of these early psychologists was systematically to vary some aspect of the environment, thereby providing a *stimulus,* and noting corresponding changes in the organism's *response.* This approach is sometimes referred to as S-R psychology.

Perhaps the two most outstanding characteristics of the early scientific approach to psychology were, first, its emphasis upon rigorous scientific methodology rather than speculation and, second, its preoccupation with the study of stimulus conditions and the physiology of the receptors. Neither of these characteristics is surprising in view of the fact that early psychologists received most of their formal training in physiology and physics. The effect of this training was to cause them to apply the research methods of these disciplines to the investigation of behavior and to seek the explanation of response in terms of physical stimuli and physiological functions.

This approach to understanding behavior contrasted markedly

with the unscientific approach of the pseudopsychologies. It removed behavior from the realm of mere speculation and made it
accesible for study by investigators grounded in the rigors of verification. Thus, the early psychologists made enormous strides by establishing the legitimacy and feasibility of a science of behavior and
developing a methodology appropriate to this science.

Although the S-R approach to behavior marked a vigorous beginning for psychology, its long-range utility was somewhat limited.
Some of the difficulties inherent in this early approach to psychology
stemmed from the fact that it attempted to become scientific by
emulating the procedures and approaches of the older sciences. Rigorous laboratory investigation can be both a strength and a weakness. It is unrealistic to assume that data uncovered in a laboratory
can always be generalized to an environment outside the laboratory.
Our attitude toward work, for example, differs when we are required
to produce in an industrial setting and when we are required to produce in a laboratory. In the latter instance, we are participating in
an experiment; in the former, we are doing our job and earning our
income. The incentives for performance in these two situations may
be quite different even though the physical setting in the laboratory
may attempt to duplicate the work setting.

In addition, stimulus-response relationships are exceedingly complex. A given stimulus may evoke different responses from different
persons, or even from the same person on different occasions. To understand behavior it is necessary to discover and understand the
roles of the variables intervening between stimuli and responses.

Modern Psychology

A clue to the subject matter of psychology as viewed by present-
day psychologists is the observation that a given stimulus typically
evokes quite a range and variety of responses. This can be simply illustrated by word association in which respondents are asked to reply with the first word that they think of in response to a stimulus
word like "round." Some of the responses to this stimulus are cited
in the illustration on page 9. You can probably think of others.

If individual respondents were asked to explain their association
between stimulus and response, we might get such varied explanations as "Columbus thought the world was round, not flat"; "I heard
the word 'round' and thought of its opposite, 'square' "; "It made me
think of a prizefight," and so on. Without further laboring the point,

it is apparent that the respondents were not replying to a single stimulus word which was uniformly interpreted. Rather, they responded in terms of their personal interpretations of the stimulus word.

It is therefore convenient to think of modern psychology as fitting more nearly into an *S-I-R* formulation as opposed to the earlier *S-R* formulation. The Response (*R*) is a function of both the stimulus (*S*) and the respondent's interpretation (*I*) of that stimulus. Almost any stimulus, whether it be a word or a more involved stimulus-pattern like a memorandum from the supervisor exhorting employees to use safety equipment provided on their machines, may produce a variety of responses depending upon the significance of that

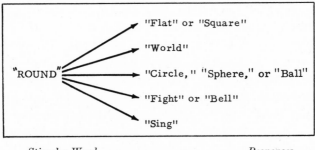

Stimulus Word   *Responses*

stimulus for, and the interpretation of the stimulus by, each individual respondent.

Let us apply the *S-I-R* framework to exploring the range of potential responses employees might make to the aforementioned memorandum regarding safety practices. The stimulus condition (S) is identical for all employees; they all receive the same memorandum. This stimulus is evaluated by each employee against the background of his own past experience and attitudes. This evaluation leads each employee to a personal interpretation of the significance of the memorandum for him (I) and to a consequent response (R). Several alternative interpretative frameworks and consequent responses are schematically indicated in Figure 1–1.

The relationship between the interpretation of the stimulus-condition and the consequent response is considerably oversimplified in the illustration outlined in Figure 1–1. First, many gradations of response other than those indicated in the illustration would be anticipated. And secondly, the memorandum would be interpreted by each employee in the light of other factors in addition to the ones of

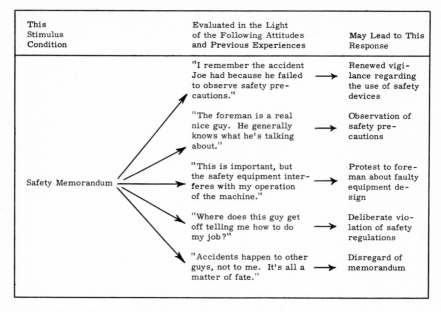

This Stimulus Condition	Evaluated in the Light of the Following Attitudes and Previous Experiences	May Lead to This Response
Safety Memorandum	"I remember the accident Joe had because he failed to observe safety precautions."	Renewed vigilance regarding the use of safety devices
	"The foreman is a real nice guy. He generally knows what he's talking about."	Observation of safety precautions
	"This is important, but the safety equipment interferes with my operation of the machine."	Protest to foreman about faulty equipment design
	"Where does this guy get off telling me how to do my job?"	Deliberate violation of safety regulations
	"Accidents happen to other guys, not to me. It's all a matter of fate."	Disregard of memorandum

FIGURE 1–1. Multiple Responses to a Uniform Stimulus Condition.

attitude and past experience. The employee's general satisfaction or dissatisfaction with the job, his physical and mental health, his mood as a result of specific experiences during the day, as well as other variables, may influence his reaction to this apparently simple stimulus-condition.

The foregoing discussion has merely hinted at the complexity of human behavior and the challenge of working within the vital and dynamic area of human behavior. Let us now bring the activities of the industrial psychologist, as opposed to specialists in other areas of psychology, into somewhat sharper focus.

PSYCHOLOGY APPLIED TO INDUSTRIAL PROBLEMS

We have already defined psychology as "the study of behavior" and have indicated that the industrial psychologist specializes in studying human behavior as it occurs in business and industrial settings. Perhaps the greatest barrier to understanding the functions of the industrial psychologist is the fairly prevalent confusion between industrial psychologists and "efficiency experts." The latter term calls to mind an image of a man more stopwatch than human. The stereotype of an "efficiency expert" is that he equates efficiency with production and regards acceleration or speedup of the activities of each employee as the least expensive road to increased productivity.

Such a stereotype is invalid, bearing no relationship to the activities of the industrial psychologist. He is committed to promoting individual initiative and in strengthening personal dignity. The successful realization of these objectives may, of course, be reflected in higher productivity, decreased absenteeism, and other objective criteria of improved performance. The essential point, however, is that the psychologist is interested in maximizing the realization of potential for accomplishment and personal satisfaction. Thus, he has a responsibility to all men, employees as well as employers.

It is difficult to date the beginnings of activity that might properly be designated as industrial psychology. The most reasonable date to assign to the formulation of this as an area of specialization within the broader framework of general psychology is 1913 when Hugo Munsterberg's *Psychology and Industrial Efficiency* was published.[1] Efficiency as defined in it involved the dual notions of output or productivity as a function of input or effort.

The specific kinds of problems industrial psychologists are called upon to solve are extensive in scope. It will be convenient to indicate something of the range of industrial problems amenable to psychological analysis by presenting what is, in essence, an overview of the chapters that follow.

Although a book is, of necessity, divided into chapters and topics, we all realize that people and problems are not neatly segmented in similar fashion. The industrial complex involves interactions cutting across the specific chapter headings and topical organization of any book. Realizing this, let us preview the major topics with which we will subsequently be concerned.

Part I: Scope and Methods

Before we can plunge into a discussion of the applications of psychological principles and methods to industrial problems, we need to know something about psychologists and the ways in which they work. A statement like: "The importance of salary as a determinant of job satisfaction has been vastly overrated by management" is

---

[1] H. Munsterberg, *Psychology and Industrial Efficiency* (Boston: Houghton Mifflin Co., 1913).

meaningless if the conclusion is predicated upon incomplete or faulty evidence. Thus, the present chapter and the one following are designed to familiarize you with the psychologist's orientation and discipline. These chapters discuss the subject matter and methodology of psychology in general and industrial psychology in particular.

Industrial psychology is an applied discipline. Its practitioner makes direct applications of sound principles underlying knowledge about human behavior gained both from other areas within the broad field of psychology (for example, clinical, experimental, and social psychology) and such other disciplines as sociology, economics, and physiology. These applications are ultimately directed either toward predicting behavior in advance of its occurrence or toward invoking some kind of change in behavior as presently constituted. These two objectives, prediction and change, are a kind of payoff. They represent a practical test of theory.

The point of view taken in this book is that the science and profession of psychology can contribute positively to all elements of the industrial complex. It is for this reason that separate sections are devoted to discussions of psychological problems related to employee recruitment and efficiency, management efficiency, and consumer behavior.

Part II: Selecting, Placing, and Training Employees

This part focuses upon the job applicant and the new employee. The company is often confronted first by the problem of selecting from a group of job applicants those who will best fulfill certain requirements. Which applicants, if hired, will most likely prove to be efficient and reasonably well-satisfied employees and which ones will find the job too easy, too difficult, or otherwise unsuited to their particular needs and desires?

This is a prediction problem requiring that the psychologist be familiar with the tools and techniques of personnel selection and placement. It may lead him into studies of the predictive efficiency of tests, inventories, interviews, application blanks, and letters of recommendation. He may have to devise new predictive instruments or to modify already existing devices. He must also develop adequate criteria of the outcomes he is attempting to predict, including industrial efficiency and job satisfaction.

Most companies place considerable emphasis upon training programs of various kinds for both new and experienced employees. The primary purpose of industrial training is to develop certain knowledges, skills, and attitudes and to alter working behaviors demonstrated to be relatively inefficient.

A systematic training program is mandatory when a company is compelled to hire inexperienced employees. New employees with prior job experience also benefit from training with respect to company policies and practices. Psychologists can make important contributions to the conduct of such programs. Problems concerning training methods, simulation of working conditions, and teaching approaches have been of significant concern to psychologists for many years.

Industrial training is by no means restricted to new employees. Management may have a number of problems for which a continual program of training for employees already on the job is the only feasible solution. Among these we may simply list as representative the problems of job enlargement, development of potential supervisory personnel, maintenance and improvement of quality as well as output, management development, and preparing employees to take on new jobs created by an ever-expanding technocracy.

Part III: Worker Efficiency

This series of chapters is concerned with a constellation of factors affecting the efficiency of employees on the job, and with certain criteria for appraising worker efficiency.

The physical working environment presents a number of problems concerning such things as optimal ventilation, illumination, machine location, and so on. More recently, psychologists have contributed significantly to problems of machine design and the structure of man-machine systems. This activity is particularly critical whenever the complexity of the equipment is such that careless design would strain or exceed human capability. Consider, for example, some of the design problems in developing high-speed aircraft in which a five-second delay during which the pilot fumbles to find a particular lever, knob, button, or dial, may well represent a traveled distance of one mile. Less dramatic perhaps, but equally important, are engineering psychology studies of the optimal location of controls and dials on automobile dashboards and industrial equipment.

In spite of technological advances, and often because of them, fa-

tigue and boredom are often characteristic of work. The deleterious
effect of these conditions upon morale, output, and safety are self-
evident as problems for psychological analysis.

Part IV: Organizational Management

Our emphasis shifts in this part from workers to management.
Management has a responsibility for maintaining both industrial
harmony and efficiency. A part of this responsibility is exercised by
pursuing justifiable wage and promotional policies.

However, effective organizational management involves much
more than this. One of the factors conditioning an employee's responses to almost anything that transpires in the industrial setting is
his relative degree of job satisfaction or dissatisfaction. Employees
who feel secure, enjoy their work, and feel amply rewarded both in
terms of personal recognition and in terms of salary are predisposed
to react favorably to management policies and practices.

This does not mean that such employees always agree with or endorse decisions by management. As a matter of fact they may feel
sufficiently comfortable in their working environment to be quite
vociferous in voicing objections or criticisms to particular practices.
They do not, however, regard every new decision with the suspicion
and mistrust characteristic of employees who are dissatisfied with
their jobs. Consequently, industrial psychologists are frequently
called upon to investigate the sources of dissatisfaction in a particular working environment.

Industrial behavior is often clarified by a study of group affiliations and allegiances of the employees. Union and nonunion employees, for example, may react quite differently to salary and promotion
policies. Similarly subgroups of employees by sex, seniority, and
level of skill may be responding from different frames of reference.

Part IV is terminated with a discussion of leadership in industry.
The fact that a man occupies a leadership position by no means
guarantees that he will have a willing group of followers. The selection and training of management personnel are generally regarded
as critical problems in most companies.

Although effective leadership at all levels of the company hierarchy is a requirement for industrial harmony, it does not guarantee
such harmony. Every company is segmented, to some degree, into
management and worker subgroups. The needs and vested interests
of these subgroups may, on occasion, be in essential conflict erupting

as a dispute. Industrial disharmony is always costly both to labor and management. The field of social psychology, in particular, has made noteworthy contributions to understanding the dynamics of such conflict.

Part V: Consumer Behavior

A company survives because consumers buy its products or services. Thus, all parties to the manufacture, distribution, and sale of products or services have a vital interest in predicting and controlling consumer behavior.

One of the psychologist's unique contributions in this general area is his application of rigorous scientific methods of inquiry to such diverse problems as the size and constituency of markets, the effectiveness of advertising campaigns, consumer reactions to the product and the company manufacturing it, and the needs and motives underlying consumer behavior, to list a few.

To the extent that there is a psychology of consumer behavior, it has been significantly bolstered by activities of psychologists in the clinical and experimental areas. Clinical tools have been used by motivation researchers to discover the "hidden" or unconscious reasons underlying consumer behavior. Advertising has capitalized for years upon well-established findings from traditional laboratory-type research in experimental psychology. More recently considerable attention has been focused upon the possibility of subliminally presented advertising.

Although psychologists have, to the present, devoted relatively little attention to studying the process of salesmanship, considerable research has been directed toward the problems of selecting and training salesmen.

INDUSTRIAL PSYCHOLOGY AS A PROFESSION

We have thus far described something of the scope of activities of the industrial psychologist. It is apparent from the foregoing discussion that he must possess general knowledge about human behavior and the factors influencing it. In addition, he must have at his command certain rather specific skills. He is a researcher and consequently must be conversant with techniques of assessment including psychological tests, attitude scales, and merit rating. He must know how to design experiments and evaluate the results in the broad area of industrial behavior. He must know how to draw representative samples from a population in order to perform certain kinds of market research and opinion studies. And we could list other skills as well. It is appropriate now to inquire into the development of these skills. How is the industrial psychologist trained, and how may we differentiate between the well-qualified practitioner and the glib but untrained charlatan?

Certification and Licensing

The classified section of the telephone directory for almost any large city contains listings under "psychologist." Unfortunately, it is legal in most states for anyone to represent himself to the public through the classified directory or any other outlet as a psychologist. This unhappy state of affairs is gradually being rectified by legislation. Thus, a few states *license* psychologists in the same way as physicians, dentists, and lawyers are licensed. It is a criminal offense in such states for an individual without a license to practice psychology or to offer psychological service to the public. Other states *certify* psychologists. Certification involves less legislative control than licensing since it prohibits unqualified persons merely from representing themselves as "certified psychologists." It is perfectly legal in states with certification laws for an untrained and unqualified person to represent himself as a "psychologist" as long as he makes no claim to certification.

Most states do not, at the present time, either license or certify psychologists. This means that if you were seeking the services of a bona fide industrial psychologist solely from the listing in a telephone directory in most communities, you might come up with a totally unqualified person. It is important, then, to know something about the training and professional affiliations of qualified industrial psychologists.

Professional Training

Since the public is not adequately protected against fraudulent psychological practice, the primary responsibility for specifying and maintaining standards rests with the psychological profession itself. Most qualified psychologists in this country are members of the American Psychological Association, which is the professional counterpart of such organizations as the American Medical Association and the American Dental Association. The purpose of the American Psychological Association is ". . . to advance psychology as a science, as a profession and as a means of promoting human welfare."[2] Although the Association does not endorse the professional qualifications of any of its members, it has developed a code of ethical practice to which all of its members are required to adhere. The minimum standard for acceptability as a *member* is roughly the master's degree in psychology from an accredited institution and one year of professional experience. *Fellows* of the Association usually have the Ph.D. degree and a minimum of five years of professional experience. The total of both classes of members is approximately 20,000.

The Association is composed of 23 divisions representing specialized fields of interest and activities of the members. One of these is designated the Division of Industrial Psychology. It is composed of approximately 800 members. The Division has as its stated purposes:

1. Establishing and maintaining high standards of practice in business, industry, public service, and related fields.
2. Encouraging research and publication in these fields.
3. Facilitating the exchange of information and experience among its members and with the general public.
4. Expediting the development of professional opportunities.
5. Fostering cooperative relations with allied professions.
6. Protecting the public from untrained and/or unethical practitioners.
7. Contributing to the advancement of psychology in general.[3]

The Division issues a Directory of its members, containing information about professional training and employment history. The most recent directory was published in 1958.

An additional kind of professional recognition is the diploma awarded by the American Board of Examiners for Professional Psychology. This diploma is awarded to psychologists who are judged to be well-trained, highly competent, and very responsible practitioners. The requirements for status as a diplomate in the fields of clinical psychology, counseling, and guidance, or industrial psychology are the Ph.D. and five years of professional experience. In addition, the diplomate has successfully passed written and oral examinations in his specialized field.

---

[2] Bylaws for the American Psychological Association, Article I.1.

[3] Bylaws of Division 14 of the American Psychological Association, Article I.2.

Employment of Industrial Psychologists

Industrial psychologists typically are employed in one of three kinds of settings. They may be employed as full-time staff members of a particular industry; they may be a full-time member of an organization of consulting psychologists; or they may hold an academic position in a university or college. Many industrial psychologists employed in the academic setting also consult on a part-time basis.

Industrial psychologists are employed as full-time staff members of quite a variety of industries, including oil companies, automotive companies, insurance companies, and so on. These psychologists are most often designated by some title other than "industrial psychologist." Several are Personnel Directors, Vice Presidents, and Directors of Research.

A number of organizations of psychologists offer consultive service to industry. These organizations typically perform studies under contract to a particular industry, business, or government agency. An industrial corporation may, for example, let a contract to a consulting organization to conduct a morale survey, or to develop a personnel selection battery, or to establish a training program. A member or team from the consulting group is then assigned to work on the problem for the contracting agency on a temporary basis. They are reassigned when the project is completed.

Although the primary emphasis in the employment of industrial psychologists is an *applied* emphasis involving a service commitment, this does not imply the absence of theoretical or pure research in this area. Industrial psychologists, whether employed by industry, a consulting organization, or a university have a commitment to further the development of psychology as a science. Thus, they continuously maintain a research orientation toward such basic problems in the field as improving the techniques of test construction and evaluation procedures, furthering scientific knowledge about human motivation, gaining a more comprehensive understanding of the learning process and, in fact, toward the entire vista of human behavior.

SUMMARY

Industrial psychology is the scientific study of behavior as it occurs in business and industrial settings. Thus, it is concerned with the behavior of three broad classifications of individuals: workers, management, and consumers.

The application of sound psychological principles differs from both the pseudopsychologies and the stereotype of the "efficiency expert." Pseudopsychologies are founded upon a presumed relationship between character traits and external signs like lines in the palm or size of the ears. This presumption is entirely unfounded.

Modern industrial psychology studies behavior with a view to maximizing the realization of potential for accomplishment and personal satisfaction. Thus, it has a responsibility to employees as well as to employers. The psychologist views behavior as a function of precipitating factors (the stimulus conditions) and of intervening variables which determine the way in which particular individuals will perceive and interpret the stimulus.

Most states have no legislation designed to protect the public from fraudulent psychological practice. Consequently, the primary responsibility for specifying and maintaining standards rests with the profession of psychology itself. Most qualified psychologists in this country are members of the American Psychological Association. Membership in this organization is predicated upon satisfactory completion of certain minimum requirements of graduate training and experience.

An industrial psychologist may be employed as a full-time staff member of a particular industrial organization, as a full-time consultant, or as a faculty member in a university or college. Many of the psychologists employed in the academic setting also consult in industry on a part-time basis.

How the Industrial Psychologist Works

2 Frequent reference was made in the previous chapter to the fact that psychology is the *scientific* study of behavior. Some persons find it difficult to conceive of a "science" without the trappings of a laboratory, including sparkling glassware, bunsen burners, microscopes, and perhaps a cyclotron or two. Reference to a scientific study of behavior is regarded by them as a basic contradiction in terms. They argue that the complexity and variability of human behavior precludes its study in scientific fashion.

Reasoning like this is erroneous because it rests upon an incorrect definition of "science." A science is characterized by the methods it employs rather than by the phenomena it studies or the physical setting in which it operates. The complexity of human behavior creates special problems for the psychologist, to be sure, but it does not itself dictate the application of methods that are unscientific. In essence, the methods employed by psychologists are identical with those employed by researchers in such disciplines as chemistry and physics.

It will be helpful to know something about the characteristics of scientific method in general before considering the specific ways in which the industrial psychologist employs these methods.

ESSENTIALS OF SCIENTIFIC METHOD

You will recall that the pseudopsychologies were primarily based upon speculation rather than upon observation. There is nothing inherently wrong with speculation in itself. Many brilliant ideas originate as figments of someone's vivid imagination. So, too, do many ideas that are not so brilliant! Consider, for example, some of the delusions experienced by certain mental patients who believe they have discovered the secret of perpetual life or have "proven" that the world is flat after all.

Scientific method requires that we go one step beyond speculation.

The investigator's educated guess about relationships between phenomena must be cast into the form of an hypothesis. The hypothesis is a statement of possible relationship that is amenable to investigation by observation.

Objectivity

Scientific observations for the purpose of substantiating or refuting hypotheses must be made in objective rather than subjective fashion. The investigator does not have an axe to grind. He attempts to discover whether or not an hypothesized relationship exists. He is not committed to proving the existence of the relationship.

During the course of everyday living, most of us make observations that are quite subjective in nature and hence are unscientific. We hold certain biases and preconceived notions which color our observations. If, for example, you fear airplane travel, you may find support for your fear in newspaper accounts of airplane accidents. In so doing, however, you are failing to consider all of the data. What about the vast majority of flights which are successful and hence are not newsworthy?

Subjectivity may influence our observations in yet another way. The observer's biases and misconceptions may actually cause him to misinterpret what he sees and hears. Suppose that an employee is convinced that his supervisor is unfair and guilty of favoritism. The fact that this supervisor recommends pay raises for certain of his subordinates and not for others may be incorrectly interpreted by this employee as another sign of favoritism rather than as a reflection of the fact that some employees are truly more deserving of salary increases than others.

Controlled Observation

In addition to objectivity, scientific methods require the exertion of careful controls. This was one of the vital elements missing from the observations offered in support of pseudopsychological notions about behavior.

It is insufficient, for example, merely to speculate that there is a criminal "type" easily recognized on the basis of facial characteristics. Casual observations of a few known criminals would not contribute to the scientific validity of this speculative conclusion. What is required, of course, is a systematic investigation of the accuracy with which known criminals and noncriminals can be differentiated solely on the basis of facial characteristics. The influence of factors other than the critical one of facial characteristics would have to be *controlled* (eliminated) if the investigation were to have meaning. It is one thing to look at a known criminal and conclude that he has a "mean looking face." It is quite another thing, however, to look at photographs of 50 persons, some of whom are criminals and some of whom are not, and successfully differentiate between the honest citizens and prison inmates.

The Independent Variable. The elements of scientific method—observation, objectivity, and control—are translated by the researcher into an investigation of the relationship between two basic kinds of variables. One of these, the independent variable, is the factor whose effects are being investigated.

The range of independent variables of interest to the industrial psychologist is quite extensive. He may, for example, be interested in studying the effects of changes in the physical working environment, or of a new safety program, or of a training program for supervisors. Any factor that is systematically controlled so that it operates under certain circumstances and not under others (or is operative for certain groups and not for others) may be investigated as an independent variable.

The Dependent Variable. The behaviors studied as possible functions of the independent variable are referred to as dependent variables. The investigator is interested in determining whether certain aspects of behavior can be shown to depend upon manipulation of the independent variable.

The dependent variables of greatest concern to industrial psychologists have been classified as (*a*) performance and (*b*) satisfaction.[1] The importance of performance measures as dependent variables is almost self-evident. In investigating the effect of some change in the working environment or some new job practice it is logical to inquire whether performance is improved, diminished, or unaffected as a consequence of the change. The kinds of performance measures used for this purpose are exceedingly diverse, including such things as productivity, absenteeism, turnover, spoilage, suspensions, and accidents.

The importance of "satisfaction" as a dependent variable may not be quite as obvious unless we recognize that management and work-

---

[1] R. A. Katzell, "Industrial Psychology," in P. R. Farnsworth and Quinn McNemar (eds.), *Annual Review of Psychology,* Vol. VIII (Palo Alto, Calif.: Annual Reviews, Inc., 1957), p. 237.

ers do not always share similar objectives. Although increased output may be regarded by management as a desirable consequence of altered working conditions, such alterations sometimes lead to considerable worker dissatisfaction. Dissatisfaction can be fertile soil for low morale, increased turnover, and absenteeism. Hence, it often is imperative to ascertain the impact of independent variable manipulations upon criteria of both satisfaction and output.

Causality?

The scientist is acutely aware of the fact that he may demonstrate a relationship between two variables but can never actually prove that one *causes* the other. Cause-effect relationships are, to be sure, frequently inferred from a set of observations. Quite often, however, we can demonstrate a relationship between variables without having any indication of which one is cause and which is effect.

Suppose, for example, that the psychologist makes the observation that in general, insurance salesmen who have been with a company for more than one year sell more insurance (that is, are more productive) than salesmen who have been with the company for less than a year. The factors of length of time with the company and productivity are thus related, but which is cause and which is effect? Does experience with the company improve selling technique? Perhaps. It is just as plausible, however, to hypothesize that highly productive salesmen are rewarded both in terms of salary and job satisfaction, causing them to remain with the company for a relatively long period of time. Unproductive salesmen, on the other hand, may receive lower commissions and become sufficiently discouraged with the job to seek employment elsewhere within a year or less. Finally, we cannot discount the possibility that *neither* experience nor productivity is a causal factor, since both may themselves be caused by some third factor held in common.

The foregoing discussion has been offered in the nature of a hasty overview of some of the essentials of scientific methodology. Let us now see how the industrial psychologist applies scientific methods to the study of human behavior in three basic ways: naturalistic observation, correlational analysis, and experimental observation.

NATURALISTIC OBSERVATION

We have already stated that the scientist attempts to discover relationships between independent and dependent variables. This requires that the independent variable be so manipulated as to reveal corresponding variations in the dependent variable.

Some kinds of independent variables, however, are not amenable to manipulation by the investigator. This situation is perhaps most apparent in astronomy where the observer cannot alter the course of the stars and planets to fulfill the needs of his experimentation. The independent variables of interest to the astronomer are manipulated, so to speak, by nature. The scientist makes his observations whenever conditions existing in their natural state are favorable to the study of the particular phenomenon that he wishes to investigate. Naturalistic observation, then, is characterized by the fact that the researcher does not control the independent variable. Rather, he is compelled to study it as and when it occurs in its natural state.

An Illustration of Naturalistic Observation

Naturalistic observations are frequently made by psychologists. One investigation of this type was concerned with studying the relative effectiveness of a stop sign and a red blinker light at an intersection.[2] State law required that a driver bring his car to a full stop at or before such a sign or blinker light.

The independent variable in this study was the signal to stop (sign or light); the dependent variable was the action of the driver in adhering to or disobeying these signals. It would have been extremely difficult for the investigators to study the relationship between these variables in any setting other than the natural environment. Consequently, observations were made at two intersections in the same neighborhood: one intersection had a stop sign while the other had a red blinker light. The observations were made from a sheltered doorway and the responses of the drivers were classified and tabulated as illustrated in Table 2–1.

The investigators drew the following conclusions: (1) Only about one half of the drivers in the neighborhood studied stopped their cars completely when required to do so by the stop sign or blinker light. (2) A significantly greater percentage of drivers stopped too late (past the intersection) at the stop sign than at the blinker light. (This is interpreted as meaning that the blinker is more readily visible from a distance.) (3) The percentage of drivers who

    [2] C. F. Hummel and G. R. Schmeidler, "Driver Behavior at Dangerous Intersections Marked by Stop Signs or by Red Blinker Lights," *Journal of Applied Psychology*, Vol. XXXIX, No. 1 (1955), pp. 17–19.

TABLE 2–1

STOPS AND SLOWDOWNS OF CARS AT INTERSECTIONS WITH A STOP SIGN AND WITH A BLINKER LIGHT

Category of Response	Stop Sign 3–4 Weeks after Erection	Stop Sign 3–4 Months after Erection	Red Blinker Light
Full stop with no more than half the car past the intersection line	22%	29%	44%
Full stop with more than half the car past the intersection line	30	19	9
Slowing down but not a full stop	31	35	25
No perceptible slowing down	17	17	22
Total	100%	100%	100%

stopped or slowed down for a newly erected sign was about the same as the percentage stopping or slowing down for a sign that had been standing for several months.

The fact that investigators employing naturalistic observation do not themselves manipulate the independent variable does not make the method or the findings unscientific. As long as observations are made systematically and objectively, and as long as extraneous factors are controlled, the results of naturalistic investigations can be both meaningful and useful.

Extraneous factors are those potentially affecting the dependent variable but not currently the subject of investigation. Hence, the control of these factors is extremely important and sometimes difficult to achieve in natural situations. The investigators comparing the relative effectiveness of the stop sign and blinker light had to control at least four such factors which might have influenced driver behavior. First, they had to take reasonable precautions to prevent drivers from knowing that their behavior was being studied. It is likely that a higher percentage of drivers would have complied with the law had they known that they were being observed. Secondly, the neighborhood was controlled by making observations at two intersections in the same vicinity. There are undoubtedly differences between neighborhoods in the extent to which drivers adhere to the letter of the law. A third controlled variable was the factor of restraints apart from the stop sign and blinker light. Obviously the experimenters would have contaminated their findings if they had selected one intersection that was regularly patrolled by a policeman (in addition to having a stop sign) and another intersection not similarly patrolled. Finally, the investigators observed that some drivers were

compelled to slow down or to stop at the intersection in order to
avoid a collision with the car in front. Since it was impossible to determine whether these drivers would have stopped or slowed down
for the sign or blinker light, these cases were eliminated from the
data analysis.

Evaluation of the Naturalistic Method

The psychologist has certain reservations about using the naturalistic method. Since he has not directly manipulated the independent variable, it is difficult to repeat a set of naturalistic observations
under exactly the same conditions as prevailed the first time. What
would happen, for example, if we wished to verify the findings cited
in Table 2–1? Even if we followed a procedure identical with that
originally used, and made our observations at the same two intersections, we might obtain different results because of changes in the
natural situation. A series of accidents, for example, at the stop sign
intersection might have led to the posting of a policeman at this intersection for several weeks. Even though he were no longer present
when we recorded driver behavior, his former presence there may
have encouraged better driving habits. Furthermore, the sign itself
will have been up for a longer time when we repeat our observations.
The time of the year at which observations are made may influence
our findings. Many high school students take part-time jobs requiring that they drive a car or truck during the summer. Their behavior
may be quite different from that of older, more experienced drivers.
You can undoubtedly think of other subtle variations that may creep
into the natural situation, making it difficult or even impossible to repeat and verify a set of naturalistic observations.

There are nevertheless situations in which the naturalistic method
is the best method available to the industrial psychologist. Persons
who know that they are being observed in an experimental situation
will sometimes deliberately behave in a way calculated to impress
the investigator. Such alterations of behavior might be noted, for example, if we were to conduct a study of the kinds of programs TV
viewers prefer to watch. We could administer a questionnaire dealing with viewing habits, but the obtained responses might not be
trustworthy. An alternative procedure would be to develop an experimental situation in which viewers have access to several TV
channels under controlled circumstances and to tabulate the percentage of viewers watching each kind of program. Here again,

though, the investigator could not be certain that the viewers had not altered their behavior because they knew they were being observed. Consequently, naturalistic observation would be the method of choice for the study of this problem. Persons might be interviewed in their homes to determine whether or not they were watching TV at the moment and if so, the particular program being viewed.

CORRELATIONAL ANALYSIS

Correlational analysis reveals the magnitude and direction of the relationship between variables. If measures of these variables parallel each other closely, they are strongly correlated. However, when there is little or no parallelism between these measures, correlation is weak or absent. The statistics underlying correlational analysis are discussed in a later section. For the moment we will merely accept as fact the availability of statistical techniques for this purpose.

Suppose we wished to determine whether there is a relationship between seniority (defined by years of experience on the job) and supervisory ratings of employee efficiency. It would be possible to make this determination by comparing data on seniority for a sample of employees with the corresponding supervisory ratings assigned to these employees. Thus, in a way, correlational analysis may be regarded as a special variant of naturalistic observation. The investigator using either method does not manipulate the variables with which he is working.

It is imperative to emphasize again that although correlation implies a relationship between things, it does not provide evidence regarding causation. Assuming the existence of a correlation between two variables, either one may be cause and the other effect. Furthermore, it is quite possible to obtain a correlation when *neither* of them is cause or effect. This occurs whenever the correlated variables are themselves dependent upon some third or fourth variable underlying the two particular ones correlated by the investigator.

Predictive Studies

Investigations of the accuracy of predictions generally require some kind of correlational analysis. The data for such studies are of two kinds: predictor and criterion measures. Predictive scores or measures are acquired for each subject in advance of his placement on the job. Then, after a period of time, his job performance is evaluated on the basis of relevant criteria. The correlation between predictors and criteria indicates the accuracy to be anticipated in the future when the predictors are used as a basis for making personnel decisions.

The most obvious application of this kind of predictive study occurs in the case of personnel selection. Utilization of test scores or interview data as a basis for deciding whether to hire or reject individual job applicants must be supported by preliminary research demonstrating the existence of a relationship between performance on these predictors and ultimate job performance.

Correlational analysis is not limited to establishing relationships between two variables. The usual predictive study involves an attempt to maximize the efficiency with which the criterion is predicted by utilizing several predictors, each weighted optimally. The statistical technique appropriate to this kind of problem is *multiple correlation.*

Nonpredictive Applications

Correlational analysis is not limited in application either to predictive studies or, in a broader sense, to test development. It is, in its own right, an important research tool contributing to our understanding of various kinds of phenomena.

Discovery of a relationship between variables often precipitates fruitful research focusing upon the question of causation. Thus, the discovery of a correlation between cigarette smoking and the incidence of certain kinds of cancer has led to investigation of the reasons for this relationship.

THE EXPERIMENTAL METHOD

The primary difference between the experimental and naturalistic methods is that the former places the investigator in charge of the situation. He manipulates the independent variable and controls extraneous factors. This kind of regulation by the experimenter makes it possible to repeat observations under identical conditions in order to verify the findings. It also means that the investigator is in a somewhat stronger position to infer cause-effect relationships, because he may systematically vary one factor at a time and note corresponding changes, if any, in other factors that he suspects might be affected.

Experimental Design

The experimental method may be employed in either a laboratory setting or in a real-life setting like an office or industrial plant. The advantage of doing research in a laboratory is that the investigator can arrange his materials and experimental conditions with precision. Since the laboratory is, however, an artificial environment generalizations from laboratory findings to the industrial setting may be erroneous. Therefore, the industrial psychologist most often accepts laboratory findings as suggestive and attempts to verify them in the plant before attempting to apply the results of his experimentation.

The simplest kind of experimental design requires a study of two groups of *subjects* (persons being investigated). One of these groups, the *control group,* serves as a standard for comparative purposes. The *experimental group,* on the other hand, is the one in which the independent variable is manipulated. A simple illustration will serve to clarify the difference between these groups.

Let us assume that we wish to investigate the effect of increased illumination upon the typewriting proficiency of secretaries. The independent variable is level of illumination. Hence, secretaries working under the changed level of illumination would constitute the experimental group. The effectiveness of this variable would be investigated by comparing the typing proficiency of subjects in the experimental group with the performance of secretaries working under normal illumination. Consequently a second group of subjects working under normal illumination conditions would constitute the control group.

The dependent variable in this investigation would be some criterion of typing proficiency like the number of words typed per unit of time and corrected for errors or erasures. It is apparent, however, that many factors aside from the specific independent variable under investigation (illumination) may affect typing speed. Such factors as finger dexterity, length of experience as a typist, and kind of copy being typed may be reflected in speed and accuracy of secretarial performance but are really extraneous to the specific problem under investigation. It would therefore be necessary to insure the similarity of the experimental and control groups with respect to all such extraneous factors before we could attribute any observed differences in typing speed solely to the independent variable.

Matched Group Design. One procedure for eliminating the effects of extraneous factors is to match or equate the groups of subjects on the basis of such factors. For example, if we wish to investigate only the effects of illumination, it would be necessary somehow to eliminate the potential effect of differences in finger dexterity. This would be accomplished in a matched-groups design by administering a finger dexterity test to a pool of available subjects before assigning anyone to the experimental or control group. Pairs of persons with identical scores would be identified, and one member of the pair would be assigned to the experimental group while her counterpart would be assigned to the control group.

It is exceedingly difficult to implement a matched-groups design for a number of reasons. First, it is necessary to have a large pool of potential subjects available in order to identify pairs that match. Second, the process of constructing equated groups becomes increasingly difficult as the number of extraneous variables to be controlled increases. You will recall that our hypothetical investigation requires that we eliminate from consideration both the factors of finger dexterity and length of experience. Thus, we would have to identify pairs of subjects who not only have the same scores on a finger dexterity test, but also are identical in length of secretarial experience. As we attempt to match for still more variables, the process becomes unmanageable. Third, we have been considering a design involving only two groups of subjects. If, however, our design required more than two groups (and many *do*) the task of matching is still further complicated. Finally, even when a matched-groups design is feasible, it would be erroneous to assume that matching has really accomplished what we set out to do: that is, to eliminate the effects of potentially contaminating factors. There is always the possibility that factors other than the ones on which we equated our groups will exert some consistent and uncontrolled effect upon the dependent variable.

It is for these reasons that most experimental investigations utilize a random group design rather than a matched group design.

Random Group Design. In this procedure subjects are randomly assigned to the experimental and control groups. Randomization requires that every subject have an equal chance for assignment to each of the groups required for an experiment. Since no biases of any kind are permitted into the assignment of subjects to groups, we may assume that each randomly constructed group is essentially like every other randomly constructed group drawn from the same original pool of subjects.

Once the subjects are randomly assigned to groups, there remains only the decision about which should be treated experimentally and which should serve as a control. This again should be decided without bias, perhaps by flipping a coin.

An Illustrative Laboratory Experiment

A considerable amount of research in the general area of improving machine design has, as you might suspect, been directed toward facilitating aircraft pilot efficiency. As aircraft become increasingly complex and as their speed increases, the pilot must make correct decisions with increased rapidity. This in turn means that new techniques must be discovered for relaying information about the functioning of aircraft components to the pilot in a way that is readily comprehensible.

The location of various kinds of dials and the "normal" position of the pointers has been shown to be a critical factor affecting the speed and accuracy with which the dials are read. The best configuration of 16 dials in multiengined aircraft has been demonstrated to be four banks of four dials each, with the normal position of each pointer at the "nine o'clock" position as indicated in Figure 2–1.

Starting with this arrangement of dials, an experiment was performed to determine whether or not speed and accuracy of dial reading could be further improved by combining a deviating pointer (indicating some kind of malfunction or condition that must be corrected) with a change in illumination of the specific dial in question.[3]

The independent variable, then, was change in illumination accompanying a deviating dial pointer. Cockpit dials are normally illuminated in red. The illuminant of deviating dials changed from red to green.

One of the dependent variables was the speed with which the subjects could identify the number of deviating dials (which was varied by the investigator between 1 and 8) in each cluster of 16.

The control condition consisted of presenting the clusters of 16 dials with varying numbers and configurations of discrepancies but

---

[3] A. E. Bartz, "Attention Value as a Function of Illuminant Color Change," *Journal of Applied Psychology*, Vol. XLI (1957), pp. 82–84.

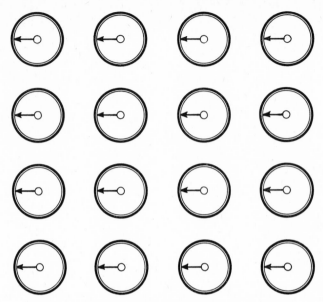

Source: M. J. Warrick and W. F. Grether, "The Effect of Pointer Alignment on Check Reading of Instrument Panels," Aero Medical Laboratory, *AMCMCREXD 694–17* (June, 1948).

FIGURE 2–1.   Optimal Arrangement of 16 Aircraft Dials, Each Pointing to the Normal Condition.

without changing the illuminant. The experimental condition consisted of the presentation of the same configuration of discrepancies with a red-to-green illuminant for discrepant dials. The same subjects were used under the two conditions, making it unnecessary to equate the experimental and control groups on extraneous factors.

The average times required to count the number of deviating dials under the experimental and control conditions are graphed in Figure 2–2.

Two conclusions follow from these data. First, the time required to count deviant dials increases as a function of the number of such dials. Secondly, this time is considerably reduced when deviation of the pointer is accompanied by changing the illuminant from red to green. The implication of these findings for the design of aircraft instrument panels is obvious.

Speed of discrepancy identification was not the only dependent variable investigated. The experimenter was interested also in comparing the *accuracy* of identification under the experimental and control conditions. He noted that the subjects averaged 1.05 errors (in identifying a total of 36 discrepant dials) with constant red il-

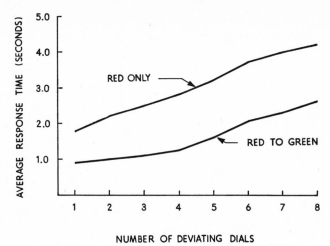

FIGURE 2–2.   Average Response Times to Configurations Containing One through Eight Error Dials.

lumination, while they only averaged 0.38 errors with the red-to-green illuminant shift. The interpretation of the average number of errors under these two conditions required a statistical analysis in order to determine that the difference between them was attributable to the experimental conditions rather than to chance. It is to the general matter of types and applications of statistics that we now turn our attention.

STATISTICS

Statistics of various kinds are used in conjunction with almost any experiment performed by the industrial psychologist. The investigator typically measures change in the dependent variable associated with manipulation of the independent variable. Hence, the outcome of an experiment is usually expressed in numerical form: that is, test scores, production records, accident rates, numbers of persons answering "yes" to a questionnaire item, and so on. The summary and interpretation of numerical results is facilitated by statistical analysis.

Statistical techniques fall generally into two classes. *Descriptive statistics* provide a kind of shorthand description of a mass of data. This is a kind of statistic with which you are most familiar. When we speak of an average score or a range of scores, we are really summarizing a mass of data in a simple and convenient way.

A second kind of statistic is required to facilitate the interpretation of obtained averages or ranges of scores. You will recall that the results of the dial reading experiment indicated that subjects made fewer errors when the illuminant was changed than when it remained constant. Before interpreting these findings as indicative of the superiority of illuminant change, however, we must be certain that the difference between the number of errors under the two conditions did not arise solely as a function of chance. *Statistical inference* provides us with an indication of the likelihood that our experimental findings are merely chance findings. As the likelihood of attributing obtained findings to chance is reduced, we may have increased confidence in the conclusion that these findings resulted from the manipulation of the independent variable.

The ensuing discussion concerns some of the simpler statistics. The computation of these statistics is not described. Rather, we will illustrate some of the ways in which both summary and interpretive statistics are applied.

Descriptive Statistics

Many kinds of data may be conveniently summarized by counting the number of persons (or computing the percentage of persons) obtaining each score. This summary may be visually presented by plotting a *frequency polygon* or a *histogram* as illustrated in Figure 2–3.

Both of the plots in Figure 2–3 were derived from the same set of

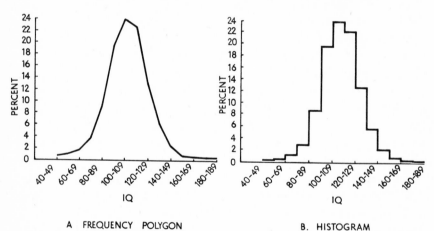

A FREQUENCY POLYGON   B. HISTOGRAM

Source: L. M. Terman and Maud A. Merrill, *Measuring Intelligence* (Cambridge: Riverside Press, 1937), p. 37.

FIGURE 2–3. Frequency Distribution of Intelligence Quotients of 2,904 Children.

IQ data. They show the percentage of youngsters earning IQs within each 10-point interval starting with the interval 40 to 49.

The Normal Distribution Curve. As the number of observations plotted on a graph is increased, the resultant distribution tends more and more to approximate a curve rather than a polygon. When we have made a substantial number of observations free of biasing factors, the obtained curve often has the characteristics of the normal distribution. Such a normal distribution curve is illustrated in Figure 2–4. You will note that very few persons have IQs as low as 40

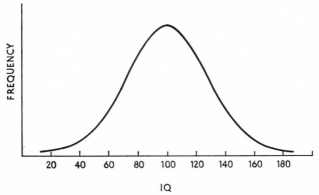

FIGURE 2–4. A Normal Distribution Curve Obtained from Measurement of IQ.

or as high as 160. The highest percentage of persons have IQs which cluster closely about 100.

Graphed data do not always take the form of a normal distribution. Some characteristics are not normally distributed even when data are plotted for the entire population. In addition, when the sample of persons is not randomly selected (that is, is somehow biased), the resultant distribution of data is usually asymmetrical. If, for example, we plotted the IQs of youngsters in a home for the feebleminded or of freshman university students, we might obtain curves like the ones in Figure 2–5. These distributions are *skewed* (unsymmetrical) because we have made measurements in restricted and selected groups of persons. We expect the distribution to be normal only when selective factors are absent.

Although it is possible to summarize a set of data in the form of a graphed distribution, this kind of summary can be rather inconvenient on occasion. We can pretty well summarize the data presented in

Figure 2–4, for example, in terms of two critical features: the "average" IQ, and the spread of IQs away from this "average." The typical or "average" score is statistically expressed by a measure of *central tendency*. The spread of scores is expressed by a measure of *variability*.

Central Tendency. The three primary measures of central tendency are the mean, median, and mode.

The *mean* ($\overline{X}$) is the measure with which you are probably most familiar. It is simply the arithmetic average computed by adding the

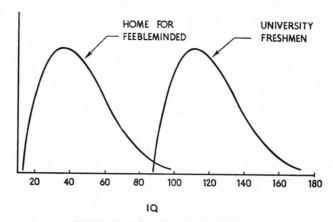

FIGURE 2–5.   Skewed Distributions.

scores and dividing by the number of cases or observations. The computational formula for the mean is written

$$\overline{X} = \frac{\Sigma X}{N}$$

where X is used to denote a score, Σ is the process of summing, and N is the number of cases.

The *median* (*Med*) is the score falling precisely at the middle of the distribution. If a distribution of IQs earned by 501 employees were arranged in order from lowest to highest, the median IQ would be the one earned by the 251st worker. Two hundred fifty employees will have earned IQs below the median and 250 would have earned IQs above the median.

The *mode* (*Mo*) is simply the score that occurs most frequently within a distribution. It is little used as a measure of central tendency except under special circumstances. A shoe buyer, for example, would find it useful to know the modal shoe size worn by men in order to place his orders wisely.

The mean, median, and mode are identical when the distribution of data is normal. These three measures of central tendency diverge, however, when the distribution is skewed. The relationships between mean, median, and mode in normal and skewed distributions are illustrated in Figure 2–6.

You will note that the mean is more sensitive to the "tail" of the distribution than is the median. The fact that the mean is highly in-

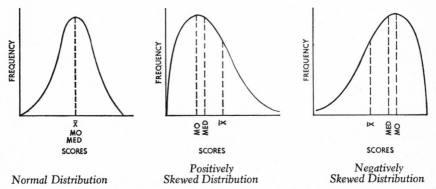

| Normal Distribution | Positively Skewed Distribution | Negatively Skewed Distribution |

FIGURE. 2–6. Measures of Central Tendency in Normal and in Skewed Distributions.

fluenced by extreme or unusual cases in a distribution implies that its use should be limited to situations in which the distribution of data is not seriously skewed. You can readily see that the median, which is less influenced by extreme cases in a distribution, is a more representative measure of central tendency than the mean when distributions are skewed.

Consider, for example, the interpretation of the statement that the average annual income of the 10 persons employed in a particular industrial capacity is $5,000.00. The first question we might raise would concern the type of "average" computed. Was it a mean, median, or mode? Secondly, the interpretation of this "average" would depend upon the shape of the distribution. Is it normal or skewed? Suppose $5,000.00 represents the mean income derived from the following set of figures: $3,900.00, $4,000.00, $4,100.00, $4,200.00, $4,-400.00, $4,400.00, $4,500.00, $4,500.00, $11,500.00. The fact that one of the 10 men is receiving an atypically high salary has acted to increase the mean as computed for the entire department to a figure that does not truly reflect typical earnings. A more realistic kind of average under such circumstances would be the median, here computed as $4,400.00.

A Measure of Variability. An indication of central tendency does not, by itself, provide an adequate description of a distribution of scores. It is perfectly possible, for example, for the means of two normal distributions to be identical even though these distributions may be quite different with respect to variability (or spread of scores away from the mean). This kind of situation is illustrated in Figure

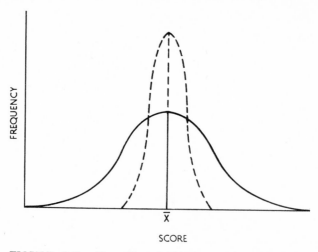

FIGURE 2–7. Two Normal Distributions with Identical
Means but Different Variabilities.

2–7, in which the data in the dotted-line distribution cluster more closely about the mean than do the data in the solid line distribution.

There are a number of different statistical measures of variability, all of which describe the spread of data away from the measure of central tendency. The statistic most often used for this purpose, and the only one with which we will be here concerned, is the *standard deviation* (σ).

The formula for standard deviation is

$$\sigma = \sqrt{\frac{\Sigma(X - \overline{X})^2}{N}}$$

Thus, to compute the standard deviation it is necessary first to determine the extent to which each score deviates from the mean ($X - \overline{X}$). These values are then squared, and the sum of the squared deviations is divided by the number of cases. Finally, extracting the square root yields the standard deviation.

Approximately 68 percent (actually 68.26 percent) of the scores in a normal distribution fall within the scores delimited by one standard deviation on either side of the mean. This percentage is constant regardless of the type of score that is plotted and of the computed mean, *provided that the distribution of data is normal.*

Suppose we have calculated the mean of a set of mechanical aptitude test scores as 50.00 and the standard deviation of the distribution of scores as 10.00. The limits defined by ±1σ (one standard deviation on either side of the mean) are thus 40.00 and 60.00, and

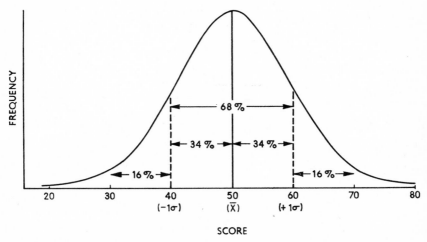

FIGURE 2–8. A Distribution of Test Scores in Which the Mean Is 50.00 and the Standard Deviation is 10.00.

approximately 68 per cent of the obtained scores fall between these limits. The remaining 32 percent of the scores are equally divided, with 16 percent falling below the score corresponding to −1σ (40.00) and 16 percent falling above the scores corresponding to +1σ (60.00). The distribution of scores obtained on this test of mechanical aptitude is schematically represented in Figure 2–8.

If we administered the same test to another group of persons, and found here that the mean was still 50.00 but that the standard deviation was only 5.00, the middle 68 percent of the scores would fall between the limits of 45.00 to 55.00. Similarly, if we had a third distribution of data also with a mean of 50.00 but with a standard deviation of 15.00, the middle 68 percent of the cases would fall between scores of 35.00 and 65.00. Thus, the larger the standard deviation the greater is the spread of scores away from the mean. Conversely, as the size of the standard deviation decreases, the scores cluster more tightly about the mean.

Just as the percentage of cases between the limits of $\pm 1\sigma$ is constant for normal distributions, so too is the percentage of cases between the limits defined by two and three standard deviations on either side of the mean. The scores between -2σ and $+2\sigma$ include 95.44 percent of the cases, while virtually all of the cases in normal distributions (99.74 percent) are included between the score limits defined by three standard deviations on either side of the mean.

Knowledge about the standard deviation of a distribution of data is useful in a number of ways. One application of this statistic relates to the interpretation of test scores. Let us assume that we have administered two tests to an individual, a test of mechanical aptitude and a test of manual dexterity. This person, we will further assume, earned a score of 80 on the mechanical aptitude test and a score of 115 on the dexterity test. Did he score better on the mechanical or manual test? It is obvious that the information thus far presented is insufficient to make a judgment.

A partial answer to this question is provided by comparing his performance with the mean performance of large groups of persons who have previously taken both tests. Suppose the mean mechanical aptitude score earned by such groups was 60 and the mean manual dexterity score was 105. It is apparent now, that this person scored somewhat better than average on both the mechanical aptitude and on the dexterity test. In order to find out *how much* better than average he scored on these tests we might want to examine the standard deviations of the two distributions of test scores. We will assume that the standard deviation as computed for the mechanical aptitude test is 20 while the standard deviation for the manual dexterity test is 30. The distributions of scores for these two tests are shown in Figure 2–9.

When the test scores are converted to standard deviation units, as shown in Figure 2–9, this person's mechanical aptitude score converts to $+1\sigma$ (1 standard deviation above the mean) while his manual dexterity score converts to $+0.33\sigma$ (one third of a standard deviation above the mean). Since a standard deviation is uniformly interpreted regardless of the test or the unit of measurement, provided that the distributions are normal, it is apparent that this person scored better on the mechanical test than on the manual test. In addition, we can see how much better he scored on mechanical aptitude by comparing the percentage of persons scoring below $+1\sigma$ (84 percent) with the percentage scoring below $+.33\sigma$ (62 percent).

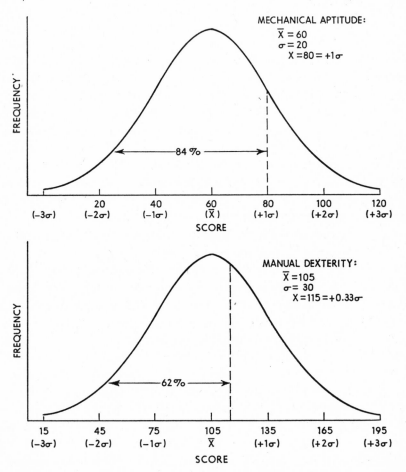

FIGURE 2–9. Distributions of Scores on a Test of Mechanical Aptitude and a Test of Manual Dexterity Showing the Relative Position of Individual X in Each Distribution.

By way of summary to the present point, then, we can completely describe any set of normally distributed data by indicating the mean and standard deviation of the distribution and the number of subjects upon whom observations were made. The typical experiment yields at least two distributions of data: one for the experimental group and one for the control group. These distributions must be evaluated by the investigator in order to determine whether they are similar (or related) or dissimilar (or unrelated). It is to this matter of interpreting the outcomes of experimentation that we next turn our attention.

Statistical Inference

The interpretation of data presents two general kinds of problems. The first of these occurs in the usual control-group experiment in which the investigator has made two sets of observations: one in the experimental group and one in the control group. He wishes to determine whether differences between the distributions of data in these two groups can be attributed to the influence of the independent variable. The second general kind of problem involves the kind of investigation in which two sets of observations are made on the same group of persons (for example, intelligence test scores and grades earned in school). In such cases the investigator may wish to determine whether or not the two variables are related. We will consider these problems one at a time.

The Difference between Means. One way in which to evaluate the effectiveness of an industrial training program is periodically to test the employees' knowledge as the training progresses. This is quite comparable to the usual practice in colleges and universities of testing students' knowledge during the course of the academic year.

Suppose we were interested in comparing the effectiveness of two kinds of industrial training programs. The first kind, which we will refer to as "distributed training," requires that employees attend training sessions two hours a day for five days. The second kind of program, "massed training," also offers a total of 10 hours of instruction. Employees under this program, however, attend class five hours a day for two consecutive days. The trainees are randomly assigned to the two groups to control extraneous factors, and a test of their knowledge at the end of 10 hours of training yields a mean score in the distributed group of 52.5 while the mean for the massed group is only 50.0. Although it appears, upon superficial examination, that distributed training is superior to massed training, it is impossible to interpret these data properly until we apply a test of statistical significance to the obtained difference between means.

The fundamental problem underlying statistical inference stems from the fact that experimental data are accumulated over a finite period of time and from limited numbers of experimental subjects.

In the illustrative training program experiment we are dealing with *samples* of employees receiving massed and distributed training rather than with the *population* (all employees to whom such training might be given). Furthermore, the criterion measure of knowledge after 10 hours of training must, of necessity, sample this knowledge rather than measure all of its components. Thus, the criterion instrument itself samples from the population of information and skills constituting "job knowledge."

However, our interest in experimental findings is not limited to the performance of samples of persons upon samples of possible test questions. We wish instead to make inferences of a more general nature from our data. We want to be able, for example, to formulate generalizations about the performance on the *population* of test questions measuring job knowledge by the *population* of employees.

The extent to which we can confidently make such generalizations is largely dependent upon the magnitude of our sampling errors. The smaller such errors, the more confidence we may place in generalizations about the population. When we statistically test the significance of the difference between means, we are in effect asking: "What is the probability of obtaining a difference between means as great or greater than the one we have noted for our samples *when there is no difference between the population means?*" In other words, what is the likelihood that we have obtained a chance rather than a statistically significant difference?

In addition to the magnitude of sampling errors influencing the means, the answer to this question is dependent upon the errors of measurement itself (which are usually small), and the size of the obtained difference between sample means. Sampling and measurement errors affect the accuracy of the mean and their influence can be estimated by formula from the standard deviation of the scores in the distribution and the number of subjects in the group.

Let us assume that there were 100 trainees in each group, that the standard deviation as computed for the distributed group was 17.0 and that the standard deviation as computed for the massed group was 18.0. The distributions of data for the two groups are shown in Figure 2–10.

The two distributions shown in Figure 2–10 overlap to a considerable extent. Virtually every test score was earned by some of the trainees in both groups. Since the distributions are so much alike, we cannot be at all confident that the 2.5 point difference between

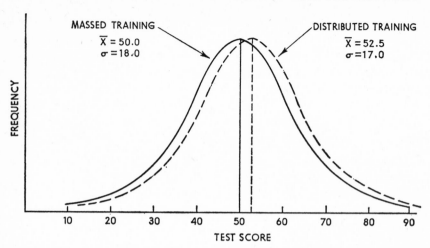

FIGURE 2–10. Distributions of Test Scores after Massed and Distributed Training
Sessions: The Effect of Large Standard Deviations.

means would be obtained again if the experiment were repeated.

By way of contrast, however, if the standard deviations were smaller, say 0.50 for the distributed group and 0.40 for the massed group, the plotted distributions of scores would look like those illustrated in Figure 2–11. You notice, in this instance, that the distri-

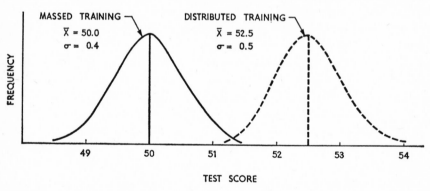

FIGURE 2–11. Distributions of Test Scores after Massed and Distributed Training
Sessions: The Effect of Relatively Small Standard Deviations.

butions of scores are quite independent of one another. Little overlap exists, indicating that most of the scores were obtained either by trainees in the distributed group or the massed group, but not by trainees in both groups. Such data indicate that the two distributions of scores are independent. In this instance we would conclude that distributed training is really superior to massed training.

Statistical Significance. Let us probe this matter of testing the difference between means in somewhat greater depth.

Suppose we drew two random samples from the same population and subjected each group to the *identical* condition. Under such circumstances we would expect the mean scores in the two groups to be very similar. These means would not be identical because of chance factors operating when individuals are assigned to groups. Sometimes the mean of one group would be higher, and vice versa.

Thus, if we assume the operation only of chance factors, we would anticipate a certain amount of fluctuation between sample means and, as a consequence, a certain amount of fluctuation in the size of the difference between pairs of sample means. If the samples are randomly drawn from the same population, the differences between pairs of means should be distributed closely about a value of zero.

Expectations about the fluctuation of mean differences attributable *solely to chance* can be determined statistically. The "standard error of the difference" tells us how much chance variation to anticipate in a distribution of differences between pairs of means for groups randomly drawn from the same population. The standard error of the difference is, in effect, a standard deviation of a distribution of mean differences attributable to chance for randomly drawn groups.

In actual experimentation, we begin with random groups and subject them to *different* conditions. What would happen if these conditions had no effect at all upon performance? The obtained difference between the group means would fall within the range of differences anticipated solely on the basis of chance. However, if the obtained difference exceeds differences attributable to chance fluctuations, we have evidence for a "statistically significant" difference.

In practice, the investigator applies a statistical test to his obtained difference between means in order to determine whether this difference is a real or chance finding. This statistic, the *t ratio,* involves a comparison between the obtained mean difference and the standard error of the difference (that is, the amount of mean fluctuation attributable to chance variation).

The *t* ratio indicates the likelihood that the mean difference for the population is *smaller* than the one actually obtained from the experimental samples. Convention dictates that when this probability exceeds 5 percent, we regard the obtained difference as not significant. We must, in other words, have evidence that a difference as great or greater than the one we obtained would occur by chance only five times in a hundred before attributing this difference to manipulation of the independent variable rather than to chance. Although a probability of 0.05 is generally accepted as indicating a statistically significant difference, lower probabilities on the order of 0.01 or 0.001 often are obtained and give cause for still greater confidence in the experimental conclusion.

Statistical versus Practical Significance. The distinction between statistical and practical significance is of great importance in applied research. To illustrate, consider again the hypothetical investigation of the effects of increased illumination upon typing speed. Even if the mean performance in the experimental group (with increased illumination) was statistically superior to that in the control group, we still must inquire whether the amount of improvement justifies the expense of rewiring and installing new fixtures in the office.

A relatively small difference between means may be statistically significant when the groups are large, but lack statistical significance when the groups are small. If very large groups are required to demonstrate statistical significance, the practical utility of the finding may be questionable.

Correlation

Another kind of interpretive problem involves the determination of the extent of relationship between any two variables. Such a relationship is statistically expressed by a coefficient of correlation (r). Industrial psychologists use this statistic most often for estimating the reliability and validity of psychological tests.

A *reliable* test is one that yields essentially the same rank ordering of persons taking the test on different occasions. Thus, if we administered the same intelligence test to a class today and again next week, we would expect the person who earned the highest score on the first occasion to score at or very near the top on the second occasion if the test is reliable. A *valid* test measures what it purports to measure. Scores on a test of academic ability, for example, should be related to earned grade-point average in school if the test is valid.

The extent to which scores obtained from two administrations of the same test are related (reliability) or the extent to which test scores are related to a criterion of the trait that the test is supposed to measure (validity) is typically expressed as a correlation coefficient.

A *Perfect Positive Correlation.* Two sets of observations made under comparable circumstances may be conveniently presented in the form of a crossplot or *scattergram.* Such a scattergram showing the relationship between inches and centimeters is illustrated in Figure 2–12. Measurement of distance in inches is shown on the Y-axis; corresponding distances in centimeters show on X-axis.

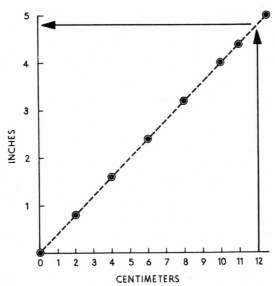

FIGURE 2–12.   A Scattergram for Inches Plotted against Centimeters.

This scattergram shows eight pairs of observations, each indicated by a dot. Each of these points shows the distance on a centimeter scale corresponding to a particular distance on an inch scale.

You will note that all of the plotted points in this scattergram can be joined by a straight line (the *regression line*). The fact that all pairs of observations fall on the regression line is indicative of the existence of a perfect correlation between the two variables under consideration. When computed, the numerical value of the coefficient of correlation would be 1.00, which is the maximum value that this statistic may attain.

What does a correlation coefficient of 1.00 tell us? It indicates, in the first place, that there is a complete and inflexible relationship between the two variables. One centimeter, for example, always corresponds to 0.3937 inch; two centimeters to 0.7874 inch, and so on. Secondly, differences between pairs of measurements of one variable are reflected in proportional differences between pairs of measurements of the second variable. In our illustration, every increase or decrease of 1 centimeter corresponds to an increase or decrease of 0.3937 inch. The effect of proportional change in the two variables is to produce the straight line relationship illustrated in Figure 2–12.

A perfect relationship, like the one illustrated, enables us to predict one variable from the other without error. Suppose, for example, that we lost the ruler that measures in inches and had only the one that measures in centimeters. We could transform a measured distance of 12 centimeters to 4.72 inches simply by inspection of the scattergram. We could, in other words, predict what the measurement would have been if we had used a scale calibrated in inches. As long as the correlation between the variables is perfect (1.00), such predictions will be entirely free of error.

In addition to being perfect, the correlation for data like those presented in Figure 2–12 is positive; the computed value of the coefficient will be + 1.00. The fact that the obtained correlation carries a + sign indicates that there is a *direct* relationship between the two variables. Increases in score on either of the variables are paralleled by increases in score on the other variable. Similarly, a decrease in score on one variable is paralleled by a corresponding decrease on the other variable.

A Perfect Negative Correlation. Correlation coefficients are not always positive. An illustration of a scattergram yielding a perfect negative correlation (− 1.00) is presented in Figure 2–13.

Again, all pairs of observations fall on a straight line indicating a perfect relationship between variables X and Y and hence errorless predictability of one variable from the other. Knowing, for example, that an individual scored 7.0 on variable X we would predict that his score on variable Y would be 4.5.

The variables in this illustration are, however, inversely rather than directly related. An increase in scores on variable X is paralleled by a corresponding decrease in Y-scores; and a decrease in X-scores is paralleled by a corresponding increase in Y-scores. This inverse relationship would be reflected in the computation of r by the assignment of a negative sign to the correlation coefficient.

A High Correlation. Perfect correlations do not occur when we deal with psychological phenomena. Let us assume that we have constructed a test for selecting personnel and wish to validate it against the criterion of supervisor's rating of efficiency at the end

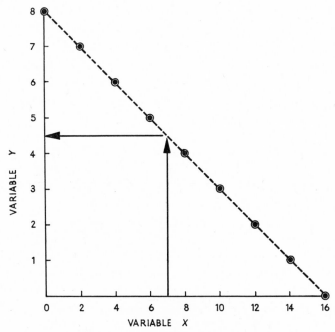

FIGURE 2–13. Scattergram Indicating a Perfect Negative Correlation.

of six months of employment. We would administer the test to all new employees and correlate the scores with the supervisor's ratings which would be available six months later. Figure 2–14 shows a hypothetical scattergram of such data.

This scattergram indicates that four of the 36 employees tested earned test scores of 60; their ratings six months later ranged between 5.50 and 7.00. Similarly, five employees earned test scores of 50 and received ratings ranging between 4.30 and 6.50 and so on.

It is obvious that the 36 points do not fall on a straight line; hence the correlation between the two variables is not perfect. The points do, however, tend to cluster about a line as indicated in Figure 2–

14. The computed correlation would be somewhat less than perfect and it would be positive, indicating that as test scores increase, supervisor's ratings tend to be more favorable. The actual coefficient in this illustration is + 0.74.

Can we use an imperfect correlation like this one as a basis for making predictions? Yes, but our predictions will contain a certain

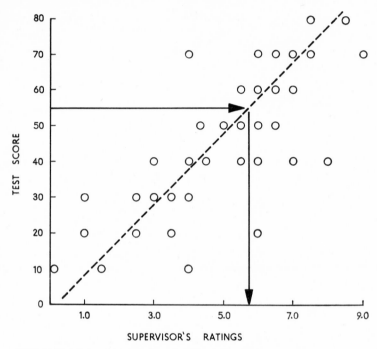

FIGURE 2–14. A Crossplot of Scores on a Personnel Selection Test against Supervisory Ratings of Efficiency.

amount of error If a job applicant scored 55 on the test, our best point prediction about his efficiency rating is that it will be 5.70. The more closely the observations cluster about the regression line (the higher the correlation), the more confidence we can have in the accuracy of this prediction. Conversely, the more dispersed are the observations from the regression line (the lower the correlation), the less confident we will be of the accuracy of this prediction.

What would happen to the obtained correlation coefficient if we had plotted the test scores in terms of the number of items answered incorrectly, instead of in terms of the number of correct answers. The strength of the relationship between the test and criterion would be unaffected. The direction of this relationship would, however, be reversed. In other words, as error scores increased, efficiency ratings would decrease. The resultant value of *r* would be negative, although the numerical value of the coefficient would be unchanged. Thus, the coefficient computed under these circumstances would be −0.74.

A Zero Correlation. Suppose we wish to determine the extent of relationship between the heights of college students and their grade-point averages. We could plot these variables against each

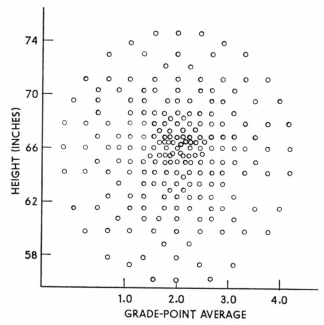

FIGURE 2–15. Heights of College Students Plotted against Grade-Point Averages Indicating a Correlation Coefficient of 0.00.

other and would obtain results approximating those displayed in Figure 2–15. This scattergram indicates that there is no relationship between the two variables in question. The grade-point averages of tall students are no different from those of short students, and in consequence, the computed *r* is 0.00. This minimum value of the correlation coefficient indicates that it is impossible to fit any regression line to the data. As a result, predictions of one variable from the other will have only chance accuracy.

Interpretation of Correlation Coefficients. A correlation coefficient is most properly interpreted in the light of the purpose for which it was computed. When estimating the validity of a test, coefficients in the vicinity of 0.40 are generally acceptable. Reliability studies, however, must demonstrate the existence of a more substantial correlation. The manuals for most published tests generally report reliability coefficients within the range 0.80–0.95.

As indicated earlier, correlational analysis has numerous applications aside from those related to the reliability and validity of tests. One such application utilizes the coefficient to provide an index of the amount of overlapping variance. The higher the correlation, the greater is the amount of overlap between variables. When the obtained correlation is 1.00, the variances overlap completely; when the correlation is 0.00, the variables do not overlap at all.

It is unfortunate that correlation coefficients look like percentages. The resemblance is entirely superficial. The percentage of overlapping variance is given by the *coefficient of determination* (r^2) rather than by the r itself. A correlation of 0.60, for example, indicates 36 percent overlapping variance. Conversely, the *coefficient of nondetermination* ($1 - r^2$) in this instance indicates that 64 percent of the variance is independent (that is, does not overlap).

We have already said that correlations do not imply causality. Thus, the coefficient of determination must be interpreted cautiously. Although a correlation of 0.60 means we have 36 percent overlapping variance, this amount of overlap might have resulted from any one of four conditions:

1. Changes in one variable caused changes to occur in the second variable.
2. Changes in the second variable caused changes to occur in the first variable.
3. The two correlated variables co-vary as a function of changes in some third, more basic underlying variable, but are themselves unrelated in causative fashion.
4. The relationship between the correlated variables is interactive in nature. An obtained correlation between productivity of piece-rate workers and their job satisfaction might reflect such an interaction. High productivity results in higher pay and may therefore lead to increased job satisfaction. Dissatisfaction with the job, however, may be responsible for diminished interest in the work and hence for lowered output.

Regardless of the conditions responsible for correlation, covariation enables us to predict scores on one variable from knowledge about scores on the other variable. The accuracy of these predictions is a function of the magnitude of r. As the numerical value of r decreases, our predictions become less and less accurate until, with a correlation of 0.00, all predictions have chance accuracy.

Assume, for example, we find a 0.00 correlation between students' heights and their grade-point averages. This means that 50 percent of the students who are taller than average earn above-average grade-points, and 50 percent of the shorter than average students also earn above-average grade-points. Clearly, then, knowledge about height will not aid us in predicting grade-point.

If, however, we used a test of academic ability as a predictor of scholastic performance we could make predictions with better than chance accuracy. Suppose we obtain a correlation between the test and grade-point of 0.40. It has been shown that with such a correlation 63 percent of the students earning above-average predictor scores also earn above-average criterion scores. If the correlation were 0.60, 70 percent of the students earning above-average test scores also earn above-average grade-points.

We will mention just one other application of the correlation coefficient. Sometimes the investigator merely wishes to determine whether the relationship between variables exceeds expectations on the basis of chance. Any r in excess of what would be expected as a chance deviation from a correlation of 0.00 could be meaningful under such circumstances.

In this regard it is important to recall the distinction made earlier between statistical and practical significance. A relatively low correlation may be statistically different from a correlation of 0.00 but lack practical significance for predictive applications.

SUMMARY

The basic approaches to the study of behavior utilized by the industrial psychologist are identical to the methodological approaches utilized in any of the other sciences. These methods are characterized by observation rather than by speculation, by objectivity rather than subjectivity, and by controls making it possible to repeat a set of observations and to draw meaningful conclusions. These elements of scientific method are translated by the researcher into an investigation of the relationship between two basic kinds of variables. One of these, the independent variable, is the factor whose effects are being investigated. The behaviors studied as possible functions of the independent variable are referred to as dependent variables. Thus, in an experiment concerning the effects of illumination upon industrial productivity, illumination is the independent variable and productivity is the dependent variable.

The relationship between independent and dependent variables may be studied by means of the naturalistic method, correlational analysis, and the experimental method. Naturalistic observations are made whenever the independent variable is not amenable to manipulation by the investigator. Under these circumstances the effects of the independent variable must be studied in natural surroundings without interference by the researcher. Correlational analysis reveals the magnitude and direction of the relationship between two or more variables. The experimental method, on the other hand, requires that the investigator manipulate the independent variable and control extraneous factors. The simplest kind of experimental design utilizes two groups of subjects: a control group, which serves as a standard for comparative purposes, and an experimental group, in which the independent variable is manipulated.

The summary and interpretation of data gathered by either the naturalistic or experimental method requires that they be submitted to a statistical analysis. Data may be statistically summarized by measures of central tendency and variability. Measures of central tendency indicate the typical or "average" score; measures of variability indicate the spread of scores away from this "average." The primary measures of central tendency are the mean (the arithmetic average), the median (the middle score in the distribution), and the mode (the score that occurs most frequently). The only measure of variability discussed in the chapter is the standard deviation.

Two statistical techniques valuable for interpreting data are the t ratio and the coefficient of correlation. The t ratio is a test of the likelihood that an obtained difference between means is attributable to chance rather than to the independent variable. The correlation coefficient expresses the strength and direction of the relationship between variables.

II.

Selecting, Placing, and Training Employees

The fundamental objective of selection, placement, and training programs in industry is to best utilize the specific capabilities and interests of the employees. Every individual is unique with respect to the pattern of his abilities and his history of past experiences. Such individual differences result from the interaction of inherited predispositions and environmental influences. The former may, for example, impose maximum limits upon intellectual and physical capabilities. The latter may determine the extent to which these capabilities are realized. Both hereditarian and environmental factors determine our interests, which, in turn, influence the kinds of satisfactions we seek from work and from life in general.

Employers generally consider several factors when hiring a new worker. First, there must be some evidence that the applicant has the capabilities and knowledges required for satisfactory job performance and completion of the company's training program. Second, employers seek workers who will be interested in and stimulated by their work to the maximum extent possible. A third consideration in many instances is the applicant's potential for advancement to positions of greater responsibility within the company.

The reasons for regarding both ability and satisfaction as important elements in personnel selection and placement are fairly obvious. Employees who lack the required abilities, regardless of whether these requisites are intellectual or personal, simply cannot work efficiently. The salesman who cannot converse easily, the supervisor who cannot direct the activities of subordinates, the laborer who lacks the necessary physical stamina, and the teacher who does not know her subject matter are all relatively ineffectual as employees. Similarly, employees who are capable of doing their work but do not regard it as enjoyable or stimulating may reflect their dissatisfaction in lowered productivity and in high absenteeism and turnover.

The primary problem, then, in the selection and placement of personnel is predictive in nature. The employer needs to know, in advance, which of several job applicants will, if hired, be most efficient as an employee. Furthermore, he must be guided in placing employees in order to best utilize their abilities, skills, knowledge, and personal characteristics.

The relationship between selection-placement programs and training programs is almost self-evident. A fundamental purpose of training is to develop job-related knowledges, skills, and attitudes. In addition, in-service training programs often provide educational experiences of a more-or-less formal nature and are designed to provide employees with opportunities for job enlargement and intracompany promotion.

Sound selection, placement, and training programs yield substantial financial dividends. Every new employee represents a monetary investment by management. In addition to the costs of recruitment and training programs, a number of other expenses are incidental to hiring procedures. Every time an employee voluntarily terminates employment or must be fired, this investment is lost.

One of the purposes of this section is to discuss the major techniques of personnel selection and placement, including the use of interviews, application forms, letters of recommendation, and psychological tests. We will be specifically concerned with the ways in which these techniques are developed, utilized, and improved. In addition, the section terminates with a discussion of industrial training which, when properly conceived, should permeate all levels and activities of the organization.

Job Analysis and Performance Criteria

3

Management's decision to institute a program for selecting, placing, and training personnel, or to evaluate the existing programs, leads of necessity to analyses of the specific jobs in question and a delineation of criteria of effective job performance.

Job analysis provides information about the duties entailed in performing the job and the surroundings in which these duties are performed. Such an analysis involves a comprehensive description of the job and, in turn, leads to an understanding of the characteristics required of an employee if he is to perform satisfactorily.

However, "satisfactory" performance may mean a variety of things. When we say an employee is a "satisfactory" worker, do we mean his output per unit of time is high, or that he has shown a relatively rapid rate of advancement, or that he has given evidence of job satisfaction, or are we using some combination of these as well as other criteria? A selection device like the pre-employment interview, for example, may prove much less efficient for predicting certain aspects of job performance than others. Similarly, an evaluation of a given kind of training program may lead to different conclusions when the criterion of "effective" training is based upon the time required to complete the program and when the criterion reflects subsequent on-the-job performance.

The present chapter considers each of these two preliminaries to personnel selection, placement, and training programs. It begins with a discussion of the purposes and techniques of job analysis, and terminates with a discussion of some of the factors involved in establishing criteria of job proficiency.

WAYS IN WHICH JOB ANALYSIS IS USED

A job analysis is prerequisite to many of the activities of the industrial psychologist. Most often the psychologist is required to predict or change behavior in work settings with which he initially is somewhat unfamiliar. He approaches his task by performing a job analysis as a preliminary to the following activities.

Personnel Selection and Placement

It would be utterly impossible to fit men to jobs unless we knew a good deal about the jobs we were attempting to fill. The specific duties to be performed by an employee, and the circumstances under which these duties are to be performed, lead to the specification of necessary employee characteristics. Such specifications dictate the utilization of certain kinds of selection devices and criteria rather than others. Thus, a job involving the use of an electronic computer can be satisfactorily filled only by an employee who either knows how to operate such a computer or has demonstrated the abilities prerequisite to learning the job. A job, like paint mixing, that requires employees to make very fine color discriminations cannot be satisfactorily filled by a color-blind job applicant.

Job analysis sometimes reveals that existent criteria for personnel selection and placement are quite inappropriate. A personnel director may, for example, automatically reject applicants who have not graduated from high school while analysis of the job may reveal that it only requires an eighth grade education. Conversely, in the absence of a thoroughgoing job analysis, the personnel director may place his requirements for selection and placement at an unrealistically low level.

Training Programs

New employees frequently receive some kind of training during the initial period of their employment. The nature of training programs varies extensively from one industry to another and even between jobs within the same industry. Such training may be a highly formalized program consisting of several hours a week of classroom-type instruction. It may, on the other hand, be a relatively informal program in which new employees work "under the wing" of more experienced employees for a period.

The object of any training program may be to teach certain skills required to do a job, to develop certain attitudes (perhaps with respect to safety practices), or to provide other kinds of information of value to new employees. In any event, it is apparent that the structure and objectives of a training program must depend, to a large extent, upon a thoroughgoing job analysis. It is necessary to know what a job entails before employees can be properly trained for satisfactory job performance.

Job Evaluation

The purpose of job evaluation is to determine the relative worth of each job in an industrial organization. One of the primary applications of such an evaluation is the establishment of equitable salary ranges for various jobs within a company. By way of simple illustration, some jobs may expose employees to hazardous working conditions, but may not require much in the way of formal education. Other jobs may require graduate training of some sort, but do not expose employees to undue hazards. A job evaluation under such circumstances would lead to a weighting of the factors of working conditions and educational requirements in order to establish an equitable basis for paying employees on both kinds of jobs.

The determination of the worth of each job within an industrial organization is dependent upon a comparative study of the job duties and the working conditions. Thus, job evaluation must be preceded by an analysis of every job to be evaluated.

Efficient Work Methods

A job analysis may be performed as a preliminary to motion studies designed to develop more efficient methods of work. An analysis for such purposes may reveal, for example, that a particular job requires employees to do considerable walking or an excessive amount of heavy lifting. Rearrangement of the working environment or of materials may reduce the extent of such nonproductive physical activity, leading to a consequent reduction in fatigue and an increase in productivity.

Health and Safety

Certain jobs, by their very nature, expose employees to personal danger. Unnecessary exposure to noxious fumes or radiation, for example, may be discovered by the job analyst and the working conditions revised in order to reduce or eliminate such conditions. Similarly, job analysis may reveal that certain features of machine operation are unduly hazardous, leading thereby to redesign of the equipment.

Merit Rating

Merit ratings are generally supervisory evaluations of the performance of individual employees. Such ratings may be used as a partial criterion for salary increases or promotions, and as indications of employee efficiency.

An unfortunate practice sometimes followed is to administer generalized rating scales requiring that the supervisor evaluate each employee in "shotgun" fashion on a variety of characteristics ranging from *initiative* to *personal appearance*. Such rating scales may have little or no bearing upon the specific job being performed by a particular employee. It is doubtful, for example, that a rating of a lathe operator's "ability to engage in interpersonal relationships" will indicate anything about his merit as a lathe operator.

A far superior approach is to custom-tailor merit rating techniques to specific jobs. The development of rating procedures valid for a specific job must, of course, be preceded by job analysis in order to determine which factors are critical and hence ought to be included in the ratings.

Delimitation of Functions

Even small businesses and offices employing relatively few workers may utilize job analyses. A major source of bickering and discontent in such organizations results from the lack of clarification of duties of individual employees and delimitation of authority. An analysis leading to the definition of duties of each position may serve to eliminate this source of discontent.

The foregoing description of applications of job analysis is not exhaustive. It is sufficient, however, to indicate the diversity of uses for information of the type provided by such analyses. The specific emphasis in any given job analysis will, of course, reflect the purpose for which the analysis has been performed. Job analyses written for the purpose of providing clues to more efficient industrial operation will highlight different aspects of the job than will analyses prepared for the purpose of evaluating the relative worth of jobs within an industrial organization. Aside from minor differences in emphasis as a function of intended application, however, all job analyses are basically alike in that they are designed to provide a detailed description of the analyzed jobs. The ensuing discussion focuses particularly upon job analysis as a basis for clarifying employee requirements with a view to establishing new selection and placement programs or modifying existent programs. This discussion is sufficiently general, however, to apply to job analyses performed for quite a variety of intended applications.

PERFORMING THE JOB ANALYSIS

The analyst is frequently required to study jobs with which he is initially unfamiliar, in industries about which he has relatively little prior knowledge. It is apparent, then, that he must utilize many different sources of information in order to insure the accuracy and meaningfulness of his findings.

Sources of Information

A useful preliminary to the performance of almost any job analysis is to consult analyses of similar jobs prepared in other industries and to review pertinent job descriptions prepared on a national basis. A comprehensive reference for the latter type of job description is the *Dictionary of Occupational Titles*[1] which contains descriptions of more than 40,000 jobs. These descriptions are rather terse and somewhat general in nature. They represent a synthesis of the duties encompassed by a particular job title as performed by employees in a number of different industries. These descriptions may serve, however, to familiarize the analyst with the grosser elements of the job and with some of the vocabulary he is likely to encounter from employees and supervisors. Here, for example, is the description of an offset-press man presented in the *Dictionary of Occupational Titles*.

OFFSET-PRESS MAN (print. & pub.) 4–48. 050. *offset-press operator*. Makes ready and tends an offset printing press that imprints stock sheets with illustration or type material from lithograph (prepared zinc) plates: Washes plate to remove protective coating and cleans back of plate to perfect smoothness. Builds up back of plate to desired printing thickness (about 0.015 inch) with sheets of tissue paper. Clamps one edge of plate to plate cylinder, using hand tools. Operates press slowly to wrap plate and backing in place around cylinder, and clamps other edge to cylinder. Adjusts diameter of blanket cylinder exactly to diameter of plate cylinder by building up tissue paper sheets under rubber blanket (covering) of cylinder. Pours supply of ink in fountain (trough) of press and runs press

---

[1] United States Employment Service, Division of Occupational Analysis, *Dictionary of Occupational Titles, Vol. I,* Definition of Titles (Washington, D.C.: U.S. Government Printing Office, 1949).

until ink rollers are thoroughly coated. Adjusts space between blanket and impression cylinders to thickness of stock to be printed and sets water roller so as to deliver proper moisture to plate cylinder. Starts press and runs several sheets through press to prepare proofs. Scans proofs closely for flaws and cleans plate or cylinder to correct any found. Starts motor and press and tends press during production run. Removes plate from press at end of run, and cleans plate and cylinders. Lubricates and cleans press.[2]

The job analyst occasionally finds that the job he is asked to study has previously been submitted to analysis in the same industry, plant, or business in which he is working. Plant modernization and equipment changes may make it necessary to revise and update job analyses performed several years earlier. Furthermore, an analysis originally written for one purpose (for example, improving safety practices) is not always useful for other purposes. Nevertheless, the job analyst may profitably study these written analyses as a preliminary to his own analysis.

After gaining a degree of familiarity with the job by means of studying analyses of related jobs, descriptions prepared on a national basis, and earlier analyses of the specific job in question, the job analyst may use three basic techniques for assembling the data he needs. These techniques are: (1) observation, (2) a questionnaire and/or interview, (3) actually performing the job himself. These approaches are best regarded as supplemental to one another rather than as mutually exclusive. Specific elements of the job not detected by observation may be revealed by questionnaire or interview responses and by actually working on the job.[3]

Observation. This approach to gathering data about the job requires that the analyst watch employees as they work. He must be careful to be as unobtrusive as possible while making notes. Generally he takes as few notes as possible while making the observation and then expands them immediately after the observation is completed.

The observer must be constantly aware of the fact that he is to note characteristics of the job and not characteristics of individual employees. Personal idiosyncrasies will cause subtle discrepancies in the ways in which individual workers perform the same job.

---

[2] *Ibid.,* p. 903.

[3] G. L. Bryan, "Empirical Evaluation of Various Job-Analysis Methods," *Symposium on Electronics Maintainance* (Washington, D.C.: U.S. Government Printing Office, August, 1955).

An adequate sample of workers on the same job must be observed at various times during the work period. In order to generalize about the job requirements, the analyst must guard against observing only the best or worst workers, or limiting his observations to periods when workers are performing at their maximum or minimum levels.

The observations will suggest many questions to the analyst about what is being done, why it is done in a particular way, and about the skills, past training, and other prerequisites to satisfactory job performance. The purpose of interviews and questionnaires is both to elicit new information about the job as suggested by such questions and to verify the observations.

Questionnaires and Interviews. A variety of persons must be interviewed and/or complete questionnaires, including the workers, their subordinates (if any), their immediate supervisors, higher level management, service personnel, and so on. The workers themselves are often aware of small details of job performance that may pass unnoticed by their supervisors or by the job analyst. The supervisor, on the other hand, is in a somewhat better position by virtue of his responsibility for several employees, to separate out job characteristics from worker characteristics.

The primary advantage of utilization of a questionnaire rather than an interview for eliciting job information is that the former is more economical of time. Persons completing a questionnaire may do so at their leisure and, if the accompanying directions are self-explanatory, without the guidance of the job analyst. This advantage is more than offset, however, by two potential deficiencies in the questionnaire approach. First, it may be difficult to motivate respondents to fill out the questionnaire with the necessary accuracy and care. Secondly, responses to questionnaire items may be lacking in the essential detail needed by the job analyst. Consequently, wherever possible, the personal interview either by itself or in combination with administration of a questionnaire, is a more desirable method for eliciting information of value to the job analyst.

The conduct of an interview is not a simple matter. The completeness of the information elicited during an interview depends, in large measure, upon the care with which the interviewer phrases his questions and upon the rapport (mutual respect and understanding) developed between interviewer and interviewee. Certain fundamental "rules" for the conduct of the job analysis interview have been suggested as follows:

1. Make sure the interviewee knows who you represent, what your name is, and what you are there for, so he will have a broad idea of what is required of him.
2. Show that his cooperation in giving information is helping to find facts.
3. Carefully think out and word questions before asking them.
4. Be interested in the information which you are receiving.
5. Secure specific and full information as directly as possible.
6. Respect the judgment of the interviewee since he, not the analyst, is the expert.
7. Close the interview promptly.
8. Express appreciation to the one who has granted the interview.[4]

Actually Doing the Job.   Many job analysts do not, in practice, avail themselves of this additional source of information. Nevertheless, actual work on the job often provides insights about certain job demands and requirements not readily apparent either from observations or interviews.

The Job Analysis Schedule

The information obtained from observations, questionnaires, and interviews is not assembled in haphazard fashion. The analyst typically records his observations and summarizes interview responses on a worksheet, or *job analysis schedule.* This schedule serves constantly to focus the attention of the analyst upon the critical job elements. The format and contents of the schedule vary somewhat as a function of the job being analyzed and the purpose for which the analysis is being conducted. Essentially, though, all such schedules cover certain basic elements. The United States Employment Service developed its job analysis schedules with a view to obtaining the following kinds of information.

I. *Work Performed—Physical and Mental.*
   a) *What* the worker does, including physical and mental responses made in the work situation.
   b) *How* he does it. What tools, machinery, equipment, and so on does the worker use? What kinds of calculations, formulas, judgments, and so on must the worker make?
   c) *Why* is the job done? What is its overall purpose and how does each task performed relate to this purpose?

---

[4] United States Employment Service, Department of Labor, *Training and Reference Manual for Job Analysis* (Washington, D.C.: U.S. Government Printing Office, 1944), p. 57.

II. *Skill Involved.*

   a) *Responsibility.* What is the extent of the worker's supervisory responsibility for the activities of other employees? What is the extent of his nonsupervisory responsibility for preventing damage to equipment and materials, for making personal contacts (of the type made by salesmen), and for cooperating with other employees?

   b) *Job Knowledge.* This factor includes knowledge of equipment, materials, techniques, and processes. The amount of job knowledge required is inversely related to the degree of supervision and guidance received by the employee.

   c) *Mental Application.* This general designation includes such factors as versatility, judgment, and intellectual alertness.

   d) *Dexterity and Accuracy.* What kind of manual or manipulative ability is required to perform the work to the degree of accuracy and precision required by the job?

III. *Selection Factors.*

   a) *Experience and Training,* including prior job experience, or experience on related jobs, or educational requirements.

   b) *Physical Demands.* The physical activities required by the job, the environmental conditions in which the job is performed, and exposure to hazards and dangers.

   c) *Worker Characteristics* of any kind (both physical and mental) that are related to satisfactory job performance.

The organization of a job analysis schedule is illustrated by the actual forms used by job analysis of the United States Employment Service as illustrated in Figure 3–1. Portions of these forms have been completed for an analysis of the job of Bank Clerk's Wife that was anonymously prepared after World War II.[5]

JOB SPECIFICATION

The information obtained from a job analysis is rarely used in its original form. The data as recorded on the job analysis schedule is generally too cumbersome for practical purposes. It must be organized and edited in order to make pertinent information readily accessible to the reader. The resultant statement of duties, qualifications, and other information developed from a job analysis is referred to as a *job description.* When the job description is primarily prepared for specifying worker characteristics to be con-

---

[5] Anonymous, "Job Description of a Bank Clerk's Wife," *The Dime,* Union Dime Savings Bank. Reprinted in *Personnel Journal,* Vol. XXVII (1948), pp. 79–80.

Form USES-546   U. S. DEPARTMENT OF LABOR   Budget Bureau No. 44-R577.3
(2–44)   BUREAU OF EMPLOYMENT SECURITY
                                UNITED STATES EMPLOYMENT SERVICE

                                JOB ANALYSIS SCHEDULE

1. Job title __Bank Clerk's Wife_____   2. Number _____102_____

3. Number employed M ____0____ F ____1_____   4. Establishment No. _____

6. Alternate titles _____   5. Date ___1944_____

____Spouse_____   Number of sheets _____

____Darling_____   8. Industry ___Family_____

____Battleaxe_____   9. Branch ___Local_____

7. Dictionary title and code _____   10. Department ___Uxorial_____

11. WORK PERFORMED:
        Under supervision of Husband (101) and/or Children (104, 105, 106) maintains
household. Allocates funds. Purchases supplies. Contrives, invents means and
methods of making Bank Clerk's (101) salary support family. (This is considered
impossible, or at least improbable, by careful statisticians.) Entertains
intelligentsia (friends and own family) and Morons (husband's friends and
family). Supervises Dog (103) and other livestock including Husband (101) and
Children (104, 105, 106).

        Daily Duties:
        1. Awakes Clerk (101). Selects suit (selection limited to one). Selects
shirt (selection limited to one clean, one soiled and two frayed). Searches for
shoes, keys, handkerchiefs, studs. Gives detailed instructions for day's program.
        2. Prepares meal. Disburses carfare and/or lunch funds.
        3. Dresses children (104, 105, 106).
        4. Washes dishes. Scrubs floors, windows, paintwork. Polishes silver, brass,
furniture.
        5. Plans day's marketing. Calculates expenditures. Compares calculations with
available funds. Recalculates. Goes to market with Children (104, 105, 106).
Destroys market list as impractical. Improvises new menu according to
availability of materials.
        6. Arbitrates differences of opinion expressed vociferously and belligerently
by Children (104, 105, 106).
        7. Washes and irons sheets, shirts, blankets, rugs, underwear.
        8. Mends and repairs sheets, shirts, blankets, rugs, underwear, tables, chairs,
beds, radio.
        9. Compromises differences of opinion. Accepts her own opinion. Rejects
Husband's.
        10. Exercises Dog (103). Wards off seasonal acquaintances. Takes Dog out when
Dog prefers to stay in. Takes Dog in when Dog insists upon staying out.
Separates Dog from fights and other turmoils. Relegates Husband (101) to
dog-house.

                            (CONTINUE ON SUPPLEMENTARY SHEETS)

Analyst ____A. Clurk_____   Reviewer _____

FIGURE 3–1. Job Analysis Schedule Used by the United States Employment Office.

SOURCES OF WORKERS

12. Experience: None .... Acceptable ..Charm,..poise,..amatory..efficiency.--.past experience not divulged. Complete knowledge of French, piano, ballet, opera, literature. Ability to handle butlers, personal servants etc.

13. Training data: Minimum training time—(a) Inexperienced workers.   Varies
(b) Experienced workers.   Varies

TRAINING	SPECIFIC JOB SKILLS ACQUIRED THROUGH TRAINING
In-plant (on job) training Continual during the period of employment.	Ability to render first aid, medical advice and treatment and minor surgical assistance. Veterinarian ability. Ability to haggle, wash diapers, iron shirts etc.
Vocational training Continual prior to employment.	twelve hours a day and still look lovely in the evening. Ability to do the work of carpenter, painter, electrician, plumber, cleaning woman, dishwasher, chef, CPA,
Technical training Varies	arbitrator, fashion designer, advisor.
SRW Eng. General education Ability to please, charm and fascinate.	
Activities and hobbies	

14. Apprenticeship: Formal ..No.. Informal .No... Length required ....

15. Relation to other jobs:
(a) Promotions from and to, transfers, etc.: ..Promotion.from.'Teen..Eventual.promotion.to ......mother-in-law..

(b) Supervision received: General .... Close ...X....... By ..Husband.(101)...........
(Title)

(c) Supervision given: None .... Number supervised ......5....... Titles ..Husband.(101),.Children (104,.105,.106).and.Dog.(103)....

The following items must be covered on supplementary sheets.

PERFORMANCE REQUIREMENTS

16. Responsibility (consider material or product, safety of others, equipment or process, cooperation with others, instruction of others, public contacts, and the like).
17. Job knowledge (consider pre-employment and on-the-job knowledge of equipment, materials, working procedures, techniques, and processes).
18. Mental application (consider initiative, adaptability, independent judgment, and mental alertness).
19. Dexterity and accuracy (consider speed and degree of precision, dexterity, accuracy, coordination, expertness, care, and deftness of manipulation, operation, or processing of materials, tools, instruments, or gages used).

COMMENTS

20. Equipment, materials, and supplies. : Electrical equipment, vacuum cleaner, duster, mop, broom,
21. Definition of terms.   sewing machine, rolling pin, pressure cooker, snow shovel,
22. General comments.   ash cans, washing machine, black lace and other deceptive devices, eyelashes, girdles, sweaters, lipstick and perfumes.

GPO 883463

FIGURE 3–1. (Continued.)

Form ES-267 (Reverse)
(Rev. 2-44)

PHYSICAL DEMANDS FORM

Job Title_____Occupational Code_____
Dictionary Title_____
Firm Name & Address_____
Industry_____Industrial Code_____
Branch_____Department_____
Company Officer_____Analyst_____Date_____

PHYSICAL ACTIVITIES		WORKING CONDITIONS	
1 Walking	16 Throwing	51 Inside	66 Mechanical Hazards
2 Jumping	17 Pushing	52 Outside	67 Moving Objects
3 Running	18 Pulling	53 Hot	68 Cramped Quarters
4 Balancing	19 Handling	54 Cold	69 High Places
5 Climbing	20 Fingering	55 Sudden Temp. Changes	70 Exposure to Burns
6 Crawling	21 Feeling	56 Humid	71 Electrical Hazards
7 Standing	22 Talking	57 Dry	72 Explosives
8 Turning	23 Hearing	58 Wet	73 Radiant Energy
9 Stooping	24 Seeing	59 Dusty	74 Toxic Conditions
10 Crouching	25 Color Vision	60 Dirty	75 Working With Others
11 Kneeling	26 Depth Perception	61 Odors	76 Working Around Others
12 Sitting	27 Working Speed	62 Noisy	77 Working Alone
13 Reaching	28	63 Adequate Lighting	78
14 Lifting	29	64 Adequate Ventilation	79
15 Carrying	30	65 Vibration	80

DETAILS OF PHYSICAL ACTIVITIES:

7-8307 bs-final

FIGURE 3-1. (Continued.)

sidered when hiring and placing employees, it is called a *job specification*. A sample job specification presenting a brief job description followed by detailed information about worker characteristics required for satisfactory job performance is shown in Figure 3-2.

There are two basic procedures for extrapolating information about worker requirements: (1) estimation, (2) measurement.

PAYROLL TITLE ___Hand Burner_____

CLASSIFICATION TITLE _____

Acetylene Burner Operator

DEPARTMENT _____

_Plate Shop_____

OCCUPATIONAL CODE _____.

6-85.219

FOREMAN ___John Jones_____

TELEPHONE ___158_____

JOB SUMMARY: Cuts mild steel plates into various shapes with an oxyacetylene cutting torch guided by layout markings on the material. With an oxyacetylene cutting torch, cuts steel plates and shapes to various dimensions and sizes as marked and laid out by LAYOUT MAN, manually moving the cutting torch along prescribed lines so that flame will cut plates squarely or with a specified bevel, as indicated by layout symbols; occasionally heats metal to dry surface, or preheats metal for cutting, bending or shaping, or to burn off paint, rust or scale, preparatory to Arc Welding,

Works under supervision of LEADERMAN (BURNING)

EDUCATIONAL STATUS ___Speak, read, write English_____

EXPERIENCE REQUIRED ___3 months as hand burner helper_____

KNOWLEDGE AND SKILLS: Must know oxyacetylene cutting and heating procedure and how to adjust fuel pressure; must be able to select proper burning tips, to clean and adjust torch and torch tips.

PHYSICAL REQUIREMENTS ___Standard physical examination_____

PERSONAL REQUIREMENTS ___None_____

MARITAL STATUS ___Open_____

SEX ___Male_____ AGE RANGE ___18 and over___

CITIZENSHIP ___Open_____

REFERENCES REQUIRED: WORK ___Yes_____

CHARACTER ___None_____

WORKER MUST FURNISH ___8" pliers; 10" crescent wrench; gloves; helmet._____

WAGE CODE ___3a_____

HOURS ___8_____ DAYS _____6_____

SHIFT ___Day; swing; graveyard_____

TESTS: APTITUDE ___None_____

TRADE ___Performance burning test____

Source: Carroll L. Shartle, *Occupational Information* (New York: Prentice-Hall, Inc., 1952), p. 66.

FIGURE 3–2. Job Specification for Hand Burner. John Doe Shipbuilding Company.

Estimation

The earliest approaches were based simply upon the analyst's estimate of the job's requirements derived from his observations and interviews. The characteristics thus delimited tended to be rather vague and ambiguous. Furthermore, it was virtually impossible to arrange the worker characteristics identified in this fashion into a hierarchy of relative importance.

Generalized Characteristics. This procedure is an attempt to systematize estimates of worker requirements. It begins with a list of job skills, abilities, and traits that might be important for *any* job (for example, keenness of vision, memory, ability to make decisions, eye-hand coordination). Each item in the list is carefully defined and accompanied by a rating scale on which the analyst estimates the degree of importance of each characteristic for the job in question. The pattern of ratings for a given job constitutes its "profile," and a comparison of profiles for various jobs indicates the relative importance of the various worker characteristics across jobs.[6]

Although ratings of generalized characteristics eliminate some of the ambiguity from specifications of worker requirements and facilitate the arrangement of these requirements in a hierarchy of relative importance, the procedure has one shortcoming. It fails to call the analyst's attention to specific characteristics that may differentiate between efficient and inefficient workers.

The Critical Incidents Technique. This technique, developed by Flanagan,[7] emphasizes the specific (or critical) factors contributing to job success or failure. The technique has a variety of applications to psychological evaluation and is particularly well suited to developing job specifications.

Almost any job analysis will reveal something about the factors differentiating between efficient and inefficient workers and hence will suggest specifications for satisfactory job performance. Flanagan's technique, however, was developed in order to overcome the relatively slipshod way in which some of this information is obtained. It focuses the observer's attention specifically upon the critical behaviors which serve to differentiate between satisfactory and unsatisfactory job performance.

In essence, the critical incidents technique requires that the supervisor carefully observe and record employees' behaviors which are critical to satisfactory job performance. The supervisor also records specific incidents in which workers have performed unsatisfac-

---

[6] M. S. Viteles, "Job Specifications and Diagnostic Tests of Job Competency Designed for the Auditing Division of a Street Railway Company," *Psychological Clinic*, Vol. XIV (1923), pp. 83–105.

[7] J. C. Flanagan, "Critical Requirements: A New Approach to Employee Evaluation," *Personnel Psychology*, Vol. II (1949), pp. 419–25.

torily. This kind of record can be invaluable for identifying worker characteristics essential for adequate job specifications.

Measurement

Whenever a procedure depends upon estimates made by human beings it is susceptible to subjective errors in judgment. The suggestion was made over 40 years ago that job profiles could be objectively developed by relying upon the results of measurement instead of judgment. Instead of requiring analysts to estimate worker requirements, a battery of psychological tests could be administered to workers on different jobs and the resultant scores used to develop profiles of the abilities and traits associated with job performance.[8]

A number of difficulties are inherent in the measurement approach to job specification. Foremost among these is the matter of deciding which tests ought to be included in the battery. In attempting to strike a reasonable balance between cost of the program, time available for test administration, and comprehensive coverage of the psychological characteristics measured, there is always the danger that tests measuring important characteristics will not be included in the battery. Thus, although the measurement approach is more objective than the estimating approach to job specification, the latter may provide increased breadth of trait coverage.

The utilization of test scores for constructing job profiles presents another problem. One technique develops the profile from the average scores earned by groups of workers on a given job. This average is presumed to indicate the relative importance of each trait or characteristic: when it is high, the trait is important; when it is low, the trait is unimportant. However, it has been shown that groups of workers may average relatively high scores on tests that are quite unrelated to job performance.[9]

An alternative to using average scores as indications of relative importance is to weight the abilities or characteristics measured by the tests in terms of their validities. Validity, you will recall, is the correlation between test scores and a criterion of job success. Tests correlating substantially with a criterion of job performance may be presumed to be measuring more important characteristics than those measured by tests yielding low validity coefficients.

---

[8] H. C. Link, *Employment Psychology* (New York: The Macmillan Co., 1920).

[9] W. H. Stead and C. L. Shartle, *Occupational Counseling Techniques* (New York: American Book Co., 1940).

Although the validity approach holds promise, it is limited on the one hand by the scope of the test battery and, on the other, by the adequacy of the criterion of job success. The former limitation was discussed earlier as it applied to job specification by measurement in general. The matter of establishing suitable criteria of job performance requires considerably more attention.

CRITERIA OF JOB PERFORMANCE

Virtually everything the industrial psychologist does necessitates his concern with some sort of criterion of job performance. Whether he is engaged in developing techniques for selecting or training personnel, improving the working environment, developing promotional procedures, or anything else, he must come to grips with the criterion problem. It is insufficient from a research standpoint to speak of improving efficiency, job performance, or job satisfaction. These can be variously defined, the ways in which they are measured are functions of their definitions, and conditions leading to improvement judged by one criterion may prove ineffective when judged by some other criterion.

The present discussion of criteria is specifically oriented toward developing measures of job performance suitable for personnel selection programs. However, the issues raised in this discussion are sufficiently general to apply to the broader problem of assessing industrial efficiency. Specific criterion problems encountered in evaluating training programs, appraising workers on the job, and measuring job satisfaction are described in context throughout subsequent chapters.

Reliability and Validity of Criteria

A criterion is a standard against which we evaluate something. The effectiveness of a test battery for selecting workers, for example, is judged by the accuracy of hiring decisions following its use. If the battery is effective, the personnel manager basing his decisions upon it will hire mostly persons who subsequently prove to be "efficient" workers; most of those he rejects would subsequently have proven to be "inefficient" workers. In this instance the criterion would have to be some measure of "efficiency."

Particular criteria are often chosen merely because they are readily available, or have been used by other investigators confronted by a similar problem, or are thought by management to be relevant to the problem at hand.[10] Without minimizing the importance of these considerations, they are insufficient by themselves to insure adequacy of the criterion.

Whenever anything is measured the investigator needs assurance that his yardstick is both reliable and valid. We have already given one definition of reliability, that is, the consistency of measurement. Validity has been defined as the relevance of measurement to whatever it is we intend to measure.

The significance of these concepts for test development will be discussed at some length in Chapter 5. The important point here is that the criteria we expect our tests to predict must themselves be reliable and valid. It is not possible accurately to predict an unstable criterion. Furthermore, there is not much wisdom in predicting a criterion of something other than the thing we really wish to predict.

Kinds of Criteria

The diversity of available criteria for industrial research is tremendous. One listing of such criteria includes items bearing upon (*a*) output per unit of time, (*b*) quality of production, (*c*) time lost by personnel because of sickness, accidents, and so on, (*d*) personnel turnover, (*e*) training time, (*f*) promotability, and (*g*) employee satisfaction.[11] Data germane to these criteria are often available in one form or another in already existing company records. The problem from a research standpoint is that often the form in which they have been collected precludes reliability and/or validity.

Production. Undoubtedly some sort of production index is one of the most widely used criteria for industrial resaerch. This is so, in part, because of expediency; most companies maintain production records and thus they are immediately available to the researcher. Also, management generally considers high productivity to be synonymous with efficiency.

Productivity may appear, on the surface, to be a highly suitable and objective criterion. The number of armatures wound by as-

---

[10] J. Weitz, "Criteria for Criteria," *American Psychologist*, Vol. XVI (1961), pp. 228–31.

[11] R. J. Wherry, "Criteria and Validity," D. H. Fryer and E. R. Henry (eds.), *Handbook of Applied Psychology*, Vol. I (New York: Holt, Rinehart & Winston, Inc., 1950), chap. xxvii.

sembly line workers during a shift, the number of words typed per minute by a secretary, or the monthly sales record of an insurance salesman can all be readily tabulated and statistically summarized.

However, output records are often invalid in their raw form. Productivity may be a meaningless criterion unless it is corrected for spoilage. Some adjustment is necessary when comparing a secretary averaging 70 words per minute with three errors with one averaging 60 errorless words per minute. Similarly, in evaluating monthly insurance sales records, it is necessary to include some indication of policy cancellations.

Even productivity corrected for spoilage may not be comparable for different employees doing what superficially appears to be the same kind of work. Typing speed and accuracy may be influenced by the amount of noise and distraction in the office. Insurance sales undoubtedly reflect the size of the sales territory and the socioeconomic status of the residents.

Since production records are not used in their entirety, additional problems arise as a function of sampling. A sample of output records will not accurately reflect fluctuations in performance if it is not drawn from periods representative of the entire shift. Furthermore, if each output sample covers only a very brief time period, or if too few samples are drawn, the criterion may lack reliability.

Another kind of problem is encountered when the attempt is made to convert performance records to a criterion of "goodness" or "efficiency." This is somewhat analagous to the evaluative problem faced by a teacher when he attempts to judge student performance on an examination. He may be able to convert the student's answers to a numerical score (that is, an output record) but he still must decide whether the score is good enough to merit a grade of A or whether it really deserves only a B or C. The standards for such a judgment, whether it be made for a class or a group of workers, may be relativistic (median output is defined as "average") or absolutistic (anyone performing better than some specified level, like 90 percent of capacity, is "superior"). The latter kind of industrial output evaluation often uses time study results for defining "capacity."

Finally, there are a large number of jobs for which it either is impossible to count units of production, or the units when counted reveal relatively little about job performance. What production measure should be counted, for example, to appraise a foreman's proficiency? One possibility would be to use an aggregate of the output by workers within his department. However, such a criterion is contaminated by factors other than the critical one of supervisory quality and neglects a number of important aspects of supervisory proficiency.

Ratings. When objective indices of proficiency are unobtainable or insufficient because of the nature of the job, it may be necessary to build criteria upon ratings. Performance judgments may be solicited from co-workers; most often they are made by the worker's immediate superior. Reliance upon subjective performance evaluations as criteria is particularly characteristic of technical, professional, supervisory, and managerial assessments.

The problems encountered in rating and possible refinements of rating procedures are discussed at length in Chapter 11. It should be apparent that criteria based upon judgments can be extremely unreliable because raters disagree among themselves. Also, since the bases upon which such ratings are made may be unrelated to the actual quality of work performed by the ratee, these criteria may be relatively invalid.

Miscellaneous Criteria. Productivity, objectively or subjectively appraised, is neither the only nor always the most desirable indication of job performance. Consider, for example, a job requiring a very lengthy initial training period at considerable expense to the company. No company likes to contemplate the prospect of an employee accepting a job offered by a competitor shortly after completing such a training program. Job tenure may actually be a more meaningful criterion than productivity in this instance.

There are a number of jobs in which the range of productivity is so narrow that the difference in output between the best and worst producer is relatively insignificant. This is particularly true of highly repetitive work paid on a piece rate for departments in which the workers have established a "gentleman's agreement" among themselves about how much they will produce. Under these circumstances management may be more interested in predicting such criteria as absenteeism, tardiness, and turnover than output.

SUMMARY

Two activities preliminary to instituting and evaluating personnel selection and training programs are (a) job analysis and (b) delineation of performance criteria. Job analysis ultimately leads to specifications of worker skills, abilities, and characteristics prerequisite to satisfactory job performance. The standards of job performance used as yardsticks for evaluating the effectiveness of various industrial programs must be carefully defined, measured reliably, and valid for the purpose intended.

The information obtained from a job analysis may suggest important worker characteristics to be considered when selecting personnel. The analyst sometimes estimates the job's requirements on the basis of his familiarity with the activities entailed in doing the job efficiently. An alternative approach utilizes the results obtained from administering various psychological tests.

If job analysis is an initial concern in developing personnel programs, the ultimate concern is with criteria of job performance. It is insufficient to select criteria solely on the basis of expediency or perceived relevance by management. Measures of job proficiency must meet acceptable standards of reliability and validity. Although output is most frequently used as a performance measure, it must often be supplemented by or replaced with such criteria as quality, turnover, lost time, and worker satisfaction.

Application Blank and Employment Interview

4

The specific procedures employed for the selection and placement of personnel vary from one industrial or business organization to another as a function of the requirements of the specific job to be filled and of the number of job applicants in relation to the number of vacancies. In spite of variability in selection procedures, virtually all industrial organizations utilize at least an application form and some kind of interview as a partial basis upon which new personnel are selected. Indeed, many organizations rely upon these devices as the sole basis for selecting personnel.

The widespread use of application blanks and employment interviews is predicated upon the notion that job success depends upon certain critical background factors (like past experience and education) and interpersonal factors (like the ability to create and maintain a favorable impression and to converse easily).

The interpretation of the significance of certain kinds of notations on the application form and of certain kinds of behavior during the interview is highly subjective. The efforts of industrial psychologists to improve these devices have been directed toward reducing this subjectivity. This is accomplished by (1) relating interview questions and items on the application blank to the results of a thoroughgoing job analysis suggesting critical items of information to be elicited by these devices; (2) research demonstrating that such information does, in fact, correlate with some criterion of job success.

APPLICATION FORMS

Letters of application and responses to formalized application blanks are generally used as preliminary hurdles in the selection process. If, for example, the job specification indicates that a tenth-grade education is prerequisite to satisfactory job performance, and

the letter of application is written by someone who is virtually il-
literate or the "schooling" section of the application form indicates
that the applicant possesses a lesser degree of education, further investigation of the applicant's qualifications is unwarranted.

The typical application blank contains items pertaining to the
applicant's age, marital status, dependents, schooling, past experience, and references. Portions of an application form for sales applicants are shown in Figure 4–1.

The Weighted Application Blank

Research studies in recent years have indicated that careful
evaluation of the kind of information elicited by the application
blank can result in the selection of better-qualified employees and
the reduction of employee turnover. The application blank is most
useful when it is developed and analyzed in accordance with standard research procedures. This implies that the investigator must
determine the extent, if any, of the relationship between responses
to the items on the application blank and some criterion of the employee's success. Items which are shown to be related to a criterion,
for example, industrial productivity, are weighted to reflect the extent of this relationship, and the total blank is "scored" by summing
the weights of responses to the items. The usefulness of this general
technique has been demonstrated for predicting various criteria of
success for a wide range of positions, including sales personnel,[1]
seasonably employed production workers,[2] and office-clerical personnel.[3]

In one of these investigations a weighted application blank was
devised to predict turnover of clerical and secretarial employees in

---

[1] O. A. Ohmann, "A Report of Research in the Selection of Salesmen at the
Tremco Manufacturing Company," *Journal of Applied Psychology*, Vol. XXV (1941),
pp. 18–19.

R. W. Scollay, "Personal History Data as a Predictor of Success," *Personnel
Psychology*, Vol. X (1957), pp. 23–26.

[2] M. D. Dunnette and J. Maetzold, "Use of a Weighted Application Blank in
Hiring Seasonal Employees," *Journal of Applied Psychology*, Vol. XXXIX (1955),
pp. 308–10.

[3] P. H. Kreidt and M. S. Gadel, "Prediction of Turnover among Clerical Workers,"
Journal of Applied Psychology, Vol. XXXVII (1953), pp. 338–40.

W. K. Kirschner and M. D. Dunnette, "Applying the Weighted Application Blank
Technique to a Variety of Office Jobs," *Journal of Applied Psychology*, Vol. XLI
(1957), pp. 206–08.

E. A. Fleishman and J. Berniger, "One Way to Reduce Office Turnover," *Personnel*, Vol. XXXVII (1960), pp. 63–69.

a university setting. The replies to each item on an application form completed by employees hired several years earlier were studied. Although all of these employees had been hired on a "permanent" basis, it was possible to identify "long-tenure" and "short-tenure" subgroups. Persons in the former subgroup had been working from two to four years and were still on the job. Those in the "short-tenure" group had terminated employment within two years.

TABLE 4–1

COMPARISON OF ITEM RESPONSES OF LONG- AND SHORT-TENURE OFFICE EMPLOYEES

Application Blank Items	Short-Tenure Group	Long-Tenure Group	Weight Assigned to Response
Local Address			
Within city	39%	62%	+2
Outlying suburbs	50	36	−2
Age			
Under 20	35	8	−3
21–25	38	32	−1
26–30	8	2	−1
31–35	7	10	0
35 and over	11	48	+3
Previous Salary			
Under $2,000	31	30	0
$2,000–$3,000	41	38	0
$3,000–$4,000	13	12	0
Over $4,000	4	4	0
Age of Children			
Preschool	12	4	−3
Public school	53	33	−3
High school or older	35	63	+3

Each of the items on the application blank was analyzed to determine the extent to which it differentiated between the long- and short-tenure subgroups.

The responses for each group were classified, tallied, and converted to percentages. For some items the percentage of response within each classification was virtually identical for both groups. Since such items did not discriminate, they were weighted zero and hence did not contribute to the score. When it was evident that an item *did* discriminate between the long- and short-tenure groups, it was weighted to reflect both the magnitude and direction of its discrimination. Illustrative data for some discriminatory and nondiscriminatory items are shown in Table 4–1. As the table shows, local address differentiated effectively between the groups but previous salary was an ineffective differentiator.

NAME

LAST | FIRST | MIDDLE

QUALIFICATION RECORD

RADIO CORPORATION OF AMERICA

® RCA

RC891—1

INSTRUCTIONS

1. TYPE OR PRINT IN INK
2. EACH QUESTION MUST BE FULLY AND ACCURATELY ANSWERED. (USE ADDITIONAL SHEET IF NECESSARY)
3. SIGN AND DATE (LAST PAGE)

ADDRESS NEXT THREE MONTHS	NUMBER	STREET	CITY	ZONE	STATE	PHONE
PERMANENT ADDRESS	NUMBER	STREET	CITY	ZONE	STATE	PHONE

SOCIAL SECURITY NUMBER

U. S. CITIZEN?   ☐ YES   ☐ NO

ARE YOU PREPARED TO SUBMIT PROOF OF U. S. CITIZENSHIP IF EMPLOYED WITHIN NEXT 3 MONTHS?   ☐ YES   ☐ NO

MARITAL STATUS

| AGE | BIRTH DATE | NUMBER OF DEPENDENTS (INCLUDE YOURSELF) | AGES OF CHILDREN | HEALTH   ☐ EXCELLENT   ☐ GOOD   ☐ FAIR   ☐ POOR | HEIGHT | WEIGHT |

LIST HANDICAPS

% DISABILITY

LIST CHRONIC AILMENTS

% DISABILITY

NAMES OF RELATIVES EMPLOYED BY RCA

PREVIOUS RCA EMPLOYMENT APPLICATION MADE?   ☐ YES   ☐ NO

WHERE?   WHEN?

IN CASE OF EMERGENCY, NOTIFY

NAME (LAST, FIRST, MIDDLE)

| ADDRESS | NUMBER | STREET | CITY | ZONE | STATE | PHONE |

HAVE YOU EVER BEEN ARRESTED?   ☐ YES   ☐ NO   IF YES, EXPLAIN:

LOCATION PREFERENCE

ARE YOU WILLING TO RELOCATE?   ☐ YES   ☐ NO

EARLIEST DATE AVAILABLE FOR EMPLOYMENT

LATEST DATE AVAILABLE FOR EMPLOYMENT

MINIMUM SALARY REQUIREMENT FOR 40 HOUR WEEK (PER MONTH) $

NAME OR DESCRIBE THE TYPE POSITION YOU DESIRE NOW

NAME OR DESCRIBE THE TYPE POSITION YOU DESIRE EVENTUALLY

APPLICANTS FOR SCIENTIFIC OR ENGINEERING POSITIONS PLEASE COMPLETE THIS SECTION

CHECK FIELD(S) OF PROFESSIONAL INTEREST

☐ Electrical Engineering ☐ Physics ☐ Ceramics
☐ Mechanical Engineering ☐ Chemistry ☐ Industrial Engineering
☐ Mathematics

Other _____

CHECK FIELDS OF PRODUCT INTEREST BELOW

☐ Radar ☐ Gas Tubes ☐ Receiving Tubes ☐ Component Design ☐ Aviation Electronics
☐ Computer ☐ Television ☐ Phototubes ☐ Radio and TV Receivers ☐ Industrial Electronics
☐ Acoustics ☐ Power Tubes. ☐ Semi-Conductors ☐ Solid State Physics ☐ Electronics of Solids
☐ Chemistry ☐ Camera Tubes ☐ Machine Design ☐ Communications ☐ General Circuit Design
☐ Standards ☐ Storage Tubes ☐ Mechanical Design ☐ Other _____

INDICATE SPECIFICALLY YOUR INTEREST IN THE ABOVE PRODUCT FIELDS: EXAMPLE—STORAGE TECHNIQUES, DIGITAL COMPUTER; OR, FIRE CONTROL CIRCUIT DESIGN AIRBORNE RADAR

	INDICATE PREFERENCE (1, 2, 3)	NUMBER OF MONTHS EXPERIENCE	MONTHS OF SUPERVISORY EXPERIENCE
LISTED BELOW ARE RCA SCIENTIFIC OR ENGINEERING CATEGORIES. PLEASE INDICATE THE INFORMATION REQUESTED IN THE THREE COLUMNS TO THE RIGHT.			
FUNDAMENTAL PURE RESEARCH—Scientific study to discover new principles			
APPLIED RESEARCH—Application of the results of fundamental research to possible useful ends			
SYSTEMS—Integration of theory, equipments and environment to create and optimize major electronic concepts			
ADVANCED DEVELOPMENT—Integration of major innovations into systems or components (model)			
DEVELOPMENT—Reduction of new ideas to practice (model)			
DESIGN—Engineering to produce a product to specifications			
FACTORY FOLLOW-UP—Liaison to reconcile design and manufacturing problems			
MANUFACTURING OR INDUSTRIAL—Factory Layout, Production Planning, Process, Time and Motion Study, Quality, Control, etc.			
SALES—Technical product representation to the customer			
APPLICATION—Determination and solution of customers' technical requirements			
FIELD SERVICE OR INSTALLATION—Erection, instruction, modification, maintenance, operation			
THESIS, PAPERS, PUBLICATIONS, PATENTS			
SUPERVISORY EXPERIENCE IN DETAIL			

Have you a currently effective agreement with employers or others concerning inventions you make?   Yes _____   No _____
If yes, how long is agreement effective after termination of services?   (Furnish copy of agreement)

FIGURE 4-1. (Continued.)

EDUCATION (Include All Course Work And Military Service Schools)

TYPE	NAME AND ADDRESS	FROM	TO	GRADUATED?	DEGREE	MAJOR AND MINOR COURSES
HIGH SCHOOL						
COLLEGE OR UNIVERSITY						

EXPERIENCE (Include U. S. Military Service, Summer, and Part-time Jobs—AND ALL PREVIOUS RCA EMPLOYMENT)

EMPLOYER'S NAME AND ADDRESS	EMPLOYED		MONTHLY SALARY		SUPERVISOR NAME—TITLE	STARTING AND TERMINAL POSITIONS	SPECIFIC REASON FOR LEAVING	TOTAL HOURS WORKED PER WEEK
	FROM (MO-DAY-YR)	TO (MO-DAY-YR)	START	STOP				
1								
2								
3								
4								
5								
6								

DESCRIBE DUTIES FOR EACH EMPLOYER AS NUMBERED ABOVE

1
2
3
4
5
6

WHAT FOREIGN LANGUAGES DO YOU-	READ	WRITE	SPEAK

LIST TYPES AND MODEL NUMBERS OF MILITARY ELECTRONIC EQUIPMENT WITH WHICH YOU ARE FAMILIAR (EXAMPLE SCR 270, SA, SG)

LIST YOUR HOBBIES AND INDICATE ACCOMPLISHMENTS

ACTIVITIES—Social, Military, Professional, Civic, Service (Do Not Include Information Regarding Race, Creed, Color, National Origin or Ancestry)

ACTIVITY	FROM	TO	OFFICES HELD (DATE)

REFERENCES—DO NOT GIVE RELATIVES OR FORMER EMPLOYERS

NAME	OCCUPATION	ADDRESS	PHONE

COMPLETE THIS SECTION IF YOUR GRADUATION FROM COLLEGE IS PENDING OR IF YOU HAVE GRADUATED WITHIN THE LAST 4 YEARS

What is the maximum grade point average at your school?   What percent of your college expenses did you earn?

What is your grade point average?   List honors and scholarships

What is the total number of students in your graduation class? (Major Field)

What is your standing in the graduating class? (Major Field)

The information on this application is accurate and subject to check by the RADIO CORPORATION OF AMERICA. I understand that any misleading or incorrect information may render the application void and be cause for immediate dismissal in the event of my employment.

SIGN HERE _____   SIGNATURE _____   DATE _____

FIGURE 4–1. (Continued.)

The application blanks of a second sample of long- and short-tenure employees were then scored, utilizing the weights derived from this analysis. The total score was obtained simply by adding or subtracting the weights assigned to categories of response for the items. The correlation between application blank scores and subsequent tenure for this sample was 0.57. If a critical (passing) score of 4 had been used as the basis for hiring or rejecting these women when they were job applicants, it would have been possible to reduce office turnover considerably. (See Figure 4–2.)

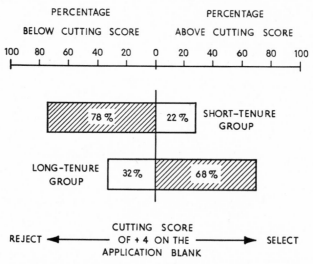

FIGURE 4–2. Percentages of Correct and Incorrect Hiring Decisions that Would Have Been Obtained for Office Employees.

It is not possible to structure a weighted application blank that will be usable for all jobs in all organizations or even for very similar jobs in different organizations. Every selection program presents a unique problem both with respect to the phrasing of items for inclusion in the blank and the weighting of responses to these items. Consequently, application forms, to be most effective, should be tailored to the needs of the specific business or industry desiring to use such a device.

THE EMPLOYMENT INTERVIEW

The primary function of the employment interview is to allow the interviewer to meet the applicant in a face-to-face relationship, thereby better permitting the interviewer to evaluate certain of the applicant's qualifications. The interview may be justified as a selection device when personal characteristics, physical appearance, and social factors are critical job requirements. Even under such circumstances, however, the subjectivity of employment interviewing seriously limits its usefulness. The interview should never be considered a substitute for psychological tests specifically designed to measure such factors as intelligence or job knowledge.

The employment interview, when placed in proper perspective, serves two functions in addition to the primary one of accepting or rejecting the applicant. Besides securing information bearing upon the applicant's status, the interviewer gives certain information to the applicant about the job and the company and he establishes a friendly relationship with the interviewee. The latter function of employment interviewing is particularly important in situations in which rejected job applicants are potential customers.

Many personnel directors pride themselves on what they consider to be their unique and uncanny ability to select employees by means of an interview. Most generally, however, the validity of their interviewing procedures has never been ascertained. A validity study would require data on the number of rejected applicants who would have been successful if they had been hired, and the number of accepted applicants who later prove to be unsuccessful employees. The results of such studies, when attempted, sometimes indicate that the well-meaning but untrained interviewer might better make his selections on the basis of revelations from a ouija board or crystal ball.[4]

Another disturbing feature of the employment interview, as usually conducted, is its unreliability. Several interviewers may differ markedly in their appraisal of the same job-applicant. One of the early studies of the reliability of employment interviews compared the ratings assigned to 57 applicants by 12 different interviewers. The interviewers were sales managers, each of whom was allowed to conduct the interview in whatever manner he wished. Each interviewer's ratings were transformed to numerical ranks ranging from 1 to 57 in terms of the suitability of the applicant for the job of salesman. The ranks assigned by the 12 interviewers to several

---

[4] J. R. Hinrichs, "Technical Selection: How to Improve Your Batting Average," *Personnel*, Vol. XXXVII (1960), pp. 56–60.

of the applicants are shown in Table 4–2.[5] Note particularly the spread or range of ranks assigned to each interviewee. In spite of the fact that the interviewers were sales managers, each with considerable interviewing experience, they disagreed extensively in their appraisal of each applicant.

Although evidence like this is disquieting, it must be remembered that the interviewers were not restricted either with respect to procedure or to the bases upon which their evaluations were to be made. This was an *unstructured* interview situation. Standardization of interviewing techniques and training of interviewers with

TABLE 4–2

RANKS ASSIGNED TO JOB APPLICANTS BY 12 SALES MANAGERS WHO INTERVIEWED THEM*

Applicant	I	II	III	IV	V	VI	VII	VIII	IX	X	XI	XII	Range
A	33	46	6	56	26	32	12	38	23	22	22	9	6–56
B	36	50	43	17	51	47	38	20	38	55	39	9	9–55
C	53	10	6	21	16	9	20	2	57	28	1	26	1–57

* A rank of 1 signifies that the interviewer believed the applicant to be the most suitable for the position; a rank of 57 means that the applicant was rated as the least suitable for the position.

respect to the proper criteria for evaluating job applicants does much to improve both the reliability and validity of employment interviews. It will be helpful to examine some of the potential sources of unreliability in interview technique before describing the methods by which the reliability of this procedure may be improved.

Sources of Unreliability

The uncontrolled interview is one in which the pattern of questions, the circumstances under which these questions are asked, and the bases for evaluation of replies to these questions are not standardized. These factors vary from one interviewer to another, and from one applicant to another. In short, the uncontrolled interview is subjective in the extreme. This subjectivity may lead different interviewers to disagree quite markedly about the suitability of a particular applicant.

[5] H. L. Hollingworth, *Vocational Psychology and Character Analysis* (New York: D. Appleton & Co., 1923), pp. 115–19.

The implications of subjectivity were outlined earlier in conjunction with the discussion of the S-I-R concept. You will recall from that discussion that responses are functions not only of the precipitating stimuli but also of the interpretation of those stimuli by the respondent. This interpretative factor is the subjective element. The employment interview involves two sets of psychologically significant responses: those made by the interviewer and those made by the job applicant. The stimuli for the interviewer's responses are provided by the applicant's replies to questions, his physical appearance, and personal mannerisms. The ways in which the applicant replies to the questions (the applicant's responses) are, in turn, a function of stimuli provided by the interviewer—the questions he asks, *his* physical appearance, and *his* personal mannerisms.

The interview, then, involves a very dynamic interpersonal relationship. The two parties react in terms of their perceptions of one another. The factors influencing these perceptions may be quite subtle, but their effects are manifest in the relatively low reliability and validity of the employment interview.

Lack of Rapport. Virtually every job applicant experiences some degree of anxiety and tension during the employment interview. His "nervousness" is well-founded! The decision about whether or not he is employed rests, at least in part, upon the impression he makes upon the interviewer. Thus, a normally fluent individual may be quite lost for words during an interview; and a normally calm person may temporarily become a finger drummer, toe tapper, or ear scratcher. The extent to which these behaviors are excused by the interviewer as being atypical and a result of an unusually tense situation, varies considerably from one interviewer to another. Similarly, there is considerable variation in the extent to which different interviewers attempt to establish *rapport*—a feeling of warmth, understanding, and relaxation—at the beginning of the interview.

The behavior of any job applicant may be quite different under circumstances in which he is interviewed by a personnel director who is himself calm, relaxed, unhurried, and gives the impression that he truly understands the kind of tension engendered by the situation, from what it is under circumstances in which the interviewer is obviously rushed, tense, and either too busy, disinclined, or personally unable to establish rapport.

Personal Bias. We all have certain biases or preconceptions about people. There are certain characteristics that immediately "rub us the wrong way." These may be physical characteristics such as overweight, red hair, dimunitive height, or a physical infirmity of some kind, or some mannerism like gum chewing, or smoking. These biases vary from one interviewer to another, influencing their appraisal of the applicant in an uncontrolled fashion. The 10 personal traits listed by untrained interviewers as being most objectionable are cited in Table 4–3.

TABLE 4–3

PERSONAL TRAITS LISTED AS MOST OBJECTIONABLE BY THREE INTERVIEWERS*

Interviewer I	*Interviewer II*	*Interviewer III*
Biting fingernails	Chewing and snapping gum	Short arms
Talking with cigarette in mouth	Being jittery or fidgety	Bad breath
Interrupting you	Nonstop talking	Shifty-eyed
Playing with articles on person	Too aggressive	Too well-groomed
Smoking chain fashion	Loud clothing	Sloppy
Being pretentious or bragging	Not meticulous about personal hygiene	Ugly
Using "I" continuously	Fresh and "smart alecky"	Jiggling legs continuously
Inconsideration	Making gestures with hands	Tapping
Avoids looking you in the eye	Foreign looking	Doodling
"Alibi"	Mousy and bashful	Acne

* American Management Association, *Manual of Employment Interviewing*, Research Report No. 9 (1946), p. 15.

Interviewers, like the rest of us, may respond in biased fashion because they identify the applicant with some group about which they have certain preconceptions or *stereotypes*. The interviewer who rejects the blonde applicant for a secretarial position because ". . . blondes are dumb," and the student who knows that ". . . professors are absent-minded," are both victims of stereotyped thinking. They subscribe to rather sweeping generalizations about groups of people which have no basis in fact. Stereotyped judgments about persons are, of course, most dangerous when any individual's qualifications are "evaluated" on the basis of ill-conceived generalizations about his particular ethnic or religious group.

The effect of personal bias is to introduce into the employment interview a highly subjective basis for the selection or rejection of particular applicants. The criteria employed by a particular interviewer may be totally unrelated to the abilities required for satisfactory job performance.

Halo Effect. The tendency to generalize from some specific characteristic or trait to an overall evaluation of the suitability of a job applicant is referred to as the "halo effect." Halo may be positive or negative. The interviewee who is neatly dressed, knocks on the door before entering the office, does not sit down until invited to do so, and is relatively free from nervous mannerisms creates a favorable initial impression. This impression may color the interviewer's perception of the entire interview, leading him to a positive evaluation of the applicant in spite of the fact that he may really be rather poorly qualified for the job in question.

Conversely, the applicant who gives the impression of being overly cocky may create negative halo. The interviewer may fail to perceive such an applicant's strengths of training and past experience because the entire proceedings are unfavorably colored by his perception of the interviewee as a "brash young man."

Certain traits are, to be sure, sufficiently important by themselves to be used as a basis for rejecting a candidate for the job. Some jobs, for example, require that the employee be tactful. An applicant who demonstrates a noticeable lack of tact could legitimately be rejected for this reason alone. An undesirable negative halo effect would be operating, however, when a tactless applicant is rejected for this reason alone in spite of the fact that he is being interviewed for a job in which personal diplomacy is not a critical requirement.

Contagious Bias. This kind of bias results from the fact that both individuals in the interview situation react to each other against the background of their own attitudes, values, feelings, and so on. Thus, as the interviewer listens to the applicant and writes up his summary and interpretation of the session, he may unconsciously misinterpret what the interviewee has actually said.

A convincing demonstration of the distortion that may occur when interpreting what has transpired during an interview was reported over 30 years ago.[6] Twelve male social workers were assigned to interview destitute men who were repeatedly applying for lodgings at charity centers. The purpose of these interviews

---

[6] S. A. Rice, "Contagious Bias in the Interview: A Methodological Note," *American Journal of Sociology,* Vol. XXXV, No. 3 (1929), pp. 420–23.

was to study the characteristics of such destitutes. The results obtained from two of the interviewers, one a socialist and one a prohibitionist, contrast markedly. (See Table 4-4.)

Two factors operated to produce results of this type. First, the personal predispositions of the interviewers led them to impart different meanings to what the interviewees were saying. Secondly, subtle differences in facial expression, posture, and phraseology of questions by the interviewer may have betrayed his own personal feelings, thereby coloring the respondent's replies.

TABLE 4-4

CONTAGIOUS BIAS: THE CAUSES OF DESTITUTION AS REPORTED BY TWO INTERVIEWERS

Interviewer's Bias	Percent Allegedly Ascribing Their Destitution to Liquor	Percent Allegedly Ascribing Their Destitution to Industrial Conditions
A (Prohibitionist)	34	42.5
B (Socialist)	11	60

One of the early studies of the influence of the form of the questions upon replies involved repeated showings of movies to subjects until they grasped the essential details of the films. Then each person was asked a series of questions about the contents of the film. The form of the inquiry was varied in order to discover the influence upon response of the wording of the questions. The investigator found that the poorest kind of question was one in which the phraseology implied something about the nature of the desired response. A question like, "Was the man carrying the umbrella?" led to fewer correct answers and fewer responses of "I don't remember" than did the question "Did you see an umbrella?" The former wording cued a response by implying that there was a man and there was an umbrella.[7]

Contagious bias, in which the interviewer leads the respondent to make a particular response, is of significant consequence during the employment interview. Quite different responses might be anticipated to the following questions, each of which is phrased to determine the reasons for which the applicant left his previous employment:

---

[7] B. Muscio, "The Influence of the Form of the Question," *British Journal of Psychology*, Vol. VIII (1916), pp. 351–89.

Why did you leave your previous job?
Did you leave your previous job voluntarily, or were you fired?
You weren't fired from your last job, were you?

The Standardized Interview

Interviewing of any kind is partly an art. Some interviewers with relatively little training and experience seem to have a knack for establishing rapport and providing an atmosphere that enables the applicant to reveal his strengths and weaknesses. Other interviewers, in spite of long experience and comprehensive training, find it relatively impossible to achieve this objective.

There are, nevertheless, certain principles of interviewing technique which, when followed, do much to improve the reliability and validity of this evaluative procedure. Several of these principles and cautions have been implied in the preceding discussion. The interviewer must be aware of the possible influence of personal and contagious bias upon his perception of the applicant's qualifications; he must guard against the operation of halo effects, either positive or negative; and he should be aware that most applicants experience some degree of tension during the interview. Consequently, he should do whatever he can in the way of "small talk" and maintenance of a general air of calm assurance to develop and maintain rapport.

These suggestions are helpful up to a point. They do not, however, overcome a basic objection to the uncontrolled interview. It is a fact that different interviewers ask different questions, and the same interviewer frequently asks different questions of various applicants for the same job. This is a critical source of unreliability which prevents the comparison of the qualifications of various applicants. The interview procedure must be uniformly structured and controlled or standardized in order to make it possible to obtain meaningful comparisons across interviewers and between interviewees.

The Patterned Interview. The "patterned interview" was designed to overcome some of the deficiencies of uncontrolled interviewing. Special interview schedules (lists of questions) were developed as guides to the interviewer in his search for relevant information about the applicant and his previous work history. This interview procedure focuses upon such character traits as "stability," "industry," "perseverance" and "leadership." It does not attempt to

PATTERNED INTERVIEW
(Short Form)

Name_____ Sex: ☐ M, ☐ F; Date of Birth_____ Soc. Sec. No._____

Address _____

SUMMARY

Rating: [1] [2] [3] [4] Comments:_____
In making final rating, be sure to consider applicant's stability, industry, perseverance, loyalty, ability

to get along with others, self-reliance, leadership, maturity, motivation; also, domestic situation and health.

Interviewer:_____ Job Considered for:_____ Date_____

Why are you applying for work in this Company?_____
Is his underlying reason a desire for prestige, security, or earnings?

If you were hired, how long
would it take you to get to work?_____ How would you do it?_____
Is there anything undesirable here?

WORK EXPERIENCE. Cover all positions. This information is very important. Interviewer should record last position first. Every month since leaving school should be accounted for. Note military service in work record in continuity with jobs held since that time.

	LAST OR PRESENT POSITION	NEXT TO LAST POSITION	SECOND FROM LAST POSITION
Name of Company			
Address			
Dates of employment	From To	From To	From To
	Do these dates check with his application?		
Nature of work			
	Will his previous experience be helpful on this job?		
Starting salary			
Salary at leaving			
	Has he made good work progress?		General or merit increases?
Was anything especially liked about the job?			
	Has he been happy and contented in his work?		
Was there anything especially disliked?			
	Were his dislikes justified?		Is he chronically dissatisfied?
Reasons for leaving			
	Are his reasons for leaving reasonable and consistent?		

OTHER POSITIONS

Name of Company	Type of Work	Salary	Date Started	Date Left	Reasons for Leaving
	Has he stayed in one line of work for the most part?				
	Has he gotten along well on his jobs?				
	Are his attitudes toward his employers loyal?				
	Was he interested in creative work? In work requiring activity?				
	Has he improved himself and his position?				

FIGURE 4–3. Patterned Interview Form.

How much unemployment compensation have you drawn?_____ When?_____ Why?_____

Does he depend on himself?

How many weeks have you been unemployed in the past five years?_____ How did you spend this time?_____

Did conditions in his occupation justify this time? Did he use his time profitably?

What accidents have you had in recent years?_____

Is he "accident-prone"? Any disabilities which will interfere with his work?

SCHOOLING

How far did you go in school? Grade: 1 2 3 4 5 6 7 8 High School: 1 2 3 4 College: 1 2 3 4 Date of leaving school_____

Is his schooling adequate for the job?

If you did not graduate from high school or college, why not?_____ Who paid for your schooling?_____

Are his reasons for not finishing sound? Self-reliant?

What special training have you taken?_____

Will this be helpful? Indications of perseverance? Industry?

Extracurricular activities_____ What offices did you hold in these groups?_____

Did he get along well with others? Indications of leadership?

FAMILY BACKGROUND	FINANCIAL SITUATION	DOMESTIC AND SOCIAL SITUATION
Father living? Mother living? _Normal background?_	Own home: $_____ Mortgage: $_____ _Stability?_	Single?_____ Engaged?_____
Father's occupation _____	Rent House: $_____ Apt.: $_____	Married?_____ When?_____
Average earnings _____	Live with friends: $_____ Relatives: $_____	Widowed?_____ Divorced?_____
Number brothers or sisters older_____ Younger_____ _Has he been babied?_	Own furniture _____ Number of Rooms _____	Ages of children _____ _Motivation?_
Financial aid to family _____	Cost of living per month $_____ _Realistic?_	How do you and your wife get along?_____ _Maturity?_
Leisure time activities _____ _Habits of industry?_	Any current debts?_____ _Mature financially?_	Recreation _____ _Maturity?_
Summer vacations_____ _Did he keep busy?_	Wages ever garnisheed?_____	Hobbies _____ _Will these help?_
Church activities _____ (Do not ask what church)	Borrow from small loan agency?_____ _Judgment?_	Entertain at home?_____ _Get along well with others?_
Group activities _____ (Exclude racial, religious,	Savings on last job $_____ Net Worth $_____	Group activities _____ (Exclude racial, religious, nationality groups) When did you have last drink?_____ _Sensible?_
and nationality groups) Positions of leadership _____ _Leader?_	Wife employed?_____ Her earnings: $_____ _Effect on motivation?_ Other income $_____	What types of people rub you the wrong way? _____ _Bias?_
How old when fully self-supporting?_____ _Self-reliant?_	Life insurance $_____ Accident insurance $_____ _Is he provident?_	Ever arrested?_____ Charges _____ _Immaturity?_

HEALTH

What serious illnesses, operations, or accidents did you have as a child?_____

Has he retained any infantile personality traits due to childhood illnesses?

What illnesses, operations, or accidents have you had in recent years?_____

Are his illnesses legitimate rather than indicating a desire to "enjoy ill health"?

How much time have you lost from work because of illness during past year?_____

Will he be able to do the job?

Does anyone in your home suffer ill health?_____

Are his wife, children, or family relatively healthy?

Do you suffer from:
- ☐ Poor Eyesight
- ☐ Rupture
- ☐ Rheumatism
- ☐ Asthma
- ☐ Heart Trouble
- ☐ Diabetes
- ☐ Ulcers
- ☐ Hay Fever
- ☐ Flat Feet
- ☐ Nervousness

ADDITIONAL INFORMATION:_____

_____

_____

Form No. OP-202

Source: The Dartnell Corporation, Chicago, 1949. Developed by Robert N. McMurry & Co.

FIGURE 4–3. (Continued.)

TELEPHONE CHECK ON SALES APPLICANT_____

Name of Applicant

Person Contacted _____   Position _____

Company _____   City and State _____   Telephone Number

1. I wish to *verify* some of the information given to us by Mr. (name) who has applied for a position with our firm. Do you remember him? What were the dates of his employment with your Company?   From_____ 19____ To_____ 19_____
                                                                                                       Do dates check?

2. What was he doing when he started? _____
                                                                   Did he exaggerate?

   When he left? _____
                                                                   Did he progress?

3. He says he was earning $_____ per_____ when he left. Is that right?   ☐ Yes,   ☐ No; $_____
                                                                   Did he falsify?

4. How much of this was salary? $_____

   How much commission? $_____

5. How was his attendance? _____
                                                      Conscientious?   Health problems?

6. What type of selling did he do? _____
                                                      To whom?   How did he get his contacts?

7. How did his sales results compare with others? _____
                                                      Industrious?   Competitive?

8. Did he supervise anyone else?   ☐ No,   ☐ Yes; How many?_____
                                                      Does this check?

   (If yes) How well did he handle it? _____
                                                      Is he a leader or a driver?

9. How closely was he supervised? _____
                                                      Was he hard to manage?

10. How hard did he work? _____
                                                      Is he habitually industrious?

11. How well did he get along with other people? _____
                                                      Is he a troublemaker?

12. What arguments did he have with customers? _____
                                                      Does he like selling?   Can he control his temper?

13. What did you think of him? _____
                                                      Did he get along with his superiors?

14. Why did he leave? _____
                                                      Good reasons?   Do they check?

15. Would you rehire him?   ☐ Yes,   ☐ No; Why Not?_____
                                                      Does this affect his suitability with us?

16. Did he have any domestic or financial difficulties that interfered with work?   ☐ No,   ☐ Yes; What?_____
                                                      Immaturity?

17. How about drinking or gambling?   ☐ No,   ☐ Yes; What?_____
                                                      Immaturity?

18. What are his outstanding strong points? _____

19. What type of saleswork do you feel he would do best? _____

20. What are his weak points? _____

Checked by_____   Date_____

Form No. 8T-103

Source: The Dartnell Corporation, Chicago, 1949. Developed by Robert N. McMurry & Co.

FIGURE 4–4. Telephone Check on Sales Applicant.

provide information about the applicant's level of job skill; this can be better appraised by methods other than the interview.

A portion of a patterned interview schedule is reproduced in Figure 4–3. Notice that there is a provision on this form for the interviewer to make notations about the applicant's responses. The questions under each response position are designed as guides for the interviewer in helping him appraise what the applicant is saying.

The patterned interview program as outlined by McMurry also includes a telephone check designed to verify statements made by the applicant on his application form, to obtain previous employer's estimates of the applicant's strengths and weaknesses, and to indicate to the interviewer the areas in which additional information must be elicited during the interview. A telephone check form for sales applicants is reproduced in Figure 4–4.

The specific advantage of the patterned interview procedure is that it provides the interviewer with a set of carefully worded questions and a sequence in which these questions are to be asked. This

TABLE 4–5

COMPARISON OF RATINGS FROM THE PATTERNED
INTERVIEW AND SUCCESS ON THE JOB

Success on the Job	Patterned Interview Rating			
	1 *Outstanding*	*2* *Good*	*3* *Average*	*4* *Poor*
Successful: Still in service.........75%		38.5%	26.1%	13.3%
Failure: Left service for any reason........................25		61.5	73.9	86.7

eliminates some of the variability of procedure between interviewers. In addition, the interview schedule contains questions designed to guide the interviewer in making his appraisal of the applicant's qualifications. The effect of this is to direct the interviewer's attention to the critical factors to be considered in making his judgment, thereby reducing the effects of personal bias and halo effect.

One indication of the validity of the patterned interview was obtained from a study of the usefulness of the technique for predicting the probable success of truck drivers.[8] One hundred and eight applicants were interviewed, and all were hired regardless of the rating assigned by the interviewers. The data comparing the initial rating by the interviewer and a criterion of employee success determined after 11 weeks are shown in Table 4–5. It is apparent that the patterned interview was quite effective in predicting the ultimate success or failure of the applicants.

---

[8] R. N. McMurry, "Validating the Patterned Interview," *Personnel*, American Management Association, Vol. XXIII, No. 4 (1947), pp. 270–71.

The Diagnostic Interviewer's Guide (D.I.G.). The D.I.G.[9] is a device which, like the patterned interview, provides a set of standardized questions to be asked of job applicants. In addition, the *Guide* contains a "scoring" system which enables the interviewer to quantify his impressions of each applicant.

The D.I.G. questions are arranged into four areas covering the applicant's work, family, social, and personal history. The questions in the *Work History* section seek information about the applicant's ability to analyze tasks assigned to him, and to profit from his work experience. *Family History* items relate to his social, economic, and educational background for the job. The section on *Social History* seeks to determine level of sociability and interest in people. Motiva-

TABLE 4–6

PERCENTAGE OF EMPLOYEES STILL ON THE JOB, RESIGNED, OR DISMISSED
BY CATEGORY OF SCORE ON THE D.I.G.

Criterion	D.I.G. SCORE CATEGORY				
	0–10	*12–16*	*18–22*	*24–28*	*30–34*
Still on job	38.9%	42.9%	47.2%	48.6%	59.2%
Resigned	22.2	25.7	29.2	29.4	34.7
Dismissed	38.9	31.4	23.6	22.0	6.1

tional factors like ambition and persistence are covered in the section on *Personal History.*

At the end of each section, there is a series of questions to be answered by the *interviewer.* One such question in the *Work History* section, for example, is: "Has the applicant indicated a serious and sincere attitude toward the work he has been doing?" The interviewer answers either "yes" or "no"; and this answer is transformed to a + or − weight. The algebraic sum of the weights of all of the interviewer's answers to the summary questions constitutes the applicant's "score."

An indication of the validity of the D.I.G. is given by a study conducted at the Household Finance Corporation. The *Guide* was completed and scored for 300 applicants, all of whom were hired. The percentages of employees who were still on the job, who had resigned, and who had been dismissed during the course of their employment are summarized in Table 4–6. These data clearly indicate

---

[9] C. I. Hovland and E. F. Wonderlic, "Prediction of Success from a Standardized Interview," *Journal of Applied Psychology,* Vol. XXXIII (1939), pp. 537–46.

that the percentage of persons still on the job is greater, the higher the D.I.G. score. Note also the marked decrease in the percentage of persons dismissed as the D.I.G. score increases.

More recently the question has been raised whether the relative success of techniques like the patterned interview and the D.I.G. is attributable primarily to control over the sequence and phraseology of questions or simply to the fact that they focus attention upon specific well-defined traits. It has been suggested that undue control over sequence and phraseology may obscure important characteristics that might become evident in a somewhat freer and more dynamic interaction between interviewer and interviewee. In a pilot study utilizing a standardized but less static format than the typical patterned interview, interviewer ratings of small groups of pharmaceutical employees were correlated with composite supervisors' ratings of job performance. The obtained validity coefficients were statistically significant for three of the five groups and positive though not significant for two of the groups. The investigator concludes that a properly used interview can play a reliable part in overall assessment of an individual's qualities.[10]

SUMMARY

The application blank and interview are the two most frequently used devices for selecting and placing personnel. The efforts of the industrial psychologist to improve these devices have, for the most part, been directed toward overcoming their inherent subjectivity.

One approach to improving the validity of application blanks is to weight the responses to individual items (for example, age, years of schooling, and so on) and to "score" the blank by summing these weights. Such weights are derived from an investigation of the relationship between specific responses and some criterion of employee success. The stronger this relationship, the higher is the weight assigned to a particular response.

The employment interview serves two purposes in addition to the primary one of providing a basis for accepting or rejecting the applicant. The interviewer gives certain information to the applicant about the job and the company, and he strives to establish a friendly relationship with the applicant. The latter function is important because even rejected applicants are potential consumers of the product or service offered.

The reliability of judgments based upon uncontrolled interviews is

---

[10] K. A. Yonge, "The Value of the Interview: An Orientation and a Pilot Study," *Journal of Applied Psychology*, Vol. XL (1956), pp. 25–31.

exceedingly poor. This is so, in part, because interviewers differ in the extent to which they can establish rapport and overcome tension. Disagreements between interviewers in their interpretations of what the applicant has said, and in their evaluations of the applicant's qualifications for the job also diminish the reliability of this technique. These disagreements result from the operation of biases of various kinds and are attributable also to the fact that the content of the interview is dependent upon the whims of the interviewer.

The standardized interview is one in which the procedure is so controlled as to reduce the extent to which interviewer biases operate. The pattern of questions to be asked of all applicants by all interviewers is specified. In addition, the factors upon which the interviewer is to base his evaluation of the applicant are clarified.

Developing
Psychological Tests

5

We have thus far described the two methods most often used for making predictions about a job applicant's likelihood of succeeding as an employee: the personal interview and the application form. Although widely used for personnel selection, both of these methods are inherently subjective. This means that the decision about whether or not to hire an applicant on the basis of information of this sort may unduly reflect the personal biases and prejudgments of the hiring official.

The purpose of testing is to provide an *objective* assessment of various kinds of psychological characteristics. When such tests are used for personnel selection, the measured characteristics are those known to be related to success on the job. Thus, a personnel testing program involves first, a preliminary study designed to identify measurable characteristics thought to be associated with job success; second, the construction of a test or *battery* (group) of tests designed to measure these characteristics; and finally, a follow-up study to determine the extent to which the measured characteristics are, in fact, related to employee efficiency. The present chapter is specifically concerned with the kinds of research implied in these three phases of testing for personnel selection.

The notion of psychological testing has caught the public fancy to a rather considerable extent. Although this kind of popularity has made it somewhat easier for management to introduce testing programs in industry, it has also had certain rather unfortunate consequences. It has, for example, led to the dissemination of so-called "tests" purporting to measure virtually everything ranging from *Your Suitability as a Marriage Partner* to *Your Susceptibility to Advertising Appeals* in Sunday supplements and pulp magazines. The questions contained in them and the suggested interpretations of responses make interesting reading. They are, however, relatively valueless as a basis for personal evaluation.

The surprising thing about such popularized pseudotests is that they appeal to and hoodwink so many otherwise hard-headed and sophisticated persons. The typical businessman, for example, tends to consider expenditures associated with engineering and raw materials supply very carefully. He may, however, be amazingly naive in the purchase of an expensive "employee selection program" that is not properly justified by an accumulation of scientific evidence supportive of its worth. The following study of the gullibility of personnel managers will serve to illustrate the point.[1]

A legitimately published personality inventory was administered to a group of personnel managers attending a conference. They each then received a fake "personality analysis" ostensibly based upon their responses to the inventory but actually consisting of 13 glittering generalities. These generalities had been collected from dream books and astrology charts.[2] The 13 general statements were interspersed with other more specific statements about personality. Both kinds of statement, the general ones and the specific ones, were duplicated, the personnel manager's name was written at the top of the sheet, the 13 general statements were encircled on every sheet, and the sheets were passed out to the respondents. Thus, every personnel manager labored under the delusion that he was receiving a personality analysis based upon the results of the inventory. Furthermore, without knowing it, every personnel manager received the identical "analysis" of his personality.

The 13 encircled statements received by each manager are shown in Table 5–1. The data in this table following each statement summarize the judgments with respect to the accuracy of each statement. Each man was asked to read the items marked for him and to rate it with respect to accuracy on the following five-step scale: (*a*) amazingly accurate, (*b*) rather good, (*c*) about half and half, (*d*) more wrong than right, (*e*) almost entirely wrong.

In addition, the personnel managers were asked to make an overall evaluation of the fake analysis. Fifty percent said that the overall description was amazingly accurate, 40 percent thought it was rather good and only 10 percent rated it as about half and half.

---

[1] Ross Stagner, "The Gullibility of Personnel Managers," *Personnel Psychology*, Vol. XI, No. 3 (1958), pp. 347–52.

[2] B. R. Forer, "The Fallacy of Personal Validations: A Classroom Demonstration of Gullibility," *Journal of Abnormal and Social Psychology*, Vol. XLIV (1949), pp. 118–23.

Since the purpose of this demonstration was to educate rather than dupe the personnel men involved, the participants were then asked to compare the personality reports they had received. The author reports, "Upon discovering that all were identical they set up a

TABLE 5-1

<small>Evaluations of 13 Glittering Generalities by Personnel Managers Who Thought They Were Receiving a Personality Analysis</small>

Item	Judgment on Accuracy of Item*				
	a	b	c	d	e
1. You have a great need for other people to like and admire you....................39%	46%	13%	1%	1%
4. You have a tendency to be critical of yourself...............................46	36	15	3	0
5. You have a great deal of unused capacity which you have not turned to your advantage......37	36	18	4	1
7. While you have some personality weaknesses, you are generally able to compensate for them..34	55	9	0	0
9. Your sexual adjustment has presented problems for you.............................15	16	16	33	19
10. Disciplined and self-controlled outside, you tend to be worrisome and insecure inside.......40	21	22	10	4
12. At times you have serious doubts as to whether you have made the right decision or done the right thing...............................27	31	19	18	4
15. You prefer a certain amount of change and variety and become dissatisfied when hemmed in by restrictions and limitations............63	28	7	1	1
16. You pride yourself as an independent thinker and do not accept others' statements without satisfactory proof.........................49	31	12	4	4
18. You have found it unwise to be too frank in revealing yourself to others.................31	37	22	6	4
20. At times you are extroverted, affable, sociable, while at other times you are introverted, wary, reserved...............................43	25	18	9	5
21. Some of your aspirations tend to be pretty unrealistic..................................12	16	22	43	7
23. Security is one of your major goals in life.....40	31	15	9	5

* Definitions of scale steps as follows: (a) amazingly accurate, (b) rather good, (c) about half and half, (d) more wrong than right, (e) almost entirely wrong.

terrific noise apparently compounded of resentment at being duped and amazement at themselves for being tricked."

The demonstration proved to be extremely valuable for convincing the participants to investigate a test or testing program thoroughly before buying it. In this instance the "test" yielded glittering generalities which apply to virtually everyone and are distinctive for no one. Such generalities do not, of course, have differential value for selection, placement, or any other personnel function.

CHARACTERISTICS OF PSYCHOLOGICAL TESTS

Useful psychological tests are distinguished from pseudotests by certain specific characteristics which are built into them. It will be helpful to outline these characteristics briefly before launching into a discussion of the ways in which they are implemented when tests are constructed.

Objectivity

You will recall that the primary objection to the use of both the uncontrolled interview and the application blank for selecting personnel is that these techniques are highly subjective in nature. The usefulness of these techniques is improved when they are made more objective.

The distinction between subjective and objective appraisal is apparent also in the area of testing. A test requiring that the scorer exercise his judgment in appraising the quality of response (for example, an essay test) is subjective in nature. A test that may be scored independently of such judgment (for example, a multiple-choice test) is objective in nature.

Regardless of the merits of subjective tests for enabling the respondent to express himself and to display a sequence of thinking, such tests do suffer from one marked deficiency. The score assigned to the person being tested may reflect an assortment of factors totally unrelated to his qualifications. Bias, halo effect, mood of the reader, as well as other subjective factors may enter into the appraisal of essay responses.

In consequence, industrial tests tend, for the most part, to be objective in nature. The score earned on such tests by the job applicant is unrelated to mood fluctuations and the personal opinions of the person scoring the test. An additional advantage of objective testing is that these tests may be scored easily and rapidly by clerks with minimal training. This factor materially reduces the cost of administering the testing program compared to what the cost would be if subjective tests were used.

Reliability

A reliable test measures with a high degree of consistency. "Consistency" has several different meanings as discussed later in the chapter. According to one interpretation, a person must rank in about the same position every time he takes a particular test (regardless of who administers it) if we are to accept it as a reliable measuring instrument.

A psychological test is no different with respect to this particular requirement from any other kind of measuring instrument. Consider, for example, the properties of a scale designed to measure weight. You wouldn't think very much of the device if you weighed yourself in your physical education class this morning and learned that you were heavier than anyone else in the class while the same scale indicated that you were lighter than 20 of your classmates yesterday morning. This amount of variation is greater than could be reasonably expected from minor weight gains or losses due to changes in exercise and diet.

Similarly, a psychological test is required to yield about the same ranking on successive testings of a given individual, showing only minor fluctuations as a result of learning or forgetting during the time interval between administrations of the test.

Validity

A valid test is one that measures whatever it was designed to measure, thereby enabling us to predict whatever it is that we wish to predict. Thus, to have predictive validity for the purpose of personnel selection, a test administered to applicants must correlate with some subsequently obtained index of employee efficiency. This index, or criterion, may take the form of production record, supervisory rating, or earnings, to name just a few.

It is perfectly possible for a test to be reliable without being valid. A yardstick, for example, is an extremely reliable measurement device. When applied several times to the same object it will yield about the same "score" or reading in inches. It is, however, totally invalid as a measure of employee efficiency. There is, for most jobs, no relationship at all between height and employee success.

It should be apparent also that a test may be valid for certain purposes but not for others. The yardstick which is extremely valid as a

measure of height, is not at all valid as a measure of muscular coordination.

Uniformity of Interpretation

Suppose we have developed a test and demonstrated that it is
both reliable and valid for selecting personnel. We now administer
this test to a job applicant and determine that his score on this test is
57. Such a score derived either from the number of correctly answered items, or the number right less a correction for guessing is referred to as a *raw score*. It cannot be interpreted properly without
reference to test *norms* which summarize the raw scores earned on
the test by a large number of persons. Knowledge about the raw
score does not, in itself, enable us to make a decision about whether
or not the job applicant ought to be hired.

What kinds of additional information do we need before properly
interpreting this score of 57? It might help, for example, to know the
maximum possible score on the test. A score of 57 out of a possible 58
points probably means something quite different than does a score of
57 out of a possible 200 points.

A detailed statistical analysis of the distribution of scores earned
on this test by persons previously tested would be even more helpful.
This might involve the calculation of the mean and standard deviation of the distribution in order to provide an indication of whether
the score of 57 is better or worse than average. In addition, the interpretation of this score is greatly facilitated when the data are
prepared in such a way as to make possible a statement about the
probability that an applicant with a score of 57 will, if hired, be a
successful rather than an unsuccessful employee.

Standardization of Testing Conditions

It is apparent that whenever a number of persons are to be compared with respect to test score, they must either take the same test
or different forms of the same test. One cannot hope, for example, to
compare the arithmetic test scores of two applicants, one of whom
has taken a test requiring that he be familiar with concepts no more
complex than long division, while the other has taken a test requiring mastery of fractions and decimals.

It is perhaps less obvious, however, that the mere fact that identical questions are presented to two applicants does not in itself guarantee that they are taking the same test! A test really consists of a set

of questions administered under certain conditions of illumination, ventilation, working space, assistance from the proctors, and preliminary directions to the person tested, to name just a few. Test scores may be markedly affected by the conditions under which the test is given. Thus, one of the characteristics of good psychological tests is that the testing conditions are *standardized*. This means that the directions for administering and scoring the test are prescribed and specified so that they may be held relatively constant from one testing session to another. A departure from the standardized testing conditions may well invalidate the test norms. The manual of directions for administering a test will most often specify the specific wording of instructions, will indicate something about the amount of assistance (if any) to be given by the proctors, the kind of physical facilities to be used for testing, the time limit if there is one, and the way in which the test should be scored and interpreted.

TEST CONSTRUCTION

The foregoing description of the required characteristics of psychological tests implies that there is considerably more to constructing a test than merely putting pen to paper and writing questions. We will be concerned in the remainder of this chapter with the implementation of these characteristics.

Step 1. Job Analysis

Nothing concrete can be done in the way of writing test questions until a clear notion of the function or functions to be measured is formulated. This is only possible after a thoroughgoing job analysis designed to clarify the differences between efficient and inefficient employees has been performed. The job analysis will provide the clues about the critical psychological functions, including specific kinds of knowledges, abilities, and personal characteristics that ought to be measured in the selection test.

Step 2. Writing the Preliminary Items

Constructing test items requires a high level of skill. Even with considerable experience, the test constructor may set performance tasks that are unsuitable for personnel testing or write questions that are defective by virtue of ambiguity or of some internal cue as to the correct answer. Thus, he prepares a preliminary set of items or tasks which he will subsequently evaluate by means of an item analysis. These items may be cast in a variety of formats including, but not limited to, the widely used multiple-choice format.

There are certain kinds of pitfalls in the construction of multiple-choice items that may be rather readily avoided. These are separately described for the *premise* (the question or phrase preceding the alternative choice) and the *alternatives* (the group of correct answer and incorrect choices).

Rules for Constructing the Premise. Perhaps the criticism most often leveled against objective tests is that the items contained in them tend so often to be ambiguous. Ambiguities can be avoided in multiple-choice items only when the premise contains a clear statement of all of the conditions necessary to interpret the item properly. It would be impossible, for example, to respond to an item beginning, "The most appropriate measure of central tendency is:" because no measure is "most appropriate" under all circumstances. The respondent needs to know whether the distribution is normal or skewed, and something about the purpose for which the measure of central tendency is to be computed.

Another source of confusion in phrasing the premise results from failure to call attention in some way to negatives. Unless such words as *not* and *never* are italicized or capitalized, the respondent may fail to notice them because of the tension and anxiety surrounding the administration of a selection test.

The test constructor must also exercise care in phrasing the premise to prevent the appearance of a grammatical cue pinpointing the correct alternative. A premise ending in the word *an*, for example, cues an alternative beginning with a vowel rather than a consonent. Similarly, a premise ending with the word *these* cues a plural rather than a singular response. Such cues, of course, make it possible for respondents to answer correctly even in the absence of knowledge called for by the item.

Rules for Constructing the Alternatives. Defects in the structure of the alternatives generally have the effect of cueing the correct answer. If the *distractors* (incorrect alternatives), for example, are not all plausible they may be eliminated by the respondent on the basis of common sense rather than actual knowledge.

It is desirable to avoid structuring the alternatives so that one is atypical in length. The atypical alternative, which may be either unusually long or unusually short, is more often the correct answer than would be expected on the basis of chance. This is probably true because the test constructor finds it possible either to phrase the correct answer very succinctly, or finds that he must add several qualifiers in order to eliminate the ambiguities.

Finally, partial parallelism should be avoided in the structure of the alternatives. *Parallel* alternatives are ones that are phrased alike with the exception of one or two key words. Often, but not always, the parallel alternatives are the converse of one another. The following alternatives are parallel:

a) The mean is higher than the median.
b) The mean is lower than the median.

A multiple-choice item with partial parallelism will often contain two parallel alternatives and two that are not parallel. In such cases, the correct answer is generally contained in the pair of parallel alternatives, thereby substantially increasing the likelihood of obtaining a correct response solely on the basis of a lucky guess.

The foregoing list of "rules" for the construction of multiple-choice items is by no means comprehensive. It serves, however, to indicate some of the kinds of errors that may creep into such items with the effect either of making the item ambiguous or of cueing the correct answer.

Step 3. Item Analysis

An item analysis provides data enabling the test constructor to evaluate the worth of each of the preliminary items he has developed. The item analysis serves as the basis for selecting those items from the preliminary item pool which are to be included in the final version of the test. The typical item analysis provides two kinds of information about each item: (1) information about the discriminatory power of the item and (2) information about the relative ease or difficulty of the item.

Item Discrimination. Every item in a test should make its contribution to the test's power to differentiate between persons on the function the test is measuring. Item discrimination (or item validity) is an indication of the extent to which the test item differentiates between persons who rank at opposite ends of the continuum with respect to the particular characteristic being measured.

This phase of the item analysis requires that the preliminary set of items be administered to a sample of persons like those who will eventually be taking the test in its final form. The persons in this item analysis group are then subdivided into high and low criterion subgroups. In practice this assignment is most often based upon the criterion of total score on the test. Thus, the objective of this phase of the analysis is to determine the extent to which each test item is measuring the function measured by the total test.

It has been determined that the optimal split for constituting the criterion subgroups is obtained by assigning the 27 percent of the persons with the highest scores to the "high" criterion group and the 27 percent of the persons with the lowest scores to the "low" criterion group.[3] Thus, if a test to be item analyzed is administered to a total group of 185 persons, each of the criterion subgroups would contain 50 persons.

It is apparent from the foregoing discussion that an item which has good discriminating power is one that differentiates between the high and low criterion subgroups. So a perfectly valid item is one that is answered correctly by everyone in the high criterion group and answered incorrectly by everyone in the low criterion group. The correlation between item response ("correct" or "incorrect") and criterion subgroup ("high" or "low") for such an item would, of course, be +1.00.

Item analysis data indicative of various degrees of discrimination power are shown in Table 5–2. The entries for the five items in the Table show the percentage of respondents within each criterion subgroup answering the item correctly and incorrectly. The correlational values represent the strength of relationship between item-response and criterion subgroup assignment.

Note particularly that the correlation between item response and total test score (as reflected in criterion subgroup assignment) decreases as the percentage of respondents from each of the subgroups answering correctly becomes increasingly similar. Finally, in item 5, in which the percentage of correct responses is identical for the two criterion subgroups, the correlational value is 0.00. This item does not differentiate at all between the high and low criterion groups.

This discussion of item-discrimination has been limited to item analyses against the internal criterion of total test score. It is quite possible, however, to establish the criterion groups on some basis that is external to the test itself. A measure of productivity, a rating

---

[3] T. L. Kelley, "The Selection of Upper and Lower Groups for the Validation of Test Items," *Journal of Educational Psychology* (1939), pp. 17–24.

of employee efficiency or any other external index may serve as a basis for separating high and low criterion groups and hence for item analysis. The use of external criteria for item analysis is much less frequent than is the use of total test score as the criterion.

Item Difficulty. Questions from the preliminary pool of items are considered for inclusion in the final version of the test only if they have demonstrated discriminative power. The items that have survived this phase of the analysis are further screened on the basis of

TABLE 5–2

PERCENTAGES WITHIN EACH CRITERION SUBGROUP CORRECTLY AND
INCORRECTLY ANSWERING ITEMS AT VARIOUS LEVELS
OF ITEM DISCRIMINATION

| Item Number | Item Response | Criterion Subgroup | | Correlation* |
		Low	High	
1.	Right	—	100%	+1.00
	Wrong	100%	—	
2.	Right	15	90	+0.73
	Wrong	85	10	
3.	Right	20	70	+0.50
	Wrong	80	30	
4.	Right	30	60	+0.31
	Wrong	70	40	
5.	Right	40	40	0.00
	Wrong	60	60	

* Correlational values from J. C. Flanagan, "A Table of the Value of the Product Moment Coefficient of Correlation in a Normal Bivariate Population Corresponding to Given Proportions of Successes" (Pittsburgh: American Institute for Research, 1950).

their relative ease or difficulty before the ultimate selection of items for the final form of the test is made.

What would be the effect, for example, if a test of numerical ability contained items, all of which were extremely easy? Since most persons would be able to answer every item, the test scores would tend to run rather high. The effect of this would be to make it difficult to separate out from the total group of persons tested those who possess a moderately high degree of numerical ability from those who possess a very high degree of such ability. The test would not have enough "top."

Conversely, a test consisting entirely of very difficult items would have too much "top." Most persons would receive low scores, making it impossible to separate out the persons of moderately low ability from those of very low ability.

To avoid either of these extreme conditions, tests are generally structured so that they contain items distributed throughout the range of difficulty. The test as finally constituted will contain some rather easy items, some rather difficult items, and a considerable number of items that are in the midrange of difficulty.

Data regarding item-difficulty are obtained by computing the percentage of persons in the total item analysis group answering each item correctly. Thus, the test in its final form will contain only those items that have been demonstrated to possess satisfactory discriminative power and a range of relative ease and difficulty. Several things remain to be done with this test, however, before it can be used for personnel selection.

Step 4. Reliability

You will recall that one of the requirements of useful measuring instruments is that they possess a satisfactory level of reliability. This generally requires a study of the consistency of test scores. Reliability studies may be performed in a number of ways, three of which are described below.

Test-Retest Method. A reliable test is one in which an individual will rank in about the same position on successive testings regardless of who administers the test. This definition of reliability suggests a simple method for determining the relative degree of consistency of measurement: that is, give the test twice to the same group of persons and correlate the scores earned on the two administrations. Ideally, the person who earned the highest score (ranked highest) when originally tested should also earn the highest score when retested. Similarly, the person who earned the lowest score the first time (ranked lowest) should earn the lowest score on the retest, and persons with intermediate scores the first time should maintain their same relative score positions the second time they take the test.

Such a perfect relationship between rankings on the original test and the retest would, of course, yield a correlation coefficient of +1.00. Although this perfect relationship is never achieved in practice, the requirement for test-retest estimates of reliability is generally set in the vicinity of +0.90.

Numerous objections have been raised to the test-retest method of estimating reliability. It is, in the first place, an uneconomical procedure since it requires that employees be excused from their work for experimental purposes on two separate occasions. Secondly, the period between original test and retest is not vacuous. New learning may occur during this time interval, causing relative rankings on the retest to be somewhat different from the rank position on the original test. Thirdly, employees may remember items from the original session when they are retested. This memory factor will enable them to respond rapidly to the remembered items and to devote proportionately more time to the items which caused them difficulty during the original testing.

The Equivalent Forms Method. This method overcomes some of the objections to the test-retest procedure, particularly those related to the possible operation of learning and memory factors. As the name implies, this method involves the administration of an equivalent form of the original test after a time interval, rather than re-administration of the original test itself.

Equivalent forms of a test are alike with respect to statistical characteristics (the distribution of item difficulty and item validity indices) and general content, although the specific items in the forms are different. The fact that the specific content of the items in equivalent forms of a test are different means that neither the memory factor nor the learning factor can operate when reliability is estimated by correlating the scores earned on the two forms.

Perhaps the primary objection to this procedure is that the expense of developing equivalent forms of a test is not justified when they are developed solely for a reliability study. There are, however, other reasons for which two or more forms of a test may be developed. It is advantageous, for example, to have multiple test forms for administration when one wishes to measure growth as a result of a formal training program or as a result of job experience. One of the forms can be given as a pretest to new employees while the other form can be given as a posttest after completion of the training program or after a certain period of time on the job. Furthermore, multiple forms of a test are extremely useful whenever a large group of persons is to be tested in a room that does not permit for adequate spacing between seats in order to prevent copying.

Split-Halves Method. A fundamental objection to both the test-retest and the equivalent forms method of estimating reliability is that these procedures require two testing sessions. The split-halves method makes it possible to estimate reliability from a single administration of a test and hence is widely used in the industrial setting.

This method requires that the total test be divided into halves in such a way that the items in each half constitute a miniature representation of the entire test. In practice, this is often accomplished by assigning the odd-numbered items to one half and the even numbered items to the other half, although any other procedure for splitting the test is acceptable provided that it yields halves that are comparable. The halves are scored separately, and the estimate of reliability is derived by correlating the scores earned by a group of persons on the halves of the test.

There are certain parallels between the split-halves method and the equivalent forms method for estimating reliability. Both procedures require the correlation of scores earned on two forms of a test. The equivalent forms method involves the correlation between two full-length forms while the split-halves method involves the correlation between two half-length forms. A fundamental difference between these procedures is the fact that while the forms are deliberately equated for the equivalent forms method, the split-halves method correlates two forms that are, at best, crudely comparable.

In appraising the split-halves method, it must be remembered that there is no time interval between administration of halves of a test, and that the correlation coefficient resulting from this procedure is based upon only half the number of items in the total test. Each of these unique aspects of the split-halves method has certain implications. The absence of a time interval has the desirable effect of eliminating the possible influences of memory and learning. It also, however, eliminates the possible effects of day-to-day fluctuations in mood, attentiveness and attitude of the respondents. This latter factor is one that should be included in estimates of test reliability. The effect of eliminating the potential influence of these daily fluctuations is to spuriously increase the reliability coefficient.

A special problem arises when the split-halves method is used to estimate the reliability of speeded tests in which the imposed time limit prevents subjects from completing all questions. Computation of an odd-even reliability under such circumstances tends to overestimate the test's reliability. This is so because the unanswered questions are distributed evenly between the two halves of the test, thereby exerting a uniform effect upon the individual's relative rank position for each half. This problem is generally resolved either by application of correction formulas estimating the lower limit of reliability for speeded tests, or by a rather simple experimental expedient. The latter requires that each half of the total test be separately administered with its own time limit.

The fact that this method yields an estimate of reliability based upon the correlation of scores on two halves of the test means that the resultant coefficient is an estimate of the reliability of a test only half as long as the one actually under consideration. Since reliability is, in part, a function of test length, estimates of reliability based upon the split-halves method must be adjusted upwards by means of a formula designed to indicate what the reliability would have been for the full-length test. The Spearman-Brown prophecy formula for a test doubled in length is:

$$R = \frac{2r_{11}}{1 + r_{11}}$$

where R is the reliability of the test doubled in length and r_{11} is the reliability of the half-length test. Thus, if the correlation between scores on the halves of a test is 0.80, the estimate of reliability for the total test would be 1.60/1.80 or 0.89.

Comparison between Methods. In the preceding sections we have described three methods for estimating the reliability of a test loosely defined as the "consistency of measurement." It is evident that each method is based upon a somewhat different concept of "consistency." Hence the methods do not yield comparable estimates of reliability.

For the test-retest procedure, consistency means *stability of scores* over a period of time. A low test-retest coefficient is evidence either for the fact that the function measured by the test is unstable over time, or that test performance is influenced by extraneous factors of an unstable nature.

The split-halves method utilizes quite a different concept of consistency. This method does not consider fluctuations over time; instead it estimates *internal consistency* or homogeneity of the test. As we have described this procedure, it indicates the extent to which one half of the test measures whatever it is that the other half measures. Variations of the general method may split the test into smaller fragments than halves. Thus it is possible, when a test is fragmented into single items, to inquire whether each item is measuring whatever is measured by each of the other items.

The equivalent forms method involves elements of both the stability and internal consistency concepts. The longer the time interval between the administration of the forms, the heavier is the emphasis upon stability over time. Conversely, with progressively shorter time intervals between test administrations, the coefficient tends increasingly to reflect internal consistency.

It is impossible, in the light of these differences, to single out a particular procedure as "best" under all circumstances. If we wish the reliability coefficient to reflect score stability over time, the split-halves method is clearly inappropriate. Since this method estimates consistency without a time interval, it overestimates stability. However, the practical consideration of available testing time may overshadow other factors and dictate the use of the split-halves method. Furthermore, there are occasions when the test constructor is more interested in estimating the internal consistency of his test than the stability of the resultant scores. When this is the case, the test-retest method and the equivalent forms method with a relatively long time interval may underestimate the kind of reliability he seeks.

Step 5. Validity

As indicated earlier, a test may be highly reliable and still be invalid or inappropriate for use under particular circumstances. A test that is valid for personnel selection must correlate with some criterion of worker success. The higher this correlation, the greater is the contribution made by the test to predicting the eventual success or failure of a group of job applicants.

Predictive Validity. The most desirable procedure by which to validate a test for selection purposes is to administer it to job applicants, all of whom are hired regardless of test score. The scores are filed until some subsequent time when a criterion measure of worker efficiency becomes available. The scores earned on the test by the applicants are then correlated with the criterion to yield an indication of the test's validity.

A graphic illustration of the meaning of test validity is presented in Figure 5–1. The data in this graph show the relationship between pilot aptitude score and elimination rate during pilot training in the United States Army Air Force. It is apparent that the psychological testing procedure predicted fitness for flight training.

Concurrent Validity. In spite of the desirability of obtaining evidence of predictive validity, resistance to the necessary procedure is often encountered in industry. Management may raise certain obvious objections to hiring all applicants regardless of their performance on the test being validated and in spite of the results of all other selection techniques including the interview and application form. Consequently, industrial tests are often validated by administering them to employees on the job and correlating the scores with an immediately available criterion of efficiency. This procedure establishes concurrent rather than predictive validity because the test and criterion measures are available simultaneously.

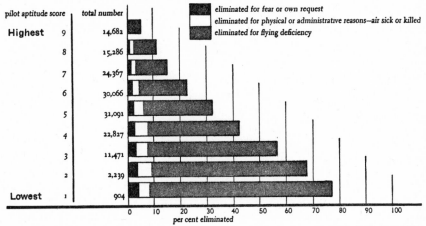

Source: "Psychological Activities in Training Command AAF," *Psychological Bulletin*, Vol. XLII (1945), p. 46.

FIGURE 5–1. Relation between Elimination Rate and Pilot Aptitude Score.

Face Validity. When a test has the *appearance* of measuring factors germane to the job it is said to have "face validity." A pilot selection test, for example, possesses face validity when the item phraseology makes reference to aircraft and flight.

The appearance of validity is entirely independent of the statistical characteristics of a test. It is a matter solely of item content. Although conceptually independent of statistical validity, face validity is generally regarded as a desirable characteristic for industrial tests. Such tests look meaningful and therefore facilitate company-wide acceptance of the testing program and heighten the motivation of persons tested.

Multiple Predictors. The discussion has thus far been limited to consideration of the relationship between a single test and a criterion of employee efficiency. However, the typical selection program uses scores earned by job applicants on a battery or group of tests. Each of the components of the battery may itself be only moderately valid. The combination, however, may be considerably more potent for predictive purposes than any of the component tests individually considered.

The validity of a battery is determined by a statistical technique known as "multiple correlation." Multiple correlation indicates the maximum validity obtainable from the optimum combination of scores on the several tests constituting the battery. It is possible, in addition, to determine the weights that must be assigned to the component tests in order to produce this optimal combination. The maximum multiple correlation obtainable from combining predictors depends upon (a) the validity of each predictor considered separately, and (b) the magnitude of the intercorrelations between predictors.[4]

Interpreting Validity Coefficients. How high must an obtained validity coefficient be in order for it to be regarded as acceptable for selection purposes? There is no ready answer to this question. The interpretation of validity coefficients depends upon a number of factors, some of which are discussed below.

One highly important consideration in this regard is the *selection ratio.* This is the ratio of job applicants to positions open; it is the percentage of applicants who must be hired to fill the available vacancies. A high selection ratio means that most applicants must be hired. Under such circumstances tests can contribute little to the accuracy of selection unless they have very high validity coefficients. However, when the ratio is low, it is possible to select only those applicants who perform exceedingly well on the selection devices. Hence, with a low ratio, tests with only moderate validity (that is, about 0.40) contribute effectively to selection.

The relationship between the selection ratio and the effectiveness of a test with a given validity coefficient can be seen by referring again to Figure 5–1. Suppose at the time this study was conducted, it was necessary to fill about 153,000 vacancies. Since approximately 153,000 men were tested, the selection ratio would be 1.00, indicating that all applicants would have to be utilized. The Pilot Aptitude Battery could not have helped at all in this case.

---

[4] M. R. Marks, R. E. Christal, and R. A. Bottenberg, "Simple Formula Aids for Understanding the Joint Action of Two Predictors," *Journal of Applied Psychology,* Vol. XLV (1961), pp. 285–88.

If, however, these 153,000 applicants were tested to fill about 115,-000 vacancies, the Pilot Aptitude Battery would have been a reasonably satisfactory selection device. By establishing a stanine of 5 as the "passing" score, about 80 percent of the selected persons would have graduated. Furthermore, if the selection ratio would have permitted utilization of a stanine of 9 as the "passing" score, over 90 percent of the selected persons would have graduated.

In addition to the selection ratio, consideration must be given to the matter of the *stringency of the criterion* of job success. If, for example, we are selecting typists, we might define a satisfactory rate as 40 words per minute or, with greater stringency, as 70 words per minute. It is possible for a device of lower validity predicting a particular criterion to be equally effective as or more effective than a device of higher validity used for predicting a more stringent criterion.

Proper interpretation of the meaning of a validity coefficient thus is impossible without reference to the specific context of the selection problem. There are, in addition, certain statistical considerations, including the reliability of the criterion and the range of ability in the sample, also influencing this interpretation. Validity coefficients reported in the literature as having "practical significance" often cluster about 0.40–0.50.

Step 6. Interpretation of Test Scores

Raw test scores are not very useful in the practical situation because they cannot be interpreted meaningfully. The industrial psychologist who has developed a test for selection purposes must perform statistical analyses designed to answer two general types of questions about every applicant's score. First, how did his score compare to the scores of other applicants who have taken the test? Secondly, did he pass the test: that is, should he be hired? The first of these questions requires that the raw score be transformed to another kind of score reflecting the performance of the specific applicant under consideration in relation to the performance of other applicants who have taken the same test. It involves the development of test *norms*. The second question requires that a *critical* (or passing) score be determined for the test.

Test Norms. Norms make possible the expression of an individual's raw test score relative to the distribution of scores earned by a group of persons known as the *standardization* or *norms* group. The development of test norms thus requires that the test first be administered to a sizable group of persons as nearly as possible like the applicants for whom the test is intended.

The distribution of scores earned by persons in the norms group may serve as the basis for converting raw scores to *percentiles*. A percentile value indicates the percentage of persons who earned a raw score at or below the specific raw score in question. Thus, if it has been determined that a raw score of 35 corresponds to the sixty-second percentile, this would mean that 62 percent of the standardization group scored 35 or less on the test.

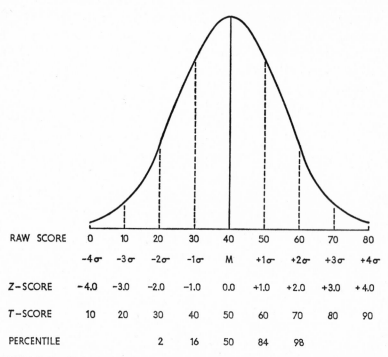

FIGURE 5–2. Relationship between Raw Scores, Percentiles, and Standard Scores.

The interpretation of raw scores may also be facilitated by converting them to some kind of standard scores. Standard scores express test performance as a function of the central tendency and variability of the distribution of scores obtained in the norm group. The most obvious kind of standard score involves the transformation of raw scores to standard deviation units. Suppose, for example, that the mean score in the norms group is 40 and the standard deviation is 10. It follows then, that a raw score of 50 would correspond to a transformed score of +1 standard deviation, a score of 30 to −1 standard deviation, and so on.

The relationships between raw scores, percentiles, and two kinds of standard scores (Z scores and T scores) are illustrated in Figure 5–2. You will note one of the major advantages of standard scores in comparison with percentiles: the former are spaced equidistantly along the measurement continuum. Hence, they are amenable to the usual kinds of arithmetic manipulations.

Critical Score. Although it is extremely useful in many situations to know how a person's test score compares with the scores earned by others who have previously taken the test, the process of person-

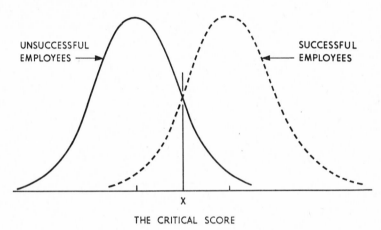

THE CRITICAL SCORE

FIGURE 5–3. Graphic Determination of the Critical Score on a Test.

nel selection requires that the test score be interpreted along with other information to produce a decision about whether or not to hire the applicant.

The critical score on a test is set at the point where the probabilities of job success favor the applicant exceeding this score over the applicant falling below this score. The meaning of the critical score can be visualized graphically by comparing the test score distributions for groups of successful and unsuccessful employees. (See Figure 5–3.) The point of intersection between these distributions is the score optimizing selection on the basis of the test *without regard for the selection ratio.*

It should be apparent that the critical score cannot be regarded as inflexible. It may be raised when there is a surplus of applicants relative to the number of vacancies, and it must often be lowered when the number of applicants is insufficient to fill the vacant positions.

SUMMARY

The steps involved in constructing psychological tests for personnel selection are designed to insure that such tests are objective rather than subjective in nature, lend themselves to uniform interpretation, and are both reliable and valid. These steps include job analysis, writing the preliminary items, performance of an item-analysis, and standardization of the test.

The standardization phase of test construction is particularly critical. A test is not useful for personnel selection unless it is demonstrated to measure consistently (reliably) and to be a useful predictor of whatever criterion we wish it to predict (to be valid). Standardized tests, in addition, are ones for which an interpretative system has been developed either in the form of test norms or in the form of a critical (passing) score.

Standardized Tests

6 Let us assume that the decision has been made to incorporate a psychological testing program into a company's personnel selection and appraisal procedures. Job analyses have been performed and some of the critical functions to be measured have been identified. There are now two courses of action to be considered. Either tests specifically designed to measure these functions can be custom-built for the company, or already existent tests available from commercial test publishers may be purchased. There is, as a matter of fact, quite a sizable pool of commercially available tests. A primary reference summarizing and reviewing virtually all developments in the field of testing is the series of *Mental Measurements Yearbooks* edited by Buros. The most recent volume in this series appeared in 1959.[1]

Several factors enter into the decision about whether to custombuild tests or to use commercially available standardized tests. Outstanding among the advantages of published instruments is the matter of economy. It is undoubtedly less expensive, particularly when the group is not too large, to purchase testing materials from a publisher than it is to engage in a program of test construction. Furthermore, the process of test development requires considerable time, thereby necessitating a delay in the actual introduction of the testing program. Commercially published tests, on the other hand, are available for virtually immediate use. Finally, many standardized tests have been administered to norms groups of various kinds, thereby facilitating the comparison between the employees now being tested with others who have previously taken the test.

There are, in spite of these virtues, certain limitations to the use of commercially available tests. The fact that a test has proven valid in one industrial setting does not guarantee that it will be equally valid even for similar jobs in other settings. It is necessary, therefore, for any test to be validated under the particular circumstances in which

---

[1] Oscar K. Buros (ed.), *The Fifth Mental Measurements Yearbook* (Highland Park, N.J.: Gryphon Press, 1959).

it is to be used. Thus, a certain amount of research must be done within the company even when the decision is made to purchase standardized tests.

Secondly, an expanding technocracy implies the creation of new jobs with novel requirements. Testing programs for such jobs may necessitate the development of unique instruments simply because the commercially available tests are not appropriate.

Finally, standardized tests may lack face validity for a particular job within a particular company.

The choice between utilization of published tests and the development of special tests is one that must be made in each individual case. It is the purpose of the present chapter to indicate something of the range of standardized tests currently available.

TEST FORMATS

Psychological tests differ from one another in the way in which they are structured, administered, and scored. Every kind of format tends to have its own peculiar strengths and weaknesses, although some are more appropriate than others for industrial testing.

Subjective versus Objective Scoring

The primary advantages and disadvantages of subjective as opposed to objective testing were discussed in some detail earlier. Industrial tests are, almost exclusively, objective in nature because of considerations of reliability and ease of scoring. The skills needed to score an objective test are minimal. The scores obtained from such tests are free from scorer bias and halo effect and are rapidly obtainable after the testing session is terminated.

Speed versus Power Tests

A *speed* test is one with a fixed time limit beyond which the respondents are not permitted to work even though they may not have attempted all of the questions, while a *power* test is administered without a time limit.

The conduct of a large-scale testing program is facilitated somewhat by the administration of time-limit tests. All of the papers are due back within a fixed period of time, thereby permitting the simultaneous scoring and processing of all of the answer sheets.

There are, in addition, certain circumstances in which speed is an essential aspect of the function being measured. Various tests of manual dexterity, for example, are designed to measure both the accuracy and speed of motor activities. These tests are administered with a time limit. Clerical speed is another function measured by means of time-limit tests. The items contained in tests of clerical speed are relatively simple, typically requiring that the respondent examine pairs of names or numbers like those illustrated below, and indicate whether they are the same or different.

149278_____149228
192278_____192278
Mary L. Jones_____Mary L. Jones
John R. Smith_____John R. Smyth

The critical function such items measure is not solely the number of pairs that the respondent can answer correctly. Given enough time, most persons would answer almost all such items correctly. The key factor here is the number that can be answered correctly within a limited period of time.

It has been shown that older persons are placed in a somewhat disadvantageous position on speed tests when compared with younger persons, although the performance of these age groups on power tests is quite comparable.[2] Aside from this finding, however, the available evidence supports the use of time-limit tests in the industrial setting.

Group versus Individual Tests

Group tests may be administered simultaneously to a large number of persons while individual tests require that an administrator be present for each person being tested. Group tests are by far the more economical to administer, provided that adequate facilities for seating and proctoring the groups being tested are available.

The unique advantages of individual testing are of greater import in clinical and vocational guidance testing than they are in industrial testing. It is easier to establish a relaxed atmosphere and to note the examinee's behavior during an individual test. It is possible to ask the kind of probing question that may be necessary during cer-

---

[2] I. Lorge, "The Influence of the Test upon the Nature of Mental Decline as a Function of Age," *Journal of Educational Psychology*, Vol. XXVII (1936), pp. 100–110.

tain kinds of personality appraisals only in the individual testing situation. Most industrial testing, however, is the type that lends itself as readily to group as to individual testing.

Performance versus Paper-and-Pencil Tests

Paper-and-pencil tests require the respondent to reply by marking or writing an answer to written questions while *performance* tests require him to manipulate apparatus or equipment. The apparatus involved in a performance test may duplicate a real-life situation. This is the case, for example, with flight simulators used for training and evaluating aircrews. A performance test may, on the other hand, require the manipulation of apparatus designed solely to measure some psychological function involving motor activity or manual dexterity.

The fact that performance tests require some kind of equipment means that such tests are generally more expensive to administer than are paper-and-pencil tests. Performance tests, furthermore, do not lend themselves readily to large-group testing. Thus, if a psychological function can be measured with equal effectiveness by means of a paper-and-pencil test and a performance test, the former will be the preferred method of measurement.

It should be apparent, however, that certain aspects of behavior can only be measured effectively by performance tests. How, for example, could a skill like typing proficiency be appraised otherwise? The only way in which to determine a typist's skill is to ask her to type a standardized passage under controlled conditions.

FUNCTIONS MEASURED BY TESTS

In addition to differences in format, psychological tests are differentiated from one another on the basis of the functions they measure. These functions are identified as intelligence, aptitude, achievement, interest, and personality. We will first distinguish between these areas of measurement and then, in a later section, describe a few specific tests of each type.

Intelligence

The definition of intelligence is complicated by the diversity of concepts included within this broad classification. Intelligence is regarded as a general kind of mental alertness. This may involve the ability to learn quickly, to solve problems not encountered previously, and to remember information learned sometime in the past. It certainly involves the ability to think in abstract as well as in concrete terms and to manipulate symbols such as mathematical and verbal concepts. The most outstanding feature of any definition of intelligence is that it involves the *general capacity* for learning and problem solving.

The fact that intelligence tests purport to measure capacity rather than knowledge means that a high score on such tests is no guarantee of the possession of the specific skills necessary for satisfactory job performance. An applicant who scores high enough on an intelligence test to be considered for the position of bookkeeper or accountant, for example, may actually know very little about bookkeeping or accounting procedures. He has merely demonstrated that he has the capability for learning these skills provided that the appropriate opportunities for training are presented to him.

The notion of minimal intellectual requirements for various kinds of work is fairly obvious. It is not so obvious, however, that certain kinds of work may be performed best by employees below some specified maximum level of intelligence. The concept of optimal intellectual levels for certain kinds of work does not imply that the ability to do the work declines as a function of increased intelligence. Rather, the job may be insufficiently demanding of the employee's intellectual capabilities. This lack of total utilization of capability may be reflected in boredom, job dissatisfaction, absenteeism, and even in increased accident rate.

The factor of optimal intellectual level for certain jobs is illustrated by a study of the average length of service of cashiers and inspector wrappers as a function of their score on an intelligence test.[3] The resultant data are shown in Table 6–1. It is apparent that the greatest stability was found for employees in the middle range of intelligence.

Aptitude

Aptitudes are *specific capacities* for acquiring particular knowledges or skills. One way of viewing the relationship between intelligence and aptitude is that the former is a kind of general aptitude. A number of studies have attempted to fragment general intelli-

---

[3] M. J. Viteles, "Selecting Cashiers and Predicting Length of Service," *Journal of Personnel Research*, Vol. II (1924), pp. 467–73.

gence into component aptitudes. An early study of this type by
Thurstone identified seven primary mental abilities (aptitudes):
Memory, Number, Perceptual, Reasoning, Spatial, Verbal, and
Word Fluency.[4] The identification of these aptitudes was accom-
plished by the statistical procedure known as *factor analysis*
whereby the intercorrelations between test scores are examined in

TABLE 6–1

INTELLIGENCE AND LENGTH OF SERVICE

Test Score	Average Length of Service in Days
10–19	3
20–29	91
30–39	156
40–49	142
50–59	107
60–69	100
70–79	96
80–89	87
90 and over	35

order to identify measured functions which cluster or "hang" together. These seven primary mental abilities cannot be regarded as
the ultimate in aptitude identification. As greater variety is introduced into the battery of tests submitted to factor analysis, more
and more specific aptitudes are identified. Thus, it has been suggested more recently that as many as 40 dimensions of intellect have
now been discovered.[5]

Again, as is the case with intelligence, aptitude tests measure capacity but not necessarily knowledge. Tests of general mechanical
aptitude attempt to measure capacity for learning to deal with mechanical devices and to perceive mechanical relationships. The person who earns a high mechanical aptitude score may not have had
any experience that will qualify him for an industrial position. Similarly, a person who earns a high muscial aptitude score may not
know how to play a musical instrument or how to compose music.
His test score reveals only a capability for learning in this area, provided that the opportunities are presented to him.

---

[4] L. L. Thurstone, *Primary Mental Abilities* (Chicago: University of Chicago
Press, 1938).

[5] J. P. Guilford, "The Structure of Intellect," *Psychological Bulletin,* Vol. LIII
(1956), pp. 267–93.

Achievement or Proficiency

Intelligence and aptitude tests are useful measures of potential. They are most helpful for selecting personnel whenever the job to be filled requires unique skills or knowledges which the company expects to teach to new employees. In addition these tests may be used for selecting personnel when the labor market is such that the company is compelled to hire employees who have certain capabilities even though these have not yet been augmented by training and experience, or when the company is specifically seeking persons who have the potential for growth and promotion within the organization.

Most often, however, the employment office will seek employees who now know how to do certain kinds of work. In such cases, the selection tests will measure achievement, knowledge, or proficiency. The specific skills or proficiencies necessary for success in particular occupations are measured by *trade tests.*

Interest

Measures of capacity (intelligence and aptitude tests) and of achievement are fundamental to a personnel testing program. However, cognitive measures alone rarely yield validity coefficients in excess of 0.40–0.50. Thus, a number of job applicants selected for employment on the basis of scores on such tests will fail as employees, and a number of rejected applicants would, if hired, have been successful employees.

The lack of perfect validity of cognitive measures is due, in part, to errors of measurement. Every kind of measuring instrument is subject to a certain amount of error. The lack of perfect validity is due in part also to the fact that factors other than capacity and achievement are partially responsible for employee success. Two such factors are measured by interest and personality inventories.

Interests are a product of the interaction of hereditary and environmental factors. It seems probable that human beings have capabilities which are never fully realized or exploited. The failure to reach the limits of our capacity in certain directions results primarily from lack of interest. The converse is also true to some extent. Heredity circumscribes the range of individual interests by limiting the range of possible achievement. Thus, we would hardly expect a color-blind person to display a strong interest in painting or other activity involving color perception or color matching. But the main limiting factor in the evolution of our interests is environmental rather than hereditary in nature.

Given two job applicants of about equal potential and prior experience, the one with the more significant vocational interests will probably be the better employee. Unfortunately, however, the measurement of interests is a much more satisfactory aid to vocational counseling with students than it is to selecting personnel. A fundamental objection to the use of interest inventories in the selection process is that the items in such inventories tend to be transparent. The applicant can often determine, by reading the item, which response will portray his interests most favorably for the job in question. He is thus able to make the "best" or "most appropriate" response even though it may not be indicative of his true interests.

Transparency is not regarded as a serious problem when students take an interest inventory for counseling purposes because it is likely that they are motivated to respond as carefully and accurately as possible. Job applicants, however, want to be accepted for employment. Thus, the validity of their replies to interest inventories may be open to question.

It follows, then, that interest inventories are probably of greater usefulness in a personnel testing program when the results are used for placement, classification, or counseling rather than selection. Once accepted for employment, the job applicant can probably be induced to respond as honestly as possible to an interest inventory on the grounds that it will facilitate his assignment to the kind of job in which he will most likely be successful.

The one noteworthy exception to this generalization is that the validity of interest inventories administered for the purpose of personnel selection has been demonstrated for certain groups of salesmen. The "salesmanship" scoring keys provided for standardized interest inventories contribute positively to selection in certain instances; in others, it has proven necessary to custom-tailor scoring keys for specific jobs.[6]

Personality

Many personnel officers regard personality as the crux of job success or failure. The feeling is rather widespread that for certain

---

[6] J. L. Hughes and W. J. McNamara, "Limitations on the Use of Strong Sales Keys for Selection and Counseling," *Journal of Applied Psychology,* Vol. XLII (1958), pp. 93–96.

types of positions, particularly those requiring the exercise of supervision, personal characteristics may be even more important than skill or job knowledge. It is likely that an employment interviewer fancies as one of his primary functions, the determination of "what the applicant is really like." There is indeed little doubt that *personality traits* (characteristic modes of reaction) are vocationally significant. It is apparent also that adjustment, goal-directedness and general mental health will all influence an employee's efficiency.

Two general types of measure are used for appraising personality: paper-and-pencil inventories and projective techniques. *Paper-and-pencil inventories* contain a series of questions or statements like:

I worry a good deal about my health.
I frequently have headaches.
I concentrate easily.

The respondent is directed to reply to each statement by answering "yes" or "no" or "always," "sometimes," or "never." Standardized paper-and-pencil personality inventories are as simple to administer and score as any other kind of objective group test. The results obtained from administration of such inventories for personnel selection have been, however, largely negative. The reason for this is that, like interest inventories, paper-and-pencil personality inventories are highly transparent.

Projective techniques confront the examinee with a relatively unstructured or ambiguous set of stimuli which, in the case of the Rorschach Test look like ink blots, and in the Murray Thematic Apperception Test are pictures. He is encouraged to respond freely, telling what he sees in the blot or making up a story about the picture. Responses to such stimuli are presumed to be projections of the subject's thoughts, wishes, desires, and needs.

Projective devices are not transparent. The subject does not know what responses are desired and hence cannot fake his replies in meaningful fashion. Administering projective techniques and interpreting responses to them does, however, require a high level of training and skill. Such instruments are typically administered individually and are both time-consuming and expensive. In addition, projective tests have consistently been shown to be less reliable than objective tests.

The transparency of paper-and-pencil inventories and the expense as well as relative unreliability of projective techniques has kept personality appraisal in industry to a minimum. More research is needed to develop such measures particularly for predicting success in different types of high-level jobs within a given professional area.[7]

It is likely that two fairly recent developments in the area will make it possible to do considerably more of this kind of appraisal in the future.

The Forced Choice Technique. The forced choice technique was designed to overcome the element of fakability in paper-and-pencil inventories and rating scales. Its application to merit rating is discussed in some detail in Chapter 11. We will be concerned now only with its use in personality assessment.

Instead of responding to every statement, the subject is forced to choose from two or more statements the one most descriptive of him. The following illustrative item taken from the *Edwards Personal Preference Schedule*[8] typifies the forced-choice format.

A. I feel depressed when I fail at something.
B. I feel nervous when giving a talk before a group.

If it appears to the respondent that both statements describe how he reacts, he must select the one that is most descriptive. If he feels that neither is descriptive, he chooses the one that is least inaccurate.

The key to the forced-choice technique is the process by which alternatives are paired. Every statement in a forced choice item has been carefully selected for pairing on the basis of preliminary research designed to insure that the statements are comparable with respect to social desirability or undesirability. The respondent cannot, in other words, deliberately respond to create a favorable impression because he is always forced to choose between pairs of alternatives which appear to be equally good or equally bad. Only one of the alternatives in each pair, however, has been demonstrated to possess item-validity and hence makes a positive contribution to the respondent's score on the inventory.

Group Projective Techniques. Considerable research has been directed toward the problem of making projective techniques more accessible to industry. This research has taken the form of restruc-

---

[7] W. B. Michael, "Differential Testing of High Level Personnel," *Educational and Psychological Measurement,* Vol. XVII (1957), pp. 475–90.

[8] A. L. Edwards, *Personal Preference Schedule* (New York: Psychological Corp., 1954).

turing such techniques for group administration and even for objective scoring.

One such modification of the Rorschach Test is the *Structured-Objective Rorschach Test* (*SORT*).[9] The *SORT* contains 10 inkblots, each of which is presented along with 10 sets of three-alternative responses representing things that might be seen in the blot. The respondent is instructed to select the one alternative from each group of three that most clearly represents something he sees. This format differs quite markedly from the usual Rorschach procedure in which the respondent is shown the blot and asked to make a free response (that is, to tell what he sees) without prompting or suggestions from the examiner. The *SORT* may be administered to groups and is scored objectively. The validity of this test and others like it is undergoing considerable study at the present time.

SOME SPECIFIC TESTS

Literally thousands of psychological tests have been reported in the professional literature, reviewed in comprehensive test bibliographies, and are available for distribution to qualified persons by test publishers. It is possible here to present only a cursory overview of some of the standardized tests most often used in industry.

Intelligence Tests

The *Otis Quick-Scoring Mental Ability Tests*[10] is a rapidly administered, paper-and-pencil group measure which, although relatively old is still widely used. It may be administered with a 20- or a 30-minute time limit, and an even briefer version has been developed by Wonderlic.[11] This test has demonstrated validity for selecting employees for quite a variety of occupations not requiring a really high level of intelligence. The *Otis* does not have sufficient "top," for example, for administration to college students.

The *Wechsler Adult Intelligence Scales*[12] is an individually administered intelligence test sometimes used for industrial purposes. The advantages of this test are related more to clinical than to industrial

---

[9] J. B. Stone, *S-O Rorschach Test* (Los Angeles: California Test Bureau, 1958).

[10] A. S. Otis, *Manuals:* Gamma (1937), Alpha, Beta (1939) (Tarrytown-on-Hudson, N.Y.: Harcourt, Brace & World, Inc.).

[11] *Personnel Test* (Northfield, Ill., 1945).

[12] D. Wechsler (New York: Psychological Corp., 1955).

applications. The fact that the examiner can probably elicit a higher level of motivation from the respondent and can better observe his behavior while he responds in the individual than in the

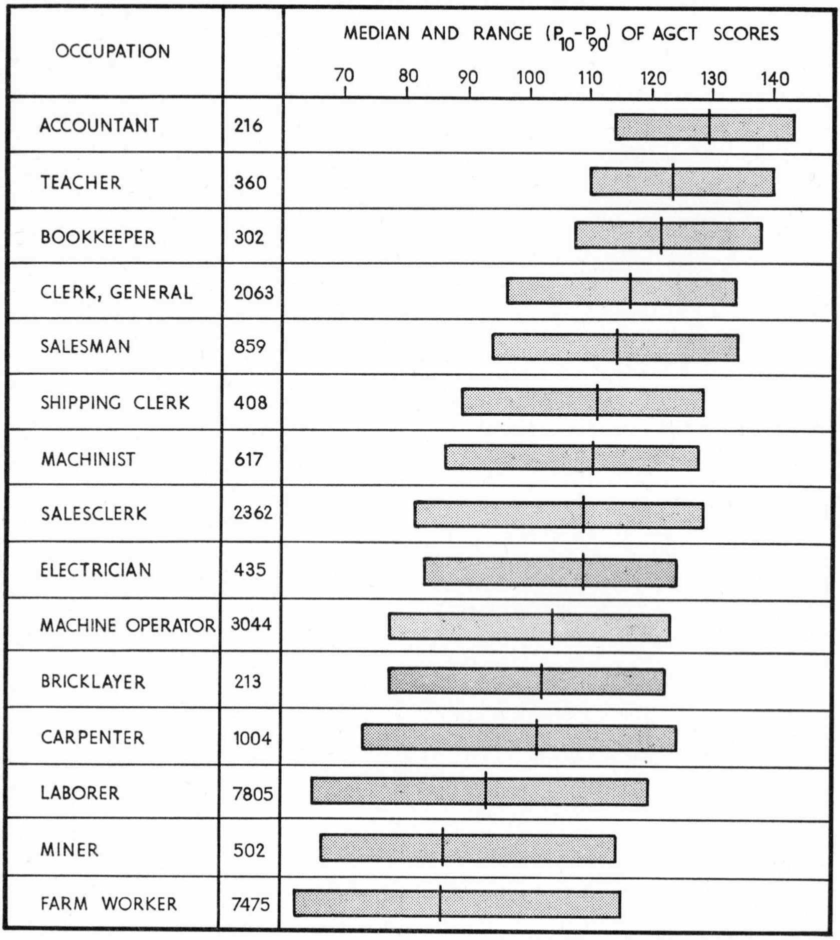

OCCUPATION		MEDIAN AND RANGE $(P_{10}-P_{90})$ OF AGCT SCORES
		70 80 90 100 110 120 130 140
ACCOUNTANT	216	
TEACHER	360	
BOOKKEEPER	302	
CLERK, GENERAL	2063	
SALESMAN	859	
SHIPPING CLERK	408	
MACHINIST	617	
SALESCLERK	2362	
ELECTRICIAN	435	
MACHINE OPERATOR	3044	
BRICKLAYER	213	
CARPENTER	1004	
LABORER	7805	
MINER	502	
FARM WORKER	7475	

Each bar shows the range of scores between the tenth and ninetieth percentiles for enlisted selectees in that occupation. The vertical bars represent median scores.

Source: N. Stewart, *Occupations*, Vol. XXVI (1947), pp. 5–13. "AGCT scores of Army personnel grouped by occupations."

FIGURE 6–1. AGCT Scores for a Selected Group of Occupations.

group testing situation probably leads to a more accurate appraisal of intelligence. Most industrial requirements can, however, be satisfied by the more economical procedure of group testing.

The fact that intelligence tests are designed to measure general rather than specific capacity implies that measures of intelligence have been found to correlate with success in quite a range of occupations. The relationship between intelligence and occupational level is illustrated by the data in Figure 6–1. These data show the range of scores from the tenth to the ninetieth percentiles and the median scores earned by inducted enlisted men from various civilian

DESCRIPTION OF THE FLANAGAN APTITUDE CLASSIFICATION TESTS

FACT NO.	NAME OF TEST	DESCRIPTION
1	INSPECTION	This test measures ability to spot flaws or imperfections in a series of articles quickly and accurately. The test was designed to measure the type of ability required in inspecting finished or semi-finished manufactured items.
2	CODING	This test measures speed and accuracy of coding typical office information. A high score can be obtained either by learning the codes quickly or by speed in performing a simple clerical task.
3	MEMORY	This test measures ability to remember the codes learned in test 2.
4	PRECISION	This test measures speed and accuracy in making very small circular finger movements with one hand and with both hands working together. The test samples ability to do precision work with small objects.
5	ASSEMBLY	This test measures ability to "see" how an object would look when put together according to instructions, without having an actual model to work with. The test samples ability to visualize the appearance of an object from a number of separate parts.
6	SCALES	This test measures speed and accuracy in reading scales, graphs, and charts. The test samples scale-reading of the type required in engineering and similar technical occupations.
7	COORDINATION	This test measures ability to coordinate hand and arm movements. It involves the ability to control movements in a smooth and accurate manner when these movements must be continually guided and readjusted in accordance with observations of their results.
8	JUDGMENT AND COMPREHENSION	This test measures ability to read with understanding, to reason logically, and to use good judgment in practical situations.
9	ARITHMETIC	This test measures skill in working with numbers—adding, subtracting, multiplying, and dividing.
10	PATTERNS	This test measures ability to reproduce simple pattern outlines in a precise and accurate way. Part of the test requires the ability to sketch a pattern as it would look if it were turned over.
11	COMPONENTS	This test measures ability to identify important component parts. The samples used are line drawings and blueprint sketches. It is believed this performance should be representative of ability to identify components in other types of complex situations.
12	TABLES	This test measures performance in reading two types of tables. The first consists entirely of numbers; the second contains only words and letters of the alphabet.
13	MECHANICS	This test measures understanding of mechanical principles and ability to analyze mechanical movements.
14	EXPRESSION	This test measures feeling for and knowledge of correct English. The test samples certain communication tasks involved in getting ideas across in writing and talking.

Flanagan Aptitude Classification Tests, *Examiner Manual* (Chicago: Science Research Associates, Inc. 1959), p. 5.

FIGURE 6–2. Description of the Flanagan Aptitude Classification Tests.

occupations on the *Army General Classification Test* during World War II. The scores on this test are not to be confused with intelligence quotients (IQs).

If we assume that these data reflect intellectual requirements for various occupations, it can be seen that there is considerable overlap between occupations with respect to these requirements. Nevertheless, there is a marked tendency for measured intelligence to increase as occupational level increases.

Aptitude Tests

The *Flanagan Aptitude Classification Tests* (*FACT*)[13] are a battery of the 14 aptitude measures described in Figure 6–2.

It was not intended that substantial importance be given to any single test score in the *FACT* battery. Rather, various combinations of the subtests in the battery have been shown to measure the significant job elements associated with specific occupations. The com-

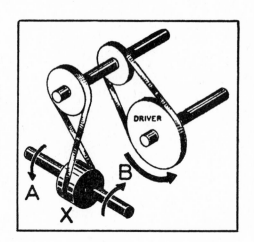

The subject marks *A* or *B* in response to the question: "If the driver turns in the direction shown, which way will the pulley at 'X' turn?"

FIGURE 6–3. Sample Item from Form B of the Bennett, Seashore, and Wesman Mechanical Reasoning Test.

bination of measures related to the job of accountant, for example, are Coding, Memory, Judgment and Comprehension, Arithmetic, and Tables. Similar patterns of aptitude based upon the significant job elements have been determined for quite a variety of occupations.

The Bennett, Seashore, and Wesman *Mechanical Reasoning Test*[14]

---

[13] Science Research Associates, Inc. (Chicago, 1959).

[14] G. K. Bennett, H. G. Seashore, and A. G. Wesman (New York: The Psychological Corp., 1947).

is a paper-and-pencil measure of mechanical aptitude. The items in this test are similar to the illustration in Figure 6–3. It is rapidly administered and scored, and likely to be of value for jobs like engineering where understanding machines is of prime importance.

The *Clerical Aptitudes Test*[15] developed by Science Research Associates is representative of the kind of measure designed to identify

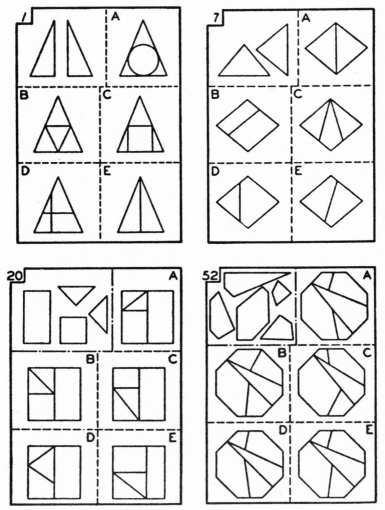

The subject must pick the figure (from *A* to *E*) which shows how the parts will look when assembled.

FIGURE 6–4. Items from the Revised Minnesota Paper Form Board Test.

[15] Science Research Associates, Inc., Chicago.

potentially successful office workers. It consists of three subtests: office vocabulary, office arithmetic, and office checking. The latter subtest is a measure of the speed and accuracy with which the respondent compares pairs of numbers.

Certain occupations, like drafting, require that the employee be able to visualize objects in space. Spatial visualization is measured by tests like the *Minnesota Paper Formboard (Revised)*[16] in which the individual responds to items similar to the one illustrated in Figure 6–4. He must select the drawing that represents what the object will look like when the components are assembled.

A study performed by Surgent[17] will serve to indicate the kind of

Courtesy: Educational Test Bureau, Minneapolis; C. H. Stoelting Co., Chicago; Science Research Associates, Inc., Chicago

FIGURE 6–5.   Minnesota Rate of Manipulation Test (above); O'Connor Finger and Tweezer Dexterity Test (right); Purdue Pegboard (left).

[16] New York: Psychological Corp., 1941.

[17] L. V. Surgent, "The Use of Aptitude Tests in the Selection of Radio Tube Mounters," *Psychological Monographs*, Vol. LXI, No. 283 (1947), p. 40.

findings that may be obtained when aptitude test scores are correlated with a criterion of employee efficiency. Four aptitude tests (yielding five scores) were administered to 233 female radio tube mounters. The predictor instruments, all of which measure manual and manipulative ability, were:

Minnesota Rate of Manipulation Test: A board with 60 round holes and 60 pegs. The "placing test" requires the subject to put each block in a hole. The "turning test" requires the subject to turn over each block.

O'Connor Finger Dexterity Test: A metal plate containing 100 holes. The subject is required to place three metal pins in each hole with his fingers.

O'Connor Tweezer Dexterity Test: Same apparatus as above. The subject uses tweezers to place one peg in each hole.

Purdue Pegboard: This test has two parts. The first measures finger dexterity by requiring the subject to assemble pins, washers, and collars. The second measures manual dexterity by having subjects insert the pins in holes. (The latter part was used in this investigation.)

The equipment required for these three tests is shown in Figure 6–5.

Test scores on these instruments were correlated with supervisory ratings of efficiency during the training period with the results shown in Table 6–2.

TABLE 6–2

CORRELATIONS BETWEEN TEST SCORES AND SUPERVISORY RATINGS OF TUBE MOUNTERS DURING THE TRAINING PERIODS

Test	Correlation
Minnesota Rate of Manipulation	
Placing test	.56
Turning test	.50
O'Connor	
Finger dexterity	.48
Tweezer dexterity	.59
Purdue Pegboard	.64

Although the Purdue Pegboard was the most efficient predictor of supervisory ratings, it was apparent that the other measures were also fairly effective predictors. Consequently, the tests were combined into a battery, and multiple correlations were computed to determine the predictive efficiency of the combined tests. The most efficient combination involving the Purdue Pegboard, the O'Conner Tweezer Dexterity Test, and the Minnesota Rate of Manipulation Placing Test yielded a multiple correlation of 0.76, which was considerably better than that obtained from any of the predictors used singly.

Achievement Tests

Many of the trade tests currently being used are not available for commercial distribution because they have been developed for and are the property of a specific company. Nevertheless, trade tests have been published in such areas as stenographic proficiency, machine-shop tools, equipment and procedures, blueprint reading, and industrial electricity.

Interest Inventories

Interest inventories can, as was pointed out earlier, be extremely helpful for the purpose of vocational guidance even though they are of rather limited utility in the industrial setting. The two most widely used inventories are the Strong *Vocational Interest Blank* and the Kuder *Preference Record.*

The items in the Strong Vocational Interest Blank[18] list occupations, school subjects, amusements, activities, and so on, which the respondent must rank in order of preference or respond to in terms of "like," "dislike," or "indifferent." Every item in the inventory carries a positive or a negative weight based upon comprehensive statistical analyses. These weights are combined to produce occupational scoring keys. When the overall positive or negative weight is determined for each occupation, it is transformed to an indication of level of interest expressed as a letter grade (A, B+, B, B—, C+, or C). An *A* rating means that the individual's interests are similar to the pattern characteristic of persons successfully engaged in that type of work. A *B* rating means that his interests bear some resemblance to those of successful workers, while a *C* rating means that his interests bear little if any resemblance to those of successful workers.

This inventory has an exceedingly thorough and comprehensive research program behind it. One of the most impressive indications of the relationship between scores on the Strong Vocational Interest

---

[18] E. K. Strong, *Manual* (Stanford, Calif.: Stanford University Press, 1927, 1938, 1951).

Blank and an occupational criterion has been reported for life insurance salesmen.[19] The obtained relationship between score on the Life Insurance Salesman Key of the *Strong*, percent of salesmen retained after one and two years, and median amount of insurance sales during the first and second year is shown in Table 6–3. Salesmen who scored at the A level on the Strong were roughly twice as productive and much more likely to be retained than were the salesmen who scored at the B level or lower.

TABLE 6–3

THE RELATIONSHIP BETWEEN VOCATIONAL INTEREST BLANK SCORE, RATE OF
RETENTION, AND ANNUAL SALES BY LIFE INSURANCE SALESMEN

	Number of Salesmen Contracted	After 1 Year		After 2 Years	
Score on Strong		Percent Remaining	Median Sales	Percent Remaining	Median Sales
A...................	228	66.5%	$155,414	42.5%	$206,680
B+...................	72	59.1	112,839	32.4	144,446
B, B−, C.............	76	34.2	73,814	15.8	133,039

The Kuder *Preference Record*[20] consists of items arranged in triads (groups of three) requiring the examinee to select the one he likes most and the one he likes least. An illustrative item is cited below:

Visit an art gallery
Browse in a library
Visit a museum

The *Preference Record* yields scores indicative of strength of interest in nine vocational areas identified as Mechanical, Computational, Scientific, Persuasive, Artistic, Literary, Musical, Social Service, and Clerical. A fundamental difference between the interest inventories developed by Kuder and by Strong is that the former indicates the relative strength of each of nine interest areas within the individual while the latter yields comparisons between an individual's interests and those of successful employees within various occupational groups.

A new form of the Kuder *Preference Record* scored by occupation

---

[19] Marion A. Bills, "A Tool for Selection That Has Stood the Test of Time," L. L. Thurstone (ed.), *Applications of Psychology* (New York: Harper & Bros., 1952), Table II, p. 133.

[20] G. F. Kuder, *Manual* (Chicago: Science Research Associates, 1939, 1943, 1953). Short Industrial Form, 1948.

rather than by vocational area has recently been published.[21] Scoring keys for 22 specific occupations are thus far available. Additional research on this form is presently under way.

Personality Inventories

The Bernreuter *Personality Inventory*[22] is probably one of the most widely used paper-and-pencil devices for assessing personality. This self-administering inventory yields scores designated Sociability, Self-Confidence, Dominance, Neurotic Tendency, Introversion, and Self-Sufficiency. Research has indicated that scoring only the first four of these six scales yields a fairly comprehensive appraisal.

The transparency of the Bernreuter when used for selecting personnel leads to the conclusion that other less fakable personality inventories may ultimately prove more satisfactory in the industrial setting. However, further evidence on this point is sorely needed.

SUMMARY

This chapter explored the range of standardized and commercially published psychological tests available for industrial application. The decision about whether to use a commercially published test or to custom-build a test must be made with reference to each individual situation. The outstanding advantages of standardized tests include economy, immediate availability, and accessibility to norms. There are, in spite of these advantages, certain limitations to the use of commercially available tests. The validity of such tests cannot be assumed; it must be established under the particular circumstance in which the test is to be used. Very often, also, commercially available tests may not be appropriate for the particular personnel selection problem confronting a company.

Psychological tests differ from one another in the way in which they are structured, administered, and scored. In addition to the previously mentioned differentiation between subjective and objective tests, some tests have a time limit (speed tests) while others do not (power tests); some are suitable for administration to groups while others are designed for administration to one individual at a time; and some require that the respondent perform on some kind of apparatus or equipment while others require the respondent to reply by marking an answer to a written question.

In addition to differences in format, psychological tests are differentiated from one another on the basis of the functions they measure. These functions are identified as intelligence, aptitude, achievement, interest, and personality.

---

[21] Chicago: Science Research Associates, 1956.

[22] R. G. Bernreuter (Stanford, Calif.: Stanford University Press, 1935).

Intelligence and aptitude tests purport to measure capacity rather than knowledge. Thus, they are most appropriate in situations in which the job to be filled requires unique skills or knowledges which the company expects to teach new employees. Most often, however, the employment office will seek employees who now know how to do certain kinds of work. In such cases, the selection tests will measure achievement, knowledge, or proficiency.

Measures of capacity, like intelligence and aptitude tests, and of achievement are fundamental to a personnel testing program. They are sometimes supplemented by devices to assess interests and personality. The primary objection to the use of interest and personality inventories for personnel selection is that these devices tend to be transparent. The respondent can often determine by reading the items, which response will portray his personality most favorably for the job in question.

One approach toward overcoming the transparency of paper-and-pencil inventories for the assessment of interests and personality is the forced-choice technique. Projective techniques for assessing personality are also free from the element of transparency, but tend to have low reliability. The validity of these approaches for industrial application is currently undergoing considerable research.

Training

7 Know all men that I, Thomas Millard, with the Consent of Henry Wolcott of Windsor unto whose custody & care at whose charge I was brought over out of England into New England, doe bynd myself as an apprentise for eight yeeres to serve William Pynchon of Springfield, his heires & assigns in all manner of lawful employmt unto the full ext of eight yeeres beginninge the 29 day of Sept 1640 & the said William doth condition to find the said Thomas meat, drinke & clothing fitting such an apprentise & at the end of his tyme one new sute of apparell & forty shillings in mony: subscribed this 28 October 1640.[1]

The kind of "on the job training" promised Thomas Millard was typical of New England apprenticeship in Colonial days. The employer's commitments were minimal. In return for receiving devoted service for "eight yeeres," he was to provide merely "meat, drinke and clothing" and, at the end of the period, "one new sute of apparell & forty shillings in mony." Little enough perhaps, but even the full extent of the generosity provided by this indenture was not realized. Apparently, Millard became itchy to strike out on his own before completing the full term of his apprenticeship. The following statement appears at the foot of the indenture:

Tho Millard by his owne consent is released & discharged of Mr. Pynchon service this 22. of May 1648 being 4 months before his tyme comes out, in Consideration whereoff he looses the 40 s in mony wch should have bin pd him, but Mr. Pynchon giveth him one New sute of Apparell he hath at present.[2]

It is apparent from the foregoing indenture agreement that industrial training is far from a new concept. However, both the scope and methods of present-day industrial training differ considerably from Colonial apprenticeship. Although development of job-related knowledges and skills has always been a fundamental objective of

---

[1] United States Department of Labor, Bureau of Apprenticeship, *Apprenticeship Past and Present*, 1952.

[2] *Ibid.*

142

training, this objective has been considerably broadened, particularly since World War II.

DETERMINING TRAINING NEEDS AND OBJECTIVES

A properly structured training program has certain well-defined objectives. These objectives follow logically from a systematic determination of training needs within the company and, in turn, suggest the ways in which training will be conducted, the persons who will be trained, and a scheme for evaluating the effectiveness of the program.

Often the need for some kind of training becomes evident because of the existence of a problem. Automation, for example, may be accompanied by layoffs and a consequent need to train displaced workers for other jobs. Rapid expansion of production or changes in the labor market may necessitate training designed to teach requisite job knowledges or skills to relatively inexperienced workers. Sometimes a company suddenly discovers a rather marked increase in accidents accompanying the introduction of new equipment and needs to institute a safety training program. Or, in anticipation of the retirement of a number of supervisory persons, the company may need to train replacements as effective leaders.

The foregoing problems merely suggest the kinds of situations that may create a need for training. The program begins with certain questions related to need: In what areas (safety, skills, supervision, and so on) is training needed? Which workers need to be trained? What are the specific training needs of these workers? Only after questions like these are answered, can the company begin to think in terms of the kind of program that will be appropriate to its needs.

Discovering Training Needs

Analyses of training needs typically begin with an overview of the entire company in an attempt to identify areas of relatively inefficient operation. Interviews, studies of company records concerning turnover, accidents and customer complaints, and observations by the training analyst may all be suggestive.[3]

Although this overview can suggest *general* areas of training need, it must be supplemented by studies to determine specific groups of

---

[3] D. H. Fryer, M. R. Feinberg, and S. S. Zalkind, *Developing People In Industry* (New York: Harper & Bros., 1956).

workers in need of training. For example, safety training may be in-dicated for a company, but it is unlikely that all groups of workers will need such training. The analyst's focus narrows during this phase of training need determination as he studies the workers in particular departments. He may consult existing job analyses or make new ones of his own; he makes systematic observations; and he interviews.

Finally, the analysis of training needs gets down to the level of in-dividual workers. Training may be necessary only for certain work-ers within a department; or differential amounts and types of train-ing may be indicated for the various department members. Various tests of ability, skill, or job knowledge may be administered if these are appropriate to the identified areas of training need. Supervisory ratings may help identify particular workers most in need of train-ing, and indicate the kinds of training they ought to receive. Com-pany records of individual productivity, accident frequency, and so on may provide further clues.

Training Objectives

A training program properly conceived permeates all levels and activities of an industrial organization. Its impact is felt by workers with varying amounts of experience and at various levels or classifi-cations.

The diversity of training needs makes it impossible to present a really comprehensive list of the objectives that can be realized as a result of training. We will consider only some that are most gener-ally applicable.

Orientation and Indoctrination. This kind of training is designed for newly hired personnel regardless of whether these workers have had prior experience. It serves primarily to explain the company's policies and practices. Secondarily, it may seek to develop attitudes of pride in the company and personal identification of the employee with it.

Job-Related Skills and Knowledges. Such training is mandatory when a company is compelled to hire relatively inexperienced em-ployees either because of conditions of the labor market or because the job to be filled is novel or unique to the particular company. A continuous program of skills-and knowledges-training for in-service personnel may be necessary also to upgrade present levels of em-ployee performance.

Personal Improvement and Enrichment. This objective extends the impact of training considerably beyond the confines of the worker's job. It is based on the assumption that more broadly educated employees handle their work more efficiently. In addition, programs with more general educational objectives lay the groundwork for teaching new skills and knowledges demanded of workers by an ever expanding technocracy. Thus, an organization like the National Secretaries Association has considered it desirable to sponsor courses for its members in such areas as Art Appreciation and Human Relations. Individual companies, likewise, provide opportunities for employees at various levels to take such courses as Speed Reading, Blueprint Reading, Speech, and Written Communication.

Management Development. The executive, administrative, and human-relations skills required for effective leadership are not acquired by virtue of seniority or demonstrated job performance. As men progress to increasingly higher management positions, their responsibilities shift from the specific to the general; they must make decisions having broad impact and affecting many other persons.

Technological and Scientific Information. Rapid technological and scientific advances have necessitated special programs designed to keep employees abreast of the most recent developments. Many accounting procedures utilizing punched-card equipment "brand new" only 15 years ago, for example, have been superseded by the development of relatively inexpensive data-processing machines capable of storing and providing ready access to vast amounts of information. In a competitive society it is imperative that industrial organizations avail themselves of all pertinent technological advances. To do so requires that scientific and professional employees be provided the opportunity and incentive to learn about such advances.

LEARNING AND FORGETTING

Industrial training is a learning situation fundamentally similar to formal kinds of schoolroom learning. To be conducted successfully, a training program must be predicated upon certain basic psychological principles of learning and forgetting. We cannot here review the very substantial body of evidence in the area of learning theory. Rather, we will attempt merely to summarize some of the highlights.

Motivation

Repetitive practice or exposure is not, by itself, a sufficient condition to produce learning. A person learns only when he is motivated to learn. The importance of motivation for learning has several implications for industrial training. New employees initially may be resentful of a training program because they may feel that the program really betrays a lack of confidence in their ability to do the work. Experienced supervisors may similarly object to the introduction of "newfangled" working procedures which are at considerable variance with their familiar and accustomed ways of doing the job.

It is necessary, then, to precede any training program with an orientation session (or a series of such sessions) in which the need for the program is clearly discussed. In addition, the program must contain provisions for the continual motivation of the trainees during the course of training.

Knowledge of Results. Trainees must be given a stream of information (or "feedback") about their performance if they are to maintain a high level of interest in the training program. The importance of feedback is evident from an investigation in which two groups of subjects were trained to aim a rifle at an unseen moving target.[4] One group was given information indicating whether or not they were aiming in the vicinity of the target. The other group received no information of this kind. At the end of the four hundredth practice trial, the dissemination of information to the "knowledge" group was terminated, and both groups operated under conditions of "no knowledge" for 400 additional trials.

The results for these two groups of subjects expressed in terms of the mean number of seconds the rifle was actually aimed on the target are shown graphically in Figure 7–1. Knowledge of results produced a more rapid increment in performance than did the control condition during the original 400 trials. Furthermore, additional learning in the "knowledge" group ceased after the four hundredth trial paralleling the cessation of information about performance. The "no knowledge" group eventually performed essentially as well as the "knowledge" group, but it required about twice as long for them to do so.

---

[4] H. C. W. Stockbridge and B. Chambers, "Aiming, Transfer of Training and Knowledge of Results," *Journal of Applied Psychology*, Vol. XLII, No. 3 (1958), pp. 148–53.

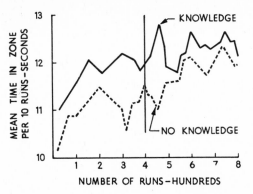

FIGURE 7–1. Effect of Knowledge of Results upon Accuracy of Rifle Aiming.

The incentive effect of knowledge of results is generally more important in the later stages of practice than during the initial stages. In the earlier stages, most trainees have a degree of enthusiasm tending to carry them forward. Later on as this intrinsic enthusiasm diminishes, it must be rekindled by such externally imposed factors as proof of progress.[5]

The provision of feedback information ought to follow the trainee's performance with as little time lapse as possible. You are aware, in your own case, of the instructional value of rapid feedback by the teacher of the correct answers to an examination. Similarly, the industrial trainee benefits most from a training environment permitting for frequent and rapid performance evaluations.

Short-Term Goals. It has been found desirable to establish a number of readily attainable short-term subgoals throughout the learning sequence in addition to the fundamental long-term goal of "completion of training" or a "certificate" or achievement of "regular salary status." It would be difficult for most university students, for example, to attend school with a high level of motivation for the full four years, if the only goal was eventual employment within a selected occupation. This goal is, to be sure, extremely important. Fortunately, from a motivational standpoint, it is supplemented by such subgoals as obtaining the diploma, earning satisfactory course grades, performing well on a specific final examination and doing well on hourly examinations and even on 10-minute quizzes in any one course. In addition, the learner may derive considerable satisfaction from having grasped a difficult concept or gaining insight into a hitherto unknown process.

[5] J. N. Mosel, "How to Feed Back Performance Results to Trainees," *Journal of American Society of Training Directors* (February, 1958).

Whole versus Part Learning.   One of the implications of the desirability of short-term goals for industrial training is that complex
tasks should, wherever possible, be divided into their significant
component parts for teaching purposes. The trainee is enabled,
thereby, to attain a measure of satisfaction from successfully learning portions of the task even though he is not yet able to perform the
entire task.

The nature of the parts to be learned, and the sequence in which
they are taught, varies from one task to another. The disassembly
of a weapon, for example, is predicated upon having the trainees
learn to handle various subassemblies. Similarly, a typist must learn
a variety of subskills including proper fingering of the keys and
proper spacing technique, which she then integrates into a total
behavioral pattern.

However, the performance of a part of a complex task by itself
sometimes is different from the performance of that part in combination with others constituting the whole task. This is especially
true when the entire task has an essential internal cohesiveness, the
integrity of which would be destroyed by decomposition into parts
or subtasks.

The entire matter of feasibility of teaching parts of a task and, if
this is done, of the optimal decomposition of the task and sequence
for presenting the parts is one that needs research in each specific
training situation. In a general way we can say that part training is
particularly useful when the responses constituting the task are not
closely integrated, or when certain portions of the total task are
much more difficult than others.[6]

Massed versus Spaced Learning.   Another aspect of the arrangement of training sessions is the matter of the optimal length of each
session. Practice periods may be *massed,* in which case training
consists of relatively few but long sessions, or they may be *spaced*
so that there are more sessions, each of shorter duration. Five hours
of training may be massed, for example, in a single session starting
at 8:00 A.M. and continuing until 1:00 P.M. The same five hours
may be spaced by setting up a 2½ hour session in the morning and
another in the afternoon, or by establishing five one-hour sessions, or
10 half-hour sessions, and so on.

---

[6] R. M. Gagné and H. Foster, "Transfer of Training from Practice on Components
in a Motor Skill," *Journal of Experimental Psychology,* Vol. XXXIX (1949), pp. 342–
54.

The primary advantage of spaced training is that it is generally easier to maintain a high level of trainee interest and to avoid fatigue during several sessions of shorter duration than during a few very long sessions. Spaced training has, in general, been demonstrated to produce more rapid learning and more permanent retention. Exceptions to this generalization occur in instances in which the skills or concepts to be learned are so simple that even massed practice periods will be of relatively brief duration.

The optimal spacing of training sessions must be determined for each task to be taught. If the time intervals between spaced practice periods are too long, the advantages of spaced practice may be more than offset by the amount of forgetting transpiring during the time interval. Similarly, if the individual practice periods are too brief in duration, they may be filled almost entirely by having the trainees check out tools and materials and receive instructions. Such periods will end just as the trainees are about to move into the task itself!

Understanding Reasons for Requirements. Given proper spacing of training sessions, an appropriate decomposition of the task into its component parts for training purposes, the creation of meaningful subgoals and the availability of knowledge of results, a high level of trainee motivation is possible, but by no means assured. There is some indication that learning is facilitated when the trainees understand the reasons for performing certain tasks in specified ways. Here again is further justification of the necessity for training the trainer how to train. Too many teachers are capable of performing a task without understanding the reasons for which the task is performed in a particular way. When such an operator attempts to train others to do the same kind of work, we are truly confronted with a situation in which the blind are leading the blind.

As a case in point, a company specializing in the manufacture of miniature motors for guidance systems in aircraft was disturbed by an unduly high rate of rejections during final inspection. The defects were attributable to poorly soldered connections. Further checking indicated that conditions caused by rapid expansion in the labor force had led management to utilize a kind of on-the-job training in which experienced solderers were teaching new employees how to do the work. None of these teachers was able, however, to explain the reason for using flux prior to applying the solder. As a result, new operators often regarded this as an unnecessary step in the soldering process. The simple expedient of explaining some elementary principles of soldering to the employees and to the new trainees led to an appreciable decrease in the rate of rejections.

Practice

It is fairly obvious that trainees must actually practice a skill if they are to learn it. Even a highly motivated student attending lectures and seeing demonstrations of automobile driving, for example, is poorly trained to drive until after he has received supervised driving practice. Similarly, the foreman who merely attends lectures on "how to train" or "how to lead" is trained incompletely either as a trainer or as a leader. The essential element of supervised practice is lacking.

Thus, a training program must make provision for the trainees actually to practice their job in the way in which they ultimately will be expected to perform it. If a motor skill, like operation of a piece of equipment, is being taught, the trainees must have an opportunity to practice the operation of the equipment. The supervisor who is learning to train, in like fashion, must receive supervised practice in actually training employees.

In spite of the widely quoted maxim, practice may make *imperfect*. Improper or inappropriate behaviors which are practiced will be learned as effectively as correct behaviors. Thus, a key feature of the practice phase is that the trainees must be very carefully supervised. Mistakes must be corrected as soon as they occur. Anyone who has attempted to teach himself to play golf, for example, and then consults a professional is well aware of the fact that he must unlearn a number of bad habits that have become established as a result of unsupervised practice.

Individual Differences

Recognition of the existence of differences in capabilities, interests, attitudes, and so on, between persons is fundamental to psychological testing programs. All men are *not* equal. Some are more capable than others of learning particular kinds of tasks. Contrary to popular belief, the effect of training is often to accentuate such differences rather than to cancel or reduce them. Thus, the spread between the best and poorest trainees in initial level of performance usually becomes progressively greater as the training program progresses. This is particularly noted when the task being learned is relatively complex or difficult.

The effect of individual differences upon subsequent performance in a training program is evident from the following study. Four groups of soldiers, classified on the basis of their scores on the Army Radiotelegraph Operator Aptitude Tests, received radiotelegraphic

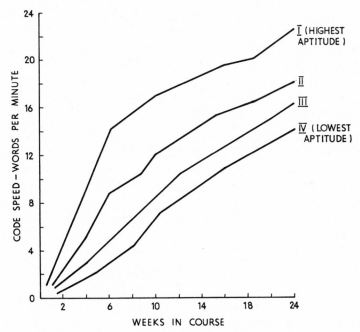

FIGURE 7-2. Radiotelegrahic Code Learning as a Function of Trainee Aptitude.

code instruction. The aptitude classifications ranged from I (highest) to IV (lowest). The rate of learning plotted for these four groups at two-week intervals during the training program is shown in Figure 7-2.[7] Note that the early differences between these groups, which were pronounced even at two weeks, became even more accentuated as training progressed.

TIME AND MOTION STUDY

We have said that the purpose of a training program is to alter behavior and to develop skills. There would be little point to developing such a program, however, unless the trainees were to be taught the most efficient ways in which to do their work. The estab-

[7] E. G. Boring, *Psychology for the Armed Services* (Washington, D.C.: Infantry Journal, 1945), p. 244.

lishment of a training program must be preceded by an intensive study of the job to determine just what it is that the program should accomplish.

The analysis of the content of a proposed training program requires a two-pronged approach. It involves, first, a job analysis to determine what employees now on the job are doing and the ways in which they are doing it. Secondly, the job must be studied with a critical eye to reveal inefficient operations and working techniques. Employees may, for example, be making unnecessarily fatiguing movements, or the sequence of operations may not be conducive to expeditious performance of the work.

Time and motion analysis, attempting to improve plant efficiency by eliminating unnecessary motions and reducing fatigue, is not inherently evil. However, it has often been misapplied. The activities of the early "efficiency expert" devoted solely to employee speed-up without commensurate compensation were repugnent both to the workers and to psychologists. The employees' primary defense against such speed-up programs is to maintain social pressures which prevent exceeding what they consider to be a fair level of production. "Rate busters" who violate tacit agreements about production level are likely to find themselves ostracized by their fellow employees.

Psychological Limitations of Time and Motion "Speed-Up"

The usual procedure for such studies is to observe and time a relatively brief sampling of cycles of a repetitive task. Time standards for performing the constituents of the cycle are then established from averages based upon these limited observations.

Psychologists reject the utilization of time and motion data to set absolute performance standards because of the fallibility of certain assumptions underlying this application.

If the average times are to be used for setting standards, we must assume that the observed performances are sufficiently consistent and have been adequately sampled to produce reliable means. This assumption fails on two counts. First, only rarely is an adequate sampling of observations recorded across employees, segments of the work day, days of the week, and so on. Second, times recorded for performance of various components of a total work cycle by individual employees tend to be characterized by a high degree of inconsistency. In view of the failure of these assumptions, we must conclude that average performance time calculated from observation is not a sufficiently reliable criterion for establishing normative performance rates.

A second psychologically fallible assumption in such utilization of time and motion data is that there is one best way for doing a task regardless of who is doing it. This assumption disregards the body of evidence concerning individual differences. Although a sequence of motions or activities proving satisfactory for many persons may be discovered, it is likely that some persons will remain who could better perform the task using a different sequence or different motions. This realization has even permeated some of the aircrew training in the Strategic Air Command in which "Standard Operating Procedures" for particular elements of a mission have given way to "Crew Operating Procedures" which, although unstandardized, work best for the particular crews in question.[8]

Thirdly, it is psychologically unsound to conceive of *rate* of production as the sole important criterion of industrial effectiveness. Increased productivity is undoubtedly extremely *inefficient* when it is accompanied by such things as heightened fatigue, worker dissatisfaction, and increased accident frequency.

There is a legitimate place for time and motion analysis in industry. It would be foolish to argue against a program designed to make operations more efficient, thereby improving the earnings of management and employees alike. The crux of the problem is the way in which this kind of program is introduced and implemented. The emphasis must be placed upon the individual and the effective utilization of his capacities, rather than upon the job without regard for the human characteristics of the workers.

VARIETIES OF SKILLS TRAINING

Assuming that the job has been studied with a view toward operations and work simplification, and that workers have been carefully selected for inclusion in a training program, management still must decide upon the kind of program it wishes to conduct.

On-the-Job Training

The oldest and simplest approach to training a new employee is to orient him directly on the job under the close supervision of a

[8] P. D. Hood, A. W. Halpin, J. J. Hanitchak, L. Siegel, and J. K. Hemphill, "Crew Member Agreement on RB-47 Crew Operating Procedure" (Lackland Air Force Base, Texas: Air Force Personnel and Training Research Center, May, 1957). Research Report AFPTRC–TN–57–64, ASTIA Document No. 126395.

foreman, a trained instructor or an experienced operator. Ideally, on-the-job training should involve a systematic program of instruction, supervision, and evaluation of trainee progress. Too often, however, this type of training is conducted unsystematically.

The defects in unsystematic on-the-job training are all too obvious. Although the trainer is a skilled and experienced operator, he may be unable to teach this skill to others. Many husbands, for example, are excellent automobile drivers but are utterly incapable of teaching this skill to their wives.

Furthermore, the skilled employee who is supposed to act as the trainer may perceive the training situation as an opportunity to enjoy a vacation with pay. He may relax, read the paper, socialize with other on-the-job "trainers" while the trainee gains experience. Thus, the learner does not get the close supervision he needs and may require an unduly long period of time to become proficient at the job. He may, in addition, practice improper work habits leading to undue spoilage, and perhaps to unnecessary injury as well as to poor productivity.

Another difficulty sometimes encountered with on-the-job training results from the fact that the employee-trainer may actually resent the presence of the trainee. Such resentment, when it occurs, often reflects insecurity. Skilled employees may, for example, fear displacement by younger men and object to teaching skills and shortcuts developed through years of experience.

The aforementioned criticisms of on-the-job training apply, of course, only to such training at its worst. At its best, when the trainer has been taught how to teach, when he is made to feel secure and needed so that he does not fear displacement, and when he is made to realize the importance of maintaining vigilant supervision, this approach to training can be exceedingly valuable.

Vestibule Training

A vestibule school is a separate room or building within a company that is equipped with production equipment and staffed by full-time instructors. It is an industrial plant in miniature in which trainees learn their jobs under conditions like those found in the working environment except that close supervision by skilled trainers is assured and production pressures are not present.

In spite of the relatively high expense of vestibule training, it offers certain rather distinct advantages. Since the focus in vestibule training is learning rather than production, a greater amount of individualized attention can be given to the trainee's problems than is possible when he is trained on the job. Furthermore, whenever there are several openings, the vestibule school can allow the trainee to try out for various jobs rather than assuming a specific job assignment right from the beginning.

The advantages of vestibule training predicated upon provision of optimal learning conditions are, of course, immediately diminished whenever the vestibule school becomes a repository for obsolete equipment. Whatever economies management may seek to effect in this fashion are countermanded by the consequence that employees are trained to do a job with equipment they will not find in the plant.

Apprenticeship

Apprenticeship training is utilized to prepare journeymen in skilled trade areas requiring relatively prolonged preparation. The period of apprenticeship varies from one to seven years, four years being quite typical.

Modern apprenticeship practices are quite different from the early practice described at the beginning of this chapter. Today's apprentice proceeds through a formal program of training, spending specified periods of time working at various kinds of jobs and taking certain courses. His hours of work are generally the same as those of employees within the department in which he is being trained, and he is paid a salary with provision for a systematic wage increase.

Satisfactory completion of apprenticeship makes the trainee eligible for admission to his trade union. Thus, apprenticeship training programs represent joint efforts of trade unions and industrial organizations to maintain a high level of preparation for certain skilled trades like carpentry and tool and die making.

Outside Training

A good deal of vocational training is given outside of industry in trade and vocational high schools and in colleges and universities. Many schools offer shop training, specific vocational preparation in fields like automotive repair, and courses in clerical skills including typing and shorthand. The danger in such training is that it may tend to emphasize outmoded practices and obsolete equipment. It is an unusual publicly supported school, indeed, which can furnish its vocational shops with the most modern equipment and staff them with personnel familiar with current vocational practices.

All of the aforementioned types of training programs have a place in current industrial practice. Research upon the relative effectiveness of these programs is pitifully slim. Although investigators have, in general, clearly demonstrated the superiority of *some* kind of training to no training at all, there have been very few studies comparing the various approaches to training.

A fairly recent study compared the scores earned on a job knowledge test by two groups of aircraft mechanic trainees.[9] One group was trained "in the field": that is, they received training by mobile training units on duty at operational sites for half of each working day. The other half-day was spent by these men at work on the job. The second group received training while in residence at an Air Force Technical School. These trainees spent no time at all on the job during the training period. The length of the training period was the same for both groups (two months), and the groups were equated on the basis of several variables which might have had some bearing upon the criterion measure. The results obtained on the job knowledge test administered after completion of the train-program clearly indicated that the two methods were comparable in effectiveness. Since this was the case, field training rather than technical school training was recommended because of the economies derived from a half-day training program.

Similar results might not have been obtained for different jobs or even for aircraft mechanic trainees learning to work on other weapons systems! Every organization maintaining a training program would find it profitable to evaluate its program to determine whether or not it is operating with maximum efficiency.

MANAGEMENT AND SUPERVISORY TRAINING

The procedures described in the preceding section are pretty much restricted in applicability to skills training for nonsupervisory workers. The skills required of management and supervisory personnel are quite different from those required of line personnel. Three

---

[9] C. J. Judy, "Field Training versus Technical School Training for Mechanics Maintaining a New Weapon System," *Journal of Applied Psychology,* Vol. XLII, No. 6 (1958), pp. 384–88.

procedures especially important in management training are: (1) case conference, (2) role playing, and (3) gaming.

Training by Means of the Case Conference

A fundamental objective in training supervisors is to develop an understanding and appreciation of human relations problems and the acquisition of skill in dealing with personnel problems. The case conference method is one way in which these objectives may be realized.

This method involves group discussions of actual business problems or cases. The case is a realistic situation requiring some kind of supervisory action. It lends itself to various solutions, none of which can be judged in absolute terms as being "right" or "wrong." Some solutions are, however, better or more appropriate than others. The following cases typify this kind of situation.

Case 1

The other day Miss Black went to the personnel office and asked to be transferred out of your section. Joe, the personnel manager, informed you that she gave as her reason that you are favoring Miss White. According to Miss Black's story, Miss White, who is of the same grade level as she but with six months' seniority, has entrenched herself in your favor by being an informer. As a result, Miss White is allowed to while away the day doing just enough work to make it look good, while she (Miss Black) carries a heavy work load and is closely supervised by you.

This is news to you. You are careful to distribute the work evenly. Miss White has a better aptitude for the work, completes it rapidly, and needs little supervision. On the other hand, Miss Black has difficulties, so you are giving her job training—not close supervision. In relation to the charge of informing, you think this might arise from the fact that Miss White often gives you good suggestions on methods improvement. You think Miss White is supervisory material, while you doubt if Miss Black is.

How are you going to handle this situation? [10]

Case 2

The other day the personnel department informed you that one of your men had quit—Smith, an operator you had hired about a month ago. During the exit interview, he told the personnel interviewer he was quitting because in your section the regular workers were a clique, there were no opportunities for an outsider, and he had been told that he was not wanted.

You began to investigate by talking to Jack White, the old-timer whom you had selected to help Smith get acquainted with the job and with the

[10] William J. McLarney, *Management Training: Cases and Principles* (Homewood, Ill.: Richard D. Irwin, Inc., 1959), p. 334.

other men. Jack informed you that he went to lunch with Smith the first day. During the meal Smith kept boasting of how he was going to be top man in the section before long because of his wonderful experience— that you had practically guaranteed him rapid advancement by stating that his past experience would be of great aid to him. Jack claimed that he tried to show Smith that this attitude wouldn't do him any good in getting along with the group. The next day Smith turned down Jack's suggestion that they go to lunch together and went instead with Bill Brown, who had recently been demoted and transferred to your section. Smith and Brown continued going to lunch together.

Then you began to check up on Smith's work. You found that he made less than normal progress during the month he was in your section. You spoke to several of the men who worked with Smith. They told you that none of the men liked him—that he criticized everything and everybody and was constantly saying that in the company where he had worked previously conditions were better and better work was turned out. One of the group said he told Smith that, if he didn't like the way things were done here, he ought to quit.

You review your actions in hiring Smith. You recall from the application blank and the interview that he came to work for a wage that was less than he had received on his previous job, also that he had received no raises on his last two jobs. During the interview he stated that he didn't mind getting less than his previous wage if he had the opportunity to advance—that the reason he quit his last two jobs was the lack of opportunity on them. You told him there were always opportunities in the company for a good man. During the month Smith was on the job, you spoke to him several times, and he told you that he was coming along fine.

1. What might be some of the things wrong with Smith, the man who quit?
2. Which of these might you have uncovered in the interview?
3. What mistakes might you have made in the induction?
4. How should you have inducted Smith?
5. Suppose he is right about the clique—that your group does try to discourage new men who are good workers. How are you going to clean up that situation?
6. What are you looking for in an induction follow-up?
7. How do you get this information? [11]

The trainees are given a period of time in which to study the case and to think about alternative solutions. They are encouraged, during the conference, to discuss the problem, to suggest solutions, and to evaluate the ramifications of the various solutions.

Training by Means of Role Playing

Role playing is, in a way, an extension of the case approach. The case conference terminates with a discussion of alternative solutions.

---

[11] *Ibid.*, p. 358.

Role playing, however, requires that the trainee actually carry out his solution in a supervised practice situation.

A problem for consideration at a role-playing session, for example, might be the case of employee Jones who has an unusually high accident rate. One of the supervisor-trainees would be assigned to the role of the employee and several others would be assigned to the supervisory role. Each of the role players would then act out his solution to the problem with the remainder of the training class as an audience. The class sees several alternative solutions acted out before it and is in a position to compare and evaluate each of them. Furthermore, the role-players have an opportunity to experience the feeling of reacting in a particular way. And the one who is assigned to the role of the employee gains some appreciation of how it feels to be on the receiving end of various kinds of supervisory reaction.

Aside from some embarrassment during the initial role-playing sessions, this technique appears to be quite valuable for helping supervisors gain an understanding of the human element in business and industry. Furthermore, it has been suggested that much of the embarrassment arising from being observed can be sharply reduced by the technique of *multiple role playing*. In this procedure the entire training class is split into small groups, each confronted by the same problem. Since every member of the group is assigned a role to play within his own group, the method tends to reduce feelings of self-consciousness. An additional advantage of multiple role playing is that subsequent discussion across groups often reveals a variety of solutions to the same problem as a function of the particular personalities interacting within each group.[12]

Management Gaming

Decision making is one of management's most critical functions. Management games attempt to develop a degree of decision-making facility by constituting groups of trainees as teams, each representing a "company," and requiring them to make decisions governing the company's operations during the next period of play. The outcome of these decisions is evaluated in terms of a "model" of the operation of the industry or economy. This evaluation is fed back to the teams at the end of each period of play and they then make new decisions for the next period. Anywhere from a week to a year

---

[12] N. R. F. Maier and L. F. Zerfoss, "MRP: A Technique for Training Large Groups of Supervisors and Its Potential Use in Social Research," *Human Relations*, Vol. V (1952), pp. 177–86.

of "real time" may be represented in periods of play ranging from a few minutes to several hours.

One such game, developed at the Carnegie Institute of Technology for use by graduate students, is played by three teams constituting the "industry." The complexity of this game is indicated by the fact that each set of decisions, covering a month of "real" time, requires two to three hours. An IBM computer is tied up for about 45 minutes each time the results of a move are computed.[13]

The players in this particular game are provided with many kinds of information, including basic background data on the history of their company's operations and constraints on its policies and operations. They receive quarterly balance sheets and income statements for their competitors. The status of the team's own company is indicated monthly by a variety of reports, including balance sheets, income statements, summaries of financial commitments, cost of raw materials, cost of goods sold, warehouse stocks and shipments, finished product inventories, and work force as well as equipment down time data. Other information including market survey data, availability of financing, results of product preference tests, and so on are available to each team as requested or required.

The teams are required to make a full range of production, marketing, and finance decisions, including such things as price levels, sales, forecasts, amount of production, applications for financing, allocation of products to regions, and others.

Management gaming has opened tremendous possibilities both for training managerial personnel and for investigating the effectiveness of various industrial policies and practices. The latter application of gaming is, of course, dependent upon the adequacy of the model upon which the game is constructed. To the extent that it realistically simulates industrial conditions, the game itself becomes a research tool whereby answers may be provided to fundamental questions about management theory and practices.

EVALUATING TRAINING OUTCOMES

The basic research design for evaluating a training program requires that measures be obtained on some sort of criterion of the

---

[13] W. R. Dill, "A New Environment for Training Decision-Makers—The Carnegie Management Game" (originally an unpublished report, Carnegie Institute of Technology, Graduate School of Industrial Administration, 1960). Reprinted in E. A. Fleishman, *Studies in Personnel and Industrial Psychology* (Homewood, Ill.: The Dorsey Press, Inc., 1961), pp. 219–30.

effectiveness of training. These criterion measures may then be compared for groups of trained versus untrained employees or for groups trained by one method versus groups trained by another method.

Lawshe has listed a number of criteria which have been utilized for such comparisons.[14] These include:

1. The number of man-hours per unit of product.
2. The amount of time required to bring new employees up to a specified quantity or quality performance level.
3. The average production per unit of time after a specified number of hours or days on the job.
4. The average production performance of employees with varying amounts of training when length of the training period is not standardized.
5. The number of employees required to do a job or to produce a specified number of units.
6. The average straight time hourly earnings when piecework or a bonus plan is in use.
7. The average amount of merit increase received after a specific period of time on the job.
8. The average merit rating score.
9. The average quantity or value of scrap produced.
10. The average number of "reworks."
11. The accident frequency rate.
12. The number of man-hours of lost time from accidents.
13. The number of hospital visitations.

Comparisons between the averages on any one of these criteria for operative personnel as a function of the kind of training program to which the employees have been exposed are useful for contrasting the relative effectiveness of the programs. Such gross comparisons, however, lack a certain amount of detail. It is often helpful to supplement comparisons between mean production, earnings, spoilage, or accident rates by plotting learning curves.

Learning Curve Analysis

A learning curve is a graph showing the relationship between amount of practice and level of performance. The amount of practice may be expressed in terms of the number of hours of training received, the number of training periods completed or the length of time on the job. Performance may be measured in terms of criteria like those cited by Lawshe.

A classic study involving learning curve analysis was the one per-

---

[14] C. H. Lawshe, Jr., "Training Operative Personnel," *Journal of Consulting Psychology*, Vol. VIII (1944), pp. 154–59.

formed in 1899 by Bryan and Harter upon telegraphic transmission
and reception.[15] The number of letters which could be sent and received in a one-minute period by apprentice telegraphic operators
was determined at weekly intervals. The learning curves for one of
the operators is shown in Figure 7–3.

Several of the features apparent in these learning curves are of
particular interest. It was obviously easier for this subject to learn
to send code than to receive it. He reached an acceptable level of
performance for sending much earlier than he did for receiving.
Secondly, both curves indicate that learning proceeded more rapidly during the initial training periods than during the subsequent

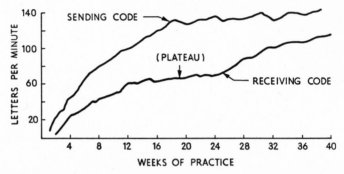

FIGURE 7–3. Learning Curves for Sending and Receiving Telegraphic Code.

periods. This is characteristic of most, but not all, industrial training. Thirdly, the curves are jagged rather than smoothly contoured.
Minor recessions and advances are always found in learning curves
plotted for individual performance. Finally, a period of virtual lack
of progress (*plateau*) is indicated on the curve for receiving. Pla-
teaus do not occur in every learning curve, but when they do appear they are worthy of study. The temporary cessation of progress
may be attributable to diminished motivation, fatigue, or the necessity for integrating previously learned habits.

Thus, the learning curve is a visual display of the effects of training upon performance at every point in the training sequence.
Learning curves may be plotted for groups of trainees as well as for
individuals. The points to be plotted for group curves would be
determined by averaging the performance at every trial in the
training sequence. Such curves may then be compared for various

---

[15] W. L. Bryan and N. Harter, "Studies in the Telegraphic Language," *Psychological Review*, Vol. VI (1899), pp. 346–76.

kinds of training (for example, on-the-job training versus vestibule training), various instructors, various training methods (for example, lecture versus demonstration versus practice), and various kinds of incentives. Figure 7–4 shows learning curves plotted for two groups of cork sorters. One of these groups had been formally trained, while the other had received no formal training.

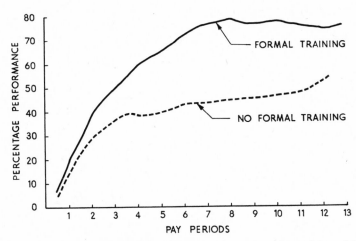

Source: W. R. Mahler and W. H. Monroe, *How Industry Determines the Need for and Effectiveness of Training;* Contract Research Report to Personnel Research Section, Adjutant General's Office, Department of the Army (New York: The Psychological Corp., 1952), p. 77.

FIGURE 7–4. Performance Curves of Trained and Untrained Cork Sorters.

TRAINING THE TRAINER

The success or failure of a training program depends, in large measure, upon the quality of instruction given to the trainees. A criticism, mentioned earlier, of many training programs is that they are founded upon the erroneous premise that men who know how to do a job are automatically qualified to teach others how to do it.

The value of training the trainer is illustrated by a study conducted by Bavelas.[16] Learning curves were plotted for three groups of trainees, all taught by the same instructor. At the time he trained the first group, the instructor had received no training in teaching methods; he had received partial instructor training in the second group; and in the third, he had completed the training program.

---

[16] A. Bavelas, in N. R. F. Maier, *Psychology in Industry* (Boston: Houghton Mifflin Co., 1946), p. 227.

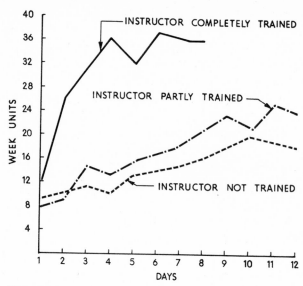

FIGURE 7–5.   Learning Curves of Trainees of an Instructor at Various Stages of the Instructor's Own Training.

The extent of instructor training is reflected in the performance of the trainees being taught by him as shown in Figure 7–5.

Granting the necessity for training the trainer, there remains the fundamental question of who should conduct the training of line personnel.

Who Should Train?

Industrial training may be regarded either as a line function or as a staff function. In the former instance, the employees are trained by their immediate supervisor. In the latter, training is administered either by a separate training department or by an outside consultant.

Although there may be certain circumstances in which training must be administered by the training department or by an outside consultant, this type of administrative arrangement is less satisfactory than is training by immediate supervisors and foremen. The danger inherent in classifying training as a staff function is that this arrangement may lead to behavioral change in the classroom but not in the working environment. The trainee learns to give the correct responses in the presence of the "expert," but does not transfer these responses to the job itself.

The immediate supervisor is, in the final analysis, the person who determines how employees will behave. He enforces certain standards of satisfactory performance and is most immediately responsible for the employee's success and job satisfaction. He is, in consequence, the most appropriate trainer.

The desirability of having the supervisor conduct training for his immediate subordinates is evident throughout the entire organizationl framework. This kind of arrangement does, however, become increasingly difficult to implement as we progress up the management hierarchy. It may be difficult to convince busy executives of the necessity for their active participation in training their immediate subordinates.

Where does the staff training expert or industrial training department fit into the picture if training is to be given at each supervisory level to the immediately subordinate level? The staff training department performs two vital and related functions. First, it is responsible for training the trainers. Secondly, the training department consults with the persons doing the training in order to develop, evaluate, and improve the quality of ongoing training programs.

SUMMARY

Training objectives follow logically from a systematic determination of training needs. These objectives, in turn, suggest the ways in which training will be conducted, the persons who will be trained, and a scheme for evaluating the effectiveness of the program.

A properly conceived training program permeates all levels of an industrial organization. The need for management and supervisory development programs has been increasingly recognized in recent years.

Successful training programs are predicated upon certain basic psychological principles of learning. The most important of these principles is that a person learns only when he *wants* to learn. Motivation for learning requires that the trainee understand the reasons for training requirements, be provided with knowledge about his progress during the program, and be permitted to achieve short-term intermediate subgoals.

Motivation is enhanced also by the proper decomposition of a task into its meaningful parts for training purposes, the presentation of these parts in an appropriate sequence, and by training sessions that are of optimal length. These matters require that research be conducted in each instance to define the parts to be taught, the sequence in which these parts are to be presented, and the most appropriate spacing of training sessions.

In addition to providing for trainee motivation, the program must include provisions for selecting trainees. Marked differences exist in the ability of individuals to profit from industrial training.

Finally, skills training is sterile unless it contains the element of closely supervised practice. The reason for requiring very careful supervision during this phase of the program is that improper or inappropriate behaviors which are practiced may be learned quite as efficiently as correct behaviors. Mistakes must therefore be corrected as soon as they occur.

Since the purpose of training is to teach the most efficient ways in which to work, institution of the training program should be preceded by an intensive study of the job to determine just what are the "most efficient" behaviors. This study generally involves a job analysis and a motion analysis. The latter may lead to rearrangement of working materials, revisions of the operations sequence, and restructuring the work load to avoid day-to-day and hour-to-hour bottlenecks.

The varieties of job skills training include on-the-job training, vestibule training, apprenticeship, and outside training. Supervisory and management training is often conducted by case conference, role playing, and gaming methods.

A key feature of any training program, regardless of its nature, is the trainer himself. He must be capable of teaching his knowledges and skills to the trainee and be willing to do so. Many training programs are open to criticism because they are founded on the erroneous premise that men who know how to do a job are automatically qualified, by virtue of this knowledge, to teach others how to do it. Nothing could be farther from the truth. It requires the possession of skill as a trainer to be an effective teacher.

However, this does not imply that industrial training should be conducted only by training specialists: that is, consultants or the staff training department. The immediate supervisor is, in the final analysis, the person who determines how employees will behave. He enforces performance standards and is most immediately responsible for the employee's success and job satisfaction. He is, in consequence, the most appropriate trainer. The role of the staff training department is to teach the supervisor how to train, and to consult with supervisors in order to develop, evaluate, and improve the quality of ongoing training programs.

In addition to various kinds of tests and ratings, evaluation of training outcomes may require an analysis of learning curves. Such curves are graphs showing the relationship between amount of practice and level of performance. Learning curves may be plotted for individual trainees or for groups of trainees. They are diagnostic aids in the sense that they provide a visual display of the effects of training upon performance at every point in the training sequence.

III.

Worker Efficiency

The chapters in the preceding section discussed selection, placement, and training procedures. The emphasis in the present group of chapters is shifted from concern with pre-employment and training practices to consideration of some job-related factors influencing an employee's efficiency after he has been hired.

The concept "efficiency" may be defined by a variety of criteria including productivity, spoilage, fatigue, absenteeism, and turnover. Although appropriate selection, placement, and training procedures can help improve efficiency, they cannot be regarded as cure-alls. These procedures must be supplemented by industrial practices designed to maximize the effectiveness of workers on the job.

The physical working environment is considered as it affects both output and subjective feelings of strain or effort necessary to maintain productivity (Chapter 8). In addition to discussing such features of the physical environment as illumination, ventilation, and noise, a major portion of this chapter is devoted to recent research upon man-machine systems.

Even a well-trained employee working under optimal environmental conditions may experience fatigue as a result of prolonged work, or boredom as a result of monotonous work. Since fatigue and boredom are both undesirable consequences of certain kinds of industrial activity, they are grouped together and discussed in Chapter 9.

Accidents (Chapter 10) are regarded as a kind of undesirable behavior due, in part, to correctible deficiencies in the working situation and, in part, to improper but correctible employee attitudes. The fact that proportionately few accidents can be attributed to equipment malfunctions seems to indicate that engineering principles related to safety have been relatively well developed and widely accepted. Thus, in this chapter, we are concerned primarily with the human factors responsible for accidents and with procedures for preventing their occurrence.

This part is terminated with a discussion of merit rating (Chapter 11) as a technique for systematizing supervisors' opinions about employee efficiency. The subjectivity of merit rating procedures is at once their strength and weakness. In the absence of more objective criteria, ratings provide the only feasible indication of efficiency. However, they tend to be exceedingly unreliable. This chapter considers several different rating procedures, their sources of unreliability, and some of the ways in which these procedures can be improved.

The Physical Working Environment

8

The physical working environment has probably been manipulated and studied by more legitimate professionals and self-styled "experts" than any other aspect of business and industry. Management is bombarded by literature describing the beneficial effects of certain color schemes and of "piped" music, and is led sometimes to expect a tremendous increase in productivity if the water cooler is moved to a different location, or if bowling alleys are installed for employee recreation.

There is no doubt that an uncomfortable or unpleasant working environment may be partially responsible for lowered productivity, increased spoilage, and unnecessary accidents. Furthermore, work may be made less fatiguing and employee morale improved by creating a more pleasant and efficient work environment. The thing that must be remembered, however, is that often a change in the physical working environment is paralleled by a temporary increase in industrial productivity because of improved morale rather than a real improvement in conditions of work. It is imperative that environmental manipulations producing only transitory effects be distinguished from environmental changes having lasting beneficial effects.

The phenomenon whereby environmental alterations lead to temporary improvements in productivity attributable to morale improvement is sometimes referred to as the "Hawthorne effect" because of the studies conducted in the Hawthorne Works of the Western Electric Company which called particular attention to it. This series of studies, begun in 1924 and spanning a 15-year period, has been reported in what is now regarded as a classic reference for industrial psychologists.[1] We will not attempt to summarize the

---

[1] F. J. Roethlisberger and W. J. Dickson, *Management and the Worker—An Account of a Research Program Conducted by the Western Electric Company, Chicago* (Cambridge: Harvard University Press, 1939).

entire set of investigations. Rather, our concern at the present time is only with the first three experiments on illumination which serve to illustrate the "Hawthorne effect."

THE HAWTHORNE STUDIES OF ILLUMINATION

The fundamental purpose of the three studies to be described was to investigate the "relation of quality and quantity of illumination to efficiency in industry." It soon became apparent, however, that implementing this objective was not as simple as one might suppose. The studies, themselves, had implications extending far beyond the matter of the relationship between illumination and industrial efficiency.

The First Study

The first experiment on illumination involved workers in three different departments of the Hawthorne Works: small parts inspection, relay assembly, and coil winding. The first step in the procedure involved establishment of a base or control rate of production within each department. Thus, the employees worked initially under the existing lighting installation.

After the base rate of productivity was established for each department, the intensity of the illumination was increased in graduated steps, and the corresponding changes in production efficiency were noted. No clear-cut relationship between productivity and intensity of illumination was evident. The report of this study concludes that the results

. . . brought out very forcibly the necessity of controlling or eliminating the various additional factors which affected production output in either the same or opposing directions to that which we can ascribe to illumination.[2]

The Second Study

This experiment, conducted only with operators in the coil winding department, was designed to overcome some of the deficiencies apparent in the first study. The workers were divided into two groups which were equated for experience and average output. The groups were housed in different buildings in order to reduce the possible effects of competition upon productivity.

---

[2] C. E. Snow, "A Discussion of the Relation of Illumination Intensity to Productive Efficiency," *The Tech Engineering News*, November, 1927.

One of the groups, the "test group," worked under three different illumination intensities (24, 46, and 70 footcandles). The other group ("control") worked under a more or less constant illumination level of 16–28 footcandles. The variations in the intensity of illumination for the control group resulted from variations in the amount of daylight which supplemented the artificial light.

Although this seemed like an excellent research design for comparing the effect of varying illumination intensities, the results were somewhat surprising. The report of the findings states:

This test resulted in very appreciable production increases in both groups and of almost identical magnitude. The difference in efficiency of the two groups was so small as to be less than the probable error of the values. Consequently, we were again unable to determine what definite part of the improvement in performance should be ascribed to improved illumination.[3]

The Third Study

The third study involved the same test and control groups but further refinements were made in the experimental design. The control group now worked under a constant illumination of 10 footcandles of purely artificial light. The test group was provided with intensity levels from 10 to 3 footcandles in steps decreasing 1 footcandle at a time. Again, quoting from the summary of findings:

After the level of illumination in the test group enclosure changed to a lower value, the efficiencies of both the test and control groups increased slowly but steadily. When the level of illumination for the test group finally reached 3 footcandles, the operatives protested, saying that they were hardly able to see what they were doing, and the production rate decreased. The operatives could and did maintain their efficiency to this point in spite of the discomfort and handicap of insufficient illumination.[4]

Implications of the Hawthorne Studies

It was apparent from the three studies cited above, and the others that followed, that something other than illumination was acting to affect employee performance. This "other" factor is clarified by referring again to the S-I-R scheme discussed in Chapter 1. You will recall that our behavior is a function not only of the stimulus condition (amount of illumination, in the case of the Hawthorne studies) but also of our interpretation of this stimulus condition. The Haw-

---

[3] *Ibid.*
[4] *Ibid.*

thorne employees interpreted the experimentation with illumination as evidence for the fact that management was interested in them and their welfare. This interpretation was responsible for the development of favorable attitudes and the consequent desire to perform at maximum capacity even when the illumination was reduced to very low levels.

There is, then, an important caution to be observed on the basis of the Hawthorne findings. One must be careful to separate out the effects attributable to the environmental change itself from the effects attributable to employee predispositions toward that change. Furthermore, short-term production or efficiency increments following the manipulation of environmental conditions are not very convincing. A valid test of such manipulation requires that the effects of environmental changes be studied over a relatively long period of time.

THE VISUAL ENVIRONMENT

The prevalance of visual defects among industrial employees is somewhat surprising. A company program to detect and correct such defects is likely to improve efficiency markedly. Motorola, Inc., for example, found that about 30 percent of the workers in one of its inspection departments had faulty vision.[5] Correction of these defects led to decreased absenteeism, diminution in complaints about the product from the field, and a lower turnover and accident rate. Thus, the relatively small expenditure by a company to check upon and correct visual defects would seem to be extremely worthwhile.

Although the Hawthorne experiments described previously were concerned solely with the intensity of illumination, this aspect of light is by no means the sole factor of importance in the visual environment. Other aspects of illumination, including the distribution and reflection of light and its hue or color, are of concern in industry.

Intensity of Illumination

Industrial requirements in terms of the amount of light on a work surface vary considerably with the nature of the task to be performed. In general, work involving precise manipulation of small objects requires more intense illumination than does work involving

---

[5] Kenneth Piper, "Motorola's Vision Program Pays Off," *Advanced Management,* September, 1951, pp. 24–25.

the manipulation of large objects for which precision is not a critical requirement.

Although illumination intensity requirements increase as the task makes increased visual demands, attempts to formulate generally useful sets of intensity recommendations have generated considerable controversy. While one investigator concluded that 40–50 footcandles is sufficient illumination for even the most severe industrial tasks,[6] others have recommended minimum intensities as high as 200 footcandles for automotive final assembly and inspection, and 2,000 footcandles for cloth inspection.[7]

Such divergent recommendations result, in part, from differing definitions of criteria of "effective seeing." The criterion problem aside, however, it is evident that any set of intensity recommendations must properly be considered rough guides rather than definitive statements of illumination requirements for specific tasks in particular work settings. It is impossible accurately to generalize about intensity requirements alone, without regard for the factors that may interact with intensity. These potentially interactive variables include not only such other characteristics of illumination as glare and spectral composition, but the entire range of physical, social, and personal factors affecting employee job performance. Once these factors are specified for a particular job, it is a relatively simple matter to determine optimal illumination requirements for that job by empirical test.

Distribution and Reflection of Light

Virtually everyone is acquainted with the visual discomfort experienced when reading directly under a lamp that is the sole source of illumination in the room. Whenever the visual field is shifted from the well-illuminated page to the poorly illuminated surroundings, the pupil of the eye dilates. Similarly, the pupil contracts when shifting from low to high illumination. Excesses of pupillary activity are fatiguing; they cause eyestrain. Consequently, it is advisable to have the light well distributed throughout the visual field. It is for precisely this reason that television viewing in a moderately lit room is preferable to viewing in a totally darkened room.

---

[6] M. A. Tinker, "Illumination Standards for Effective and Easy Seeing," *Psychological Bulletin*, Vol. XLIV (1947), pp. 435–50.

[7] *Footcandles in Modern Lighting*, Technical Publication LS–119, General Electric Co. (Nela Park, Cleveland, 1960).

Solutions to the problem of glare are relatively simple. They include the proper shading of lamps, the elimination of highly reflective surfaces from the visual field, and the diffusion of light at its source.

Color

Many extravagant claims have been made about the beneficial effects of using certain colors or color combinations in industry and in the home. Not all of these claims, however, are supported by valid evidence. It is quite true that the appropriate use of color can do much to provide a safer, more pleasant, and more efficient working atmosphere. Such benefits result from painting the equipment and background in such a way as to: (1) indicate danger zones, traffic patterns, fire and safety equipment, and so on; (2) focus attention upon the critical elements in the visual field; (3) provide ample reflection without glare; and (4) provide a restful visual relief when the employee turns momentarily from his work. About the only thing that can be said about the overall color scheme or *decor*, however, is that it should be one that is not regarded by employees as unpleasant.

Color as a Focusing Agent. The color coding of fire protection equipment (red), first aid and safety facilities (green) and danger zones (yellow) can make a valuable contribution to safety practices throughout the plant. Awareness of danger zones reduces accident frequency; facile identification of fire and first aid equipment reduces the severity of mishaps once they occur.

The equipment with which an employee works may also be painted in a way calculated to improve safety and increase productivity. The suggestion has been made that color be used to differentiate between three areas of machinery or equipment: the moving, working, or critical area; the body of the machine or noncritical area; and the controls, including buttons, levers, handles, and so on.[8] The *working area* consisting of operating parts of the machine should be painted in a color which contrasts strongly with the noncritical portion of the machine and with the material being worked on. Danger areas (moving and cutting parts) should be further spotlighted by using strips of bright color like orange or yellow. The *body* of the machine, it is suggested, ought to blend into the back-

---

[8] Robert B. Fetter, *How Color Can Increase Your Productivity*, Business Information Bulletin No. 8, Bureau of Business Research, Indiana University (Bloomington, Ind., 1950).

ground wall and ceiling color. This will prevent visual attention from being directed toward it. *Controls* should be painted to contrast sharply with the body of the machine so the worker can locate and use them with a minimum of difficulty.

Walls and Ceilings. The color of the walls and ceilings surrounding the immediate work area can do much to produce either visual comfort or discomfort. These surfaces must reflect an adequate amount of light without either producing glare or an undue contrast in brightness with the working area. Surfaces painted white, cream, or ivory reflect a considerable amount of light; pastel shades have intermediate reflectance values; and shades of brown, dark red, dark green, or dark blue have low reflectance values. The appropriate wall and ceiling color will depend, quite obviously, upon the adequacy of the lighting and the specific type of work being performed.

Another factor that may affect decisions about the wall color to be used is the color of the material upon which work is being performed. All of us rest our eyes momentarily by looking away from the work surface. You look away from the textbook occasionally, for example, when you are reading; and your eyes wander away from the instructor or demonstration during a class period. Similarly, the industrial employee looks up from his work periodically.

An interesting illustration of the relationship between these brief visual rest periods and the optimal color for painting the surrounding surfaces occurred in the inspection room of a textile mill. The inspectors were scanning bluish denim, searching for defects. The walls were painted white to provide high reflectance on the assumption that the high illumination level would facilitate the inspection process. This assumption was entirely correct, but it neglected one important feature of the job. Since the employees were staring at the denim for relatively long periods of time, they reported a disturbing visual "afterimage" (peach color, in this instance) when they looked up from their work to rest their eyes momentarily. This negative afterimage, which is always the complement of the color to which the eye has been exposed for a prolonged period, interfered with normal vision for a while after the inspectors returned to their task. The simple solution in this case was to paint the walls in the color demanded by the eyes—that is, peach.[9]

The aesthetic value of particular hues and their influence upon

[9] "Color Punches the Time Clock," *The Management Review*, American Management Association, September, 1947, p. 452. After Lloyd Stauffer, *Popular Science*, June, 1947, pp. 124–26.

behavior has been the subject of some investigation and considerable discussion. Darker hues create the illusion of pulling walls in or ceilings down; lighter hues create the visual impression of added spaciousness and airiness.

Colors on the red side of the spectrum are regarded as *warm*, exciting colors; those on the green and blue end of the spectrum are regarded as *cool*, tranquilizing colors. The distinction between warm and cool colors is regarded as extremely important by most interior decorators and color consultants and is exploited in a variety of ways. Persons are presumed to move more rapidly, to talk with greater animation and generally to maintain a higher level of excitation in a predominantly red-orange environment than in a blue-green environment. Thus, an environment that is meant to be relaxing and calming ought to be painted in cool colors. The suggestion is sometimes made that work involving the generation of considerable heat should be performed in a room painted in cool colors, while large, vaulty work areas should be painted in warm colors.[10]

Such generalizations about the effect of color upon mood or subjective experiences of warmth and coolness are not well documented. We learn to make associations relative to particular colors and attach our own personal significances to particular hues. The range of such associations is tremendous, and generalizations about them are quite tenuous.

NOISE AND MUSIC

Noise and music are aspects of the auditory environment which have been subjected to considerable study. We must be concerned with both employee output (productivity) and with the input (or energy) necessary to achieve or maintain a given level of productivity in appraising the effects of these variables. The finding, for example, that employees can adjust to noisy conditions without a production decrement would in itself be rather unimportant if this adjustment required them to expend considerable additional effort in order to maintain their productivity. Such additional effort would be reflected in undue fatigue, leading, perhaps, to job dissatisfaction and consequent personnel turnover, and to an increased accident rate.

The interpretation of the effects of any environmental condition,

---

[10] Fetter, *op. cit.* p. 4.

including noise and music, is complicated by differences in investigatory procedure. It is convenient, in this regard, to distinguish between "laboratory" and "field" studies. The former kind of investigation requires that groups of persons (either employees or persons assumed to be like employees) be removed from their actual working environment and required to perform in an artificially created environment. The task they perform for experimental purposes may be identical to the one they do on the job, or it may be a special task designed to incorporate the major elements of their job task.

"Field" studies, on the other hand, are performed in the working environment. It is possible, within certain limits, to manipulate the environmental conditions in an office or a factory. It is also possible, on occasion, to study groups of employees performing essentially the same job but working in different environments.

The fundamental difference between these experimental procedures is an important one. The "Hawthorne effect," noted earlier, may be confounded in laboratory investigations by the fact that the entire setting is artificial. Thus, the discrepancy in experimental procedure (that is, laboratory versus field investigations) may account, in part, for discrepancies in the outcomes of studies concerned with noise and music. The amount of agreement based upon solid evidence concerning these variables is not outstanding.

Noise

Sounds differ with respect to loudness, pitch, and quality. Furthermore, a given sound may be continuous or, as most often the case in industry, intermittant. These variables, considered together, serve to distinguish between "pleasant" or "desired" and "unpleasant" or "unwanted" sounds. The latter is, for practical purposes, what is meant by noise. Virtually all studies of industrial noise have been concerned with sounds that are reasonably loud, unpleasant in pitch and quality, and varying in continuity. There is, however, another aspect of sound having some bearing upon work efficiency: that is, its meaningfulness. It is considerably easier to disregard meaningless extraneous sounds (like the clatter of a typewriter) than it is to disregard meaningful sounds (like the conversation of other students in the study hall).

Psychological Studies of Noise. Several of the early laboratory investigations indicated that following the onset of noise, there is a minor decrease in productivity after which productivity increases above the level attained when the environment was relatively quiet. The maintenance of productivity is accomplished, however, at the worker's expense. He must exert additional effort to maintain his output. It has been found, for example, that noise leads to increases in muscle tension and metabolic rate.[11] These physiological changes are noted most immediately after the onset of noise. They decline, indicating diminished exertion, after a period of time during which the employee adapts to the noise.

The generalization that workers can adapt to noise and equal or surpass their former production level is, however, an artificial one. This generalization is founded upon laboratory investigations in which the participants were highly motivated and performed tasks requiring the exertion of short spurt-like efforts. These conditions are unlike those found in many industrial settings.

A more recent study examined the effects of noise upon sustained performance, leading to boredom and fatigue.[12] Groups of subjects were required to monitor a panel of dials under conditions of "relative quiet" and "noise." The former condition consisted of a background sound of approximately 80 decibel intensity (about as loud as the noise present in a typical office). The "noisy" condition consisted of sound intensity in excess of 110 decibels (about as loud as the sound of thunder).

The subjects were required to "work" for periods of two hours. Under the control condition, the laboratory was relatively quiet for the full time; under the experimental condition, the laboratory was relatively quiet for one half hour and noisy for the remaining 1½ hours. The results, showing the average performance at the end of each half hour under these conditions, are shown in Figure 8–1. It is evident that the deleterious effects of noise upon the performance of this task (which required the maintenance of vigilance) became evident only after a relatively long period of time.

We will consider the results of one additional investigation of par-

---

[11] F. L. Harmon, "The Effects of Noise Upon Certain Psychological and Psysiological Processes," *Archives of Psychology*, Vol. XXIII, No. 147 (1933).

D. A. Laird, "The Measurement of the Effects of Noise Upon Working Efficiency," *Journal of Industrial Hygiene*, Vol. IX (1927), pp. 431–34.

J. J. B. Morgan, "The Overcoming of Distraction and Other Resistances," *Archives of Psychology*, Vol. V, No. 35 (1916).

H. M. Vernon and C. G. Warner, "Objective and Subjective Tests for Noise," *Personnel Journal*, Vol. XI (1932–33), pp. 141–49.

[12] H. J. Jerison, "Effects of Noise on Human Performance," *Journal of Applied Psychology*, Vol. XLII, No. 2 (1959), pp. 96–101.

ticular interest for three reasons: (1) it was a field rather than a laboratory study, (2) the performance investigated was manual rather than mental work, (3) a deliberate attempt was made to control for the Hawthorne effect.[13] The latter was accomplished by having the same subjects work under noisy and "quiet" conditions.

The investigators studied the output and other measures of efficiency for groups of employees working for periods under pre- and postnoise reduction conditions. These workers operated equipment perforating the side of movie film. Since they normally shifted from

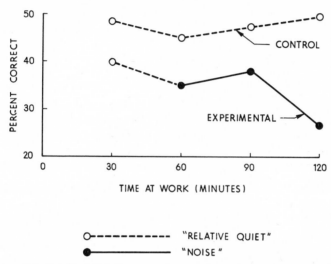

TIME AT WORK (MINUTES)

O– – – – – – – – – "RELATIVE QUIET"

●———————— "NOISE"

Note that the initial discrepancy between the experimental and control groups was maintained at a constant level for the first hour and a half. The deleterious effects of noise were apparent only after two hours.

FIGURE 8–1. Average Performance under Conditions of Relative Quiet and Noise.

one room to another in a systematic cycle of six weeks, this was chosen as the length for experimental and control periods. Noise reduction in one of the work rooms was accomplished by baffling between rows of machines and acoustic treatment of the walls and ceilings.

The outstanding finding was that although noise reduction did not improve the rate of work, it significantly reduced shutdowns due to operator error and calls for maintenance. The magnitude of reduction in human errors following noise reduction led the investigators to hypothesize an interaction between noise and other features

[13] D. E. Broadbent and E. A. J. Little, "Effects of Noise Reduction in a Work Situation," *Occupational Psychology*, Vol. XXXIV (1960), pp. 133–40.

of this particular job, including the low illumination levels required for handling film. If such an interaction existed it might have acted to magnify the effects of noise reduction beyond what would be observed in other work conditions.

Nevertheless, the conclusions from this field study are consistent with those derived from laboratory investigations of high intensity, meaningless, and continuous noise upon tasks requiring continuous attention. Noise does not markedly affect productivity defined by work rate. It does, however, increase the frequency of momentary lapses in attention and is thereby responsible for some kinds of "human error."[14]

As with other factors in the work environment, it is impossible to formulate a generalization about the psychological effects of noise applicable in all circumstances. Whether or not the potential of noise for increasing human errors is of practical importance depends upon such things as the kind of work being done, the characteristics of the noise, and other aspects of the physical and social working environment.

Physiological Damage. Noise can have serious consequences apart from those regarded as fundamentally psychological in nature. Workmen's compensation is provided persons with hearing loss attributable to industrial noise. Legal proof of auditory damage is typically based upon the factors of intensity and length of time the worker is exposed to the noise. The New York State Workmen's Compensation Board, for example, uses the following standards in evaluating claims: (1) most persons will suffer permanent damage in a matter of months if exposed to over 120 decibels of noise for several hours daily; (2) a considerable portion of workers can suffer permanent hearing damage from exposure to 100–120 decibels for several hours daily; (3) a few persons may be permanently damaged by exposure for many years to noise between 90 and 100 decibels.[15]

Opinions about the minimum intensity and exposure required to produce permanent damage vary somewhat from the standards cited above. Some of this variation is undoubtedly due to the confounding effects of a third aspect of noise: pitch. The human ear is

---

[14] D. E. Broadbent, "Effects of Noise on Behaviour," C. M. Harris (ed.), *Handbook of Noise Control* (New York: McGraw-Hill Book Co., Inc., 1957).

[15] John F. Goldsmith, "New and Noteworthy," *Factory Management and Maintenance*, February, 1954, p. 132.

most sensitive (that is, responds with sensations of pressure at a given sound intensity) to pitches at the upper and lower extremes of the auditory range.

Music

You undoubtedly have certain personal feelings about the desirability or undesirability of having a radio or a record player operating while you are studying. It is likely, also, that you know someone (perhaps your room-mate) who feels quite differently from you about this matter. The interesting thing about this kind of discrepancy in attitude toward music as a facilitator or inhibitor of work is that there is a direct relationship between attitudes toward music and productivity during music periods.

This relationship has been investigated in the following way. Two groups of subjects were each required to do arithmetic calculations during a sequence of music periods and nonmusic periods. The groups were each given a different *set* or expectation regarding the effects of music. One of the groups was informed, at the beginning of the experiment, that the music would probably interfere with its ability to do mental arithmetic. This expectation was reinforced by the presentation of "data" allegedly showing that this finding had resulted from a previously conducted experiment. The other group was told that previous research had indicated that music facilitates mental arithmetic, and appropriate "documentation" was presented to this group also. The actual arithmetic performance of the subjects in these groups indicated that their productivity was directly related to their expectations concerning the effects of the music (see Figure 8–2).[16]

Music is most likely to be beneficial for work that is of a short-cycle and highly repetitive nature. Such work often does not utilize enough of the employee's abilities. His attention is not absorbed by the task, and he regards the work as monotonous. The hours of the day tend to move slowly, and the employee may experience very little personal satisfaction. In such circumstances, music may increase productivity and worker satisfaction. It is pleasantly diverting and may make time appear to move more rapidly.

The beneficial effects of music under such circumstances were

---

[16] K. H. Baker, "Pre-experimental Set in Distraction Experiments," *Journal of General Psychology*, Vol. XVI (1937), pp. 471–86.

demonstrated quite clearly by a very careful investigation involving a large number of employees engaged in radio assembly.[17] It was found that a production increase attributable to music was considerably more marked during the night shift than during the day shift, although music was beneficial also during the day. Employee reac-

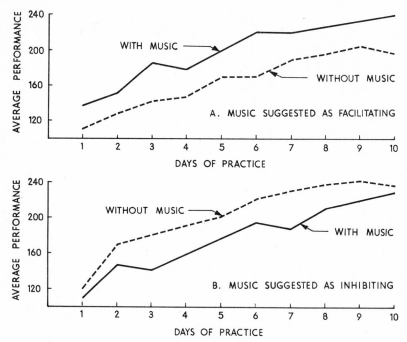

The performance of subjects during music and nonmusic sessions was compared for two groups:
A. Music was suggested as facilitating performance.
B. Music was suggested as inhibiting performance.

FIGURE 8–2.   The Effect of Expectation about the Effects of Music upon Actual Performance.

tion to the music was extremely favorable; only 2 percent of the workers indicated that they did not care at all for it.

The effect of music is, of course, to distract the worker. Music is beneficial both to productivity and morale only when such distraction is desirable. Thus, it must be emphasized that results favorable to music are generally obtained only for employees performing routine, repetitive jobs. More complex jobs requiring a greater amount

[17] H. C. Smith, *Music in Relation to Employee Attitudes, Work Production and Industrial Accidents,* Applied Psychology Monographs, No. 14, 1947.

of employee attentiveness generally are performed better in the absence of any distracting influence.

Slight differences in the effectiveness of various kinds of music appear to be a function both of the employees' personal tastes and of the rhythmic quality of the music. The average output and quality of production of operators in a glass radio tube factory was studied, for example, when three different kinds of music were played: hit-parade, waltz-Hawaiian and march-polka.[18] It was found that both output and quality were lowest on days when the waltz-Hawaiian music was played. Production and quality were about equal on hit parade and on march-polka days.

One of the very interesting findings of this study, and of some of the others reported in the literature, is that the relatively slight production increase attributable to music may be accompanied by a slight decrease in the *quality* of production. This suggests that investigations concerning the effectiveness of music that use output as the sole criterion probably lead to conclusions which overstate the value of music.

The typical practice when making use of music in an industrial setting is to restrict each music session to a 20- to 40-minute period. These periods are generally inserted into the midmorning and mid-afternoon schedule at about the time when monotony and fatigue reach a maximum. Some companies make a practice also of scheduling music periods at the beginning and at the end of the shift. This procedure is presumed to create a pleasant working environment when the employees begin and terminate the day's work.

TEMPERATURE AND VENTILATION

Industrial ventilation is of considerable interest because of the demonstrated relationship between this environmental factor and such criteria as productivity, spoilage, and accident rate. A substantial body of research has been conducted relative to the three essential components of ventilation: temperature, humidity, and air movement. It has been found that control of any one of these factors is, by itself, relatively valueless unless the others are controlled also. A temperature of 90° Fahrenheit, for example, is much less comfort-

---

[18] W. A. Kerr, *Experiments on the Effects of Music on Factory Production,* Applied Psychology Monograph, No. 5, 1945.

able when the humidity is high and the air relatively stationary, than it is when the humidity is low and the air is in motion.

Thus, it is much more meaningful to consider *effective temperature* than it is to consider absolute temperature (as measured by a dry-bulb thermometer). The effective temperature scale combines the subjective effects of temperature, humidity, and air movement. When air movement is at a minimum, a dry bulb temperature of 90° F at 10 percent humidity constitutes the same effective temperature (that is, is as comfortable as) a temperature reading of 75° F at 100 percent humidity or a reading of 80° F at 60 percent humidity.[19]

The relative comfort or discomfort experienced in a particular effective temperature is, of course, partially a function of the kind of work being performed. One reviewer concluded, as a cautious generalization, that the maximum effective temperature for the performance of simple sedentary tasks without serious impairment is 85° F.[20] Tolerance limits for heavy physical labor are, of course, much lower.

MAN-MACHINE SYSTEMS

The emphasis upon man-machine relationships is relatively recent. Machine and plant design have, for the most part, been traditionally regarded as the province of the engineer. The comfort of the person who operated the machine and, indeed, his capability for operating various kinds of "mechanical monsters" was considered (if at all) almost as an afterthought.

This rather one-sided regard for the machine could not continue indefinitely. Technological advancements made possible the design of ever more powerful machines capable of performing previously unimagined tasks with staggering speed and precision *provided they could be operated.* Such a provision removes the human operator from the realm of afterthought and makes his limitations and strengths essential considerations in machine and equipment design.

The urgent military requirements of World War II focused par-

---

[19] *Heating, Ventilating, Air Conditioning Guide,* American Society of Heating and Ventilating Engineers Comfort Chart for Still Air, 1947.

[20] L. Connell, "The Effect of Heat Upon the Performance of Men in High Speed Aircraft: A Critical Review," *USN, Special Devices Center Report* 151–1–17, 1948.

ticular attention upon the necessity for merging the talents of engineers, psychologists, physiologists, physicians, and others in designing equipment and structuring working conditions. This represented the beginning of a field designated either "Human Engineering" or "Engineering Psychology."

The point of departure for engineering psychology is information about man's capabilities and limitations. Utilizing such information, the engineering psychologist seeks to develop an optimally functioning unit of man and machine: that is, a *man-machine system*. In order to conceptualize man-machine systems, we will first examine the structure of purely mechanical systems functioning without man as a component.

Mechanical Systems

The simplest kind of system is designed to perform a specific function or group of functions indefinitely (or until it wears out) once it is triggered. This is an *open-loop* system. *Closed-loop* systems are ones in which the performance of a function by the equipment is sensed or fed back into the machine, making it self-regulating.

Open-Loop Systems. Many commercial buildings are equipped with sprinkler systems for fire control. The overhead sprinklers automatically spray water when there is a fire. The system is *controlled* by metal plugs which melt at a critical temperature. When the heat (the *input*) causes these plugs to melt, a water spray is released (the *output*).

This system is not self-regulating. It will continue to spray water as long as it is functional until it is shut down by some force external to the system itself. Figure 8–3 shows the system diagrammatically.

Closed-Loop Systems. A thermostatically controlled home freezer is a closed-loop system because it is self-regulating. (See Figure 8–3.) Once the thermostat is set for a particular temperature (say 10° F), the refrigerating motor will operate whenever the temperature rises above that level. However, the output itself serves to change the input, in turn signaling to the control when the temperature again drops to 10° F, and motor operation ceases.

Human Systems

We may consider man also as a closed-loop system. This analogy is not difficult if we substitute for the terms Stimulus-Interpretation-

Response, the mechanical concepts Input-Control-Output. Viewed as a system, man receives information, somehow processes it, and reacts to it.

Inputs for the human system take the form of receptor organ activity. These sensations are processed by such interpretive control functions as thinking, reasoning, deciding, and so on. The output, of course, is some kind of behavior. This response in turn affects the input and the cycle continues.

Consider the operation of a human system performing a relatively simple task like maintaining a constant driving speed of 55 miles per hour. (See Figure 8–4.) The basic input is a set of visual sensations from the speedometer. These are supplemented by other inputs, not

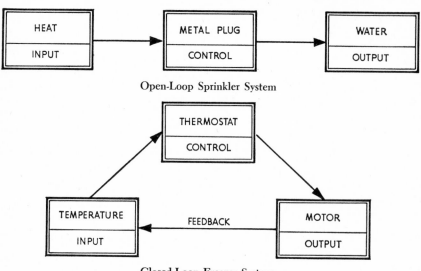

Open-Loop Sprinkler System

Closed-Loop Freezer System

FIGURE 8–3. Mechanical Systems.

considered in Figure 8–4, including the sound of wind rushing past the car, the "feel of the wheel," or the sound of certain squeaks or rattles we have learned to associate with certain speeds. The visual sensations from the speedometer are processed and, depending upon the interpretation, an appropriate response is made.

Note that the situation described and diagrammed in Figure 8–4 provides for *branching*. Instead of a system limited to a single control action and a single output, we have a variety of control decisions each eliciting a different output. Branching is not limited to human systems. Electronic computers, for example, are often controlled by

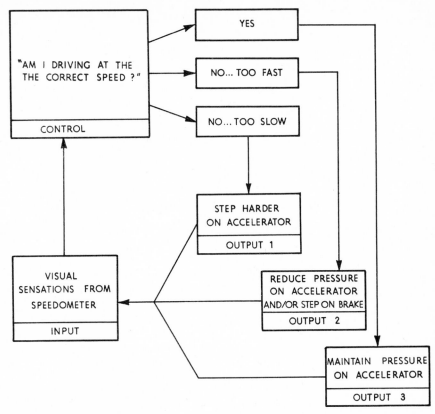

FIGURE 8–4. A Human System: Maintaining Driving Speed at 55 Miles per Hour.

branching programs permitting specified operations to occur under specified circumstances.

A Man-Machine System

It has undoubtedly occurred to you that the human system we have just described is only a part of the total system involving both the man and the machine. A portion of this man-machine system is shown diagrammatically in Figure 8–5.

The essence of this system is that the human portion with its inputs, controls, and outputs constitutes an overall control system for the mechanical portion of the system. The entire man-machine system thus is mediated by the human operator. Should he fall asleep at the wheel, the mechanical controls become useless.

This suggests what is at once the strength and weakness of man-machine systems compared with systems that are entirely mechani-

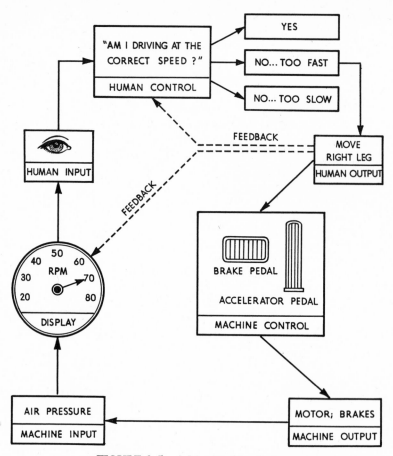

FIGURE 8–5. A Man-Machine System.

cal. The latter are foolproof except for mechanical breakdown. However, they lack the precision of control and flexibility of output that can be exerted only when the higher cognitive processes of a human being are incorporated within the system. In order for man to function as part of the system, there must be an optimal rapprochement between the human being and the machine. The inputs, controls, and outputs required of him must be facilitated by the machine's design and within the range of human capability.

HUMAN FACTORS IN MAN-MACHINE SYSTEMS

It is possible here to offer only a sketchy overview and a few illustrations of the tremendous body of information now available in this area.

Input Linkage between Man and Machine

The input subsystem has three essential components: (1) the machine input, (2) the linkage between machine functions and human inputs, (3) the human input. The first of these is entirely mechanical and therefore not of concern to us now. The human input subsystem involves the sensory processes and has been a traditional area of investigation by experimental psychologists for many years before the development of engineering psychology. Our particular concern in this section is with the linkage between man and machine.

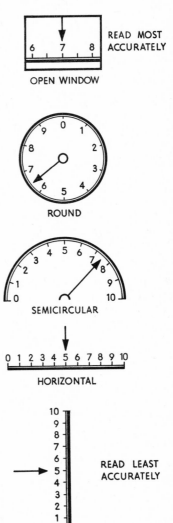

The human operator must somehow be appraised of the operation of the machine as quickly and efficiently as possible if he is to function in a partnership with it. This linkage is generally mediated by some kind of display indirectly indicating the way in which the machine is functioning.

Displays. A pilot making a landing approach needs to know whether his landing gear is down. Although he cannot see the gear directly, this information is provided him by a simple visual display: the "wheels down" light glows when the gear is in position.

The nature of the display is complicated when the operator needs to know degrees rather than categories of machine function. Thus, it requires a more complex display to provide information about how fast a car is moving than to answer the question, "Is it exceeding 55 miles per hour?"

FIGURE 8–6. Dial Shapes in the Order in Which They Are Read Most Accurately.

Matters of display design have received considerable attention by engineering psychologists. Studies of the readability of different kinds of dials, like those shown in

Figure 8–6, indicate that vertical scales are read less accurately than horizontal or circular scales.[21]

Another problem related to the display components of man-machine systems concerns the arrangement of display clusters like those on automobile dashboards and in airplane cockpits. Whenever the operator must keep abreast of information conveyed simultaneously by several different dials, his task can be simplified by patterning the dial display.[22] This is done by orienting each dial so the "normal" position of the pointer is the same for every one. Thus, the operator can quickly spot and identify a dial pointer indicating an abnormal condition.

Studies have also been conducted upon the limits of precision for particular kinds of displays, and the way in which display information ought to be coded for most facile access and accurate interpretation.

Output Linkage between Man and Machine

Man's output affecting machine function can be mediated by a wide assortment of equipment controls including levers, knobs, buttons, pedals, wheels, and so on. At least three factors must be considered in designing any control: (1) the force necessary to operate it must not exceed human capabilities; (2) it must be distinguishable from other controls performing different functions; (3) it ought to be realistic.[23]

Distinguishability is a particularly important consideration when the operator is confronted by an array of controls in close proximity and must select the appropriate one very quickly. This situation is typical in high-speed aircraft. One study of aircraft controls found that certain shapes are more readily identifiable by touch than others even when gloves are worn (see Figure 8–7).[24]

Control realism may be heightened by the shape and direction of

[21] R. B. Sleight, "The Effect of Instrument Dial Shape upon Legibility," *Journal of Applied Psychology*, Vol. XXXII (1948), pp. 170–88.
Norah E. Graham, "The Speed and Accuracy of Reading Horizontal, Vertical and Circular Scales," *Journal of Applied Psychology*, Vol. XL (1956), pp. 228–32.

[22] W. E. Woodson, *Human Engineering Guide for Equipment Designers* (Berkeley, Calif.: University of California Press, 1954).

[23] E. E. Ghiselli and C. W. Brown, *Personnel and Industrial Psychology* (New York: McGraw-Hill Book Co., Inc., 1955).

[24] W. O. Jenkins, "Tactual Discrimination of Shapes for Coding Aircraft-type Controls," in P. M. Fitts, *Psychological Research on Equipment Design* (Washington, D.C.: U.S. Government Printing Office, 1947).

movement of the control. Controls shaped as reminders of their function, and moving in the same direction as the resultant machine operation tend to facilitate man-machine linkage. The automobile steering wheel is a realistic control. You turn it to the right to move

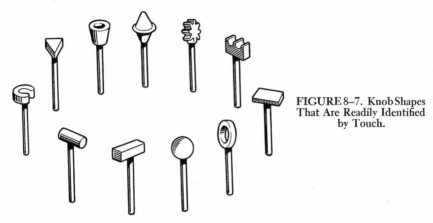

FIGURE 8–7. Knob Shapes That Are Readily Identified by Touch.

the vehicle to the right. It would be more than a trifle confusing if the control and resultant operation were to act in opposite directions.

SUMMARY

The effects of changes in the physical working environment must be interpreted cautiously for a number of reasons. First, employees respond not only to an objectively definable change in illumination or noise level, but also to their attitudes concerning such changes. If they interpret a change as evidence for the fact that management is interested in their welfare, they will respond positively and their productivity may increase. If, however, the employees interpret the change solely as an economy measure designed by management to "get more for its money," actual productivity may decline.

Related to the matter of employee attitudes are the facts that short-term effects of environmental changes are insufficient as a basis for determining the true worth of such changes, and that the results of laboratory investigations are not always verified when similar changes are instituted in the field.

Finally, environmental changes which lead to a production increase are not always desirable. It would be unwise to institute any such change, even if it increased productivity and reduced expenses, if these outcomes were accomplished by forcing a considerable increase in employee input or effort. Such additional effort may lead to job dissatisfaction, increased spoilage, and accidents, all of which may well offset the advantages relative to improved productivity and economy.

Studies of industrial illumination have indicated that the critical requirements for light intensity vary with the nature of the task being performed. Work involving the manipulation of small objects with great precision requires more intense illumination than does work involving the manipulation of large objects for which precision is not a critical feature. Light distribution and reflection are also important aspects of the visual environment. The entire visual field must be relatively evenly illuminated and glare must be eliminated if visual comfort is to be maximized.

The use of color in the working environment has been the subject of many extravagant claims, not all of which can be documented. The appropriate use of color can contribute to the safety and efficiency of the work environment. About the only thing that can be said about the overall color scheme or decor, however, is that it should not be regarded by the employees as unpleasant.

Noise may, but need not, impede industrial efficiency. Whether or not the potential of noise for increasing "human error" is of practical importance depends upon such factors as the characteristics of the noise, the kind of work being done, and other aspects of the physical and social working environment. Aside from the possibility of undesirable psychological consequences, certain kinds of noises are clearly responsible for auditory damage.

Music is a distracting factor and is thus most likely to be beneficial for work that is of a short-cycle and highly repetitive nature. More complex tasks requiring a greater amount of employee attentiveness generally are performed better in the absence of any distracting influence.

Psychologists and engineers have been concerned with three essential and interdependent components of ventilation: temperature, humidity, and air movement. These components, considered together, constitute the subjective factor of "effective temperature." The worker's tolerance for a relatively high effective temperature is greatest if he is engaged in simple sedentary tasks and lowest if he is engaged in heavy physical labor.

In an age of rapidly advancing technocracy, it has become imperative that increased attention be given to developing an optimal rapprochement between the worker and the machine he operates. Engineering psychologists view the human organism from a "systems" orientation. This orientation has led to a considerable amount of highly significant research upon the input, control, and output functions of the human component of man-machine systems.

Fatigue and Boredom

Fatigue and boredom are factors of considerable consequence in industry. The most apparent indicators of either of these conditions is diminished output and increased spoilage. Secondary effects include increased turnover and accident rate. Although the correlates of fatigue and boredom are, on the whole, somewhat similar, the nature of these conditions and the factors responsible for them are quite different.

The Nature of Fatigue

Fatigue is a complex phenomenon from both a physiological and a psychological standpoint. Prolonged muscular activity eventually produces physiological changes, including the accumulation of waste products resulting from the activity of the muscles and depletion of the reserve of carbohydrates which serve as fuel for such activity. In addition, the continuation of activity ultimately leads to unpleasant subjective feelings of strain or tension. These two types of change, the physiological and the subjective, do not, however, parallel each other very closely. Furthermore, the time at which either of these changes occurs, and the intensity of their occurrence, correlates only imperfectly with a measureable decrement in productivity.

The absence of a close relationship between the physiological changes, the subjective experiences, and productivity are evident in situations in which persons fatigued from a physiological standpoint may continue to maintain a high level of productivity and may not report feelings of "tiredness." It is apparent that strong motivation, like that encountered during athletic contests or in defense plants engaged in wartime production, may reduce or almost obliterate any noticeable deterioration in performance. Conversely, poorly motivated persons may experience subjective feelings of fatigue, and their output may decline, some time in advance of the physiological changes associated with fatigue.

It is difficult to formulate a definition of fatigue because of the imperfect relationship between its physiological and subjective components. The formulation of a definition is further complicated by the fact that the relationship between the physiological and subjective changes accompanying fatigue may be either reduced or accentuated by motivational factors. It will be satisfactory, for our purposes, to define fatigue in terms of its practical implications in the industrial setting. It is a temporary condition resulting from prolonged muscular activity and is manifest in a declining capacity for continued work.

The Nature of Boredom

Boredom is sometimes thought of as a kind of "mental fatigue," implying that it results from a psychological rather than a physiological cause. This distinction considerably oversimplifies the situation since, as we have already said, fatigue also entails a psychological or subjective component.

It is, perhaps, most meaningful to distinguish between fatigue and boredom on the basis of the kind of activity that generates these experiences. Fatigue results only when the person is engaged in prolonged muscular activity. Boredom results when the activity is regarded as monotonous or uninteresting. Prolonged muscular activity is not a necessary precursor to boredom. We may be bored, for example, when we read an uninteresting book, listen to a dull lecture, or watch a trite television program.

A further distinction between fatigue and boredom is predicated upon the fact that the former tends to generalize, while the latter is highly specific. When we are fatigued, we seek rest from all activity. When we are bored, we seek relief only from the monotonous activity. This fact should not be taken as an indication that boredom is somehow less significant or less important than fatigue. The production decrement for tasks regarded as monotonous is quite as real and as serious as that which accompanies the performance of fatigue-producing tasks. The remainder of this chapter is devoted to a discussion of the effects of each of these conditions and of certain remedial measures.

FATIGUE

The fact that fatigue reduces the capacity for further work is amply illustrated by studies of industrial productivity or output during the course of a typical working day. A schematic plot of average hourly output for an industrial task involving motor activity is shown in Figure 9–1. The irregularities which are always apparent when such a curve is plotted have been smoothed in order to make the fundamental trends more apparent. Note that prolonged motor activity is characterized by an initial period of "warm-up" followed by a decline in output during the latter hours of the morning, and again toward the end of the work period.

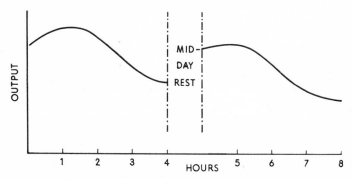

Source: R. A. Katzell, "Fatigue and its Alleviation," in D. H. Fryer and E. R. Henry, *Handbook of Applied Psychology* (New York: Holt, Rinehart & Winston, Inc., 1950), p. 75.

FIGURE 9–1.   A Schematic Plot of Average Hourly Output for Complex Motor Work.

Such a graph suggests that the examination of production records throughout the course of the work day may serve to identify the existence of fatigue. Furthermore, the comparative analysis of such records obtained under varying circumstances probably indicates something about the relative amount of fatigue experienced under these circumstances. Although output curves can be used in this way, they are not entirely satisfactory as indices of the existence of fatigue or as measures of the amount of fatigue generated by particular tasks. Any record of employee performance reflects the factor of motivation in addition to the effects of fatigue. Thus, a decline in output may be erroneously attributed to fatigue when, in fact, it may result from a progressive decline in interest. Conversely, of course, the output rate may remain high in spite of fatigue because of a high motivational level.

It is obvious, also, that many kinds of jobs do not lend themselves to work-curve analyses. It is possible to graph output only when the work is repetitive and when some kind of production unit can be counted. Work which varies in nature, like that of an office secretary, does not provide equivalent units which can be summated and graphed. Under such circumstances, the existence of fatigue must be verified by some other method.

Measurement of the Physiological Component

We have already mentioned that subjective feelings of fatigue and a decrement in output are often accompanied by changes in bodily processes. Some of the very early studies of fatigue were directed toward the measurement of the limitations upon prolonged work imposed by the musculature. The device used for such studies, known as an *ergograph*, permits for the conduct of fatigue experiments involving specific muscles or muscle groups. A weight is attached by a cord to an extremity of the body (for example, the fingertip or the hand) and the rest of the limb is strapped in order to inhibit movements of the muscles that are not under investigation. The subject is required to raise the weight periodically at a signal, and the height of each lift is automatically recorded. This recording, called an *ergogram*, is really a plot of the work decrement accompanying prolonged activity of the muscle or muscle group being studied. An ergogram produced by a subject required to lift a weight using one finger is illustrated in Figure 9–2. Note the progressive deterioration in his performance.

Ergographic studies clearly demonstrate that there is a considerable range of individual differences in the amount of prolonged muscular work that can be performed. The tracings obtained from different subjects vary tremendously with respect to the maximum level of performance, the length of the period during which near-maximum performance is maintained, and the rate at which performance deteriorates. This suggests, of course, that there are individual variations in susceptibility to the physiological components of fatigue. Again, however, it is important to realize that some portion of the differences obtained from ergographic studies must properly be attributed to variations in the motivational levels of the subjects rather than to variations in susceptibility to physiological fatigue.

A more direct approach to the measurement of the physiological aspects of fatigue requires a study of the involuntary physiological processes themselves while work is being performed. Such factors as oxygen consumption, muscular tension, and circulatory activity have been found to be related to fatigue and are relatively, although

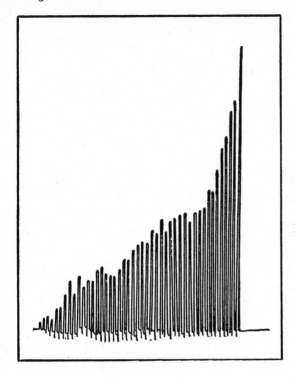

Each stroke represents a complete cycle of lifting and dropping the weight. The temporal sequence is from right to left.
Source: T. A. Ryan, *Work and Effort* (New York: The Ronald Press Co., 1947), p. 50.

FIGURE 9–2. An Ergogram

not completely, independent of motivational factors. This approach to the measurement of fatigue is, however, generally too unwieldy for use in industry.

Measurement of the Subjective Component

The subjective component of fatigue (that is, feelings of strain or tiredness) have also been explored. It has been found, for example, that feelings of weariness generally occur prior to a noticeable decrement in actual performance.[1] Such subjective fatigue does, however, tend to parallel production curves even though it anticipates them. Workers report the greatest feelings of tiredness when they begin work in the morning, immediately prior to lunch, and again immediately prior to the time that their shift ends (see Figure 9–3). You will recall that the typical curve of industrial productivity exhibits declining output also at these three periods.

Perhaps the most surprising aspect of industrial fatigue, defined

---

[1] A. T. Poffenberger, "Effects of Continuous Work Upon Output and Feelings," *Journal of Applied Psychology*, Vol. XII (1928), pp. 459–67.

either in terms of subjective feeling or in terms of output, is that it does not appear to accumulate continuously throughout the work day. Workers neither produce less nor do they feel more weary in the midafternoon than in the midmorning. Furthermore, both productivity and feelings of tiredness at the end of the shift are about the same as they are immediately prior to lunch. It is certain that a

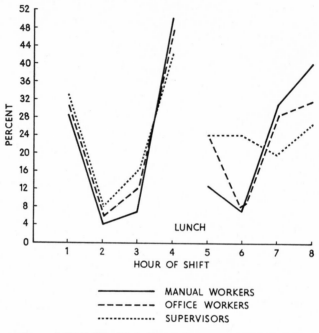

Source: J. W. Griffith, W. A. Kerr, T. B. Mayo, Jr., and J. R. Topal, "Changes in Subjective Fatigue and Readiness for Work during the Eight-Hour Shift," *Journal of Applied Psychology*, Vol. XXXIV (1950), pp. 163–66.

FIGURE 9–3. Percent of Employees Reporting Maximal Feelings of Tiredness at Each Hour of an Eight-Hour Work Shift.

45-minute or one-hour lunch period is not, itself, sufficiently long to dissipate completely the physiological component of fatigue. These findings again reinforce the importance of motivational factors in offsetting, at least partially, both feelings of fatigue and the concomitant work decrement associated with it.

Alleviation of Fatigue

It is apparent that certain difficulties are encountered when the psychologist studies fatigue. These difficulties are inherent in the formulation of a definition of fatigue, in measuring it, in reconciling discrepancies between its physiological and subjective components, and in separating out the effects of fatigue from those attributable to declining interest and motivation. In spite of these problems, however, the reduction of industrial fatigue is of extreme practical importance.

The findings of ergographic studies and of other types of observations relative to the widespread individual differences in susceptibility to fatigue suggest that appropriate selection and placement procedures can serve as a partial solution to the problem. The assignment of employees to jobs should not be predicated solely on the fulfillment by them of the necessary experiential and educational requirements. The state of their physical health and the likelihood that they will experience real satisfaction from their work are factors that must be considered also in order to minimize susceptibility to fatigue.

The attempts of the psychologist to reduce the fatigue experienced by employees presently on the job are, in general, directed toward the maintenance of productivity or output while simultaneously reducing the effort or input required of the employee. Thus, the alleviation of fatigue involves, for the most part, the manipulation of certain features of the physical working environment. It is imperative that the beneficial effects accruing from the actual reduction of effort be sorted out from those effects attributable to the improved employee motivation which often accompanies the conduct of this type of investigation. You will undoubtedly recall the implications of the Hawthorne Studies[2] in this regard.

Length of the Work Period. Since fatigue is generated by prolonged activity, one avenue to its alleviation is the reduction of the length of the working period. The length of the typical working day and work week has been progressively shortened during the past several years and, in all likelihood, will be further shortened within the next few years.

Unfortunately, the matter of the optimal length of the work period is too often approached with a background of misconceptions that appear, on the surface, to be reasonable. Management, for example, often expresses the view that the way to increase productivity is simply to increase the length of the work day or week. Representatives of management are sometimes heard to express concern

---

[2] See Chapter 8 for a discussion of the "Hawthorne Effect."

about reduction in the length of the work period on the grounds that
this will force an undue decline in productivity and create certain
social problems related to the increase in available leisure time. Union representatives, on the other hand, may perceive reductions in
the length of the work week as an indirect device for increasing employee salaries and as a means by which the number of available
jobs may be increased.

Both of these points of view stem from the erroneous assumption
that productivity is directly related to the amount of time spent at
work. The fact of the matter, however, is that changes in the length
of the work period do not yield proportional changes in productivity. It is helpful, in this regard, to differentiate between *nominal* and
actual hours worked. The "nominal" hours of work are defined by
the clock; that is, the employee checks in and out at specified times
and is nominally on the job for the number of hours elapsing between his check-in and check-out times. It is apparent, however,
that he does not actually produce during this entire period. Virtually every job entails a certain amount of unproductive time, some
of which is scheduled (for example, formally recognized rest periods) and some of which is not scheduled. We are dealing, after all,
with a human being rather than with a machine. He alters his work
pace, he has "good" days and "bad" days, he becomes tired and
must rest, he experiences boredom and takes a "break," and so on.
Thus, the critical factor affecting productivity is actual rather than
nominal hours worked. It has been found, in general, that increases
in nominal hours decrease actual hours worked and, conversely, that
decreases in nominal hours tend to be accompanied by increases in
actual hours worked. Employees for whom the work day is length-
ened spend, on the average, proportionately less time each hour in
productive work.

This generalization holds, within certain limits, even for highly
motivated employees engaged in wartime production. One of the
earliest series of studies of the effect of the length of the work period
was conducted in Great Britain during World War I. The hourly
output of women engaged in munitions work during 12- and eight-
hour shifts, for example, was 19½ per cent higher during the short
shift. Furthermore, when the nominal hours of weekly work by
women who turned fuse bodies were reduced from 63½ to 47½
hours, their total weekly output increased by 13 percent.[3]

---

[3] Industrial Fatigue Research Board, Great Britain, *Report No. 2.*

Decisions about the optimal length of the work period are, in practice, somewhat influenced by economic factors. Although there is ample evidence for the fact that hourly productivity tends to increase when nominal hours are reduced, the two factors do not balance each other entirely with respect to total productivity. A 25 percent reduction in nominal hours, for example, leading to a 15 percent increase in hourly productivity will yield a net loss in plant production unless additional employees are hired or extra shifts are run. This may be entirely feasible from an economic standpoint because of the savings resulting from the higher proportion of actual to nominal hours of work. It is a matter that must be studied, however, by each company contemplating a reduction in nominal hours.

Factors other than economic considerations also enter into decisions about the optimal length of the work period. The type of work being performed and employee reaction to altered periods of work may have considerable bearing upon the matter.

The relationship between the characteristics of the job and the actual amount of work performed is clearly apparent from a study conducted by the U.S. Department of Labor.[4] The hourly productivity of employees in the metalworking industry was compared for persons doing light work under wage incentive systems and those engaged in heavy labor. These employees worked nominally between 55 and 58 hours a week. Those doing light work averaged approximately two hours' output for every three hours worked in excess of 48. Employees engaged in heavy work, however, only averaged about one hour's output for every two hours worked in excess of 48.

The eight-hour day and the 40-hour week are generally regarded as optimal for striking a balance that maximizes industrial efficiency under normal (nonemergency) conditions. Hourly productivity in a box factory was found, for example, to be highest when the employees worked a 40-hour week, slightly reduced when they worked either a 36- or a 44-hour week, and considerably reduced when they worked a 48-hour week.[5] Another study, contrasting a 7½ hour day and a 9½ hour day, found that the former condition led to higher productivity and lowered absenteeism.[6]

---

[4] U.S. Department of Labor, "Hours of Work and Production," *Labor Information Bulletin*, No. 2, 1944, pp. 4–7.

[5] S. L. Pressey *et al.*, *Life: A Psychological Survey* (New York: Harper & Bros., 1939), p. 524.

[6] M. D. Kossoris, "Studies in the Effects of Long Working Hours," *Bureau of Labor Statistics, Bulletin No. 791*, 1944.

The desirability of decreasing the length of the working day below 8 hours and that of the work week below 40 hours is still an open issue. A certain amount of resistance to further reductions can undoubtedly be attributed to a prevailing conservatism relative to any kind of a change in the established way of doing things. It is likely, for some jobs requiring a lengthy "warm-up" building slowly to maximum output each day, that the eight-hour day is indeed optimal. Other kinds of work, particularly those generating extreme fatigue or boredom, however, will be performed most efficiently when the nominal hours are reduced below eight each day.

Rest Periods. The effect of authorized rest pauses during the day has been investigated rather extensively. It has been demonstrated that employees will rest regardless of whether or not rest periods are scheduled. A careful study of unauthorized breaks taken when formal rest periods were introduced into the work schedule of comptometer operators indicated that the effect of the authorized rest periods was to produce a sharp decline in unauthorized breaks and an increase in productivity.[7]

The beneficial effects of scheduled rest pauses accrue from the fact that such pauses provide opportunities for a partial recovery from fatigue and for a change of pace which undoubtedly helps to relieve boredom. The mere fact of a scheduled rest period is, however, an insufficient guarantee of its effectiveness. The time of the day at which such breaks are scheduled, their frequency and duration, and the employee activity during the rest period may all be of considerable importance.

There is considerable variation between companies in the number and length of scheduled rest periods, even for jobs essentially similar. The typical procedure is to schedule one rest around midmorning and another around midafternoon, each period being 10 to 15 minutes in length. The ideal schedule for rest pauses is something that must be determined for each kind of work. It is likely that each rest period ought to be somewhat longer for very strenuous tasks than for light work. It is probable, also, that rest periods should be scheduled with greater frequency when the task is monotonous or physically taxing than when it is interesting or relatively sedentary.

An examination of the production curve during the course of the day can furnish very helpful clues about the specific times at which

[7] W. McGehee and E. B. Owen, "Authorized and Unauthorized Rest Pauses in Clerical Work," *Journal of Applied Psychology*, Vol. XXIV (1940), pp. 604–13.

rest periods should be introduced if they are to be most beneficial. You will recall that the typical output curve for fatiguing work (Figure 9–1) indicates that productivity declines sometime after mid-morning and again sometime after midafternoon. The usual practice is to schedule rest periods immediately prior to these declines in productivity in order to forestall their occurrence. (See Figure 9–4.)

The time scheduled for rest must be used wisely if the break is to be most beneficial. Employees engaged in heavy labor should relax; employees engaged in sedentary activity should move about and experience a change of scene. The rest period should provide a variation in pace and an opportunity for fatigue to be dissipated.

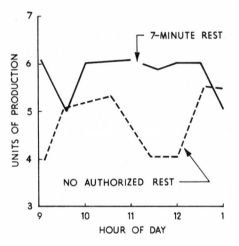

Source: J. Tiffin, *Industrial Psychology* (New York: Prentice-Hall, Inc., 1952), p. 412, drawn from data by E. Farmer and S. M. Bevington, an experiment in the introduction of rest pauses, *Journal of National Institutional and Industrial Psychology*, 1922, pp. 89–92.

FIGURE 9–4. Effects of Authorized Rest on Production during the Morning Hours.

Miscellaneous Environmental Factors. Many of the environmental conditions that serve to accelerate or retard the development of fatigue have been discussed in Chapter 8. Reduction in the prevailing noise or vibration level and improvements in illumination and ventilation may lead to both improved output and diminution in subjective feelings of tiredness. Changes in work methods or in equipment design may materially decrease industrial fatigue by making it easier for the employee to do his work.

BOREDOM

We have already mentioned that the effects of boredom and of fatigue have much in common. Both may lead to increased turnover, spoilage and accidents, lowered morale, and subjective feelings of strain or discontent. Both factors also affect productivity. The output curve for monotonous work, however, is generally differentiated from that resulting from fatiguing work by the appearance of an "end-spurt" in anticipation of release from the task. (See Figure 9–5.)

Monotonous tasks are thought of typically as being rather routine and highly repetitive. The relationship between the nature of the task and the experience of boredom is not nearly as direct, however, as the relationship between the kind of work performed and the ex-

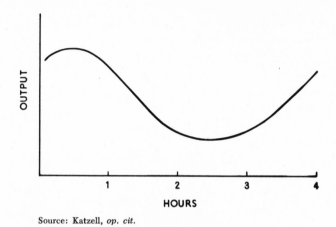

Source: Katzell, *op. cit.*

FIGURE 9–5. Schematic Plot of Average Hourly Output
for Monotonous Work.

perience of fatigue. Tasks that are monotonous for some workers may be rather interesting and challenging for others. Thus, boredom results from a lack of interest in the work. The experience of boredom is dependent upon the character of the work *as it is perceived by the worker,* rather than upon the character of the work as it may be described objectively.

Worker-Job Relationships Associated with Boredom

Remedies for boredom are predicated upon an understanding of the factors that lead workers to regard their jobs as monotonous. The factors which have been explored in this regard include intelligence, interest, and personality.

Intelligence of the Employee. It is reasonable to anticipate that jobs requiring either more or less intellectual capability than the worker possesses will prove to be monotonous. It is difficult for workers who are too intelligent for their task to maintain a continuing interest in it. The job does not challenge them sufficiently and therefore does not provide them with a feeling of satisfaction and accomplishment. Conversely, workers placed on jobs requiring more intellectual capability than they possess may also be expected to lose interest in their work because of the frustration of continual failure. It is not gratifying to be confronted continually by one's shortcomings.

It has been found, for example, that highly intelligent employees performing simple clerical tasks had a much higher turnover rate than did less intelligent employees on the same job.[8] Turnover may be regarded as a partial indication of boredom since some employees undoubtedly terminate their employment in order to accept a more interesting job. It is likely, however, that many workers leave their present employment in order to accept a higher paying, but not necessarily more interesting, position. This factor confounds the utilization of turnover as a criterion of boredom.

The relationship between intelligence and boredom has been studied more directly by comparing the average intelligence test scores of workers who completed a questionnaire appraising the degree of boredom they experienced on the job. The average intelligence of the groups of workers reporting the most boredom tended to be higher than that of workers reporting the least boredom. The differences between the mean test scores of these groups did not, however, always meet the requirements for statistical significance, and the groups utilized for the study were very small in size (four to 10 persons each).[9]

Although there is some evidence in support of a relationship between employee intelligence and boredom, this relationship is by no means as strong as one might suppose. It is apparent that other factors, including interest and personal adjustment, may operate to counteract or minimize this relationship.

Employee Interests. The kinds of activities that interest us are determined, in part, by our intellectual capacity and, to a large extent, by our past experiences. We develop our own unique pattern of interests on the basis of the successes which we have experienced in

[8] M. A. Bills, "Relation of Mental Alertness Test Score to Position and Permanency in Company," *Journal of Applied Psychology,* Vol. VII (1923), pp. 154–56.

[9] S. Wyatt, J. N. Langdon, and F. G. L. Stock, "Fatigue and Boredom in Repetitive Work," Industrial Health Research Board, Great Britain, Report No. 77, 1937.

the past and the environment to which we have been exposed. Thus, we each have proclivities toward certain kinds of industrial activities and away from other kinds of activities.

Individual differences with respect to interest were demonstrated by having workers in a candy packing department alternate on five different jobs for one month each. The employees were questioned about the amount of boredom they experienced on each of the five jobs, and highly individual patterns of boredom were discovered. A job that was the least interesting for one worker often proved to be the most interesting for another.[10]

Personality. Attempts to establish a "personality pattern" characteristic of workers who are easily bored as differentiated from those who withstand boredom have not been outstandingly successful. One investigation of the problem led to the conclusion that extroverted persons tend to experience boredom more readily that introverted persons.[11] Presumably, this relationship exists because introverted workers are less dependent upon social stimulation for personal gratification and are therefore better able to function under conditions involving repetitive activity and relative isolation. It has been found, also, that older employees and those who prefer a degree of regularity in their daily activities are least susceptible to boredom during repetitious work.[12]

These bits of evidence provide meager clues to the relationship between personality patterns and susceptibility to boredom. The relationships are neither sufficiently strong nor sufficiently consistent to permit the utilization of such measures for predictive purposes.

A more promising approach to this problem focuses upon employee needs and personal adjustment as the critical factors, rather than upon identification of a personality pattern associated with boredom. A job which is satisfying to the employee and provides him with a feeling of accomplishment and a sense of personal worth is rarely regarded as monotonous. Work, on the other hand, that does not provide the employee with a degree of job satisfaction is often boring regardless of the nature of the activity performed. In many ways, the factors responsible for job satisfaction are quite similar to those responsible for deriving satisfaction from life in general.

---

[10] Wyatt *et al., ibid.*

[11] Wyatt *et al., ibid.*

[12] P. C. Smith, "The Prediction of Individual Differences in Susceptibility to Industrial Monotony," *Journal of Applied Psychology,* Vol. XXXIX (1955), pp. 322–29.

Employees who seek variation in activities after working hours tend also to derive the greatest amount of job satisfaction when their work is varied in nature. Similarly, employees who are dissatisfied with life in general and who are poorly adjusted in their familial and home relationships tend to be dissatisfied with their work and to be most susceptible to boredom.[13]

Alleviation of Boredom

Industrial automation has made it possible, within certain limits, to eliminate many routine and highly repetitive jobs. Automated equipment cannot, however, relieve workers from all such tasks. The equipment itself generates some new jobs of a repetitive nature and many rather routine industrial activities are not amenable to automation. In addition, the fact that boredom is a function of the worker's perception of the job rather than of the characteristics of the job as objectively defined implies that a certain amount of monotonous activity will always be present in industry.

One solution to the problem of boredom entails the utilization of appropriate personnel selection and placement procedures. A gross mismatching of the job and the worker relative to such factors as his intelligence, interests, and other personal characteristics should be avoided. Even the most careful selection and placement program will not, however, be a full solution to the problem. Selection and placement procedures must be supplemented by measures designed to reduce the boredom that is an inevitable consequence of certain kinds of work for some employees.

The fundamental consideration in alleviating boredom is, of course, that of increasing the employee's interest and involvement in his work. This can be accomplished in a number of ways. Almost any job assumes additional significance for the employee when he is informed about the relationship between what he is doing and the end product being produced. It is imperative that the training program for new employees include some kind of an overview of the entire industrial operation and an indication of the role played in this operation by the individual worker.

In addition, many jobs may be made more interesting by enlarging the scope of the activities performed by the employee. It is often

---

[13] P. A. Cain, "Individual Differences in Susceptibility to Monotony" (Ph.D. dissertation, Cornell University, 1942). Cited in R. A. Ryan, *Work and Effort* (New York: Ronald Press Co., 1947), pp. 199 ff.

possible to permit employees engaged in fragmented work a greater amount of responsibility for planning and organizing their activities. Such enlargement of the scope of the work provides the worker with a degree of variety which can be very helpful in counteracting boredom.

When job enlargement is not feasible, variety may be introduced by means of job rotation. Several employees, each performing a different monotonous task, may be permitted to change jobs with each other every two hours or so. The actual change in activity combined with a change in the physical and social environment relieves the routine and enhances the maintenance of a level of interest. This may well justify the added costs incurred by job rotation.

Certain other approaches to the alleviation of boredom are based upon factors other than that of increasing the employee's interest in his work. Strategically placed rest pauses, for example, are very helpful in forestalling the experience of boredom. Similarly, music may serve as a mild diversion acting to make time seem to pass more quickly and the job itself to seem more pleasant. Finally, bonus payments for productivity in excess of some established minimum may reduce the deleterious effects of boredom upon output.

SUMMARY

Fatigue and boredom are both undesirable consequences of industrial activity. These conditions lead to diminished output and subjective feelings of strain and tension. Although the effects of fatigue and boredom are somewhat similar, the factors responsible for these conditions are quite different.

Fatigue is a temporary experience resulting from prolonged muscular activity and is characterized by a declining capacity for continued work. The physiological and subjective components of fatigue are correlated only imperfectly with each other and with a measureable work decrement. Motivational factors may act to forestall or obscure fatigue.

The alleviation of fatigue may be approached in several ways. Appropriate personnel selection and placement procedures facilitate the assignment of employees to jobs that fit their physical capabilities and from which they are likely to experience personal satisfaction. In addition, modifications in the length of the work-period and the insertion of authorized rest pauses into the schedule can be very helpful for dissipating fatigue. Improvements in certain environmental conditions including illumination and ventilation, and the reduction of undue noise or vibration may lead to both improved output and dimunition in the subjective feelings of "tiredness." Finally, changes in work methods and in equipment design can materially decrease industrial fatigue by making it easier for the employee to do his work.

Boredom is differentiated from fatigue by the kind of activity that generates it and its rather high degree of specificity. Monotonous work is uninteresting to the employee. Furthermore, the bored worker seeks relief only from the activity he regards as monotonous, while the fatigued worker seeks rest from all activity.

Boredom is dependent upon the character of the work as it is perceived by the employee, rather than upon the nature of the work as it may be objectively described. Thus, the fundamental approach to the investigation of boredom is directed toward identifying the worker characteristics associated with the perception of work as monotonous. It has been found that the workers who are most susceptible to boredom tend to be dissatisfied with life in general and to be poorly adjusted in their personal relationships outside of the job.

Monotonous work cannot be entirely eliminated from industry. Boredom, however, may be somewhat reduced by the assignment of employees to jobs that are congruent with their capabilities and interests. In addition, provision should be made in the training program for informing employees about the relationship between their particular job and the total industrial operation.

Job enlargement, permitting workers a greater amount of responsibility for planning and organizing their activities, can often provide a degree of variety in work which forestalls the experience of boredom. When job enlargement is not feasible, variety may be introduced by means of job rotation. Miscellaneous approaches to the alleviation of boredom include authorized rest pauses, music, and bonus payments for high productivity.

Accidents and Safety

10 Everyone regards war as a cause of extensive devastation, death, and injury. The weapons recently developed by man for destroying the enemy are horribly effective. Even during World War II, fought with much more rudimentary weapons, our own casualties between the start of the war and the surrender of Japan numbered in excess of 900,000 persons, almost one third of whom were killed.[1] Thus, war injuries and deaths affected a group of persons comparable to the entire population of a fair-size city.

The destructiveness of a war, however, is exceeded by the sheer waste of human resources attributable to civilian accidents. The number of deaths and injuries from civilian accidents during the period of World War II exceeded those classified as war casualties. Accidental civilian deaths during this period numbered approximately 350,000 and injuries numbered 36,000,000.[2] Accidents in the home were responsible for the greatest proportion of these injuries and deaths, but occupational and automotive accidents also contributed substantially to this enormous waste of manpower.

One other alarming statistic will suffice to set the stage for this chapter. Although we will be concerned most specifically with the matter of occupational safety, much of the discussion will be sufficiently general to apply with equal facility to nonoccupational accidents. The data relative to injuries and deaths resulting from automobile accidents provide convincing evidence for the fact that the improperly handled automobile is a lethal weapon that rivals those deliberately developed for combative purposes. Vehicular accidents alone in the United States during 1959 were responsible for in excess of 37,000 deaths and 1,500,000 nonfatal injuries.[3]

We cannot, as a society, afford to neglect the matter of accident prevention. Research and the application of knowledge in this area

---

[1] National Safety Council, Inc., *Accident Facts* (Chicago, 1946), p. 17.

[2] *Ibid.*

[3] *Automobile Facts and Figures* (Automobile Manufacturer's Association, 1959–60).

is as critical as it is in combating such medical scourges as cancer and heart disease. The fatalistic notion that accidents cannot happen to us, or that they will occur because of "bad luck" regardless of our efforts to prevent them, is contrary to the facts. The role of luck (including such things as unavoidable equipment malfunction) as a cause of accidents has been the subject of considerable study. Estimates of the percentage of accidents due to such causes, and therefore unpreventable, vary between 10 and 20 percent. The large majority of accidents are clearly due to human factors rather than to "fate." The most efficient eyeshield in the world is valueless, for example, if an employee refuses to use it. And even a smoothly functioning aircraft is subject to pilot error involving misinterpretation of its instrumentation or poor judgment relative to landing conditions.

Accident prevention requires the joint efforts of engineers and psychologists. The fact that proportionately few accidents are attributable to equipment malfunction would seem to indicate that engineering principles related to safety have been well-developed and widely accepted. The psychological factors responsible for accidents have been studied also, but there is some reticence about applying the knowledge now available in this area.

This chapter is concerned primarily with the human factors responsible for accidents and with certain procedures for preventing their occurrence. The fact that relatively little attention is given to many of the engineering problems related to safety should not be taken as an indication that these factors are unimportant. Rather, this emphasis reflects the fact that the majority of accidents are due to human factors rather than to equipment malfunction.

CAUSES OF ACCIDENTS

It is not difficult to understand management's concern for employee safety. Accidents are expensive. They are responsible for a direct cost in terms of diminished productivity, as well as for the related costs of providing medical attention and compensation. Accidents, furthermore, may have a deleterious effect upon plant morale. It is understandably disturbing to employees, for example, to know that they are working at a job that has led in the past to a substantial number of injuries.

Work in certain industries is more hazardous than in others. The lumber, mining, and construction industries characteristically rank higher with respect to accident frequency than do communications and electrical equipment.[4] This discrepancy in safety record as a function of the industry suggests at least three general factors which are potential causes of accidents. The first, and most obvious, of these is the *physical working environment*. The greater the exposure of an employee to dangerous equipment and to unfavorable working circumstances, the greater is his liability to accidents. A second causal factor suggested by interindustry differences in accident frequency is *personal* in nature. Certain industries are more selective than others in hiring and retaining employees on the basis of such personal variables as age, prior experience, and physical health. Finally, industries (and individual companies within an industry) may differ markedly in the extent of their concern about employee *attitudes* relative to safety. Workers who are unimpressed by the potential of their surroundings and job activities for causing accidents are more likely to be injured than those who have developed attitudes of appropriate caution.

The Physical Work Environment

A good deal has already been said about the working environment in Chapter 8. Unfavorable or unpleasant environments are responsible for diminishing productivity and lowering morale. It should be readily apparent also, that certain environmental conditions may be either direct or indirect causes of accidents. Improperly anchored equipment, for example, would be regarded as a direct causal agent. Such factors as improper illumination or ventilation may either act directly as causes of accidents, by making it virtually impossible for the worker to perform with safety, or may act indirectly by making the job unpleasant and the worker incautious.

Ventilation. The component of ventilation usually explored with reference to accidents is temperature. The relationship between accident frequency and temperature is shown clearly in Figure 10–1. The employees upon whom these data were based were all engaged in factory work. Fewest accidents occurred when the temperature was about 68 to 70°; a noticeable increase in accident frequency was observed when temperatures declined. The discrepancy between the accident rates noted for men and women as the temperature

---

[4] National Safety Council, Inc., *Accident Facts* (Chicago, 1955).

increased above 70° is of some interest. It suggests the possibility that the adverse effects of high temperatures may be sex-linked. This conclusion is confounded, however, by the fact that men are generally assigned to jobs requiring a greater amount of physical exertion and hence may be more vulnerable to accidents as temperature increases.

The results discussed above were based upon records of relatively minor accidents. When coal mine accidents were classified ac-

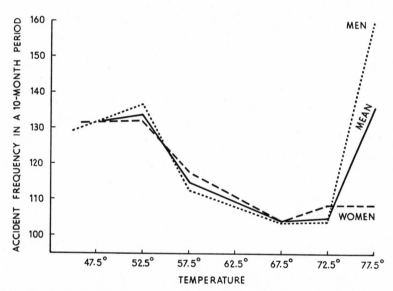

Source: E. E. Osborne and H. M. Vernon, *The Influence of Temperature and Other Conditions on the Frequency of Industrial Accidents,* Industrial Fatigue Research Board, No. 19 (London: H. M. Stationery Office, 1922).

FIGURE 10–1. Accident Frequency in Relation to Temperature.

cording to severity (that is, length of time absent from work), it was found that rising temperature increased the rate of minor accidents to a much greater extent than that of major accidents.[5] The discomfort associated with higher temperature probably leads to the kind of carelessness or indisposition toward work that is particularly responsible for minor accidents. The suggestion has been made, also, that workers may be more likely to use a minor injury as an excuse to take time off when the working environment becomes unpleasant.

One aspect of ventilation that may, on occasion, be a very direct

---

[5] H. M. Vernon, *Accidents and Their Prevention* (Cambridge, Eng., and New York: The University Press and The Macmillan Co., 1936), p. 80.

cause of accidental injury is oxygen deprivation and the accumulation of noxious fumes. Flights at an altitude of about 14,000 feet without supplemental oxygen, for example, will produce oxygen starvation. The pilot may suffer visual impairment, his muscular coordination will be poor, and he may feel giddy or euphoric. His ability to reason and to solve problems under such circumstances is affected seriously. Anoxia (oxygen deficiency) is, of course, a rare occurrence at the present time. It is not of major concern to industry because of the development of air purification equipment sufficient to cope with virtually every kind of circumstance that might produce an accumulation of noxious gases.

Illumination. Twilight is a dangerous time of the day for driving simply because it is difficult to see under conditions of inadequate illumination. Defective illumination in industry is a rather obvious and easily correctible source of accidents.

Studies made some years ago of accident frequency under conditions of daylight and artificial illumination indicated that the latter circumstance produced a considerable increase in accident rate. Enormous improvements have been made by lighting engineers, however, since these investigations were conducted. The unshielded, low intensity incandescent lamp should by now be a relic of the past. Proper artificial lighting still provides illumination that is somewhat inferior to daylight, but the differences are not great.

Equipment Design. The newspapers occasionally report an automobile accident occurring at night because the driver erroneously depressed his headlight button instead of his cigarette lighter. This kind of accident reflects the folly of poor equipment design and the sacrifice of safety in the interest of the aesthetics of dashboard arrangement. Many accidents can be avoided in circumstances in which rapid judgments are necessary by utilizing knobs of appropriate shapes and dials that are amenable to accurate interpretation. It is apparent that some automobile manufacturers are less impressed than they should be with the importance of proper equipment.

The design of manufacturing equipment with built-in safety devices and power cutoffs, and of special clothing that does not itself interfere with productivity, is a matter of very direct concern to industry. This is a particularly critical problem in circumstances in which the operation of the equipment demands continual exposure of the employee to moving parts, cutting edges, and flying debris.

Personal Characteristics of the Employee

The Metropolitan Life Insurance Company classified the causes of accidents experienced by employees of a railway company with the results noted in Table 10–1.[6] About 20 percent of the accidents were attributed to physical and personal disability (including defective vision, organic disease, worry and depression, and so on); the remainder were caused primarily by attitudinal factors.

Health. It is unnecessary to belabor the importance of physical health to safe industrial operation. An employee who is ill cannot

TABLE 10–1

CAUSES OF ACCIDENTS IN THE CLEVELAND STREET
RAILWAY COMPANY

Faulty attitude	14%
Failure to recognize potential hazards	12
Faulty judgment of speed or distance	12
Impulsiveness	10
Irresponsibility	8
Failing to keep attention constant	8
Nervousness and fear	6
Defective vision	4
Organic disease	4
Slow reaction	4
High blood pressure	2
Senility	2
Worry and depression	2
Fatigue	2
Improper distribution of attention	2
Inexperience	2
Miscellaneous	6

devote the required amount of attention to his job and is likely to be somewhat careless.

The relationship between physical disability and accident liability is, however, a somewhat different matter. If the disability interferes with satisfactory job performance, the employee may experience an accident because of his defect rather than carelessness. One of the sources of accidents that can be most readily identified and easily corrected is defective vision. A comparison between the prevalence of visual defects among good and poor drivers, for example, indicated that accident-free drivers were significantly less susceptible to

---

[6] *The Accident Prone Employee* (New York Metropolitan Life Insurance Co., 1930).

glare sensitivity, relatively free from astigmatism and more likely to have adequate visual acuity.[7]

Many companies have drawn up rather elaborate sets of physical specifications for various jobs in recognition of the fact that it would be utter foolishness to assign persons with certain disabilities to certain kinds of jobs. It is important to bear in mind, however, that the mere fact of the existence of a physical disability should not be construed as a contraindication for employment unless it is clear that the disability will interfere with satisfactory job performance. Quite often the handicapped worker, once aware of his limitations, can learn to compensate for them effectively. Thus, when handicapped workers are properly placed, employers report lower absenteeism and termination as well as accident rates than for able-bodied persons employed on similar jobs.[8]

Age. The relationship between age and accident frequency reflects the operation of at least three variables which underlie the age factor: health, experience, and attitude. Younger employees, as a group, may be in better physical health than older workers, but are more likely to be relatively inexperienced and somewhat more irresponsible. Studies of age as a cause of accidents are further complicated by the selective factors sometimes applied to older employees. Advancing age may be used by management as a reason for discharging an employee, particularly if he has a history of high accident frequency, or for reassigning him to less hazardous work.

The effect of this constellation of factors associated with aging is to produce consistent findings indicative of a lower accident rate for older than for younger employees. The data for workers in an ordinance depot, shown in Table 10-2, are typical of such studies. The incidental evidence apparent in this table, that men are more likely to have accidents than are women, is also a persistently recurring finding.

A similar pattern of accident frequency is discovered when accidents are plotted as a function of length of service or experience rather than of age. The more experienced employees (generally the older employees) have considerably fewer accidents than do the relatively inexperienced employees. A considerable diminution in

---

[7] E. D. Fletcher, *Capacity of Special Tests to Measure Driving Ability,* State of California, Department of Motor Vehicles.

[8] C. H. Stone and W. E. Kendall, *Effective Personnel Selection Procedures* (Englewood Cliffs, N.J.: Prentice-Hall, Inc., 1956).

accident frequency as a function of job experience is apparent also for relatively young employees as shown in Figure 10–2. Thus, experience makes a contribution to safety of its own beyond that explicable solely in terms of increased employee maturity.

TABLE 10–2

TABULATION OF ACCIDENT FREQUENCY
AT AN ORDINANCE DEPOT

Age Group	Male Rate Per Hundred	Female Rate Per Hundred
17–21................172		41
21–28................. 75		36
28–35................. 65		17
35–45................. 50		26
45–60................. 42		37
60+ 35		0

Source: J. Mann, "Analysis of 1,009 Consecutive Accidents at One Ordinance Depot, *Industrial Medicine*, Vol. XIII (1944), pp. 368–74.

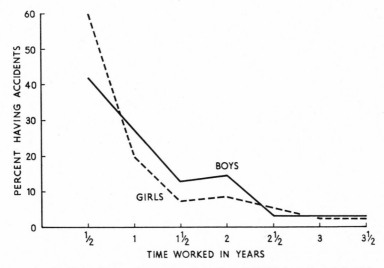

Source: H. M. Vernon, "Prevention of Accidents," *British Journal of Industrial Medicine,* Vol. II (1945), p. 3.

FIGURE 10–2. Accidents Incurred by Young Employees as a Function of Years of Experience.

In spite of the favorable safety record accumulated by older employees by virtue of experiential and attitudinal factors, there is a particular set of circumstances in which age must be regarded as a detrimental factor. Whenever the job makes physical demands upon the employee which are more readily satisfied by younger workers, the older employee is likely to be particularly susceptible to accidents. Thus, as shown in Figure 10–3, age is positively correlated with accident frequency under adverse temperature conditions when the work is strenuous.

The entire matter of the employment of older personnel is one that requires serious consideration by management because medical

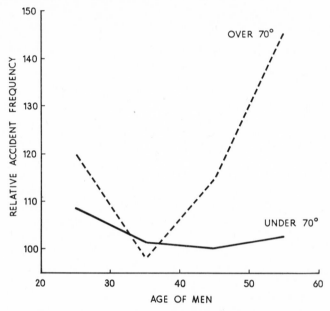

Source: H. M. Vernon and T. Bedford, *The Absenteeism of Miners in Relation to Short Time and Other Conditions,* Industrial Health Research Board, No. 62 (London: H. M. Stationery Office, 1931).

FIGURE 10–3. Accident Frequency of Coal Face Workers in Relation to Age and Temperature.

advances have increased our span of active, healthy years. There is no magic inherent in the number "65" dictating this as an age for mandatory retirement. Certain physical abilities, including vision and speed of reaction, are known to decrease with advancing age. There are, however, widespread individual differences in the rate and severity of such impairments. Furthermore, the depth of job knowledge accumulated by virtue of experience may act, in many instances, to offset the physical accompaniments of aging. It is probably sensible to reassign many older employees to jobs that require relatively little physical exertion and are not dependent upon rapidity of response, but it is both unwise and uneconomical to put all older employees "out to pasture."

Fatigue. You will recall from the discussion in Chapter 9 that one of the effects of fatigue is to decrease productivity. This decline in the output curve typically is observed during the periods immediately preceding lunch and the termination of the work day. The same general kind of curve has been found to result when accidents (rather than output) are plotted as a function of time of the day.[9] Thus, there appears to be a relationship between production rate and accident frequency.

It is necessary, therefore, in investigating the relationship between fatigue and accident rate, to somehow separate out the influence of output which is related both to fatigue and to accident frequency. This has been done by utilizing a simple index of accident frequency per unit of production. The resultant data, obtained over a relatively long period of time in plants working eight- and 10-hour shifts, are exhibited in Figure 10–4. The accident index was found to parallel the output curve very closely during the eight-hour shift, indicating that production increases tend to be accompanied by an increment in accident frequency. The 10-hour shift, however, provided for the development of considerable fatigue leading to a rise in the accident index during the last two hours of the shift in spite of declining productivity.[10]

Evidence of this sort leads to the conclusion that although fatigue can be rather directly responsible for accidents, it is not a causal factor of significant concern in most industrial settings. The eight-hour work day, which tends to prevent the occurrence of the kind of extreme fatigue associated with accidental injury, is fairly well standardized.

Attitudes, Adjustment, and Emotional Factors

An employee who is free from debilitating physical characteristics, who works under optimal environmental conditions, and who is aware of the limitations of his equipment is still quite likely to have an accident if his attitudinal pattern is one of recklessness, irre-

---

[9] H. M. Vernon, *op. cit.*

[10] J. Goldmark, M. D. Hopkins, P. S. Florence, and F. S. Lee, "Studies in Industrial Physiology: Fatigue in Relation to Working Capacity, No. 1 (Comparison of an Eight-Hour Plant and a Ten-Hour Plant)," *Public Health Bulletin No. 106,* U.S. Public Health Service, 1920.

sponsibility, or uncooperativeness. Such attitudes are, of course, symptomatic of more fundamental kinds of personal maladjustment. A mature, well-adjusted employee does not regard it as "sissified" to observe safety precautions and to avoid unnecessary risks. Thus, the entire matter of the relationship between attitudes and liability to accidents has generally been investigated within the broader context of adjustmental and emotional factors.

There is some evidence, for example, that high accident frequency is associated with neuroticism. This evidence is predicated upon the observed correlation between accident frequency and the number

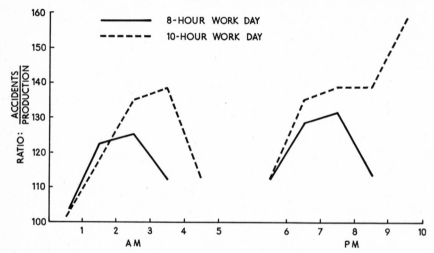

FIGURE 10-4. Accident Ratio for Eight-Hour and 10-Hour Day with Production Rate Constant.

of visits to the dispensary for the treatment of relatively minor conditions. Since absences for reasons of sickness were not found to correlate with accident frequency, the investigator interpreted his data as indicative of something other than a relationship between general health and accidents. A continual history of minor medical complaints is often associated with neurotic instability. Hence, it appears that this underlying personality pattern is a factor of some importance in causing accidents.[11]

More concrete evidence relative to the relationship between personal maladjustment and susceptibility to accidents was provided

---

[11] H. M. Vernon, *op. cit.*

by a study of over 100 workers who had experienced more than 400 minor accidents. More than half of these accidents occurred when the worker was emotionally disturbed, that is, worried, apprehensive, and so on. Such emotional states resulted either from concerns about the job or represented a transference of difficulties being experienced in the home. Some of the workers who experienced accidents were found also to be susceptible to rather regular periodic fluctuations in mood or emotional tone.[12]

Efforts to identify a "personality type" or a constellation of personality traits associated with high accident liability have not been particularly successful. Although the data from such studies have not proven to be especially useful for predictive purposes, they have provided some important clues about the personalities of individuals who have repetitive accidents. Accident repeaters were found, in one study, to be differentiated from other workers by being overly fearful, fatalistic (feeling that they were unlucky), overly ambitious, revengeful, and desirous of pampering.[13] A similarly unhealthy emotional pattern involving feelings of hostility and lack of concern for the social consequences of actions was discovered as a correlate of automotive accidents.[14] Emotional immaturity, as evidenced by a tendency to become easily disturbed by minor irritations, to "blow off steam" in excess of that required by the situation, and by a kind of general irresponsibility and lack of considerateness, was found to be related to accident frequency for route salesmen.[15]

It must be reiterated that the above noted relationships between personality and accident frequency are not strong. Were they more potent, we should have some basis for a statement to the effect that certain kinds of persons are "accident-prone": that is, that their personality is such that we would expect them to have accidents with considerably greater frequency than dictated solely on the basis of chance. The issue of accident-proneness has received considerable attention in the professional literature, and it is appropriate that we direct our attention next to this matter.

---

[12] R. B. Hersey, "Emotional Factors in Accidents," *Personnel Journal*, Vol. XV (1936), pp. 59–65.

[13] A. Adler, "The Psychology of Repeated Accidents in Industry," *American Journal of Psychiatry*, Vol. XCVIII (1941), pp. 99–101.

[14] P. L. Brown and R. P. Berdie, "Driver Behavior and Scores on the MMPI," *Journal of Applied Psychology*, Vol. XLIV (1960), pp. 18–21.

[15] A. H. Malo, "New Light on the Accident Prone," *Personnel*, July, 1954, p. 65.

ACCIDENT-PRONENESS

The reasons for interest in, and even excitement about, the possibility of demonstrating the existence of an accident-prone personality are relatively apparent. If it could be demonstrated that certain kinds of persons are much more susceptible than others to accidents, we would be provided with a powerful tool for the prevention of accidents. Accident-prone employees could presumably be identified and assigned to nonhazardous jobs.

The tenability of the principle of accident-proneness hinges upon the demonstration that some persons have many more accidents than one would forecast for them on the basis of chance, while others have many fewer accidents than one would expect if chance factors alone were operative. The typical evidence in support of the principle is based upon the demonstration that a relatively small percentage of employees have a disproportionately large percentage of accidents. One study of accidents in which taxicab drivers were involved, for example, found that 40 percent of the drivers had 70 percent of the accidents.[16] Thus, the argument was made that since some drivers never had an accident while others had several accidents, the latter must be accident-prone.

The critical feature overlooked in such "demonstrations" of accident-proneness is the proper definition of chance. The question of the number of accidents to be expected solely on the basis of chance is a little like asking how many heads in a row would result from flipping a coin. Assuming no bias in the coin or in the flipping procedure, we would expect to observe 50 percent heads and 50 percent tails *in the long run.* You are well aware, however, that it would be possible to observe five heads in a row on five consecutive flips just by chance. The odds against this occurring are high, but it can happen! The fact that it does happen occasionally is what tempts the inveterate gambler to try the "long shots."

Mintz and Blum have been most articulate in pointing out the defect inherent in the interpretation of accident data like those cited for taxicab drivers as supportive of the principle of proneness. They write:

The method of percentages of people and accidents implies an incorrect assumption, *viz.,* that chance expectation requires that all people in

---

[16] *Preventing Taxicab Accidents* (New York: Metropolitan Life Insurance Company, 1931).

a population should have the same number of accidents. This is not the case. An obvious limitation that has often been overlooked is the fact that very often the reported total number of accidents in a population is smaller than the number of people in the population. For example, if a group of one hundred factory workers had fifty accidents in one year, then a maximum of fifty people could have contributed to the accident record and accordingly a maximum of 50% of the population would have contributed to 100% of the accidents. Obviously, a small percentage of the population in this case does not establish the principle of accident proneness.[17]

They follow this argument with another predicated upon the fact that there is no reason to assume that one accident immunizes the victim against the possibility of having other accidents. It is perfectly plausible to expect that some persons will, just by chance, have several accidents while others may not have any. The application of these arguments was used to develop an appropriate chance distribution of accident frequency for the taxicab accidents cited earlier, with the result shown in Figure 10–5. You will note that the obtained accident frequency and the chance expectancies are very similar in shape. There is some evidence for the fact that something other than chance was operating to produce the observed distribution of accidents because the discrepancy between the obtained and chance distributions is statistically significant. It is quite clear, however, that the principle of accident-proneness is not nearly as formidable as it was once thought to be. Mintz and Blum concluded, from the examination of these and similar sets of data, that the variance attributable to differences in accident liability is about 20 to 40 percent. The effect of this factor is small when compared with the estimated 60 to 80 percent attributable to unpredictable (chance) factors.

The impact of this important study along with several more recent ones has been to place the principle of accident-proneness in perspective. It was thought, at one time, that the primary route to the prevention of accidents was the utilization of appropriate personnel selection procedures designed to identify and eliminate those applicants who would tend to be accident-prone under virtually all circumstances. The most recent evidence, however, supports the contention that an individual's liability to accidents is highly specific. The fact that he is accident-prone under a given set of circum-

---

[17] A. Mintz and M. L. Blum, "A Reexamination of the Accident Proneness Concept," *Journal of Applied Psychology*, Vol. XXXIII (1949), p. 196.

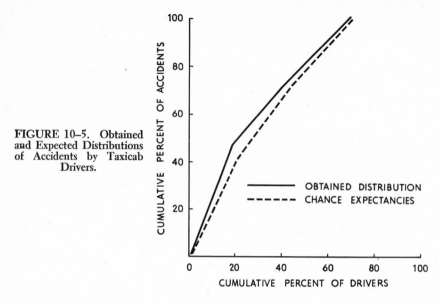

FIGURE 10–5. Obtained and Expected Distributions of Accidents by Taxicab Drivers.

stances does not mean that he will be accident-prone under other circumstances.

Thus, the focus of activity in the area of industrial safety has changed from that of a fundamental emphasis upon the identification of potential accident victims to a multidimensional approach emphasizing accident prevention.

ACCIDENT PREVENTION

An industrial safety program must contain at least three elements in order to be of maximum effectiveness. Such a program must include provisions for (1) the identification and correction of unsafe working practices and conditions; (2) the specification of employee characteristics required for safe performance on certain jobs, and the consequent implementation of these specifications by means of appropriate selection procedures; and (3) a continuing program of pre-service and in-service training.

Eliminating Unsafe Practices and Environmental Conditions

Certain environmental conditions which are potential sources of accidents are controlled by state regulations of various kinds. The placement of fire extinguishers and mandatory inspections of elevators and other moving equipment are illustrative of this kind of control. Ultimately, however, the responsibility for identifying and eliminating unsafe work practices rests with management and with every employee. It is management's responsibility to arrange the physical working environment in such a way that it provides adequate ventilation, illumination and the safest possible equipment. Management must arrange also to staff and equip a maintenance department adequate to the task of keeping the plant and its equipment in excellent working order. The fact that maintenance was too overworked to repair a defective rung on a ladder is small consolation to the painter who falls when the rung gives way.

The entire burden of accident prevention cannot, however, be placed upon management alone. Each employee must assume responsibility for reporting defective equipment or unsafe practices. In addition, every worker must appreciate and implement his own personal stake in a safe environment by observing certain rudimentary principles of industrial housekeeping, including mopping floors to prevent the accumulation of water or grease, piling materials properly, and removing loose objects from floors, stairs, and platforms.

There is some evidence for the fact that the psychological environment in which work is performed may be as important a consideration in accident prevention as is the physical environment. A comparison between employees in factory departments who had variable safety records indicated that accidents tended to occur with the greatest frequency in those departments with the lowest intracompany transfer mobility rates and the least promotion possibility for the typical employee. These factors are interpreted as symptomatic of an unwholesome psychological work environment. The lack of intracompany mobility and of promotional opportunities may lead to the development of attitudes of indifference toward the work. A more favorable psychological climate can provide incentives which act to raise the general level of alertness to potential hazards and to promote a desire to cooperate with safety personnel.[18]

Appropriate Personnel Selection Procedures

A comprehensive job analysis leading to an adequate set of worker specifications can quite often suggest certain of the physical or personal employee characteristics which are associated with accidents.

---

[18] W. A. Kerr, "Accident Proneness of Factory Departments," *Journal of Applied Psychology*, Vol. XXXIV (1950), pp. 167–70.

Some of these kinds of characteristics, like defective vision or health, are self-evident. Others are a little more obscure but may nevertheless be of considerable importance. It has been suggested, for example, that accidents in certain kinds of activities are especially likely when the employee's perceptual speed is slow in relation to his motor speed.[19] Since both of these factors appear to represent inherited capacities or limitations, and are not amenable to training, they can be controlled only by the utilization of appropriate selection procedures.

Training

The discussion, earlier in this chapter, of the causes of accidents indicated that the majority of accidents are attributable to "faulty attitude." Although this is a rather vague classification, it implies that the utilization of selection procedures and the modification of the working environment can, at best, prevent only a relatively small proportion of industrial accidents. The most fundamental cause of accidents appears to be attitudinal in nature. Consequently, workers, and supervisors must be taught to be safety-minded.

Such safety-mindedness does not always accompany the acquisition of skill or knowledge about equipment operation. Most persons learn how to drive an automobile, for example, with relatively little difficulty. An attitude of maturity in its operation, however, is quite a different matter as shown by the comparison in Table 10–3 between the violations recorded for samples of accident-free and accident-repeater drivers.

Virtually all of the accumulated evidence about automobile accidents indicates that the safe driver is one who is skillful, knows the limitations of his equipment, and has a high degree of social awareness, including consideration for others. Safe drivers are neither resentful of authority, nor do they regard the automobile as a tool for the extension of their own power. The National Safety Council's admonition that we reveal a good deal about our level of maturity by the way in which we drive is based upon solid evidence. It is likely that the relatively low proportion of accidents among drivers who are trained in a high school driver-training program can be attributed to the fact that such training emphasizes the acquisition of appropriate attitudes as well as of driving skills.

[19] C. A. Drake, "Accident Proneness: A Hypothesis," *Character and Personality*, Vol. VIII (1940), pp. 335–41.

Since accident prevention is largely dependent upon the development of appropriate attitudes, industrial safety requires a continuing program designed to alert all personnel to the potential sources of accidents and to reinforce safe practices. The safety program

TABLE 10–3

Motor Vehicle Violations Recorded for Driver Samples

	Number of Drivers	
	Accident Free (N = 59)	Accident Repeater (N = 88)
Minor Offenses		
Leaving vehicle running and unattended...............	1	1
Driving within 8 feet of streetcar stopped for passengers....	7	20
Not reasonably right for vehicle coming from opposite direction..	4	15
Not keeping to right half of road when view is obstructed..	2	5
Crossing throughway without stopping................	7	16
Failure to obey traffic signal.........................	1	11
Speeding...24		50
Left of streetcar....................................	0	2
Violation of traffic rules.............................	6	8
Mechanical defect...................................	0	1
Without proper lights...............................	1	5
Without proper brakes..............................	0	2
Without proper muffler..............................	0	1
No vehicle inspection sticker........................	4	19
Improper operation.................................	5	7
Negligent collision..................................	3	5
Serious Offenses		
Operating under influence of liquor...................	8	13
Operating so as to endanger lives and safety...........	8	15
Going away after injury to property..................	1	7
Going away after injury to persons...................	0	1
Operating after license suspension...................	0	7
Operating without proper registration................	0	10
Operating without being properly licensed.............	4	9
Violation of compulsory insurance law................	0	6
Operating without authority.........................	0	4

Source: R. A. McFarland and A. L. Moseley, *Human Factors in Highway Transport Safety* (Cambridge, Mass.: Harvard University Press, 1954).

must make provision for the systematic study of accident reports and regular inspections to detect unsafe procedures. The findings from such reports and inspections provide a firm base for the development of safety training programs.

Training of foremen relative to accident prevention has been shown to be highly effective. (See Figure 10–6.) The foreman, after all, is the person who is in the best possible position to see to it that safety precautions are observed.

The training of foremen alone, however, is not sufficient. It is important, also, that a continuing program of in-service training be directed toward the workers. Such a program typically consists of several elements, all of which are designed to impress constantly the matter of industrial safety upon the individual employee. Publicity

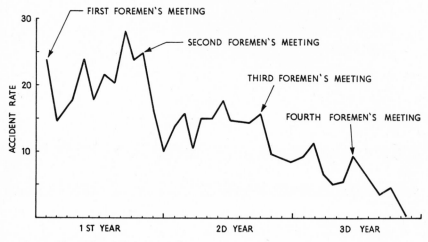

Source: Metropolitan Life Insurance Co.

FIGURE 10–6. Monthly Accident Frequency When Foremen Are Trained.

including safety bulletins, payroll envelope inserts, charts, displays, and articles in the house organ can be highly effective in this regard. It is difficult to remain callous to the kind of evidence contained in the bulletin shown in Figure 10–7, for example. Other devices for encouraging safe work practices include the conduct of contests and the provision of awards to personnel or departments with outstanding safety records.

These apparently simple devices should not be dismissed lightly. The data on the effectiveness of organized safety programs are extremely impressive. Proctor and Gamble, for example, was able to reduce the frequency of disabling injuries from 36 per million man-hours in 1930 to 1 per million man-hours in 1955 by means of a program in which everyone was encouraged to "think" and "work" safety.[20] This kind of record is quite typical. The essence of success-

[20] J. M. Ewell, *Safety Bulletin* (Cincinnati, Ohio: Proctor and Gamble, January, 1956).

WHAT HAPPENED?

NEAR-ACCIDENT REPORT — INDIANA HARBOR WORKS

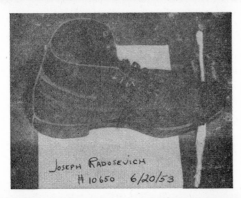

Joseph Radosevich
10650 6/20/53

Joe Radosevich, #10650, missed losing his big toe by 55/1000th of an inch. He and another man were using a dolly bar to loosen a work roll. Joe lost his balance and the dolly bar went through his shoe, as shown in the picture.

HOW INJURY WAS PREVENTED

The dolly bar came within 55/1000th of an inch of Joe's big toe. This is the thickness of the safety cap in his shoe. The steel bar went between the leather and the safety cap. Wearing of safety shoes saved a toe or more for Joe.

76" Hot Strip Mechanical
Bulletin #35
July 1953

 Issued by . . . SAFETY DEPARTMENT

FIGURE 10–7. "What Happened?" A Near-Accident Report.

ful safety training is the philosophy underlying the program rather than the specific methods whereby the program is implemented. Some companies with successful programs favor contests, others favor bulletin bombardments, and still others lean toward the use of the house organ for this purpose. All programs that work, however, are directed toward the fundamental objective of creating an attitude of pride in individual and company safety records, and of consideration and respect for one's fellow employees.

SUMMARY

The majority of accidents are attributable to three factors: (1) defective working environment; (2) human limitations in the operation of equipment; and (3) improper worker attitudes relative to safety.

The role of the physical environment, including such factors as illumination, ventilation, and equipment malfunction, has been the subject of considerable study by engineers and psychologists. Although there is still room for further improvements in this area, it cannot be regarded any longer as a primary cause of accidents. The more fundamental problem in accident prevention is a human one and requires the application of appropriate selection and training procedures.

Efforts to identify a personality type associated with high accident liability have not been outstandingly successful. There is some evidence that the accident-repeater tends to be emotionally immature, somewhat hostile, and socially irresponsible. This pattern is not sufficiently consistent, however, to support the principle of accident proneness as the basic factor underlying accidents.

The importance of accident-proneness has quite often been overstated because of misinterpretations of studies, indicating that a relatively small percentage of employees have a relatively large proportion of the accidents. The proper application of chance expectancies to observed distributions of accident frequency leads to the conclusion that accident-proneness accounts for about 20 to 40 percent of the total accident variance. Thus, although of some consequence, this factor must be placed in proper perspective.

The most satisfactory approach to industrial safety involves the development of a comprehensive program of pre-service training and in-service education relative to accident prevention. Such a program must place a continuing emphasis upon the study of the causes of accidents and near-accidents, the identification and correction of unsafe working procedures, and the development of an employee attitude best described as "safety-mindedness."

Merit Rating

11

The three preceding chapters have discussed various factors affecting worker efficiency. We made frequent reference throughout these chapters to such criteria of worker efficiency as output, spoilage, absenteeism, turnover, and accident rate.

The present chapter discusses another aspect of worker evaluation: procedures designed to summarize and systematize *subjectively* held opinions about employees. The purpose of merit rating is to distinguish between levels of efficiency of employees on a given job or within a particular job classification. These ratings are used as a basis for ordering workers along subjective continua of relative efficiency or trait possession.

APPLICATIONS OF MERIT RATINGS

The element of subjectivity is at once the peculiar weakness and strength of rating techniques. Rating procedures tend to be much less reliable than psychological tests or objective performance criteria. Thus, if a supervisor wished to obtain a meaningful index of efficiency for factory assemblers, he might do better to utilize an output measure involving a count of production per unit of time adjusted for spoilage, than to trust his personal opinion about employee efficiency.

There are circumstances, however, when a reliable criterion measure is not available. The decision must be made, in such instances, either to measure with a relatively subjective device or to forego measurement entirely. What can the office supervisor count, for example, when she wishes to appraise the overall efficiency of a statistical clerk in her section? Similarly, what objective measures can be applied to assessing the efficiency of office receptionists or Army officers? The diversity and nature of tasks performed by such workers prevents their assessment by objective indicators. Rating procedures must, of necessity, be used to provide criteria of performance.

Even without a proliferation of examples showing the need for subjective assessment in industry, it is apparent that merit ratings have a wide range of possible applications.

Wages

Since it is generally assumed that efficiency ought to be rewarded financially, merit ratings may be used as a partial determinant of wages. This use of merit ratings supplements, but does not vitiate, periodic wage increments based upon such things as seniority or changes in the cost-of-living index. Most employees want to feel that their own personal efforts are recognized and rewarded by management. A lockstep wage system in which all employees on a particular job or in a particular level are paid essentially the same wage reduces individual initiative.

Promotions

The identification of employees who ought to be advanced to a supervisory position or to a higher job classification is a management problem of considerable significance. Union contracts often specify consideration of seniority as a criterion for promotion. However, prolonged experience does not, by itself, guarantee the employee's readiness for a more responsible position. The most experienced welder in the world may be totally unqualified for promotion to a position in which he is required to direct the activities of other welders.

Most union contracts recognize this fact and specify that seniority should be the deciding factor in promotion only when such things as skill and the job proficiency of the eligible employees are equal. Merit rating can be helpful in deciding whether the applicants for promotion are equally qualified on grounds other than seniority. These ratings must, where appropriate, be supplemented by consideration of factors like ability as measured by psychological tests, age, physical health, and formal education.

Layoffs

The use of information from merit ratings during periods when personnel must be dismissed, either temporarily or permanently, parallels its use for employee promotions. If the labor force must be reduced, management benefits most by retaining only those employees who have demonstrated a satisfactory level of proficiency. Although seniority must be considered during layoffs, some union contracts recognize management's prerogative to weight skill and ability more heavily than mere tenure on the job.

Employee Transfer

Management has two alternatives in the case of dissatisfied or inefficient personnel. Such employees may either be dismissed or transferred to another job within the organization. If a transfer is to be effective, the employee must be moved to a job which is more congruent with his abilities and hence more conducive to job satisfaction. Merit ratings may reveal certain of the worker's strengths that can be utilized more effectively in another position within the company.

Employee transfers sometimes are necessitated by the creation of new positions within the company or by the development of critical vacancies on other jobs or in other departments. Screening by management of all employees in a given grade or classification may be desirable under these circumstances in order to identify persons who have the requisite skills and abilities to fill these positions. Merit ratings can help management match present personnel with positions requiring transferees.

Knowledge of Progress

Most of us are interested in knowing how our supervisor appraises our performance. A student, for example, is understandably distressed if he attends an entire course believing that he is doing satisfactory work only to learn, after the final examination, that he has failed the course. Similarly, employees cannot be expected to perform at maximum efficiency, and high plant morale cannot be maintained, unless the workers are systematically informed about their supervisors' opinions. In the absence of knowledge of progress or standing, the employees may feel considerable tension disruptive of industrial efficiency. The fact that merit ratings are performed and the results discussed with individual employees can do much to quell unfounded rumors of dismissal or transfer. Furthermore, a wisely conducted systematic program of employee appraisal injects the very important element of personal recognition into the industrial situation.

Diagnostic Applications

The use of merit ratings for diagnostic purposes is closely related to their use for informing workers about their supervisors' perceptions of them. The company stands to benefit whenever an employee is made aware of his own particular strengths and weaknesses in a constructive manner. Tactful criticism can alert the employee to previously unrecognized deficiencies. Unfortunately, it is very difficult to implement this potential use of merit ratings. When it is attempted, its value is dependent upon the skill and understanding displayed by the supervisor.

When merit ratings for an entire unit, section, or department are collated, the summary may occasionally reveal a rather prevalent area of employee deficiency. Entire groups of workers responsible for handling small and delicate subassemblies, for example, may receive low ratings on such an important characteristic as *carefulness*. In this instance, the prevalence of low ratings might suggest modifications in the training program for such employees. Thus, it may be advisable to institute a program of in-service training concerning the extent, type, and consequences of damage caused by improper handling of the subassemblies. The training program for newly hired employees would, of course, also have to be bolstered in this regard.

Merit Ratings as Validation Criteria

You will recall that validation is the most critical phase in the construction of tests or batteries for personnel selection and placement. Management must have adequate assurance that its selection procedures do, in reality, lead to the rejection of applicants for whom the probability of unsuccessful job performance is high.

The usual procedure in validating a test is to try it out on the present group of employees and to compare the test performance with some criterion of employee efficiency. A better procedure requires the administration of the test to applicants, all of whom are hired, and the correlation of test scores with a criterion measure subsequently obtained.

In either case, the validation procedure rests upon the availability of some criterion of employee efficiency. Supervisory judgments, in the form of merit ratings, may provide at least a partial criterion for this purpose.

PRELIMINARY PLANNING

Regardless of its objectives, a merit rating program cannot be instituted within a company without considerable preliminary planning. Decisions must be made about who is to rate and be rated, what traits to evaluate, when and how often ratings will be made, and the procedures for making the ratings and feeding back the results to the ratees.

Many employees and employee organizations are strenuously opposed to merit rating, particularly when used for the purposes of wage and promotional determination. Hence, preliminary decisions about the mechanics of a merit rating program must be accompanied by a concerted effort to "sell" the program, both to the prospective ratees and raters. The specific way in which the program is sold will vary with the particular situation encountered in a given company. As generalizations, the following points have been suggested as helpful:

1. Merit ratings should be sold first at the top levels of supervision. The lower supervisory levels, comprised of the majority of raters, should be approached only after the top levels have endorsed the program.
2. The raters ought to be involved as early as possible in developing the rating procedure. Such participation encourages identification with the program and its success.
3. Delegations of raters might be sent to other companies to investigate their rating programs and report back to a meeting of all supervisors.
4. The program should not be started prematurely: that is, until the groundwork has been properly laid.[1]

MERIT RATING PROCEDURES

All of us constantly evaluate the persons with whom we come in contact. We form first impressions often based upon physical appearance, dress, personal mannerisms, and speech. Subsequent contacts may either reinforce our original impression or cause us to change it. In any event, we continually appraise others and are, in turn, ourselves appraised, in a highly subjective and uncontrolled fashion.

Figure 11–1 shows a "horrible" but historically interesting example of unsystematic efficiency rating. It is difficult to ascertain the bases that were used by General Cass in forming his judgments, but it is apparent that he was responding to certain factors extraneous to "efficiency."

---

[1] R. Bittner, "Developing an Employee Merit Rating Procedure," *Personnel Psychology*, Vol. I (1948), pp. 403–32.

Sir: Lower Senaca Town
                                                        August 15, 1813

     I forward a list of the officers of the 27th Regt. of Infty. arranged agreeably to rank. An-
nexed thereto you will find all the observations I deem necessary to make.

                                                Respectfully,
                                                I am, Sir,
                                                Yo. Obt. Servt.

                                                Lewis Cass
                                                Brig. Gen.

                        ****

                        27th Infantry Regiment

Alex Denniston	- Lieut. Col., Comdg.	- A good natured man.
Clarkson Crolins	- First Major	- a good man, but no officer.
Jesse D. Wadsworth	- 2nd Major	- an excellent officer.
Captain Christian Martel) " Aaron T. Crane) " Benj. Wood) " Maxwell)		- all good officers.
" Shotwell		- a man of whom all unite in speaking ill. a knave despised by all.
" Allen Reynolds		- An officer of capacity, but imprudent and a man of most violent passions.
" Danl. Warren Porter		- Stranger but little known in the regiment.
First Lieut. Jas. Kerr) " " Thos. Darling)		- Merely good, nothing promising.
" " Wm. Perrin) " " Danl. Scott) " " Jas. I. Ryan) " " Robt. McElwrath)		- Low vulgar men, with exception of Perrin, Irish and from the meanest walks of life -- Possessing nothing of character of officers or gentlemen.
" " Robt P. Ross		- Willing enough - has much to learn -- with small capacity.
" " Hall		- Not joined the regiment.
2nd Lieut. Nicholas G. Carner		- a good officer but drinks hard and dis- graces himself and the service.
" " Stewart Elder		- An ignorant unoffending irishman.
" " McConkey		- Raised from the ranks, ignorant, vulgar and incompetent.

FIGURE 11–1. The First Recorded Efficiency Report in the Files of the
War Department.

    Fortunately, we have come a considerable distance in the applica-
tion of merit rating procedures during the past 150 years. Rather
than permitting the rater to use his own idiosyncratic standards of
judgment, the present application of merit rating attempts to impose
a degree of uniformity on these standards. To the extent that rating
procedures are successful in accomplishing this end, the rater is
provided with a yardstick for appraisal that is appropriate to the

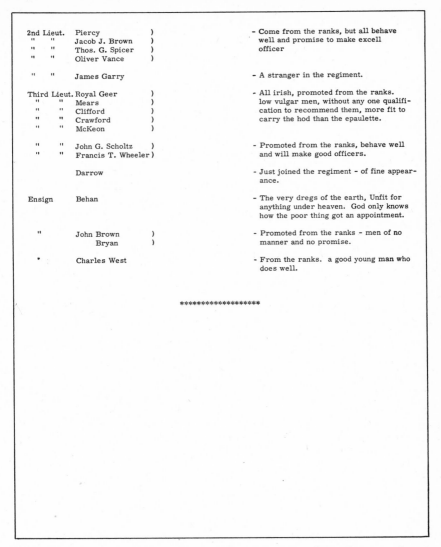

2nd Lieut.	Piercy)	- Come from the ranks, but all behave
" "	Jacob J. Brown)	well and promise to make excell
" "	Thos. G. Spicer)	officer
" "	Oliver Vance)	
" "	James Garry	- A stranger in the regiment.
Third Lieut.	Royal Geer)	- All irish, promoted from the ranks.
" "	Mears)	low vulgar men, without any one qualifi-
" "	Clifford)	cation to recommend them, more fit to
" "	Crawford)	carry the hod than the epaulette.
" "	McKeon)	
" "	John G. Scholtz)	- Promoted from the ranks, behave well
" "	Francis T. Wheeler)	and will make good officers.
	Darrow	- Just joined the regiment - of fine appear-ance.
Ensign	Behan	- The very dregs of the earth, Unfit for anything under heaven. God only knows how the poor thing got an appointment.
"	John Brown)	- Promoted from the ranks - men of no
	Bryan)	manner and no promise.
"	Charles West	- From the ranks. a good young man who does well.

****

particular characteristics he is attempting to describe. In short, effective merit rating procedures encourage an increased degree of objectivity, reliability, and validity in appraising human behavior.

The Ranking Method

The rater using this technique merely orders the ratees from best to worst, generally assigning a rank of 1 to the person he judges to be highest or best, a rank of 2 to the second best, and so on. The method is a simple one, and may be applied either by assigning "man-as-a-whole" ratings or "trait" ratings. In the former case, the employee is assigned a rank on the basis of the supervisor's overall impression about his efficiency. Ratings of traits, on the other hand, may require the supervisor to rank his employees on several specific characteristics like "cooperativeness," "initiative," or "versatility." Such trait ratings are sometimes averaged to yield a composite index of the supervisor's opinions.

Appraisal of the Ranking Method. The ranking method is susceptible to two deficiencies that may have deleterious effects upon the validity of the resultant information: (1) the hair splitting necessitated by differentiating between adjacent ranks in the middle of the continuum, and (2) the fallacious appearance of equal intervals along a scale of ranks. Thus, if 50 employees are to be ranked, the supervisor very likely will experience difficulty in differentiating between the one who should be ranked 23 and the one who should be ranked 24. Furthermore, it is unlikely that the magnitude of the difference between employees ranked 2 and 3 is of the same order as the difference between the employees ranked 26 and 27, even though only one rank separates each of these pairs.

Certain procedures for minimizing these deficiencies have been suggested. It often is desirable, for instance, to differentiate ranks only for persons in the upper and lower quarter of the total group, assigning a common middle rank to the remaining 50 percent of the group. This modification of the ranking procedure obviates the necessity for making impossibly fine discriminations between persons in the middle of the range.

It should be apparent, however, that the ranking method is a crude one. Its usefulness is limited to situations in which relatively few employees are to be rated. Furthermore, it is applicable only when merit rating is intended to order employees from best to worst without providing an indication of *how much* better or worse one employee is than another.

Paired Comparisons Method

This procedure for making and summarizing judgments has numerous psychological applications. Fundamentally, the procedure requires the evaluator to compare two objects or events and to judge which is the heavier, rounder, sharper, louder, and so on. The paired comparisons method has enjoyed extensive use in studies of sensation and perception.

The application of the paired comparisons method to merit rating leads to a certain degree of systematization in the assignment of ranks to employees.[2] Every employee to be rated is compared with every other employee, and the rater judges which member of the pair is the better. The supervisor generally predicates this judgment upon his overall impression of the employees' efficiency, but the method may be used also in a more analytical fashion by requiring the rater to consider specific traits one at a time.

To illustrate this procedure, let us assume that five employees (designated A, B, C, D, E) are to be rated relative to "overall performance." The supervisor would compare each employee with every other employee and check the name of the member of each pair judged to be superior. The comparisons required, and a hypothetical set of judgments are shown below.

A with B✓	✓B with C	✓C with D	D with E✓
A with C✓	✓B with D	C with E✓	
✓A with D	✓B with E		
A with E✓			

It is a rather simple matter to transmute these judgments to ranks for the purpose of summary. In the illustration above, the best worker is judged to be B, the second best is E, and so on. Thus, the resultant rank order for these employees would be $B = 1$, $E = 2$, $C = 3$, $A = 4$, and $D = 5$.

Appraisal of the Paired Comparisons Method. The fundamental advantage of this method over the ranking procedure is that it simplifies the kind of judgment required of the rater. Instead of necessitating simultaneous consideration of all members of the group, the paired comparisons method narrows the field for consideration by the supervisor to just two workers at a time.

A very important practical objection to the procedure, however, is that it is quite unwieldy. The number of pairs of employees to be considered is given by the general formula $N(N-1)/2$, where N is the number of workers included in the evaluation. Thus, if a supervisor applies the paired comparisons method to 20 employees, he must make 20 (19)/2 or 190 comparisons. It is not surprising that

---

[2] C. H. Lawshe, Jr., N. C. Kephart, and E. J. McCormick, "The paired Comparisons Technique for Rating Performance of Industrial Employees," *Journal of Applied Psychology*, Vol. XXXIII (1949), pp. 69–77.

the use of this procedure is generally limited to assignment of man-as-a-whole ratings rather than analytical or trait ratings. The latter application in a 20-man department would, of course, require the supervisor to make 190 comparisons for each of the several traits or dimensions of behavior being appraised.

Man-to-Man Rating

Although this procedure is no longer used very extensively, it is of interest both from an historical standpoint and because it further clarifies some of the difficulties experienced in attempts to objectify merit ratings.

With man-to-man ratings subjective judgments are recorded on a scale consisting of something like equal units. In this respect the procedure is superior to techniques converting judgments to ranks. Unfortunately, however, the man-to-man rating method has some unique deficiencies of its own that diminish its value considerably.

The procedure can be easily illustrated by assuming that you are required for some reason to evaluate the teaching effectiveness of each of your present instructors. Once general agreement is reached on a definition of "teaching effectiveness," you would proceed to establish and differentiate between several levels (generally five) of teaching effectiveness. These levels might be identified as follows:

1. The very best college teacher you have ever known.
2. A good college teacher.
3. An average or run-of-the-mill college teacher.
4. A poor college teacher.
5. The worst college teacher you have ever known.

Next to each of these descriptive levels, write in the name of a particular teacher. In doing this, you are to draw from the entire pool of college teachers you have known, selecting one as typical of each level. The five names you have written constitute a kind of master scale which can serve as a yardstick for evaluating the teachers you have during the present term. You need simply compare each of the teachers you are rating with the five teachers in your master scale, and decide where, on the master scale, he fits. You can assign the ratee the corresponding classification level (1, 2, 3, 4, 5), or you can convert these levels to points (for example, 15 points for level 1, 12 points for level 2, and so on). In any event, the master scale provides you with a standard for ordering your present teachers along a continuum of effectiveness.

The procedure, as we have illustrated it, involved an overall efficiency rating. It would, however, be perfectly possible to use the method in similar fashion to provide ratings of particular traits or specific characteristics. One of the earliest applications of man-to-man rating, for example, required that U.S. Army officers and prospective officers be rated separately in this manner on physical qualities, intelligence, leadership, personal qualities, and general value to the service. A composite rating was derived by adding the weights received by a particular ratee for each of these five characteristics.[3]

Appraisal of Man-to-Man Rating. The primary objection to this procedure is that although the scheme helps to objectify supervisory judgments, it does so in a way that prevents comparisons between the ratings assigned by different raters. To clarify this point, let us return to the earlier illustration in which you were rating college teachers. If you compare the master scale that you developed with the master scales developed by any of your classmates, you will undoubtedly find some startling discrepancies. The teacher that you have named as typical of level 2 of your master scale, for example, may not appear at all on your classmate's scale; or, if he does appear, he may have been cited as typifying a level either above or below level 2. Since the master scales from which various raters operate are not comparable, the resultant ratings cannot be collated.

The reasons for the lack of uniformity in the master scales constructed by different raters are simple to comprehend. First, every rater has his own unique perception of what constitutes a high, intermediate, or low level of almost any kind of human behavior. These differential perceptions may lead him to interpret the definitions of the various levels for the master scale differently from the interpretations made by some other rater.

Secondly, all raters do not share a common base of experience from which to identify persons for inclusion in their master scale. Just as you have received instruction from a different set of teachers than any of your classmates, industrial supervisors have each been exposed to different sets of workers. This experiential factor causes some supervisors to be acquainted with workers who are either markedly superior or inferior to those known by other supervisors.

---

[3] Committee on Classification of Personnel, Adjutant General's Department, *Personnel Manual* (Washington, D.C.: U.S. Government Printing Office, 1919).

As a result, the master scales constructed by different supervisors may differ considerably in the amount of "top" or "bottom" contained in them.

Graphic Rating Scales

This approach to merit rating is very widely used in one form or another. The procedure for constructing graphic rating scales requires that levels or degrees of trait possession be established and defined as unambiguously as possible.

There are so many variations of this procedure now in use that it is possible only to indicate something of the diversity of graphic formats. These formats can be conveniently grouped into two classes: continuous scales and discontinuous scales. *Continuous scales* require the supervisor to inspect a rating continuum and to indicate his evaluation of the employee by making a mark somewhere along that continuum. *Discontinuous scales* require the rater to consider only selected points on the rating continuum. A few illustrations of each type of format are shown in Table 11–1.

Appraisal of Graphic Rating. All rating procedures, including graphic scales, have certain deficiencies. In spite of these deficiencies, the graphic scale approach to rating has much to recommend it. Its use entails consideration of scale units that can be made more or less comparable across raters if the supervisors are adequately trained. Furthermore, graphic rating scales are easily understood by all persons within the company.

A major source of unreliability in graphic ratings is halo effect. This, you will recall, is the tendency for a ratee to receive consistently high or low ratings as a result of generalization by the rater.

This phenomenon operates in many kinds of situations requiring subjective appraisal. We have already discussed its potential influence during job interviews (Chapter 4) and grading of subjective examinations (Chapter 5). Halo effects may operate in any kind of merit rating scheme including, but not limited to, graphic procedures. Hence, we will reserve a more extensive discussion of this source of unreliability for a later section in which we will consider the shortcomings of merit rating procedures in general.

The Weighted Checklist

It has been suggested that the Thurstone scaling procedure for measuring attitudes can be adapted to provide a scheme for merit

TABLE 11-1

ILLUSTRATIVE FORMATS FOR GRAPHIC SCALES REQUIRING RATINGS OF "DEPENDABILITY"

Instructions to the rater: Consider the manner and extent to which the employee is "dependable," using the definition given below, and place a check mark indicating your opinion at the appropriate point (or in the appropriate box) of the scale.

Dependability is evidenced by the following behaviors: (1) follows instructions, (2) completes job on time, (3) is punctual and regular in attendance, (4) does not require excessive supervision.

Illustrative Continuous Scales

0   5   10

A   F   K

Extremely
Dependable

About
Average

Extremely
Undependable

Illustrative Discontinuous Scales

In the highest 10% of workers.	In the next 20% of workers.	In the middle 50% of workers.	In the next 20% of workers.	In the lowest 10% of workers.
☐	☐	☐	☐	☐

Exceedingly dependable; follows instructions with only minimal supervision.	Generally dependable but sometimes needs supervision.	About average.	Usually undependable. Needs more than average supervision.	Exceedingly undependable, requires continual supervision.

rating.[4] This scaling procedure assigns differential weights to statements of opinion. The respondent's attitude is converted to a numerical value by averaging the weights of the statements with which he agrees (see Chapter 14).

A set of statements describing various employee behaviors can be prepared and each one weighted relative to employee efficiency by means of the Thurstone procedure. These statements can then be submitted to the supervisor in the form of a checklist with instructions to check the ones that are descriptive of the employee being rated. Since each of the statements carries a scale value, this checklist can be scored by averaging the weights of the descriptive statements checked by the supervisor.

This procedure has been utilized for obtaining merit ratings of salesmen. The scale underlying the assignment of weights to each descriptive statement was based upon a seven-point continuum ranging from a low weight of 10 to a maximum weight of 70. A few of the items included in the checklist are reproduced below:

Is weak on planning. (weighted 29)
Is a good worker. (weighted 46)
Is making exceptional progress. (weighted 69)[5]

Appraisal of the Weighted Checklist. A considerable amount of preliminary investigation is required to develop statements with the necessary properties: that is, low ambiguity and a spread of scale values. Hence, the development of a weighted checklist may be relatively costly.

Nevertheless weighted checklists have certain distinct advantages. The rater records his obervations of behavior instead of making judgments along sometimes ambiguous and often incomparable rating continua. Thus, as reported by Kuder and Richardson, weighted checklists probably have higher levels of reliability than the methods heretofore described.

Forced-Choice Ratings

This procedure for merit rating evolved, in the main, from research conducted for the military services during World War II. The forced-choice procedure was specifically designed to overcome a

---

[4] M. W. Richardson and G. F. Kuder, "Making a Rating Scale That Measures," *Personnel Journal,* Vol. XII (1933), pp. 36–40.

[5] *Ibid.*

major deficiency inherent in all of the other rating techniques: that is, the fact that the rater knows whether he is giving either a high or low rating. This kind of awareness permits the rater to slant his recorded judgment in any direction he chooses. The effects of personal biases and favoritism can be only partly eliminated from rating procedures by a training program for supervisors. The forced-choice procedure is an attempt to increase the objectivity of ratings by preventing the rater from knowing whether he is assigning a favorable or an unfavorable rating.

In its simplest form, a forced-choice format requires the rater to select the one statement from a pair that is either most or least descriptive of the person he is rating. A supervisor might, for example, be required to select the statement from each of the following pairs that he feels best describes the employee he is rating.

1. *a*) Is punctual.
   b) Is careful.

2. *a*) Hard worker.
   b) Cooperative worker.

Similarly, he may be required to select the least descriptive statements from pairs of undesirable behaviors like the following:

3. *a*) Is dishonest.
   b) Is disloyal.

4. *a*) Is overbearing.
   b) Is disinterested in his work.

Alternative arrangements for forced-choice items may consist of groupings of three or four statements with instructions to the rater to mark the one least descriptive and the one most descriptive statement from each triad or tetrad.

The key to the development of forced-choice scales is that the statements within any item are equally attractive or unattractive, but differ in discriminative power. In the preceding illustrations, for example, the two statements constituting each pair are grouped together partly because the results of a preliminary investigation have indicated that these statements have similar *preference values:* that is, raters tend to interpret these behaviors as being about equally desirable or undesirable. A second basis for pairing alternatives is that they have been demonstrated to have different *discriminative power:* that is, only one of the alternatives differentiates between efficient and inefficient employees. Each of the alternatives in a forced-choice scale is weighted in terms of its discriminative power, and the entire rating form can thus be scored by summing the weights of the statements marked by the supervisor.

The supervisor who deliberately attempts to overrate or underrate an employee is likely to find that it is very difficult to display intentional bias on a forced-choice scale. The format compels him to choose between alternatives that look equally attractive or unattractive; the rater does not, of course, know which of the alternatives contribute positively or negatively to the scale score. Thus, in theory at least, it would be quite possible for a supervisor to mark only desirable behaviors for a ratee without assigning a favorable rating to him.

Appraisal of the Forced-Choice Technique. The rationale underlying forced-choice procedures is rather ingenious. The available evidence supports the particular usefulness of this technique for developing personality inventories. Studies conducted by the Personnel Research Section of the Adjutant General's Office indicate also that the application of forced-choice procedures to merit rating tends to reduce halo and bias and to yield improved validity and reliability.[6]

In spite of these findings, forced-choice merit ratings have not been extensively used in industry. A primary reason for the reluctance to use this procedure is that the development of forced-choice scales is relatively time-consuming and costly.

Raters sometimes express objections to the procedure because it compels them to select a descriptive statement from a limited number of alternatives. The supervisor responding to such a scale sometimes feels that he is being forced to choose between alternatives, none of which are applicable. This kind of objection is a relatively superficial one. It can usually be overcome by care in pairing alternatives and training raters.

It has been suggested that one of the major limitations of forced-choice merit rating is its failure to provide the kind of information that can be used for diagnostic feedback to the employee.[7] This can

---

[6] D. E. Baier, "Reply to Travers' 'A Critical Review of the Validity and Rationale of the Forced-Choice Technique,'" *Psychological Bulletin,* Vol. XLVIII (1951), pp. 421–34.

[7] J. A. Patton and C. L. Littlefield, *Job Evaluation* (Homewood, Ill.: Richard D. Irwin, Inc., 1957), p. 306.

be a serious objection to the procedure if the rating is to be used for informing individual employees about their own particular strengths and weaknesses.

Forced-choice merit rating should not be regarded as a panacea. The primary advantages of the technique involve possible reductions in the influence of rater bias and halo. The operation of these undesirable factors can, however, be reduced also for the more usual and less expensive graphic rating procedures. Thus, it is appropriate to consider some of the major sources of unreliability in merit rating procedures, with particular reference to graphic scales, and some of the steps leading to improved reliability.

IMPROVING MERIT RATING PROCEDURES

Merit rating procedures are subjective and hence unreliable by the standards applied to psychological tests. The reliability of a composite rating derived for a 12-item scale completed by different raters, for example, was estimated at 0.55.[8] This value is far different from the reliability coefficients usually required for standardized tests, and suggests that different raters really use different subjective yardsticks for appraising human behavior. A fundamental problem, then, in improving merit rating procedures is to increase the uniformity with which subjective evaluations are made. To the extent that this is accomplished, the agreement between raters (reliability) will be increased, and the correlations between merit ratings and other industrial criteria will be improved. We will focus, in this section, upon the major sources of unreliability in merit rating and suggest the importance both of training raters and of modifying the techniques themselves to overcome this difficulty.

Halo Effect

You are well aware of the lasting consequences of first impressions because of the halo effect. We tend to generalize from our present experiences to our subsequent experiences. This kind of generalization may exert a pronounced effect upon assigned merit ratings. Thus, although a rating form may contain 10 or 15 separate scales, the supervisor may respond carefully only to the first one or two of

---

[8] J. Tiffin, *Industrial Psychology* (Englewood Cliffs, N.J.: Prentice-Hall, Inc., 1952), p. 345.

these, marking the remaining ones on the basis of the impressions he has recorded earlier.

Reversal of the Poles.   One solution to this problem is to random-ize the location of the favorable and unfavorable ends of each scale. By designating the left end of some scales as the "high" or "favor-able" pole, and of others as the "low" or "unfavorable" pole, the rater is at least compelled to examine each scale carefully enough to determine which end is favorable.

Horizontal Rating.   Although reversal of the poles probably re-duces the operation of halo effects somewhat, it is not as effective as horizontal rating. Horizontal rating requires that all employees be rated on a single trait or characteristic at a time.[9] Thus, if employees were to be rated on 10 different graphic scales, the supervisor would be asked to rate every one of the employees on the first scale before moving on to the subsequent ones. This procedure is superior to "vertical rating" in which all trait ratings are assigned in immediate succession to one employee, then to a second employee, and so on.

Systematic Bias

Specific raters sometimes exhibit consistently favorable or un-favorable biases in appraising the performance of virtually all of their subordinates. Such a predilection for using either the high or the low end of the rating continuum defeats the fundamental pur-pose of merit rating by making it virtually impossible to differentiate between the ratees.

Forcing the Distribution.   If a relatively large number of persons are to be rated by a particular supervisor, we might expect the distribution of the ratings he assigns to approximate a normal dis-tribution. If a five-point graphic scale is used, for example, rather few employees ought to be assigned ratings at either the top or bottom pole. Assuming a perfectly normal distribution, we would anticipate that about 7 percent would receive ratings at each of the poles, 38 percent in the middle or "average" category, and 24 per-cent in each of the remaining categories.

Supervisors can be forced to adhere to a normal distribution when making their ratings. Such forcing will, of course, overcome any systematic rating bias that the supervisor may have. There is the danger, however, that forced distributions of ratings may actually

---

[9] S. N. Stevens and E. F. Wonderlic, "An Effective Revision of the Rating Tech-nique," *Personnel Journal*, Vol. XIII (1934), pp. 125–34.

produce some unfairly harsh appraisals when the department as a whole is better than average. Similarly, a forced distribution will produce a number of overly lenient ratings in departments with a large number of inefficient employees.

The dilemma of forced distributions for merit ratings is quite analogous to "curved" grades. It is advisable to make a study of the legitimacy of requiring a normal distribution before deciding to force either merit ratings or course grades to such a distribution. How can we know whether or not it is legitimate to impose a normal distribution upon merit ratings? We would have to examine both the personnel selection program and the training program before answering this question. If employees were carefully selected through the application of rather rigorous standards, and if they were carefully trained, it would be erroneous to require the supervisor's appraisals of their performance to conform to a normal distribution. The anticipated distribution, under these circumstances, should contain a relatively large proportion of favorable ratings. Conversely, if the selection and training programs were relatively weak, we should anticipate a skew in the opposite direction.

Ambiguity in the Scale

This is one of the most obvious sources of unreliability in merit rating. If the trait descriptions or guideposts along the continuum are ambiguous, various raters cannot possibly respond to them uniformly. A trait designation like "cooperativeness," for example, may mean quite different things to different raters. Hence, it is imperative that the characteristics to be rated be defined with extreme care, and that the raters themselves be trained to interpret these definitions in the intended manner.

Ratings Based upon Inadequate Information

Supervisors often feel compelled to assign ratings even though they have not had an adequate opportunity to observe the employee relative to the particular characteristic in question. In many instances, this feeling probably reflects the supervisor's own insecurity. He may be concerned lest an admission that he is not sufficiently familiar with one of his subordinates be interpreted by management as an indication of his inadequacy as a supervisor.

Ratings made on the basis of inadequate information are relatively valueless to management and may do considerable harm to the employee so rated. Thus, it is advisable for the rating scheme to embody a provision whereby the supervisor can refuse to rate any subordinate if he feels that he possesses insufficient or inadequate information to make a valid rating. This provision must be accompanied by a program of management education and supervisory training, however, if it is to work effectively. Management must not impose the impossible demand that supervisors know enough about every salient characteristic of every employee to rate him; supervisors must be informed about the deleterious effects of assigning ratings predicated upon inadequate information, and reassured that their unwillingness to rate under such circumstances will not reflect unfavorably upon them.

Ratings Reflecting Uncontrolled Factors

Assuming that the merit rating procedures have been developed to maximize their reliability and validity, and that the raters are carefully trained to make their ratings as objective and useful as possible, the interpretation of the ratings may be confounded by a variety of uncontrolled factors. The rater is required to appraise certain of the employee's behaviors. Unfortunately, this appraisal may reflect the influence of factors that really are unrelated to the dimensions supposedly under consideration. The supervisor may be unduly influenced, for example, by such things as the employee's job level or classification, the department within which he works, his age and seniority, and even by the employee's sex.

It is generally desirable, therefore, to interpret the merit ratings received by an employee in relation to those received by others in his own reference group: that is, other employees in similar departments, on similar jobs who are of about the same age, and so on.

SUMMARY

Merit ratings are designed to summarize and systematize subjectively held opinions about employees. They may supplement more objective measures of performance (like output records) or, on occasion, may provide the only feasible criterion of worker efficiency.

Data obtained from supervisors' ratings have a wide range of possible administrative applications in the areas of wages, promotions, layoffs, and transfers. In addition, feedback of information from merit ratings can provide employees with an indication of their job-related strengths and weaknesses. Finally, such ratings are often used as a criterion against which to validate selection and placement procedures.

Several different rating techniques, each with its own peculiar strengths and weaknesses, have been described in this chapter. The weighted checklist and the forced-choice approach to rating have special advantages, but these are often offset by the relatively high cost involved in the development of such scales.

The fundamental problem in improving rating procedures is to effect a higher level of reliability. Various sources of unreliability including halo effect, systematic bias, ambiguity, and others were discussed. It is imperative that the scales be properly structured and the raters trained in their use if the reliability of rating procedures is to approach satisfactory levels.

IV.

Organizational Management

Industrial management has responsibilities in many directions. There is, of course, its responsibility to the company, business, or stockholders to improve overall efficiency in order to increase profits. The reduction of all management or supervisory behavior to this level, and the attempted explanation of all industrial behavior in terms of the ledger and the balance sheet would, however, be a gross oversimplification. The responsibilities of management extend considerably beyond that of increasing the financial gains accruing to the company.

Management has a vital commitment to its employees. Workers are engaged in company activities for more than a third of their waking hours each week. Furthermore, as we have already indicated, work itself is an important aspect of life and contributes to man's sense of general well-being and feeling of personal worth. For this reason alone, and apart from any benefits that may be derived in terms of increased efficiency, industrial leadership has a responsibility to each employee to help him derive the maximum possible satisfaction from this important constituent of his life.

Finally, management must accept its responsibility to the community and to society. Large companies must consider, for example, their dependence upon higher education and basic research, and support these accordingly, if we are to maintain a superior level of technological and theoretical progress. Management must be aware also of the impact upon the community when plants are relocated or closed down, when sizable numbers of employees are laid off even temporarily, and when a breakdown in labor-management relations leads to a strike.

It is with an awareness of responsibilities like these that we approach the discussion of certain aspects of organizational management.

Job Evaluation

12 Job evaluation procedures are designed to assist management in establishing equitable rates of pay. Every employer, regardless of the size of his business or company, must make certain decisions about the salaries to be paid to his employees. The implementation of an equitable salary structure is important to the maintenance of job satisfaction and high morale. Thus, the wages paid by a company may have some bearing upon such critical factors as level and quality of production, employee turnover, and absenteeism.

COMPANY SIZE AND WAGE PRACTICES

The typical wage practice in small business organizations employing relatively few workers tends to be a simple one. The basic wage is often determined by the "going rate" for similar jobs in comparable businesses operating in the same general locale. Although this basic wage may be increased periodically in the case of employees whom management wishes to retain, the matter of wage determination in small business often rests upon the relationship between the available supply of workers and the demand exerted by competitive employers.

The salary structure within a company becomes increasingly complex as the industrial organization increases in size. This added complexity is due, in part, to the fact that a larger number of workers will be affected by any revision in salary policy. Furthermore, the direct relationship between wages and the supply and demand of workers breaks down in large organizations because of the unions' attempts to stabilize base wage levels. Such wage stabilization tends to prevent salary reduction when labor is in overabundant supply, and to inhibit the release of highly paid employees when cheaper labor becomes available.

Diversity of Jobs

Another difference between large and small companies contributing to the added complexity of the salary structure in larger
organizations is the relative diversity of the jobs performed in such
organizations. A small business may, for example, employ two or
three salesclerks, each of whom has essentially the same qualifications for his work and performs essentially similar tasks. The matter
of maintaining internally equitable wage scales is not a serious one
in this type of organization.

As companies become larger, however, the work performed by the
individual employees tends to become increasingly diverse. This
diversity of tasks, and the consequent diversity in experiential and
educational requirements for satisfactory job performance, creates
certain rather serious problems. To illustrate: what salaries should
be established within a given company for chemists on the research
staff, plumbers on the maintenance staff, and line personnel engaged in assembly? Certain of the jobs within almost any company
will require a high level of formal education or training, while others
may expose employees to unusual physical hazards or unpleasant
working conditions. It is imperative, if industrial harmony is to be
maintained, that salary schedules be established in a manner that
takes account of the unique requirements of each of the jobs within
the company.

RELATIONSHIP BETWEEN JOB EVALUATION
AND MERIT RATING

The primary function of job evaluation is to provide a systematic
study of all jobs within the company with a view toward establishing equitable salary ranges or pay rates. The assumption underlying
all job evaluation procedures is that it is possible to determine the
relative worth of the various jobs within a company, and to translate
job worth into a monetary value.

It is important to recognize that job evaluation is concerned with
the job or position rather than with the relative level of efficiency or
inefficiency of the individual workers filling this position. The
evaluative scheme makes it possible to consider every job in relation
to every other job, and to arrange the various jobs in some kind of
hierarchy of overall worth to the company. Thus, the results of a job

evaluation typically indicate a range of salaries for all employees filling a particular position.

The determination of the particular salary to be paid to an individual worker requires an analysis beyond the job evaluation itself. Let us assume that a job evaluation has been performed, leading to the establishment of a base hourly wage range for lathe operators between $1.80 and $2.10. What specific salary should be paid to Harry Oliphant who is a lathe operator in this particular company? Should he receive $1.80 an hour, $2.10 an hour, or some rate between these extremes?

The particular base wage paid to an individual employee is often determined by considering his seniority and his efficiency as an employee. Other things being equal, a newer and less experienced employee will be paid at a lower base rate than one who has been with the company for a period of time. Similarly, a less efficient employee will be paid less than a more efficient one. Although it is a relatively simple matter to determine seniority, the appraisal of employee efficiency can be a difficult matter. This appraisal often requires some kind of quantification of the supervisor's opinion about the employee in the form of a merit rating. Thus, job evaluation is an aid to determining the range of base salaries to be paid to employees filling a particular position; merit rating, on the other hand, may aid in determining the particular base rate within this range to be paid to each employee within a job classification.

Quite often the base rate, reflecting the results both of job evaluation and merit rating, is supplemented by incentive earnings based upon actual productivity in relation to some standard of productivity. This standard may be established by a motion and time study. The amount of additional payment for "overproduction" relative to the standard will reflect a variety of factors, including the results of labor-management negotiations on this matter as well as the outcomes of the job evaluation and merit rating procedures.

The present chapter discusses the techniques for assembling one of the fundamental kinds of information critical to the establishment of equitable rates of pay: that is, job evaluation. Merit rating procedures were considered in the last chapter. It is well to emphasize at the outset that job evaluation procedures are exceedingly subjective; they rest entirely upon the rather frail foundation of human judgment. The discussion that follows will call attention to some of the major pitfalls in these procedures and will describe certain techniques for reducing some of the undesirable consequences of their inherent subjectivity.

JOB EVALUATION IN PERSPECTIVE

Job evaluation has not been embraced wholeheartedly either by management or by the unions, although there has been a growing realization of its value, particularly since World War II. As is the case with many other techniques, job evaluation too often has been oversold by some of its well-meaning enthusiastic advocates. Its fundamental value inheres in the fact that it provides a systematic approach to the development of a wage yardstick applicable throughout the range of diverse jobs within a sizable company. It has value also in pegging wages for newly created positions, because the evaluative scheme provides a standard against which the value of a new position can be appraised. If the job evaluation is accepted by both management and employees, grievances about wages may be materially reduced. However, management and the union may have legitimate reservations about the desirability of performing a job evaluation.

Reservations by Management

Management's reluctance to engage in job evaluation is often explicable, in part, by lethargy and a reluctance to "rock the boat" of existing salary structure. In addition, complacency about the present salary scheme may make the cost of performing a job evaluation seem unduly high.

Reservations by Unions

Much union opposition to job evaluation is founded upon the suspicion that it will lead to a certain amount of wage-cutting. The union may be concerned, for example, about what will happen to the salaries of employees who are presently being "overpaid" in the light of the results of an evaluation. Furthermore, unions often are reluctant to embrace or endorse any procedure that appears to interfere with their prerogatives in collective bargaining.

The concerns expressed both by management and the unions are legitimate ones. Job evaluation cannot be sold to a company as a replacement for wage negotiation because, in fact, it cannot be substituted for such negotiation. Provision must be made in the evaluative scheme to protect the salaries of employees now on the job whose earnings exceed the standards established by the job evaluation. Finally, management must be sensitized to the deleterious effects of an inequitable wage structure upon job satisfaction and morale before it will be ready to accept and implement a company-wide job evaluation.

Job Evaluation Not a Panacea

Even when the performance of a job evaluation gains company-wide acceptance, the results of the evaluation must not be expected to resolve all industrial wage problems. Job evaluation procedures are founded upon subjective judgments which sometimes neglect consideration of a number of factors related to wage rate.

The fact that evaluative procedures do not resolve all wage problems is illustrated in the following case. A job requiring only a moderate amount of skills, training, and prior experience will generally show up in the evaluation as being of less worth to the company than one requiring a high level of professional or technical competence. This discrepancy will, of course, be translated into differential salary schedules for the two positions. It may be necessary, however, to deviate from the established wage plan for these jobs because of the supply of workers relative to the demand for their services. Relatively unskilled employees in a plant devoted to the separation of radioactive metals from the raw ore, for example, may have to be highly paid because of the unattractive working conditions to which they are subjected. Although the work itself does not require particularly valuable skills or abilities, the shortage of workers willing to undertake this activity may necessitate the payment of wages which are disproportionate to the job's experiential and skills requirements.

Another factor generally neglected by job evaluation schemes is the possibility for employees on particular jobs to advance within the company. Assume, for example, that a company has two positions which have very similar requirements and make similar demands upon the workers. Such positions would be assigned essentially similar base rates by the job evaluation. If, however, one of these jobs presented substantial opportunities for advancement within the company, while the other was regarded as a "dead-end" position, they would prove to be unequally attractive to employees. It might be necessary, under such circumstances, to adjust the base rate for the less attractive position.

PRELIMINARIES TO PERFORMING A JOB EVALUATION

It will be helpful, before considering the specific procedures for conducting a job evaluation, to discuss some of the general principles and approaches held in common by all of the procedures. Job evaluation can be a touchy area of management activity. Certain preliminaries to the institution of the evaluative program are critical to its acceptance by the employees.

Introducing the Job Evaluation

Considerable spadework must be done within the company to prepare both management and employees for the installation of a job evaluation plan. This preparatory groundwork prior to the actual conduct of the evaluation will require joint meetings of labor and management representatives directed toward the formulation and dissemination of a clear-cut policy statement concerning the way in which the evaluation is to be conducted, and the uses to be made of the findings. This statement of policy will vary somewhat from one company to another but should generally contain information of the type listed below.

1. *The Fundamental Objective of Job Evaluation and the Critical Assumption Underlying It.*   The objective, of course, is to appraise the relative worth of the jobs within the company. The underlying assumption is that the worth of a job, and hence the pay for it, should be a function of the requirements for satisfactory job performance.

2. *The Company's Stake in the Plan.*   The company, particularly top management, must make explicit its endorsement of the plan and its willingness to abide by the results of the evaluation. Furthermore, provisions must be made for periodic reappraisal and appropriate revision of wage policies.

3. *Labor's Stake in the Plan.*   The policy statement should define labor's role in the conduct of the job evaluation. Representatives of labor should, ideally, become sufficiently involved in the plan to function as effective partners along with management.

4. *The Effects of the Plan upon Individual Employees.* This section of the policy statement will be particularly critical to acceptance of the job evaluation plan and implementation of its findings. There must be a clear-cut agreement between management and labor on the following points, and the implications of this agreement must be understood by the employees.

a) The policy statement should contain assurance that although the job evaluation will establish maximum and minimum rate ranges for the job classifications, adequate provisions will be made also for rewarding both seniority and merit.

b) The employees now on the job must be assured that no worker's base rate will be reduced because of the results of the evaluation. If an employee is found to be overpaid, he may be transferred or promoted to a new position in conformance with his present salary, or else he will be retained on his present job at his current base rate.

c) If the results of the job evaluation indicate that an employee is being underpaid for the work he does, his salary will be adjusted upward.

d) The effect of the job evaluation will not be to reduce the general level of company rates below that currently being paid within the community and the industry in general.

5. *The Constituency of the Committee and the Nature of the Plan.* The policy statement should describe the procedures to be used in implementing the job evaluation plan, and specify the persons who are to be responsible for the conduct of the evaluation (that is, the committee).

The Job Evaluation Committee

The committee is the heart of any job evaluation scheme. It is the combined judgment of the members of this committee that will decide the relative worth of each job, and hence determine the appropriate rate schedules to be applied to it. A typical arrangement is to constitute the committee of company representatives, union, or labor representatives, and an outside consultant specializing in job evaluation procedures. Resource persons (for example, departmental supervisors) familiar with a particular job or a group of jobs can be consulted by the committee as it engages in deliberations about jobs within particular departments or sections. The entire committee must recognize and accept each other's stake in the evaluation. It cannot function well if it is loaded by members representing either management or labor, since satisfactory implementation of the job evaluation plan will require a truly cooperative endeavor by all of the committee members.

Regardless of the specific technique of job evaluation finally accepted by the committee, it must understand and accept the following assumptions about the relationship between work performed and the base rate justified by that work:

1. The salary schedule for a particular job should reflect the effort expended by employees and the nature of the work performed.

2. All jobs being evaluated can be reduced to certain elements (like Skill, Responsibility, and so on) which are held in common but to varying degrees.

3. The degree to which a job is characterized by these elements should be correlated with the salaries paid to employees on the job.

4. The results of the job evaluation should lead, ultimately, to the establishment of a maximum and minimum rate for every job. The establishment of such rate ranges recognizes the existence of individual differences in the efficiency with which the same job is performed by different employees, and makes it possible to provide additional rewards to particular employees deserving them. Thus, an equitable wage structure requires that job evaluation be supplemented by merit rating.[1]

The committee must be trained both in the conduct of the specific evaluative scheme they are going to use and in the fundamental intent of job evaluation in general. One of the most prevalent kinds of error unintentionally committed during the course of job evaluation can be attributed to halo effect. Unless the members of the committee are specifically trained to eliminate this factor, they will exhibit a tendency to appraise the job's worth in terms of the salary now being paid to employees on that job. Such a basis for judgment, of course, obviates the intent of the evaluation. The committee members must be trained, therefore, to discard their prior conceptions about particular jobs based upon present wage rate, and to approach the appraisal of every job with completely open minds.

The Job Description and Job Specification

The committee members must be provided with accurate and complete information about each of the jobs they are evaluating. It has already been suggested that the committee may wish to consult with departmental supervisors in order to clarify the requirements

---

[1] H. Moore, "Problems and Methods of Job Evaluation," *Journal of Consulting Psychology*, Vol. VIII (1944), pp. 90–99.

of particular jobs. The fundamental sources of information about each job included in the evaluation, however, are the job description and job specification. The former, you will recall from the discussion in Chapter 3, outlines the duties involved in the performance of the job; the latter specifies the worker requirements for satisfactory job performance. It is virtually impossible for any job evaluation plan to proceed satisfactorily if it is built upon sketchy or inaccurate job descriptions and specifications.

TECHNIQUES OF JOB EVALUATION

The purpose of job evaluation is to order or scale the jobs within the company along a continuum of overall worth. The translation of this rating of job worth into a monetary value cannot be undertaken until the entire job evaluation is completed. These two phases of wage determination, the job evaluation and the translation to base rates, are separated with good reason. The committee members can generally appraise jobs with less partiality when they are dealing with numerical values like points or ratings than when they are dealing with actual monetary values. Personal biases, intentional and otherwise, are somewhat less likely to influence a decision about whether a job is worth 300 or 320 points than they are to influence a decision about whether employees on the job ought to be started at a base rate of $1.60 or $1.70 an hour. Thus, the ensuing discussion of the techniques for performing a job evaluation makes only occasional reference to wages. The procedures for translating the numerical index of job worth derived from the evaluation to dollars and cents are discussed in a subsequent section.

Four basic methods of job evaluation are now in use: the Ranking method, Classification method, Factor Comparison method, and Points method.[2]

The Ranking Method

This is the simplest and poorest method for ordering jobs along a continuum of worth. The general procedure, without going into its many possible variations, is to require the committee members to rank the jobs under consideration in order from most to least important. Thus, if 30 jobs were included in the plan, the most im-

---

[2] L. C. Pigage and J. L. Tucker, *Job Evaluation*, University of Illinois Bulletin, Vol. XLIX, No. 36 (January, 1952), 43 pp.

portant job would be assigned a rank of 1, and the least important a rank of 30. This ranking may be accomplished by the committee as a whole engaging in a group discussion of each job, or it may be done independently by each committee member. In the latter case, the rankings by each member must be collated and the discrepancies arbitrated to arrive at a consensus of opinion about each job.

Appraisal of the Ranking Method. The ranking approach to job evaluation is subject to many kinds of error. Its usefulness, to the extent that it is at all useful, is limited to the situation in which relatively few jobs are to be evaluated. The primary reason for this limitation upon the usefulness of the Ranking method is that it is exceedingly difficult to differentiate between adjacent ranks in the middle of the continuum when a large number of jobs are being simultaneously evaluated. The differences between jobs relative to their overall worth requires considerable hair-splitting when the committee is attempting to decide, for example, which of 70 jobs ought to be assigned a rank of 31 and which deserves a rank of 32.

A further limitation of this procedure results from the fact that the committee is attempting to rank the jobs in terms of their *overall* worth, rather than on the basis of more specific critical elements like the skill or experiential requirements of the job. The necessity for making gross judgments about each job often leads the committee to the assignment of ranks based, at least in part, upon the salaries currently being paid, or upon the level of performance of the persons presently employed in these positions. The utilization of these factors, even as partial determinants of the assigned ranks, contradicts the intent of the job evaluation plan.

A final deficiency of the Ranking method is related to the fact that adjacent ranks are not spaced equidistantly along a scale. The actual difference in overall worth between the jobs ranked 3 and 4, for example, may be either considerably greater or less than the actual difference in worth between the jobs ranked 4 and 5. The absence of equal scale units along the rank continuum can create rather serious problems when the attempt is made to convert job ranks to monetary values.

The Classification Method

This procedure is also a very simple one and overcomes the necessity, sometimes present when the Ranking method is used, for making overly fine discriminations between jobs. The Classification method is rather widely used, particularly for Civil Service jobs.

The comittee using this method begins by establishing a master rating scale consisting of broad labor grades or job classifications. The number of classifications or grades is not of particular consequence as long as the number of levels is sufficient to permit the assignment of all jobs under consideration. To illustrate, The Classification Act of 1949 established 18 levels of Federal Civil Service positions in a General Schedule covering professional and scientific service, clerical, and administrative positions. The range of levels embodied within this classification is evident in Table 12–1.

TABLE 12–1

SELECTED FEDERAL GENERAL SCHEDULE CLASSIFICATION LEVELS

Grade GS-1 includes all classes of positions the duties of which are to perform, under immediate supervision, with little or no latitude for the exercise of independent judgment, (1) the simplest routine work in office, business, or fiscal operations, or (2) elementary work of a subordinate technical character in a professional, scientific, or technical field.

Grade GS-2 includes all classes of positions the duties of which are (1) to perform, under immediate supervision, with limited latitude for the exercise of independent judgment, routine work in office, business, or fiscal operations, or comparable subordinate technical work of limited scope in a professional, scientific, or technical field, requiring some training or experience, or (2) to perform other work of equal importance, difficulty, and responsibility, and requiring comparable qualifications.

Grade GS-8 includes all classes of positions the duties of which are (1) to perform, under general supervision, very difficult and responsible work along special technical or supervisor lines in office, business, or fiscal administration, requiring (*a*) considerable specialized or supervisory training and experience, (*b*) comprehensive and thorough working knowledge of a specialized and complex subject matter, procedure, or practice, or of the principles of the profession, art, or science involved, and (*c*) to a considerable extent the exercise of independent judgment; or (2) to perform other work of equal importance, difficulty, and responsibility, and requiring comparable qualifications.

Grade GS-13 includes all classes of positions the duties of which are (1) to perform, under administrative direction, with wide latitude for the exercise of independent judgment, work of unusual difficulty and responsibility along special technical, supervisory, or administrative lines, requiring extended specialized, supervisory, or administrative training and experience which has demonstrated leadership and marked attainments; (2) to serve as assistant head of a major organization involving work of comparable level within a bureau; (3) to perform, under administrative direction, with wide latitude for the exercise of independent judgment, work of unusual difficulty and responsibility requiring extended professional, scientific, or technical training and experience which has demonstrated leadership and marked attainments in professional, scientific, or technical research, practice, or administration; or (4) to perform other work of equal importance, difficulty, and responsibility, and requiring comparable qualifications.

Grade GS-18 includes all classes of positions the duties of which are (1) to serve as the head of a bureau where the position, considering the kind and extent of the authorities and responsibilities vested in it, and the scope, complexity, and degree of difficulty of the activities carried on, is exceptional and outstanding among the whole group of positions of heads of bureaus; (2) to plan and direct or to plan and execute frontier or unprecedented professional, scientific technical, administrative, fiscal, or other specialized programs of outstanding difficulty, responsibility, and national significance, requiring extended training and experience which has demonstrated outstanding leadership and attainments in professional, scientific, or technical research, practice, or administration, or in administractive, fiscal, or other specialized activities; or (3) to perform consulting or other professional, scientific, technical, administrative, fiscal, or other specialized work of equal importance, difficulty, and responsibility, and requiring comparable qualifications.

The committee matches each of the jobs included within the evaluation against the classification scheme and assigns it to the particular classification with which it corresponds most closely. In effect, this procedure leads to an ordering of jobs along a continuum consisting of as many units as there are levels or classifications in the master rating scale.

Appraisal of the Classification Method. This method is similar to the Ranking method in that the committee in both instances evaluates the jobs in terms of their overall worth rather than in terms of the specific factors that contribute to overall worth. Thus, the Classification method and the Ranking method share a common deficiency: that is, committee judgment of job worth may be based, at least in part, upon the performance of incumbents and the salaries they are receiving.

The Factor Comparison method and the Points method, discussed in the following sections, attempt to circumvent this difficulty by starting from the assumption that certain common factors are present in varying degrees in all jobs. Thus, instead of requiring the committee to rank or classify jobs on the basis of "overall worth," these methods require consideration of each of the jobs relative to these commonly held factors. The composite appraisal of the factorial components of each job serves as the basis for differentiation between the "overall worth" of the jobs. The specific ways in which this composite may be effected are clarified in the discussion that follows.

The Factor Comparison Method

In broad outline, this method requires the committee to identify the factors or elements common to all of the jobs included within the evaluation, to rank the jobs relative to each of these factors, and to apportion wages on the basis of this ranking.

Selection of the Factors. It has been suggested that five factors are applicable to the evaluation of a diversity of jobs by means of the Factor Comparison method. These factors, which thread their way in varying degrees through almost every job, have been identified as:

1. Mental requirements.
2. Skill requirements.
3. Physical requirements.
4. Responsibility.
5. Working conditions.[3]

The five factors are intentionally broad in order to permit for their adaptation to a diversity of companies and industrial situations. As a general rule, the Factor Comparison method is predicated upon the use of these five factors defined appropriately to make them specifically applicable to the particular company in which the evaluation is being performed. Although it sometimes is necessary to add another factor or two to this basic list in order to encompass all jobs included within the evaluation, the number of factors rarely is permitted to exceed six or seven.

Identifying the Key Jobs. After the committee has selected and defined the factors it will use, it selects a number (generally 15–20) of "key" jobs within the company. These jobs are selected in accord with two primary requirements: (1) They cover virtually the entire

[3] E. J. Benge, S. L. H. Burk, and E. N. Hay, *Manual of Job Evaluation* (New York: Harper & Bros., 1941).

range of jobs included in the evaluative plan. The key jobs selected by the committee run the gamut of "overall worth." (2) The committee members agree that the present rates of pay assigned to these jobs are fair in relation to other jobs within the company and the community at large. Thus, the list of key jobs will serve as a frame of reference for the committee in its deliberations about all other jobs included within the evaluation. It should be apparent that the validity of the Factor Comparison method rests upon the identification of appropriate key jobs. If the rates now paid for these jobs are in error, the entire evaluation for all other jobs may also be invalid.

Ranking the Key Jobs. The Factor Comparison method requires that the committee members rank the key jobs in two ways. First, each member working independently, must rank the jobs with respect to each of the factors. He considers each of these jobs, for example, relative to its Mental Requirements, and orders them from highest to lowest on this factor. This procedure is repeated for each of the other factors with which the committee has agreed to work. Typically these rankings-by-factor are made two or three times with a period of several weeks intervening between rankings. Wide discrepancies between the ranks assigned by individual committee members are discussed to correct possible misunderstandings either about the job's requirements or the definitions of the factors. Finally, the average of the ranks assigned by the committee members is computed to yield results similar to those shown in Table 12–2.

TABLE 12–2

AVERAGE RANKINGS OF KEY JOBS ON EACH OF THE CRITICAL FACTORS

	Factors				
Key Job	Mental Requirements	Skill	Physical Requirements	Responsi- bilities	Working Conditions
Patternmaker	1	1	6	1	7
Electrician	3	3	5	2	3
Machinist	2	2	7	3	6
Painter	4	4	4	4	5
Drill press operator	7	5	8	6	8
Inspector	5	6	10	5	10
Bench assembler	6	7	9	10	9
Carpenter's helper	8	8	2	7	4
Janitor	9	9	3	8	2
Laborer	10	10	1	9	1

The second kind of ranking involves wage apportionment and must be performed without reference to the factor rankings. Each committee member must consider the total hourly rate for each of the key jobs and decide how much of this hourly rate is paid for the possession of each of the factors critical to the job. How much of the patternmaker's hourly rate, for example, is paid for possession of the necessary mental requirements, skill, physical requirements, and so on. The apportionments made individually by the committee members are then averaged and these averages are converted to ranks.

The results from the two independent ranking procedures, one based upon wage apportionment (*$ rank*) and the other based upon the jobs' factorial components (*job rank*), are compared as shown in Table 12–3.

Discrepancies of the order noted in Table 12–3 are to be anticipated. Further discussion by the committee members will frequently lead either to resolution of such discrepancies or to a decision to drop the particular job from the list of key jobs.

Use of the Master Scale. The final list of key jobs and the ranks assigned to them constitutes a master scale for the establishment of wage rates for all other jobs included within the evaluative plan. Let us assume, for example, that the committee wishes to establish a base rate for lathe operators. The factorial composition of this job would be compared with the master scale, perhaps with the following results: The Mental Requirements for lathe operators fall between those of painters and electricians ($0.72); the Skills are roughly comparable to those required of electricians ($0.90); the Physical Requirements exceed those of drill press operators but not those of machinists ($0.23); the Responsibilities involved and the Working Conditions are about the same as those of machinists ($0.40, $0.25). The total of the base rates apportioned by factors would thus be $2.50.

You will note from examination of Table 12–3 that the factors Mental Requirements and Skill have been weighted more heavily by the committee than have the other three factors. The patternmaker's rate, for example, was broken down to $0.95 for Mental Requirements and $0.95 for Skill, but only $0.50 for Responsibility even though this position was ranked highest on all three factors. This tendency by job evaluation committees to weight Skill and Mental Requirements more heavily than most other factors is rather preva-

TABLE 12-3

AVERAGE MONEY APPORTIONMENT, RANKED MONEY APPORTIONMENT, AND OVERALL RANKINGS ASSIGNED TO KEY JOBS ON EACH FACTOR

Key Job	Average Hourly Rate	Mental Requirements		Skill			Physical Requirements			Responsibility			Working Conditions		
		$*	Job Rank‡	$	$ Rank	Job Rank	$	$ Rank	Job Rank	$	$ Rank	Job Rank	$	$ Rank	Job Rank
Patternmaker	$3.05	.95	1	.95	1	1	.35	5	6§	.50	1	1	.30	6	7§
Electrician	2.90	.75	3	.90	2	3§	.30	6	5§	.45	2	2	.50	3	3
Machinist	2.65	.90	2	.85	3	2§	.25	7	7	.40	3	3	.25	7	6§
Painter	2.60	.70	4	.80	4	4	.40	4	4	.30	5	4§	.40	5	5
Drill press operator	2.05	.65	5	.75	5	5	.20	8	8	.25	6	6	.20	8	8
Inspector	1.90	.60	6	.70	6	6	.15	9	10§	.35	4	5§	.10	10	10
Bench Assembler	1.50	.55	7	.60	7	7	.10	10	9§	.10	9	10§	.15	9	9
Carpenter's helper	1.75	.40	8	.15	8	8	.55	2	2	.20	7	7	.45	4	4
Janitor	1.45	.15	9	.10	9	9	.50	3	3	.15	8	8	.55	2	2
Laborer	1.40	.10	10	.05	10	10	.60	1	1	.05	10	9§	.60	1	1

* Portion of hourly rate paid for this factor.
† Ranking of monetary apportionment.
‡ Job Ranking as indicated in Table 12–2.
§ Discrepancy existing between $ Rank and Job Rank must be adjusted.

lent, and is a matter to which we will return in subsequent discussion.

The Points Method

The Points method is used more frequently for job evaluation than any other scheme.[4] The objective of this procedure is to assign to each job a point value representing the committee's opinion about the job's overall worth. The more valuable the job, the higher will be the total number of points assigned to it. The conversion of points to dollars is not undertaken until point allocations have been made for all jobs included within the evaluation.

The Points method and the Factor Comparison method are similar in that both procedures are based upon the assumption that certain factors are common to all jobs in varying degrees. Thus, the method presently under consideration leads to the assignment of a point total to each job predicated upon the point allocations for each of the specific factors selected for analytic purposes.

Selecting the Factors. The number and type of factors used in various Point evaluation plans varies considerably as a function of the specific jobs encompassed by the evaluation. Attempts to formulate a set of general factors applicable to all kinds of jobs, including factory and clerical work, have generally been relatively unsuccessful. A factor like Working Conditions, for example, may be rather critical in the evaluation of certain kinds of factory work but inconsequential for most clerical work.

Most Points plans are based upon the use of about 10 to 15 relatively specific factors like: Education, Experience, Physical Effort, Mental Effort, Physical Working Conditions, Hazards, Responsibility for Equipment, Initiative, Precision, Manual Skill, Tact, or Diplomacy. The foregoing list of factors is by no means exhaustive.

Constructing the Points Table. Since it is anticipated that each of the factors will be present in varying degrees for the different jobs, the committee must decide upon the number of levels to be differentiated for each factor. It is fairly common practice to identify five factor levels, although, on occasion, a particular set of jobs may require as many as seven or eight levels or as few as three levels for each factor.

Once the factors have been agreed upon, and the number of levels

[4] C. W. Lytle, *Job Evaluation Methods* (New York: The Ronald Press, Co., 1946).

to be differentiated for each factor is established, the committee is
ready to construct a points table. Such a table indicates the number
of points to be assigned for possession of a particular factor at a particular level. The points table for the widely used National Electrical Manufacturers' Association (NEMA) plan for shop jobs is
shown in Table 12–4.

TABLE 12–4

The Points Allocations and Factor Weights Used in the Plan of the National
Electrical Manufacturers' Association

Factor	First Level	Second Level	Third Level	Fourth Level	Fifth Level	Factor Weight
Skill:						
Education................14	28	42	56	70	14%
Experience................22	44	66	88	110	22
Initiative and Ingenuity......14	28	42	56	70	14
Effort:						
Physical demands............10	20	30	40	50	10
Mental/visual demands....... 5	10	15	20	25	5
Responsibility:						
For equipment or process..... 5	10	15	20	25	5
For material or product....... 5	10	15	20	25	5
For safety of others.......... 5	10	15	20	25	5
For work of others.......... 5	10	15	20	25	5
Job Conditions:						
Working conditions.........10	20	30	40	50	10
Hazards.................... 5	10	15	20	25	5

Source: National Electrical Manufacturers Association, New York.

The NEMA plan is based upon 11 factors, each with five levels.
You will note that this plan makes a deliberate attempt to weight
the factors unequally: the maximum number of possible points for
"Experience" exceeds the maximum for any of the other factors.

The decision about whether to weight factors equally or, as in the
case of the NEMA plan, to weight them unequally, rests squarely
with the committee. Its initial decision in this matter may have to be
revised if it is found that the plan they establish does not permit for
a sufficient point spread between the various jobs included in the
evaluation. Furthermore, the practice of establishing differential
points allocations for the various factor levels does not guarantee the
desired weighting of the factors when points totals are determined.

Applying the Points Table. The total number of points allocated
to each job is determined by rating the job against the points tables.
This rating is performed for each factor, and the points derived

from the factor ratings are summed. To illustrate, the job of Drill-Press Operator might be rated in the following manner by the committee using the NEMA Points Table (shown in Table 12–4):

Factor	Degree	Points
Skill:		
Education	2	28
Experience	2	44
Initiative and ingenuity	2	28
Effort:		
Physical demands	2	20
Mental/visual demands	3	15
Responsibility:		
For equipment or process	2	10
For material or product	2	10
For safety of others	2	10
For work of others	1	5
Job Conditions:		
Working conditions	2	20
Hazards	2	10
Total		200

Every job within the evaluative plan would be assigned its own point total in similar fashion, and the differences between the total point allocations would serve as the basis for establishing wage scales.

CONVERTING JOB EVALUATION RESULTS TO WAGES

The job evaluation schemes described thus far, with the exception of the Factor Comparison method, are designed to order jobs along a continuum of worth without reference to the monetary value that ought to be assigned to each job. The Ranking method expresses relative worth in terms of simple ranks; the Classification method assigns each job to one of the classifications of the master rating scale; and the Points method reflects differential worth in the total number of points allocated to each job. It remains now to convert these numerical indices of worth to hourly, daily, weekly, monthly, or annual rates of pay. The procedures for such conversion will be described for the Points method. They are applicable, with minor modifications, to the other evaluative plans.

The Wage Curve for Key Jobs

Certain of the jobs that have been included in the Points evaluation are identified as "key" jobs because: (1) they represent a considerable range of total point allocations; (2) they are sufficiently common to exist in many plants other than the one in which the evaluation has been performed; (3) there is general agreement that the present base rate for each of these jobs is a fair one. The point allocations for these key jobs is plotted against the present base rate, yielding the kind of wage curve shown in Figure 12–1.

The wage curve, shown as a heavy line in this figure, is fitted to the plotted points either statistically or by inspection. This curve is then used as the basis for establishing base rates for the remaining jobs included in the evaluation. If, for example, the committee had allocated 160 points to the job Carpenter's Helper, an hourly rate of $1.70 could be read directly from the graph.

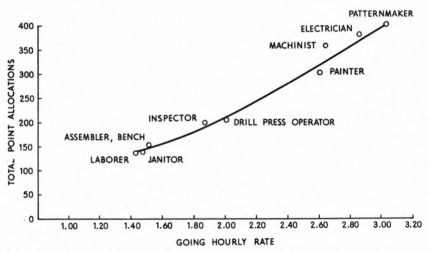

FIGURE 12–1. Point Allocations for Key Jobs Plotted against Going Rate of Pay.

Since it is generally the intent of a job evaluation to determine wage *ranges* rather than a specific wage for the various jobs, groups of jobs are usually clustered into gross labor grades. Each of these grades contains all jobs with similar point allocations, and is assigned a band of wages. The wage bands permit for periodic rate increases on the basis of seniority and/or merit without necessitating promotion to the next higher grade level. The structure of wage bands, the desirability of overlapping wages between adjacent labor grades, and the extent of such overlapping if it is permitted, are

matters that must be decided in the light of past company practices, labor traditions, and union sentiment.

RESEARCH ON JOB EVALUATION

We have described four fundamental plans for job evaluation in
the preceding sections. Other plans in current use involve, for the
most part, variations in or combinations of these fundamental
schemes. Thus, research on job evaluation has involved comparative
studies of these schemes in the attempt to identify the "best" plan,
and the "ideal" number and type of factors underlying judgments of
jobs' overall worth.

No Best Plan

Research comparing the relative efficiency of the several plans for
job evaluation has indicated that there is no "best" or "ideal" plan.
One such study, for example, compared the results obtained from
the plans in use by six different companies: two companies were
using Factor Comparison systems; two were using a Point plan
based upon 15 factors; one was using a 13-factor Point plan; and
one was using a combination of the Ranking and Classification
plans. The intercorrelations between the results obtained from these
six systems were exceedingly high, ranging between 0.89 to 0.93.[5] It
is apparent that as long as the raters are well-trained, it makes relatively little difference which system of job evaluation is used. Thus,
the actual selection of a particular plan ought to be based on such
practical considerations as cost and its adaptability to company
needs rather than upon a desire to use the "best" procedure.

Factors Underlying "Overall Worth"

The issue of the number and type of factors included in the job
evaluation scheme has been the subject of considerable study, particularly by Lawshe and his associates. The single factor making the
most important contribution to the results of a job evaluation is
Skill Demands. This factor was found to account for between 77.5
percent and 99 percent of the variance in total point ratings for

---

[5] D. J. Chesler, "Reliability and Comparability of Different Job Evaluation Systems," *Journal of Applied Psychology*, Vol. XXXII (1948), pp. 465–75.

hourly paid jobs,[6] and 95.6 percent of the total variance for salaried jobs.[7] It is apparent from results like these that the number of factors necessary for a satisfactory job evaluation need not be very large. If Skill Demands accounts for more than 90 percent of the variance of total point allocations, there is not much additional information that can be obtained from using a large number of other factors.

Reduction of the number of factors with a consequent savings of time and without any marked alteration in the outcomes of the job evaluation is supported by the results of other studies in this series. In one such investigation, a five-factor scale of the Factor Comparison type was abbreviated to three factors. The results obtained with the abbreviated and the longer scale correlated 0.99.[8] Another study compared the results obtained with an abbreviated points scale and the longer original version of this scale. The scale under investigation was the 11-factor NEMA points scale for hourly paid jobs. The results obtained with the full scale were compared with the results from an abbreviated version of the scale consisting of just three factors: Experience, Hazards, and Initiative. It was found that the abbreviated scale yielded results that would have maintained the same labor grade for 62 percent of the jobs, with virtually all of the remaining jobs being displaced by only one labor grade.[9] Another investigation, this time of the NEMA points scale for salaried employees, found that three of the original 11 factors were sufficient to account for 96 percent of the total variance in point allocations. These three factors were Experience, Complexity of Duties, and Character of Supervision.[10]

The results of such investigations of job evaluation procedures exhibit a high degree of consistency. The frequent practice with the Points method, of using 10 or more factors, appears to be relatively

---

[6] C. H. Lawshe, Jr., and G. A. Satler, "Studies in Job Evaluation No. 1: Factor Analyses of Point Ratings for Hourly Paid Jobs in Three Industrial Plants," *Journal of Applied Psychology*, Vol. XXVIII (1944), pp. 189–98.

[7] C. H. Lawshe, Jr., and A. A. Maleski, "Studies in Job Evaluation No. 3: An Analysis of Point Ratings for Salary Paid Jobs in an Industrial Plant," *Journal of Applied Psychology*, Vol. XXX (1946), pp. 117–28.

[8] C. H. Lawshe, Jr., and R. F. Wilson, "Studies in Job Evaluation No. 5: An Analysis of the Factor Comparison System as It Functions in a Paper Mill," *Journal of Applied Psychology*, Vol. XXX (1946), pp. 426–34.

[9] C. H. Lawshe, Jr., "Studies in Job Evaluation No. 2: The Adequacy of Abbreviated Point Ratings for Hourly Paid Jobs in Three Industrial Plants," *Journal of Applied Psychology* Vol. XXIX (1945), pp. 177–84.

[10] Lawshe and Maleski, *op. cit.*

inefficient. Such a large number of factors does not contribute either to the overall validity or reliability of the method.[11] Three or four carefully chosen factors would appear to be satisfactory for the conduct either of a Points or a Factor Comparison evaluation.

SUMMARY

Job evaluation procedures are designed to assist management in establishing equitable rates of pay. The utility of such procedures is limited to rather large companies embodying diverse jobs.

Job evaluation should not be regarded as a panacea for correcting wage inequities. Both management and the union may raise pertinent and valid objections to the procedure and the rationale underlying it. Thus, if a job evaluation is to succeed at all, it must be preceded by a comprehensive program of labor and management preparation. This program must clarify the objectives of the evaluation, and the possible effects of the plan upon individual employees.

Four specific procedures for job evaluation were described in this chapter: the Ranking, Classification, Factor Comparison, and Points methods. All of these methods order the jobs under consideration along a continuum of overall worth. The position of each job on this continuum is subsequently converted to a monetary value.

Job evaluation is, of necessity, a highly subjective procedure. Is is imperative, therefore, that the committee members who actually perform the evaluation be carefully selected and adequately trained.

---

[11] C. H. Lawshe, Jr., and R. F. Wilson, "Studies in Job Evaluation No. 6: The Reliability of Two Point Rating Systems," *Journal of Applied Psychology,* Vol. XXXI (1947), pp. 355–65.

Job Satisfaction

13 It was stated earlier, when defining the role of the industrial psychologist, that ". . . the psychologist is interested in maximizing the realization of [the employee's and employer's] potential for accomplishment and personal satisfaction." Appropriate training procedures and a favorable work environment may contribute positively to employee efficiency by increasing output and diminishing fatigue, accidents, turnover, spoilage, and absenteeism. Reference has been made from time to time to the relationship also between such factors and job satisfaction. We will now bring this matter into somewhat sharper focus. Just what is it that employees seek from their work, and how can the realization of personal satisfactions be facilitated? This important question requires that we first discuss some general principles of human motivation and then apply these principles to the matter of job satisfaction.

MOTIVATION

Motivation is a fundamental explanatory concept related to the *why* of behavior. Organisms continually experience needs or wants which impel them to action. When the individual is driven either to attain some goal or to avoid some undesirable consequence, we have evidence for motivation. A simple illustration will serve to clarify the semantics of motivation. A hungry person *needs* food, he is *driven* by hunger, and *motivated* by a desire to obtain food in order to satisfy his need.

Differences in motivation often account for the fact that various persons may react quite differently when confronted by the same set of circumstances and, indeed, a given person may behave differently when confronted by a particular set of circumstances on different occasions. You will recall the S-I-R scheme introduced in Chapter 1. We stated then that in order to understand behavior, we had to know something about the determinants of the way in which a

278

respondent interprets and perceives a particular stimulus condition. Motivation is, of course, one of the keys to such understanding.

The Complexity of Motivation

Motives related to work have quite generally been oversimplified. The typical response of uninformed management to the question, "Why do employees work?" is "To earn money." If this were correct, it would be a relatively simple matter to increase job satisfaction by raising salaries. The fact that this approach does not work in the long run is indicative of the complexity of industrial motivation.

Motives have often been classified on the basis of the need or want that generates activity. *Primary drives* are linked to physiological imbalance and are responsible for motives in the direction of such incentives as food, water, and sleep. These drives can be extremely powerful as determinants of behavior, but they generally are easily satisfied under normal conditions of life in our society. The *secondary drives* are socially derived (that is, learned) and include such things as the desire for acceptance by the group, status, and personal recognition. The fact that these drives are learned, and that their satisfaction is not a requirement for survival in the physiological sense, does not diminish their importance as determinants of behavior.

Since social motives are not a product of the physiology of the organism, it is reasonable to anticipate considerable diversity among them. We each have a somewhat unique environmental history which has led us to develop our own special and particular pattern of secondary drives. Certain patterns of socially derived motives do, however, appear to occur with a high degree of consistency because of gross similarities in environmental patterns within a culture. Almost everyone, for example, has learned needs for some kind of social approval. Persons who do not respond in terms of such needs (that is, who flout society) are, in fact, generally regarded as deviant.

Work can be a very important source of satisfaction for socially derived needs and, in consequence, a means toward the realization of satisfaction with life in general. The job is not, however, the only means by which such needs can be satisfied. The relationship between job satisfaction and general adjustment, for example, has been found to be more pronounced for men than for women.[1] This finding supports the contention that most male employees do not work simply in order to earn a livelihood. The producing role is important to them for maintaining their sense of general well-being.[2] Most women have other roles to fulfill aside from that of breadwinner, and other important routes to the derivation of personal satisfactions outside of the work environment.

The assumption that employees can best be motivated to produce by financial incentives disregards the complexity of human motivation. It is predicated, in part, upon the erroneous belief that whatever goals we seek can be bought or, at least, are attainable by means of increased income. It is founded also on the untenable notion that the needs of employees and employers coincide. These assumptions have been evaluated critically in an excellent article by Brayfield and Crockett.[3] The authors discuss motivation as a function of three social systems within which virtually every employee operates: (1) fellow workers, (2) the company, (3) the community.

Relations with Other Workers. There is considerable evidence for the fact that an individual's productivity tends to conform to a group norm. Standards of output, once established by the work group, are often imposed upon new employees. The individual who attempts to deviate from the group norm of a "fair day's work" by overproducing may be ostracized by his fellow employees.

This situation, when it exists, represents a conflict of interests between employees and employers. The latter may wish to increase productivity in order to improve the economic position of the company and, parenthetically, to improve the wage schedule. The employees, however, may perceive such increased productivity as a threat to full employment. Social acceptance by fellow workers often proves to be a more powerful incentive for maintaining the present level of production than does the promise of increased wages for improving productivity.

---

[1] A. H. Brayfield, R. V. Wells, and M. W. Strate, "Interrelationships Among Measures of Job Satisfaction and General Satisfaction," *Journal of Applied Psychology*, Vol. XLI (1957), pp. 201–5.

[2] Nancy Morse and R. S. Weiss, "The Function and Meaning of Work and the Job," *American Sociological Review*, Vol. XX (1955), p. 198.

[3] A. H. Brayfield and W. H. Crockett, "Employee Attitudes and Employee Performance," *Psychological Bulletin*, Vol. LII, (1955), pp. 396–424.

Relations within the Company Structure. Improved productivity is perceived by some employees to be a path leading to promotion and improvement of status within the company structure. Not all employees, however, are motivated by the incentive of promotion within the company. Workers who are reasonably well-satisfied with their present position and earnings are not likely to respond by increasing production in order to improve their salary or to gain a promotion.

An additional factor that diminishes the effectiveness of financial or status incentives is sometimes operative in unionized plants. The worker may be oriented more toward advancement within the framework of the union hierarchy than the company hierarchy. There is no evidence that the realization of this objective is dependent upon high productivity. Financial incentives provided to such employees by management do not bear upon the goals which they have elected to pursue.

Relations outside of the Company. The generalization is sometimes made that all employees desire to improve their status in the community. Since community status is somewhat dependent upon the possession of tangible wealth (house, car, clothes, furniture), it follows that the desire for status ought to lead the employee to increase his output in order to reap financial gain.

This line of reasoning is erroneous on two counts. First, many employees do not desire to improve their status within the community. Unless the employee is upwardly mobile, he probably evaluates his status in terms of some segment of the community rather than in the light of the total community. Thus, an individual may compare himself with others in his neighborhood, his religious or ethnic group, his occupational classification, his high school graduating class, or from his own particular environmental background and conclude that he has done quite well indeed. Furthermore, an improvement in his wage leading to the acquisition of additional tangible wealth may actually be regarded as undesirable because it may lead to his exclusion from the social group with which he chooses to identify.

Secondly, it is incorrect to assume that the attainment of socially rewarding goals outside of the plant is necessarily dependent upon financial or status gains within the company. Individuals who are active participants in community activities may have their needs fulfilled by such activities regardless of their income level or their position within the company.

Need Hierarchy

An overall view of motivation is that it directs behavior in two ways: (1) by causing the individual to seek one of several available goals, and (2) by causing him to seek certain goals not present at the moment.

The former is illustrated by an employee who must choose between remaining in his present position or accepting advancement within the company entailing greater income but less security than he presently enjoys. Other things being equal, the choice he makes will reflect a discrepancy in the value he places upon income and security. Similarly, an employee dissatisfied with his present position because it provides little opportunity for advancement may be motivated to seek a job with another company providing greater opportunities.

It is evident that needs, and hence the goals we seek, are arranged in a hierarchy of importance. At any given time certain needs are stronger than others. However, this hierarchy is flexible rather than static because of the interdependence of needs. Relatively less important goals may assume real importance after previously more basic ones have been satisfied.[4]

We will have occasion to invoke the notion of interdependence of needs throughout the ensuing discussion of job satisfaction. Attempts to generalize about the perceived importance of specific job factors must take into account the overall job picture.[5] As an illustration, in certain job situations pay and security may be reasonably satisfactory while physical working conditions are poor; in others working conditions may be good but pay and security are unsatisfactory. Workers in the former situation would probably perceive working conditions as more important than pay and security while the converse would be characteristic of workers in the latter.

The fact that human motivation is complex makes it difficult to generalize about the factors contributing to job satisfaction or dissatisfaction. There are widespread individual differences between employees in the goals which they seek (individual need-hier-

---

[4] M. Haire and J. S. Gottsdanker, "Factors Influencing Industrial Morale," *Personnel*, Vol. XXVII (1951), pp. 445–54.

[5] F. Herzberg, B. Mausner, R. O. Peterson, and D. F. Capwell, *Job Attitudes: Review of Research and Opinion* (Pittsburgh: Psychological Service of Pittsburgh, 1957).

archies) and hence in the effectiveness of specific factors as determinants of job satisfaction. Furthermore, as we have already pointed out, need-hierarchies are exceedingly flexible.

It is important, nevertheless, to learn as much as we can about the factors contributing to job satisfaction because of its bearing upon such critical issues as morale and labor-management relations.

JOB SATISFACTION AND JOB PERFORMANCE

Particular mention has not yet been made of a relationship between job satisfaction and productivity or output, although such a relationship might be anticipated on the basis of common sense. As is often the case with common sense, however, the available evidence is somewhat counter to expectations. Quite a number of investigators have correlated a measure of job satisfaction with supervisory ratings of employee performance and been forced to the conclusion that these two factors are not particularly related. The correlations actually obtained for groups of office clerical workers, for example, ranged between −0.06 and +0.13.[6] Similarly low values have been reported for plumber apprentices, farmers, IBM operators,[7] retail sales clerks,[8] and other employee groups.

Such studies are open to a certain amount of criticism because of the nature of the criterion of employee performance utilized. Supervisory ratings of performance leave something to be desired in the way of reliability and validity. An objective criterion, sales volume, was correlated with an index of job satisfaction for insurance agents with positive results. The two measures yielded a correlation coefficient of 0.26.[9] Although this value is not high, it does provide some support for the contention that there is a slight tendency for satisfied employees to be more productive than dissatisfied employees. The important fact, of course, is that this relationship is not stronger.

---

[6] Brayfield and Crockett, *op. cit.*

[7] M. S. Gadel and P. H. Kriedt, "Relationships of Aptitude, Interest, Performance and Job Satisfaction of IBM Operators," *Personnel Psychology*, Vol. V (1952), pp. 207–12.

[8] A. C. Mossin, *Selling Performance and Contentment in Relation to School Background* (New York: Bureau of Publications, Teachers' College, Columbia University, 1949).

[9] B. Baxter, A. A. Taaffe, and J. F. Hughes, "A Training Evaluation Study," *Personnel Psychology*, Vol. VI (1953), pp. 403–17.

Other investigators have attempted to discover a relationship between job dissatisfaction and such criteria as absenteeism and turnover without notable success.[10] Although it seems reasonable to expect that the worker who is unhappy with his job ought, whenever possible, to seek other employment and to avoid coming to work, the data concerning these relationships point again to (a) the complexity of motivation and perhaps also to (b) difficulties in assembling reliable criterion measures.

The foregoing discussion is intended to call attention to some of the difficulties inherent in applied research. It should not be construed as an indication that job satisfaction is relatively unimportant as a consideration in industry. The reported correlations between measures of satisfaction and industrial efficiency are probably underestimates because of procedural problems related to record-keeping and the development of criterion measures of employee efficiency. Nevertheless, it is apparent also that other factors in addition to job satisfaction are operative as determinants of employee efficiency.

This situation is quite analagous to your own experience in the educational setting. It is unlikely that the amount of effort you expend in a particular course is affected solely by your feelings about that course. Regardless of whether you are happy or unhappy in it, and whether you have elected to take it or have been compelled to take it in order to fulfill a university requirement, you are under a certain amount of pressure to produce (that is, to earn a passing grade) in order to be graduated.

Employees also function under conditions of constraint. Productivity or job stability may be no more of an ultimate goal for them than earning a satisfactory grade is for you. High productivity or job stability may, for some employees, be a means toward the realization of certain other goals like status or ownership of a new car. When the pressure for productivity is high, the employee may perform efficiently either in the absence of any real job satisfaction or even when he is quite dissatisfied.[11]

---

[10] W. J. Giese and H. W. Ruter, "An Objective Analysis of Morale," *Journal of Applied Psychology*, Vol. XXXIII (1949), pp. 421–27.

W. A. Kerr, "Summary of Validity Studies of the Tear Ballot," *Personnel Psychology*, Vol. V (1952), pp. 105–13.

[11] H. C. Triandis, "A Critique and Experimental Design for the Study of the Relationship between Productivity and Job Satisfaction," *Psychological Bulletin*, Vol. LVI (1959), pp. 309–12.

It must be recognized also that efficient production is not the only means of goal realization for all employees. The worker who is highly motivated by a desire for social acceptance by his fellow employees, for example, may actually derive increased satisfactions by limiting his productivity and thereby gaining group acceptance.

STUDIES OF JOB SATISFACTION

The results of job satisfaction studies may be conveniently grouped under two headings on the basis of their pertinence to factors (1) intrinsic or (2) extrinsic to the job itself. The former classification includes investigations of the relative importance of various job-related incentives and features of the work environment. Extrinsic factors include such aspects of the broader job context as company policies, practices, and supervision as well as the workers' personal characteristics.

The relative importance of intrinsic and extrinsic factors to job satisfaction has been investigated for accountants and engineers. Intrinsic factors including the nature of the work itself, responsibility, recognition, and advancement were most frequently cited by these workers as sources of satisfaction. The greatest sources of dissatisfaction for them involved certain of the extrinsic factors. Thus, the authors concluded that although factors intrinsic to the job may bring about job satisfaction, their absence does not result in dissatisfaction. Conversely, factors within the broader job context can produce dissatisfaction but not satisfaction.[12]

This conclusion has been questioned because of the introspective nature of the data underlying it. It has been argued that when individuals are asked the sources of their satisfaction and dissatisfaction, they may attribute the former to their personal accomplishments and the latter to factors beyond their control as a defensive reaction.[13]

The relative contributions of intrinsic and extrinsic factors to feelings of satisfaction or dissatisfaction is not now resolved. Nevertheless, it is evident that both the more specific aspects of the job and

---

[12] F. Herzberg, B. Mausner, and B. B. Snyderman, *The Motivation to Work* (New York: John Wiley & Sons, Inc., 1959).

[13] G. Gurin, J. Veroff, and S. Feld, *Americans View Their Mental Health* (New York: Basic Books, Inc., 1960).

the general context in which work is performed have considerable bearing upon workers' attitudes.

Factors Intrinsic to the Job

One of the typical procedures utilized for this type of study is to require that employees consider a list of job characteristics and rank or rate them in order of their perceived importance. The 10 factors ranked as most important by employees in six companies is shown in Table 13–1. This table also shows the expectations of executives in these companies and labor leaders about the ranks that the employees would assign to these factors.

TABLE 13–1

THE 10 MOST IMPORTANT FACTORS CONTRIBUTING TO JOB SATISFACTION AS RANKED BY EMPLOYEES, EXECUTIVES, AND LABOR LEADERS

Rank	By Employees	Expected by Executives	Expected by Labor Leaders
1.........	Security	Pay	Pay
2.........	Advancement	Security	Security
3.........	Pay	Vacations	Hours
4.........	Benefits	Advancement	Working conditions
5.........	Information on success or failure at job	Working conditions	Unions
6.........	Type of work	Company attitude	Company attitude
7.........	Vacation and holiday practices	Type of work	Handling of grievances
8.........	Supervisor	Benefits	Vacations
9.........	Profit sharing	Supervisor	Union-management relations
10.........	Working conditions	Hours	Job evaluation programs

Source: National Industrial Conference Board, *Factors Affecting Employee Morale*, Studies in Personnel Policy No. 85, (1947), p. 21.

One very important conclusion from such studies is that the needs of employees often are not well understood either by executives or by labor leaders. A factor, for example, like "information on success or failure at the job," was ranked as quite important by workers but excluded from the top 10 ranks expected by executives and labor leaders. The latter group, in particular, tended to overestimate the extent of employee concern about union matters.

The rank assigned by employee groups to any job factor is, of course, a function of the specific factors that employees are asked to consider. The perceived importance of certain intrinsic factors has, however, been explored with sufficient frequency to permit for generalizations about the extent to which they bear upon job satisfaction.

Pay. It is evident in Table 13–1 that management tends to overemphasize the importance of pay as a determinant of job satisfaction. Quite elaborate incentive pay systems have been developed to recompense employees on the basis of productivity (either as individuals or in groups) or some related criterion. Employees rarely, however, rank pay as the most important determinant of their satisfaction with the job.

The relative importance attached to this factor by workers is undoubtedly a function of the wage currently being received in rela-

TABLE 13–2

IMPORTANCE OF VARIOUS JOB FACTORS AS RATED BY WORKERS

	Percentage of 7,000 Workers Including This Item in the First Five	Percent Assigning It First Choice
A steady job	61.9%	36.1%
Pay rate	52.6	7.2
A chance to get ahead	41.9	6.9
A square boss	39.6	4.8
Working on the job you prefer	35.3	15.2
Credit for the job you do	29.6	2.2
Vacations and holidays	21.5	0.4
Friendly working companions	21.3	0.7
Medical and health facilities	20.8	0.6
Pension	9.7	7.1

Source: R. Stagner "Psychological Aspects of Industrial Conflict, II: Motivation." *Personnel Psychology*, Vol. III (1950), pp. 1–16.

tion to that being paid to other employees in similar jobs or requiring similar training and experience. Its perceived importance is also a function of the employee's needs relative to what he can purchase with the wage he is receiving.

The fact that employees quite often rate factors related to ego-satisfaction and personal recognition as more important than salary is apparent from the results obtained from a large group of workers and shown in Table 13–2.

It would be incorrect, of course, to maintain that rate of pay is unrelated to job satisfaction. The point, however, is that once the employee surpasses some minimum income, his feelings about the job tend to reflect the extent to which it satisfies certain of his socially derived needs. Thus, financial rewards cannot be regarded as a panacea or even as the most important incentive governing employee motivation.

Job Security. The importance attached by workers to the factor of security is clearly evident in Table 13–2 and substantiated by other investigations of a similar nature.[14]

The relative importance of security in comparison with other intrinsic aspects of the job, such as pay or personal recognition, varies as a function of the job classification and the extent to which the workers actually do feel secure in their job. It is likely that workers who are not confronted by the possibility of precipitous dismissal will regard factors other than security as being of primary importance. Many employees, however, remember the widespread unemployment and the real economic pinch of the depression and, in consequence, place a very high value upon job security.

Participation and Personal Recognition. Improvements in industrial efficiency are often accompanied by fragmentation of the task performed by each employee. The craftsman's feeling of satisfaction and personal pride derived from his ability to transform raw materials into a finished product is rarely experienced within our present factory structure. The employee today has the same needs for a feeling of accomplishment, pride, and personal worth as did his artisan predecessor. The importance of these factors is evident from the high ratings consistently assigned by workers to such questionnaire items as "opportunity to use own ideas" and "credit for the job you do."

Although it is often impossible to enable each employee to experience the pride of a craftsman, it is both possible and necessary to provide the kind of training that will enable each worker to see how his sometimes miniscule task fits into the manufacture of the total product. This kind of training has been found, by way of illustration, to improve materially the net good yield produced by a manufacturer of miniature motors utilized in guidance systems and on space satellites. Prior to training, the assemblers tended to be somewhat careless in handling components. This lack of caution often pro-

---

[14] R. Hersey, "Psychology of Workers," *The Personnel Journal,* Vol. XIV (1936), pp. 291–96.

S. Wyatt and J. N. Langdon, "Fatigue and Boredom in Repetitive Work," *Industrial Health Research Board,* No. 77 (London: H.M. Stationery Office, 1937).

duced microscopic chips which were ultimately responsible for motor malfunctions. The solution developed by the company was to organize a training program in which all employees became aware of the importance of their motor to the successful performance of the satellite, and of the importance of their own job to the proper functioning of the motor.

Hours and Working Conditions. It is of some interest to note that the hours worked and the physical conditions under which work is performed are generally not regarded by employees as very important determinants of job satisfaction. The consistently low ratings assigned to these factors probably indicates that most jobs are performed on a tolerable work schedule and under, at least, minimally adequate working conditions.

TABLE 13–3

JOB SATISFACTION AS A FUNCTION OF OCCUPATIONAL CLASSIFICATION

Classification	Number of Cases	Range of Indices	Mean Index
Unskilled manual	55	100–650	401
Semiskilled	74	125–650	483
Skilled manual and white collar	84	125–675	510
Subprofessional, business, and minor supervisory	32	250–700	548
Professional, management, and executive	23	300–700	560

Source: R. Hoppock, *Job Satisfaction* (New York: Harper & Bros., 1935).

Occupational Status. It has been estimated that approximately 13 percent of employees are dissatisfied with their jobs. This percentage is a median value based upon the results of a large number of job satisfaction studies spanning many years.[15]

Although most employees either are satisfied with their jobs or else maintain a feeling of relative neutrality toward them, the degree of job satisfaction reported varies with the worker's occupational status. The higher his position in the job hierarchy, the more likely he is to report satisfaction with his job. This generalization is evident from the results of studies like the one reported in Table 13–3. The index of job satisfaction utilized in this investigation extends from a low of 100 (extreme dissatisfaction) to a high of 700 (extreme satisfaction) with a neutral or indifference point at 400.

---

[15] H. A. Robinson, "Job Satisfaction Researches of 1958," *Personnel and Guidance Journal*, Vol. XXXVII (1959), pp. 669–73.

The progression of satisfaction indices as a function of occupational classification is self-evident.

This kind of finding tends to substantiate the point made earlier that ego-satisfaction is an important contributor to job satisfaction. The occupational levels delineated in this study represent a hierarchy with respect to social prestige and status. It is quite likely that the worker's reported level of satisfaction with his job is related to the value placed upon his services by the community at large.

Occupational differences have been found also in the priority assigned by workers to the importance of specific intrinsic factors as determinants of job satisfaction. Security, for example, is of much greater concern to unskilled and semiskilled employees than it is to personnel at the higher end of the occupational scale. Conversely, the opportunity for self-expression is weighted more heavily by professionals and business personnel than by laborers.[16] In another study, college graduates ranked both pay and opportunity for advancement above security in importance to job satisfaction.[17] It is quite likely that such findings reflect both the fact that highly trained persons are less susceptible to precipitous job termination and the likelihood that, should their employment be terminated, they anticipate relatively little difficulty in obtaining other employment.

Factors Extrinsic to the Job

The relative importance of various elements of the job as determinants of worker satisfaction, and the overall level of job satisfaction reported by employees has been shown to vary as a function of certain factors extrinsic to the job itself. This is quite a reasonable finding since perceptions about work are, in part, influenced by the totality of the worker's past experiences and his present group affiliations. Thus, it is appropriate to examine the matter of job satisfaction as it is affected by the context in which work is done (including perceptions about supervision) and certain of the worker's personal characteristics.

Supervision. One of the significant findings of the Hawthorne study was that it was possible to change the attitudes of the em-

---

[16] R. Centers, "Motivational Aspects of Occupational Stratification," *Journal of Social Psychology*, Vol. XXVIII (1948), pp. 187–217.

[17] Stanford Research Institute, "Tomorrow's Manpower," *Research for Industry News Bulletin*, May, 1955, pp. 8–9.

ployees by developing a cooperative spirit between workers and supervisors.[18] A friendly supervisory-subordinate relationship appeared to generalize to a favorable work climate. The importance attached by workers to the quality of supervision probably results from the fact that the supervisor is, in a way, a representative of the company. When perceived in this light, he is a primary force facilitating or inhibiting the satisfaction by the employee of his needs for personal recognition.

TABLE 13–4

RESPONSES OF GROUPS OF INSURANCE SALESMEN TO SELECTED ITEMS CONCERNING SUPERVISION

	Percent of Survivors	Percent of Terminators
Like freedom from supervision	56	34
Like helpfulness of supervision	62	41
Like personal friendship with the manager	70	53
Dislike manager misrepresenting or failing to explain all provisions of the contract	6	16
Manager doesn't devote enough time to the agent's problems	4	12
My job was misrepresented by the manager during the hiring interview	9	19
Feel free to talk over personal problems with the manager	94	74
Feel free to discuss selling problems with the manager	99	90
Manager makes you feel you are doing a worthwhile job	90	78
Enjoy manager socially	92	83
Manager spends part of his time handling agents' personal problems and grievances	83	64
Manager gives each agent a detailed explanation of changes in company policy or procedure	88	73

A strong relationship has been found, for example, between dissatisfaction with certain aspects of supervision and the subsequent termination of employment by life insurance salesmen. Two groups of salesmen, equated for length of service, age, and company for which they worked, were differentiated on the basis of survival or termination of employment during the year subsequent to completion of a job satisfaction questionnaire. The comparison between the responses made by these groups relative to certain supervisory matters is shown in Table 13–4.[19]

---

[18] F. W. Roethlisberger and W. J. Dickson, *Management and the Worker* (Cambridge, Mass.: Harvard University Press, 1939).

[19] J. Weitz and R. C. Nuckols, "Job Satisfaction and Job Survival," *Journal of Applied Psychology*, Vol. XXXIX (1955), pp. 294–300.

Sex. A higher overall level of job satisfaction has been reported for women than for men.[20] Work is generally a less consuming element in the lives of women and hence of somewhat lesser importance to their status in the community.

Differences in the relative importance attached by men and women to specific aspects of the job have also been investigated. A sample of workers completed a questionnaire in which the following five factors were presented in various combinations as pairs: advancement, hours of work, salary, security, and supervisor. The respondent was required to check the item in each pair of statements that he (or she) regarded as most important in a job.[21] The choices, expressed as percentages of the total number of choices attainable, are summarized by sex and by marital status in Table 13–5.

TABLE 13–5

ATTITUDE TOWARD VARIOUS INCENTIVES BY SEX AND MARITAL STATUS

	Men			Women		
	Married	*Single*	*Total*	*Married*	*Single*	*Total*
Salary............46%	46%	46%	34%	36%	39%
Security...........76	65	69	65	73	72
Supervisor.........32	34	33	51	45	45
Hours of work......13	16	15	29	18	21
Advancement......83	89	87	71	78	76

Men attached considerably more importance than women to advancement possibilities and somewhat greater importance to salary. The women, on the other hand, regarded the supervisor as a more potent determinant of job satisfaction than did the men.

The replies of unmarried female workers corresponded, in some ways, more closely to those of men than to those of married women. This is particularly apparent for the ratings assigned to the supervisor, hours of work, and advancement. Thus, these data are suggestive of some fundamental differences in the gratifications which employees seek from their job and of the role of work in overall life adjustment as a function of sex and marital status.

---

[20] N. C. Morse, *Satisfactions in the White Collar Job* (Ann Arbor, Mich.: Institute for Social Research, University of Michigan, 1953), p. 72.

[21] M. L. Blum and J. Russ, "A Study of Employee Attitudes towards Various Incentives," *Personnel,* Vol. XIX (1942), pp. 438–44.

Age. There is some evidence indicative of increased job satisfaction with increased employee age.[22] This relationship has been attributed to a combination of factors, including the termination of employment by dissatisfied older personnel and a kind of conservatism or resignation with advancing age to the realities of life and the job. In addition, some of the factors responsible for job dissatisfaction, like lack of opportunity for advancement and low salary, are of somewhat lesser importance to older workers than to younger employees who are in the midst of raising a family.

Miscellaneous Factors. Other factors extrinsic to the job which have been studied with reference to job satisfaction include intelligence and job experience.

The level of intelligence does not itself appear to be a determinant of job satisfaction or dissatisfaction. The employee's intelligence in relation to the nature of the job he performs is, however, a factor of considerable consequence. Employees who are either insufficiently challenged by their work or who are engaged in activities that are too demanding relative to their intellectual capabilities are often dissatisfied with their job. The implication of this relationship for the implementation of adequate personnel selection procedures is self-evident.

Job experience is related to satisfaction in a rather interesting fashion. As one might expect, new employees tend to be relatively well-satisfied with their jobs. This "honeymoon" terminates after a period of time, however, unless the worker feels that he is making rather steady progress toward the satisfaction of his occupational and social needs.

Almost every company employs a number of persons who, after several years with the company, feel that advancement or salary increases have not been forthcoming with sufficient regularity and that they are working at a dead-end job. The effect of this is to cause a perceptible decline in the prevailing level of job satisfaction during the several years following the start of employment. The level of job satisfaction appears to increase again after six or seven years and reaches a maximum for workers who have remained with a company for about 20 years.[23] This is undoubtedly due to the fact

---

[22] Morse, *op. cit.*

R. Hoppock, "Age and Job Satisfaction," *Psychological Monographs*, Vol. XLVII, No. 212 (1936).

[23] R. L. Hull and A. Kolstad, "Morale on the Job," in W. Goodwin (ed.), *Civilian Morale* (New York: Reynal & Hitchcock, Inc., 1942).

that the most dissatisfied employees have sought other employment either voluntarily or involuntarily. In addition, employees who have been encouraged to remain with the company for as long a period as 20 years have probably been provided with the kind of incentives that lead to feelings of job satisfaction.

LIFE ADJUSTMENT AND JOB ADJUSTMENT

"Adjustment" is a word that is bandied about a good deal in Sunday Supplements and popular magazines. Writers of such articles sometimes erroneously equate it with conformity. This equation implies that the well-adjusted person is one who submerges his own individuality, often disregarding the fulfillment of his own needs, in order to gain or maintain acceptance by some group.

There is no doubt that well-adjusted individuals often do conform to societal and group pressures. Their conformity is, however, to be regarded as evidence for, but not as identical with, personal adjustment. The well-adjusted person is one who, after weighing the issues, may feel quite free to be a nonconformist if such behavior best satisfies his fundamental needs and does not deprive others of the right to satisfy their needs. Thus, from a psychological standpoint, adjustment is more nearly equated with personal satisfaction than it is with conformity.

The existence of a relationship between job satisfaction and adjustment to, or satisfaction with, life in general has been implied throughout the preceding sections of this chapter. The interpretation of such a relationship in terms of cause and effect is somewhat risky. It might be assumed that a worker who is personally maladjusted and unhappy about circumstances outside of the plant will generalize this attitude to include dissatisfaction with his company and his job. There is some evidence, however, that the relationship may also work the other way: that is, job satisfaction is partly responsible for a general feeling of well-being and satisfaction with life.[24] In any event, either as cause or effect or as some combination of the two, management has reason to be concerned with the worker's adjustment to the job itself and, in a larger sense, to life.

Almost any industrial organization will occasionally hire an employee who is seriously maladjusted. The treatment of such persons

---

[24] Brayfield, Wells, and Strate, *op. cit.*

is a matter that extends considerably beyond the scope of the present discussion and, in fact, beyond the limits of the counseling activities usually undertaken by the company. Employees who suffer from major personality disturbances are generally referred to more appropriate agencies for treatment.

Persons who are, however, reasonably well-adjusted may experience a certain amount of job dissatisfaction because of situational factors in the environment. Since it is not always possible for an individual to achieve his goals or to satisfy his needs, most employees are occasionally confronted by circumstances which temporarily produce tension and feelings of dissatisfaction. Schaffer[25] and Morse[26] have suggested that job satisfaction is a function of the relationship between drive-strength and the availability of appropriate goals. The stronger the drive, the more critical it is to provide the employee with an appropriate and attainable goal if he is to experience satisfaction.

INCREASING JOB SATISFACTION

The preceding discussion has, in the main, been descriptive. We have summarized some empirical findings relevant particularly to (1) the importance attributed by workers to specific incentives and job conditions, and (2) differences in job satisfaction attributable to factors extrinsic to the job itself.

Our emphasis changes now from describing factors related to job satisfaction to manipulating these factors. What can management do to increase employee feelings of job satisfaction?

The entire matter of increasing job satisfaction and of facilitating personal adjustment requires that the employee be recognized and accepted as an individual with his own unique pattern of needs, strengths, and weaknesses. He cannot be expected to compartmentalize and separate his "job life" from his "home life"; and he cannot be regarded by management at any level solely as a statistic or as a component in the organization.

A traditional approach has been to assume employees are satisfied until such time as they express a grievance of some kind and then to cope specifically with the expressed dissatisfactions. This

---

[25] R. H. Schaffer, "Job Satisfaction as Related to Need Satisfaction in Work," *Psychological Monographs*, Vol. LXVII, No. 14 (1953).

[26] Morse, *op. cit.*

approach is unsatisfactory on two counts. First, it is probably less efficient, from management's standpoint, to cope with grievances than to prevent their occurrence. Second, the grievance presented to management may not truly reflect the underlying sources of dissatisfaction. In the latter regard, complaints about such things as wages or working conditions cannot always be accepted at face value. Unless the fundamental sources of dissatisfaction are corrected, wage increases or modifications in the work environment will improve job satisfaction only temporarily.

Communication and Participation

Many potential sources of grievance can be avoided by adequate communication throughout the entire company structure. If the employee is made aware of the reasons for certain company policies, practices, and decisions, he is more likely to accept them. Similarly when management is receptive to expressions of employee feeling and attitude, appropriate measures can be taken to prevent the explosion of potential sources of dissatisfaction.

Actual employee participation in programs of industrial change goes one step beyond such communication. The workers do not merely learn of an impending change and the reasons for it; they may actually participate in working out some of the details of the program. In addition to the positive effects upon job satisfaction, employee participation tends to produce feelings of group solidarity and personal identification with the program.

The conduct and effects of one such employee participation program have been described for workers engaged in manufacturing men's apparel.[27] Management had decided to make major changes in production methods in order to (1) reduce the in-process inventory and shorten the time required to produce a given garment, (2) attain more flexible control of production, (3) reduce manufacturing costs, and (4) improve the quality of the garments.

Although a general plan had been evolved for re-engineering the production lines in order to accomplish these objectives, the precise changes to be made were not known at the outset. The program was introduced to the workers in two smaller plants in a series of meetings conducted by local plant management. Following the initial

---

[27] J. R. P. French, Jr., I. C. Ross, S. Kirby, J. R. Nelson, and P. Smyth, "Employee Participation in a Program of Industrial Change," *Personnel*, Vol. XXXV (1958), pp. 16–29.

meeting, changes were gradually introduced on the production floor.

After the new system had been in effect long enough to be stable, another series of meetings was called to discuss revised wage rates. Care was taken to protect earning opportunities and compensate for any economic loss brought about by the new methods. At these meetings, the workers also raised a number of complaints about equipment and mechanical difficulties. These were investigated and remedied. After the new system had been developed and refined in the smaller plants, the change was successfully introduced into the third and largest plant.

The economic goals anticipated by management at the beginning of the program were realized with minimal expressions of employee dissatisfaction. Throughout the process of change, management did not forego its right to make the changes it contemplated, but it also remained aware of what the changes meant to the employees.

Job Design

Job design specifies the individual tasks assigned to individual workers and the method by which these tasks are to be performed. Typically the criteria for job design are consistent with specialization: that is, minimizing immediate cost and maximizing immediate productivity.

These criteria have been criticized on the ground that "minimum *immediate* cost" is not the same as minimum *economic* cost. The latter includes social costs attendant upon depersonalization of the job and enforcement of worker anonymity. These social costs attributable to overfractionalization in job design are reflected in worker dissatisfaction. Hence, there is a growing emphasis upon what has been termed a *job-centered approach* to job design taking into account (1) the processes to be accomplished, (2) the unique capacity of human beings to make decisions, and (3) optimal organizational groupings of workers to maintain continuity of production.[28]

Miscellaneous Solutions

At least three additional practices bear upon job satisfaction: initial employee selection and placement; provision of evidence to the

---

[28] L. E. Davis, "Job Design and Productivity: A New Approach," *Personnel,* Vol. XXXIII (1957), pp. 418–30.

employee that management recognizes and appreciates his contribution to the company; and provision of opportunities for industrial counseling. Counseling in industry is not geared to treating serious psychological disorders. It is intended, rather, to help employees cope with the less severe kinds of emotional problems that may interfere with his behavioral effectiveness in the company, family, and community.

SUMMARY

Motivation is a fundamental explanatory concept underlying the understanding of behavior. A person's needs or wants, and the drives generated by them, sensitize him to awareness of particular stimulus conditions and influence the way in which he perceives and responds to these conditions.

Motives related to work have quite generally been oversimplified. Employees do not work solely or, in most instances, even primarily to earn money. The work role is central to the maintenance of an individual's sense of general well-being.

The satisfying job is one that contributes to the employee's feelings of accomplishment and purposefulness. Thus, there is no reason to expect that job satisfaction must invariably lead to increased productivity. The reward for high production is most often financial in nature. This incentive may be relatively unimportant to the individual in comparison with other kinds of incentives provided by his personal interactions with fellow employees and in his community.

The needs of employees are generally not well understood, either by executives or by labor leaders. The latter group tends to overestimate the extent of employee concern about union matters. Executives, on the other hand, often overestimate the importance attached by workers to such factors as pay and working conditions. Neither executives nor labor leaders appear to be well informed about the employees' needs for personal recognition.

The overall level of job satisfaction varies with such factors as occupational status, sex, age, and experience. Intelligence *per se* is not related to job satisfaction except as the level of intelligence is considered in relation to the nature and demands of the job. Employees who are either insufficiently challenged by their work, or who are engaged in activities that are too demanding, tend to feel dissatisfied.

There is a rather strong relationship between job adjustment and life adjustment. This interaction probably works in both directions: that is, job satisfaction contributes positively to satisfaction with life, and adjustment to factors outside of the working environment reinforces the worker's adjustment to his job.

A traditional approach to increasing job satisfaction is to deal with grievances as they arise. It is important to note, however, that the grievances typically presented to management may obscure the fundamental sources of employee dissatisfaction. Employees who make complaints about pay or working conditions may often be reacting to other sources of frustration.

. Ameliorative measures predicated solely upon the expressed sources of dissatisfaction may therefore provide only temporary relief from strained labor-management relations. Consequently, it is imperative that consideration be given the matters of increasing employee involvement, redesigning overly fractionated jobs, providing individual recognition, improving personnel selection and placement procedures, and making industrial counseling available to employees.

The ultimate responsibility for maintaining or increasing job satisfaction rests with management and supervisory personnel. The employee must be recognized and accepted as an individual rather than as a statistic or as a mere extension of the mechanical equipment with which he works.

Morale

14

In the preceding chapter we considered several elements associated with job satisfaction. Such satisfaction (or dissatisfaction) is, as you will recall, a highly individual matter. It is dependent upon the extent to which the job is perceived by the employee as fulfilling his needs and as providing the gratifications he desires.

It has been suggested that morale is the combination of attitudes held by the employee toward his job, company, and immediate supervisor.[1] This definition is, in a sense, an operational one describing the way in which morale is characteristically appraised. An *attitude* predisposes a person to behave in either a favorable or an unfavorable fashion. Thus, a typical approach to the assessment of morale involves a kind of "averaging" of employee attitudes in several critical areas. Presumably, an employee who is unfavorably disposed toward his job, his company, or his supervisor will lack the sense of company identification that is associated with high morale.

The definition of morale as a composite of employee attitudes does, however, appear to miss two essential components of the concept. First, we generally think of morale as a relatively stable attribute. Employee attitudes toward various aspects of the job may be transitory, reflecting conditions of the moment rather than a more basic orientation. Secondly, a combination of job-related attitudes misses the flavor of interaction between the individual and the group usually associated with morale. High morale implies that ". . . the individual perceives a probability of satisfying his own motives through cooperation with the group."[2] Thus, the state of an individual's morale is gaged relative to a specific group like his company, informal work group, or union.

In this chapter we will be particularly interested in understanding

---

[1] R. L. Kahn and D. Katz, "Leadership Practices in Relation to Productivity and Morale," in D. Cartwright and A. Zander (eds.), *Group Dynamics* (Evanston, Ill.: Row, Peterson & Company, 1953), p. 616.

[2] R. Stagner, "Motivational Aspects of Industrial Morale," from "Industrial Morale (A Symposium)," *Personnel Psychology*, Vol. XI (1958), p. 64.

the factors responsible for high and low morale and in the implications of morale for various criteria of industrial efficiency. To approach these objectives, we must first describe some of the procedures for assessing morale.

MORALE ASSESSMENT

Attempts to measure or otherwise to assess morale can be classified on the basis of the definition of morale upon which they are predicated. Morale is, on the one hand, a function of the group's cohesiveness. High morale cannot exist unless the group is well integrated and the members accept one another. Morale, considered in this light, must be assessed by studying the pattern of group interactions.

Cohesion of group members is not, however, the sole requirement for high morale. An originally cohesive group that lacks focusing goals may begin to disintegrate rather rapidly. This often occurs, for example, when an athletic team becomes convinced that it cannot win. In order for morale to be high, the goals must be clearly perceived by each member of the group. The members must, in addition, be convinced of the importance of their own task to the successful attainment of the goals, and must feel that the group as a whole is making satisfactory progress in the direction of goal attainment.

It is necessary, in view of all of the components of morale, that a multidimensional approach be taken in the matter of its assessment. The work group must be studied as a unit to determine the extent to which it functions as a cohesive whole; the individuals within the group must be studied to determine the level of their awareness of the existence of a goal and the extent to which they perceive themselves as contributing substantially to the overall group endeavor.

Sociometry

From one viewpoint, high morale depends upon the existence of shared feelings of belonging and participation by the employees. Thus, in a high morale group, we would expect group structure to be relatively cohesive. Conversely, where morale is low, we might anticipate that there will be some employees who are assigned to, but not integrated within, the work unit.

Sociometry is a technique developed by Moreno[3] for studying a variety of group structures. It has been rather extensively used both for assessing morale and suggesting possible modifications in group structure.

When sociometric procedures are utilized in work groups, each individual assigned to the group is asked to name the person who, in his judgment, would be the best supervisor, makes the greatest contribution to the total group effort, or is the best worker. This fundamental procedure can be modified easily by requiring respondents, for example, to choose two persons rather than one, or by requiring them to "nominate" persons who they feel are inefficient as well as those who are efficient. The application of the latter *nominating technique* is illustrated by the following questions asked during interviews with naval pilots:

Assume that you are to be shifted to a new air group tomorrow and that you may select your own combat mates to go with you to this new air group. Of all the men known to you in Naval Aviation—living or dead —what two men would you like most to fly wing in your new combat assignment? Why would you select these men?
What two men would you least like to have flying wing on you? Why?[4]

The resultant choices and rejections are summarized visually in a map of the group's structure called a *sociogram*. Every person is represented in the sociogram by some kind of symbol, like a circle. Choices and rejections are often represented by connecting pairs of circles with solid lines to represent positive choices and dotted lines to represent negative choices. Some representative sociometric patterns are shown in Figure 14–1.

Application of Sociometric Findings. It is impossible to perform a sociometric analysis of group structure unless the group satisfies certain requirements. The members of the group must be closely associated for a sufficient period of time to have formulated evaluations of each other. The circumstances of their association, furthermore, must be such that they are familiar with one another's capabilities and limitations. Finally, the group must share a common task or objective if sociometric evidence is to be regarded as a valid index of morale.

---

[3] J. L. Moreno, "Foundations of Sociometry," *Sociometry Monograph*, No. 4 (Boston: Beacon House, 1943).

[4] J. G. Jenkins, *The Nominating Technique: Its Uses and Limitations* (Paper presented to meetings of the Eastern Psychological Association, 1947).

This latter point is an important one and, perhaps, not self-evident. Workers who are grouped together for administrative purposes but do not share a common objective may have high morale in spite of sociometric evidence for the existence of cliques and self-contained

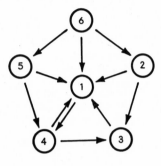

A. A COHESIVE GROUP
WITH A STAR

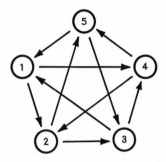

B. A COHESIVE GROUP
WITHOUT A STAR

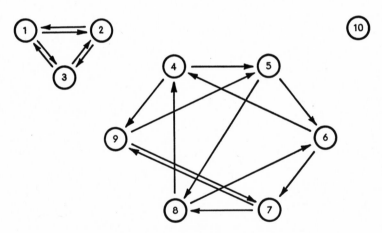

C. A NONCOHESIVE GROUP WITH A CLIQUE (1,2, AND 3)
AND AN ISOLATE (10)

FIGURE 14–1. Some Typical Sociometric Patterns.

subgroups. These subgroups may have been formed because of common interests and activities. Thus, the very fact of their existence under such circumstances could be indicative of high morale.

The information relative to group structure provided by a sociogram yields valuable clues about ways in which industrial morale may be improved. Any procedure that eliminates cliques or isolates, either by integrating them within the group structure or severing them from the group, may well improve morale by increasing cohesiveness. Furthermore, the sociogram can be extremely potent for the purposes of identifying persons who are potential leaders, and paving the way for newly assigned supervisors by familiarizing them with the structure of the group they are to lead.

It frequently is desirable to implement sociometric choices by assigning employees to work with the persons whom they have chosen. A good deal of industrial activity is organized about the work team consisting of two or more employees. This is, perhaps, most evident in the case of an aircrew executing a military mission, but is a factor also in many other kinds of settings. When carpenters and bricklayers were permitted to choose their work partners sociometrically, for example, production costs decreased by about 5 percent and the workers reported increased interest in and satisfaction with their work.[5]

Surveys

Morale is, as we have already pointed out, dependent upon certain factors in addition to the one of cohesiveness. Knowledge of the employee's feelings about the job, the company, and the supervisor is important to the assessment of morale. In order for morale to be high, the employees must perceive their job to be of importance to the welfare of the company, the company to be sincerely interested in them as individuals, and the supervisor to be an individual who acts fairly in his role as intermediary between the employee and the company.

Employee attitudes and opinions may be surveyed by a variety of questionnaire, interview, and attitude scaling procedures. Such surveys serve three purposes in addition to the fundamental one of appraising morale. (1) The properly designed morale survey is a diagnostic device which helps to identify some of the sources of friction between management and the worker. (2) Action predicated upon the results of such a survey can do much to improve group solidarity and morale. (3) It provides concrete evidence to the employees that management is really interested in them and in their opinions.

---

[5] R. H. Van Zelst, "Sociometrically Selected Work Teams Increase Production," *Personnel Psychology*, Vol. V (1952), pp. 175–85.

Questionnaires. A questionnaire is the most economical and probably the most frequently used procedure for soliciting employee opinion. The format of the questionnaire can be varied in accord with the kind of information desired from each respondent, the amount of time available for summarizing the responses, and the occupational level of the employees. The principal dimension differentiating between various kinds of formats is the extent to which the questionnaire is structured.

A *highly structured questionnaire* asks very specific questions and limits the nature of the response that can be made by the employee. The percentage of employees marking each alternative of a structured questionnaire can be summarized easily. In addition, such forms are sometimes "scored" by assigning weights to each of the alternatives and averaging the weights of the alternatives marked by each respondent.

The *Tear Ballot for Industry* is a generalized questionnaire designed for administration in a variety of industrial situations. The test consists of 11 five-alternative items, is simple to administer, and guarantees anonymity to the respondent.[6] Replies to the *Tear Ballot* questions were correlated with job tenure rate for a sample of 98 workers in diverse industries. Job tenure rate was determined by dividing the total time the worker had been in the labor market by the number of different jobs he had held. The resultant correlations for each of the items are shown in Table 14–1.

Highly structured questionnaires have been criticized on the grounds that the areas of opinion investigated are too narrowly defined by the specific questions asked, and the replies are limited by the choices offered by the item. The respondent generally cannot indicate subtle gradations of feeling or qualify his answers. *Unstructured questionnaires* offer the respondent considerably more leeway in making comments related to his attitudes and opinions. An illustrative item from such a questionnaire might read as follows:

How do you feel about the flow of information from management? Do you get all of the information you want or need? Does this information reach you rapidly enough or does it come to you to slowly? How could the flow of information in your section be improved?

The response to such a sequence of questions must, of course, be written out. Hence, it is considerably more difficult to summarize

---

[6] W. A. Kerr, "On the Validity and Reliability of the Job Satisfaction Tear Ballot," *Journal of Applied Psychology*, Vol. XXXII (1948), pp. 275–81.

and integrate the replies than it is when highly structured questionnaires are administered. This type of open-ended question, however, often elicits considerably more information of greater depth
and significance than that obtained from structured morale surveys.

   Interviews. The employee interview for the purpose of morale
assessment, in a way, involves the verbal administration of a
questionnaire. In fact, the two procedures often are combined. The
preliminary administration of a questionnaire may suggest areas
that merit further discussion during the course of the subsequent interview.

   The interview has the unique advantage over the questionnaire of
providing direct contact between the employee and the interviewer.

TABLE 14–1

CORRELATIONS BETWEEN ITEMS IN THE "TEAR BALLOT FOR INDUSTRY"
AND JOB TENURE RATE

1. Does the company make you feel that your job is reasonably secure as long as you
   do good work?... .45
2. In your opinion, how does this company compare with others in its interest in
   the welfare of the employees?... .14
3. How does your immediate supervisor compare with other managers, foremen,
   or section leaders as to supervisory ability?............................ .18
4. Consider your work; are your working conditions comfortable and healthful?.... .26
5. Are most of the workers around you the kind who still remember you when you
   pass them on the street?.. .63
6. Do you think your income is adequate for your living needs?............... .26
7. Do you feel that you have proper opportunity to present a problem, complaint,
   or suggestion to the management?.. .33
8. Do you have confidence in the *good intentions* of management?............. .33
9. Do you have confidence in the *good sense* of management?................. .32
10. What effect is your experience with the company having upon your personal
    happiness?... .17

Thus, if it is skillfully conducted, the interview will permit considerable probing of feeling and may lead to the discovery of previously unsuspected sources of low morale. The interview, furthermore, provides the employee with opportunities to indicate not only
how he feels, but also *why* he feels the way he does, and to make
positive suggestions about the ways in which morale might be improved.

   Interviews are, however, subject to a number of sources of difficulty which may interfere with their utility for morale assessment.
The validity of the interview is highly dependent upon the establishment of good rapport. Unless this is accomplished, the inter-

viewee may fear reprisals by management and, in consequence, the usefulness of his replies will be diminished.

Successful interviewing requires considerable skill and experience. A number of pitfalls attributable to the extreme subjectivity of this procedure have already been discussed in Chapter 4. Management may decide against using interviews for morale assessment also because of the relative costliness of this procedure in comparison with questionnaire surveys. Questionnaires can be administered simultaneously to groups of employees and, on occasion, may be given to the employees with instructions to complete the form at home. Interviews, on the other hand, are generally conducted with just one employee at a time and hence entail considerable expense in terms of both released work time and consultant or interviewer time.

Attitude Scales. This approach to morale assessment is founded upon many of the concepts underlying psychological testing procedures. Attitude scaling is a measurement technique as differentiated from procedures, like questionnaires and interviews, that are designed primarily to yield qualitative information about employee opinions. The attitude scale is a psychological yardstick. Employee responses are scored, and the resultant value is indicative of the degree to which the employee holds favorable or unfavorable attitudes. These scores may be averaged for groups of employees, and the attitude scales themselves may be submitted to the same kinds of studies of reliability and validity which are applied to tests.

One scaling technique, originally proposed by Thurstone and Chave,[7] results in identifying a group of relatively unambiguous statements expressing a range of attitudes from "extremely favorable" ones to "extremely unfavorable" ones. Each statement is weighted in accord with its position on the favorability-unfavorability continuum, and scores are computed for respondents by averaging the weights of the statements with which they agree.

An illustrative scale of this type measuring employee attitudes toward company policies and practices is shown in Table 14–2.

In Uhrbrock's study using this scale, 3,934 factory workers earned an average score of 6.34 and 400 foremen earned an average score of 7.19. When these scores are interpreted in the light of the con-

---

[7] L. L. Thurstone and E. J. Chave, *The Measurement of Attitude* (Chicago: University of Chicago Press, 1929).

tinuum about which the scale is based, it is apparent that foremen's attitudes were more favorable than those of factory workers.

Indirect Methods

One of the most serious obstacles to assessing attitudes and opinions by means of the three approaches thus far described (questionnaires, interviews, and attitude scales) is the possible discrepancy

TABLE 14–2

STATEMENTS SELECTED FOR INCLUSION IN A SCALE FOR MEASURING EMPLOYEE ATTITUDES TOWARD THEIR COMPANY

Scale Value*	Statement
10.4	I think this company treats its employees better than any other company does.
9.5	If I had it to do over again, I'd still work for this company.
9.3	They don't play favorites in this company.
8.9	A man can get ahead in this company if he tries.
8.7	I have as much confidence in the company physician as I do in my own doctor.
8.5	The company is sincere in wanting to know what its employees think about.
7.9	A wage incentive plan offers a just reward for the faster worker.
7.4	On the whole, the company treats us about as well as we deserve.
6.3	I think a man should go to the hospital for even a scratch, as it may stop blood poisoning.
5.4	I believe accidents will happen no matter what you do about them.
5.1	The workers put as much over on the company as the company puts over on them.
4.4	The company does too much welfare work.
4.1	Soldiering on the job is increasing.
3.6	I do not think applicants for employment are treated courteously.
3.2	I believe many good suggestions are killed by the bosses.
2.9	My boss gives all the breaks to his lodge and church friends.
2.5	I think the company goes outside to fill good jobs instead of promoting men who are here.
2.1	You've got to have "pull" with certain people around here to get ahead.
1.5	In the long run, this company will "put it over" on you.
1.0	The pay in the company is terrible.
0.8	An honest man fails in this company.

* The scale values are not presented to respondents actually required to fill out the attitude scale.

Source: R. S. Uhrbrock, "Attitudes of 4,430 Employees," *Journal of Social Psychology*, Vol. V (1934), pp. 365–77.

between the manifest and latent contents of verbalized attitudes. The *manifest* content is evidenced by what people say; the *latent* content is the hidden, deeper feeling underlying what they say.

The fact that the verbal expressions of attitude or opinion do not always reveal the respondent's real feelings or predispositions does not necessarily imply that he has been untruthful. Psychotherapists are often confronted with instances of "unconscious motivation" in which the client is quite unaware of the real reasons for his behavior. We all, as a matter of fact, possess certain underlying feelings and attitudes which we cannot verbalize.

The indirect methods of attitude assessment are designed to identify the latent as well as the manifest attitudes. Although they have been used somewhat more extensively in consumer research (Chapter 16) than for morale assessment, we will here be concerned only with the latter application.

Ethical Considerations. Attempts to discover underlying feelings have recently been given the generic designation "motivation research," particularly when such efforts are directed toward furthering our understanding of the effectiveness of advertising appeals and the images typically associated with particular brands. The approach taken by such research is subtle and regarded, by some, as deceptive. The persons serving as subjects for study are generally unaware of the real purpose of the investigation.

The conduct of motivation research has led to the publication of attacks upon the methodology in the popular literature,[8] and to the discussion of certain ethical considerations in the professional literature.[9] Two of the most significant issues in this regard deal with the legitimacy of investigation involving some kind of "deception," and the possibility that powerful tools for the indirect assessment of attitudes may be used by unscrupulous political leaders or others with vested interests which may be harmful to society.

These issues are serious ones and cannot be disposed of glibly. We must, however, assume that the ethical and professional standards of psychologists will guard against the misuse of indirect methods of attitude assessment. The history of science is punctuated by many discoveries that can be used for both beneficial and destructive purposes. It is necessary that we trust the integrity of the discoverers if we are to continue to expand beyond the frontiers of our present knowledge.

---

[8] See, for example, V. Packard, *Hidden Persuaders* (New York: D. McKay Co., 1957).

[9] I. R. Wechsler, "Problems in the Use of Indirect Methods of Attitude Measurements," *Public Opinion Quarterly*, 1951, pp. 133–38.

Illustrative Procedures. The "My Job Contest" conducted by General Motors is illustrative of the application of an indirect approach to the assessment of employee attitudes.[10] This contest, complete with prizes, required that the participants write a letter on "My Job and Why I Like It." The themes contained in these letters were analyzed as evidences of employee attitudes, and the resultant summary of findings was reported to each division of the company.

The "error-choice" technique has been suggested as another interesting and novel approach to investigating attitudes.[11] This method requires the respondent to choose between two alternatives for each item, both of which are wrong or controversial. Since a correct alternative is not presented, the answer selected is presumed to indicate the direction of the respondent's attitude.

Other indirect procedures, including word-association methods, incomplete sentence blanks, and projective tests like the Thematic Apperception Test, involve techniques that were developed primarily for clinical purposes. The rationale for the utilization of such methods is that predisposition to action, both within the industrial setting and out of it, is best revealed by probing personality in depth.

EFFECTS OF MORALE

It is erroneous to assume that poor productivity is necessarily symptomatic of low morale or that high morale must perforce be accompanied by a high level of output. A study of the relationship between these variables for employees of a mail order company, for example, has indicated that the correlation between morale and productivity is, at best, a weak one.[12] Other investigators have found that certain elements of morale, namely pride in the work group[13] and attitude toward the supervisor,[14] correlate with productivity while other elements appear to be unrelated to output.

---

[10] C. E. Evans and L. N. Landau, "My Job Contest," *Personnel Psychology Monograph, No. 1,* Washington, 1950.

[11] K. Hammond, "Measuring Attitudes by Error-Choice," *Journal of Abnormal and Social Psychology,* Vol. XLVIII (1948), pp. 38–49.

[12] W. J. Giese and H. W. Ruter, "An Objective Analysis of Morale," *Journal of Applied Psychology,* Vol. XXXIII (1949), pp. 421–27.

[13] D. Katz, N. Maccoby, and N. Morse, *Productivity, Supervision and Morale in an Office Situation* (Ann Arbor, Mich.: University of Michigan, Survey Research Center, 1950).

[14] C. H. Lawshe and B. F. Nagle, "Productivity and Attitude toward Supervisor," *Journal of Applied Psychology,* Vol. XXXVII (1953), pp. 159–62.

In a comprehensive survey of 26 studies relating morale to productivity, the authors concluded that 14 demonstrated a positive relationship, nine demonstrated no relationship, and three demonstrated a negative relationship.[15] This discrepancy leads to the generalization that high morale is just one of a multiplex of factors responsible for high productivity.

Labor turnover and absenteeism similarly cannot always be attributed to low morale. Such undesirable employee behaviors may result from a shoddy selection program, improper training procedures, unpleasant working conditions, or any one of a host of other factors ranging from inclement weather to the opening of a new plant in an adjacent community.

Thus, although high morale predisposes employees to efficient industrial behavior, it is too often erroneously regarded by management as the sole factor underlying efficiency. It is significant that often a problem which is presented to the psychologist as symptomatic of low morale proves, upon further study, to stem from deficiencies in other elements of the industrial configuration.

Management is well advised when it is concerned about morale. It cannot, however, anticipate that a simple prescription like piping music into the plant or repainting the rest rooms will invoke fundamental improvements either in morale or in output. Any company that is seriously interested in improving employee morale must, in effect, be concerned with improving every aspect of its organizational structure and activities.

ORGANIZATIONAL STRUCTURE AND MORALE

The unique characteristic of an organization, as opposed to other kinds of social groups, is the fact that its members are differentiated with respect to their functions in achieving the common goal.[16] Thus, the members of any organization, be it a military group, governmental agency, school, or industrial plant, have assigned responsibilities involving both the work they are expected to do and the persons (peers, subordinates, and superordinates) with whom they

---

[15] F. Herzberg, B. Mausner, R. O. Peterson, and Dora F. Capwell, *Job Attitudes: Review of Research and Opinion* (Pittsburgh: Psychological Service of Pittsburgh, 1957).

[16] R. M. Stogdill, "Leadership, Membership and Organization," *Psychological Bulletin*, Vol. XLVII (1950), pp. 1–14.

are expected to work. These formal assignments are often represented in the form of organizational charts showing both the division of work responsibility among members of the organization (the
horizontal dimension) and the division of decision-making or leadership responsibility (the vertical dimension).

Although the usual organizational charts show the formal organization, they do not clarify the informal organization consisting of
the tasks *actually* performed by group members and the persons
with whom they *actually* work. This informal structure reflects the
operation of a variety of factors, including production demands,
supervision, size of the organization, capabilities and limitations of
individual workers, and cohesiveness of the group.

The traditional view of organizational structure is that it is
founded almost entirely upon superior-subordinate relationships.
However, the realization that organizations are generally characterized by an informal structure superimposed upon the formal
"charted" structure has led to abandonment of the traditional view
in favor of a more dynamic one. In addition to the usual "vertical"
or "chain of command" relationships, current literature recognizes
the existence and importance of "horizontal" relationships between
workers at the same hierarchical level and "diagonal" relationships
cutting across functional divisions.[17]

Organizational structure perceived in this more dynamic fashion has highly significant implications both for industrial leadership
and morale. Since leadership will be discussed in the next chapter,
we will restrict our present concern to the implications of certain
aspects of organizational structure and function for morale.

An Overview of the Relationship

You may ask at the outset, "Why does organizational structure
have any bearing at all upon morale?" You will recall that high morale implies that the group is perceived by its members as a cohesive
unit in which they share a feeling of "belongingness" and participation in pursuing common goals regarded as desirable. Thus, although individual employees experience job satisfaction, morale
may be low if the group lacks cohesion. Conversely, a few dissatisfied employees in an otherwise cohesive group may have little or no
effect upon morale.

---

[17] F. J. Jasinki, "Adapting Organization to New Technology," *Harvard Business
Review,* Vol. XXXVII (1959), pp. 79–86.

Cohesiveness is rarely self-generating, except when there is an externally imposed focusing agent for group activity. The singleness of purpose and the solidarity of workers directed toward attaining production goals during a war illustrates this exception. However, under normal circumstances it is not at all correct to assume that management and the employees share a common interest in productivity. Thus, a major function of good management is to develop a smoothly functioning, well-integrated organization in which employees cooperate with one another in pursuing goals benefiting the company as well as themselves.

Organizational Size

The relationship between the complexity of organizational structure and morale has been investigated rather extensively at Sears, Roebuck and Company.[18] One of the important conclusions of this study is that personal involvement of the employees is a much simpler matter in small than in large organizations. The smaller organization is a simpler social system permitting for closer contact between executives and employees and easier relationships between them.

The results of such investigations suggest that overcomplexity of organizational structure is a major cause of poor management-employee relations. The workers in such a setting are required to perform highly fragmented and specialized tasks, thereby depriving them of a feeling of goal-directedness. The subunits within a complex organizational structure tend to be poorly integrated and the supervisors tend, therefore, to exert control by pressures and threats rather than by exhibiting leadership based upon cooperation and team effort.

Thus, a certain amount of administrative reorganization may be required in order to increase the involvement of each employee in company activities. Worthy states, in summarizing the results of his study of organizational structure, that:

Flatter, less complex structures, with a maximum of administrative decentralization, tend to create a potential for improved attitudes, more effective supervision, and greater individual responsibility and initiative among employees. Moreover, arrangements of this type encourage the development of individual self-expression and creativity which are so

---

[18] J. C. Worthy, "Organizational Structure and Employee Morale," *American Sociological Review*, Vol. XV, No. 2 (1950), pp. 169–79.

necessary to the personal satisfaction of employees and which are an essential ingredient of the democratic way of life.[19]

This conclusion is reinforced by other studies showing generally positive relationships between organizational size and absenteeism, accidents, lateness and strikes, and a curvilinear relationship between size and job performance. (In the latter relationship, job performance is maximized in moderately sized organizations.)[20]

Employee Participation

Organizational changes involving alterations in methods of work and established work groups are frequently associated with low morale. Such changes disrupt the cohesiveness of the work unit and engender unfavorable attitudes by virtue of enforced departure from the accustomed way of doing things.

It has been demonstrated that low morale is not an inevitable consequence of organizational change when employees participate in discussions of the necessity for change and alternative solutions. Two problems treated in this fashion by the management of a men's apparel manufacturing company were: (1) supervisors' reluctance to hire female employees; (2) excessive turnover among workers forced to transfer from one job task to another because of changing market conditions. Both problems were successfully resolved by having employees participate in the changes.[21]

When groups of persons work together to arrive at the solution of some common problem, they tend to experience a feeling of solidarity. This, of course, is one of the crucial elements of morale. Moreover, when employees are encouraged to engage in group discussions of work-related problems, they are better able to understand some of the limiting constraints experienced by management, and management in its turn is better able to understand what it is that employees need and want from their job.

Employee discussion groups are not to be confused with gripe sessions. The discussion leader focuses the entire discussion upon the solution of a single problem. He does not lead the discussion to a

---

[19] Worthy, *op. cit.*, p. 179.

[20] R. W. Revans, "Human Relations Management and Size," in E. M. Hugh-Jones (ed.), *Human Relations and Modern Management* (Amsterdam, Netherlands: North-Holland Publishing Co., 1958), pp. 177–220.

[21] L. Coch and J. R. P. French, Jr., "Overcoming Resistance to Change," *Human Relations*, Vol. I (1948), pp. 512–32.

preordained conclusion or decision, but rather handles it in an entirely democratic fashion. Resource persons with specific areas of competence (consultants, representatives of management or of the union) may be requested by the employees to sit in during the session to clarify matters of policy or to help the discussion group evaluate the feasibility of a number of proposed solutions. If the discussion procedure is to work effectively, however, neither management nor an outside consultant can be permitted to grab the ball and run with it. The employees alone must share the responsibility for developing a final solution to the problem. Once the solution is voted upon and accepted by the group, little if any enforcement by management will be required. It is unnecessary for anyone to see to it that we do something that we ourselves have decided to do.

It cannot be assumed that amount of participation *per se* determines the level of satisfaction of participants. In fact, a nonindustrial study of this issue led to the suggestion that the *opportunity* to participate rather than the amount of participation may be the critical variable. Small groups of undergraduate students were allotted a specified number of grade-points to distribute among the individual group members. These points were added to course examination scores, engendering a conflict of interest. The solution arrived at by three fourths of the groups was to allocate these points according to need. Each member was asked to express his feelings about the decision. The degree of satisfaction reported by individual members was related to the extent to which they felt they had an opportunity to participate in and affect the group's decision. The number of points received and the actual degree of participation were not similarly related to members' feelings.[22]

Participation, or at least the opportunity to participate, is essentially a democratic process. Therefore, there has been some speculation that results favoring participation might be culturally limited to the United States. A review of recent studies in certain other countries, including Norway, Japan, and England, supports a degree of generality for the beneficial effects of participation upon employee attitudes.[23] Whether or not participation would be either

[22] L. R. Hoffman and N. R. F. Maier, "The Use of Group Decision to Resolve a Problem of Fairness," *Personnel Psychology*, Vol. XII (1959), pp. 545–59.

[23] V. H. Vroom and N. R. F. Maier, "Industrial Social Psychology," in P. R. Farnsworth, O. McNemar, and Q. McNemar, *Annual Review of Psychology*, Vol. XII (Palo Alto, Calif.: Annual Review, Inc., 1961), p. 421.

possible or similarly effective in other more restrictive nations is
still an open question.

Communication

Communication, or the transmission of information throughout an
organization, is an exceedingly important factor in industrial morale. Erroneous or delayed transmission of facts may serve as the
groundwork for rumor. Furthermore, even without rumor, employees who are not well informed about company policies and practices
can hardly develop a sense of identification with the "company
team." Finally, poor communication can lead to an utter breakdown of activities requiring coordinated action, and consequent inefficiency quite apart from its deleterious effects upon morale.

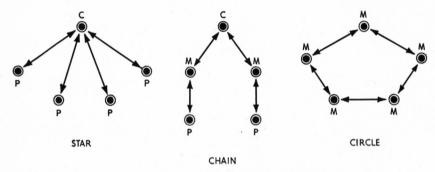

FIGURE 14–2. Three Communication Networks.

Communication Networks. A communication net describes the
pathways for transmitting information among members of the
group.[24] Three such networks are shown in Figure 14–2:

The Star Group: All information is sent to a central figure (C) who in
turn relays it to the persons on the periphery of the group (P). This is a
miniature representation of a simple autocratic communication structure.

The Chain: The communication pattern is complicated by placing
middlemen (M) between the star and the men on the periphery.

The Circle: This pattern permits communication between adjacent
group members but lacks centralized organization.

The relative efficiency of these and other communication nets is

24 A. Bavelas, "Communication Patterns in Task-Oriented Groups," *Journal of
Acoustical Society of America,* Vol. XXII (1950), pp. 725–30.

typically investigated in a particular kind of laboratory setting. The subjects in each group are seated around a table but are separated from one another by partitions. They can communicate only by passing notes through slots in the partitions, and the experimenter establishes the network by opening and closing the slots. The group must solve problems utilizing only the channels of communication open to it.

With reference to the three networks shown in Figure 14–2, it has been demonstrated that the "star" group solved problems most efficiently but tended to have the poorest morale. The "circle" group was least efficient in solving problems but had the highest morale. An additional finding of interest was that persons occupying central positions expressed greater job satisfaction and were perceived as having higher status than persons either at the middle or peripheral positions.[25]

Subsequent investigation attempted to separate out the effect of communication restrictions upon performance of the task from its effects upon the group's ability to organize itself for such performance. This study essentially repeated the procedure described above for the "star" and "circle" groups. In addition, an "all-channel" group in which every member was free to communicate with every other member was established. The results confirmed the hypothesis that communication nets affect the efficiency with which groups perform because of the influence they exert upon the development of adequate organizations. The "star" is most efficient because organization is imposed upon the group; the "circle" least efficient because the strictures upon communication operate to prevent such groups from developing organizational hierarchies.[26]

Generalizations about the superiority of particular kinds of communication networks, judged either by the criterion of task-performance or morale, must be tempered by consideration of the constituency of the group and the purpose for which it is formed. A highly centralized network is probably most efficient when the task is routine and collation of individual activities is necessary from the very beginning.

---

[25] H. J. Leavitt, "Some Effects of Certain Communication Patterns upon Performance," *Journal of Abnormal Social Psychology*, Vol. XLVI (1951), pp. 38–50.

[26] H. Guetzkow and H. A. Simon, "The Impact of Certain Communication Nets in Task-Oriented Groups," *Management Science*, Vol. I (1955), pp. 233–50.

There are circumstances, however, in which a freer network permitting for more active participation by the group members is highly desirable. It would probably be unwise to impose a rigidly patterned communication network when flexibility is required of the group by virtue of the complexity of the problem confronting it and/or the diversity of knowledges possessed by its members.

Feedback. When communication proceeds along an open channel in which members of the organization have access to each other, we have an instance of feedback. In its simplest form feedback involves just two persons; Person A communicates something to B and in turn receives back from B some form of communication indicating, for example, that B understands or misunderstands what A has said. Feedback is not limited to a cognitive level. B may, either by words or expression, feed back a range of attitudes, value judgments, and so on.

It is obvious that some kind of feedback is an aid to the original communicator. He can judge from the behavior of the recipient whether or not he has made himself understood. Moreover, feedback permits a sense of amity to develop between sender and receiver.[27]

Feedback, or its absence, has important consequences also for cohesiveness within organizations involving more than just two persons. Feedback of the results of an industrial morale survey is a case in point. It seems self-evident that such a survey ought to be a starting point rather than a terminus for management's efforts relative to morale. Yet, in spite of what seems to be a statement of the obvious, neatly bound results of morale surveys are often distributed throughout the company with a cover memorandum to the effect that ". . . this will provide interesting and informative reading" and without any concrete effort to implement the survey findings or to feed them back to the employees.

Without feedback the respondents may be left with the feeling that they have been shouting into an empty rain barrel. Its absence may be construed by some employees as evidence that management is not really interested in their opinions and probably has not even bothered to read a summary of the results of the survey. Feedback and discussion of the results of an attitude survey has, in fact, been

---

[27] H. J. Leavitt and R. A. H. Mueller, "Some Effects of Feedback on Communication," *Human Relations,* Vol. IV (1951), pp. 401–10.

found to produce attitudes which were markedly improved over what they were at the time the survey originally was conducted.[28]

SUMMARY

One of the fundamental objectives of good management is to develop smoothly functioning, well-integrated groups of employees in which the members cooperate in the pursuit of goals that are of benefit to the company. Such "team spirit" is rarely self-generating. The development of high morale requires that employees hold favorable attitudes toward the job, the company, and the supervisor. In addition, the members must share a feeling of communality of purpose and of group participation.

A variety of procedures are utilized for assessing morale. Sociometric techniques are designed to study the work group in order to determine the extent to which it functions as a cohesive unit. The attitudes and opinions of individuals within the work group may be appraised by means of questionnaires, interviews, attitude scales, and a number of other "indirect" procedures.

Low morale predisposes employees to such undesirable behaviors as absenteeism, turnover, and diminished productivity. Morale is not, however, the sole factor underlying these criteria of industrial efficiency. Frequently a problem that is presented to the psychologist as symptomatic of low morale proves, upon further study, to stem from deficiencies in other elements of the industrial configuration.

The relationship between three aspects of organizational structure and morale were considered: size, participation, and communication. The group's structure as a factor in morale was discussed also, but in the context of assessment procedures. A fifth factor, leadership, is treated in the next chapter.

---

[28] H. Baumgartel, *The Survey Feedback Experiment: A Study of a Program for the Use of Attitude Survey Data in a Large Organization* (Ann Arbor, Mich.: Survey Research Center, University of Michigan, 1953).

Leadership and
Industrial Relations

15

An effective leader establishes goals for the group, initiates action toward the achievement of these goals, and is largely responsible for maintaining or improving the prevailing level of group morale. Most industrial leadership is exercised through a bureaucratic type of organization. The chain of command is such that persons at successively lower levels in the hierarchy wield progressively less power and have lesser degrees of status. Thus, the distinction is often made between top management (the "big boss" or bosses), middle management, and line management including foremen and supervisors.

The identification and training of effective line supervisors is a particularly critical problem because these are the leaders who exert the most direct influence upon individual employees. An understanding of the specific problems involved in selecting and training supervisors requires an appreciation of the functions, requirements, and methods of exercising leadership in a broader context. Thus, it is to this more general discussion of the leadership process that we must first direct our attention.

THE LEADERSHIP PROCESS

The specific functions performed by the leader, and the expectations of subordinates about what constitutes "good" leadership, vary with the level of leadership and the setting in which it is operative. The line supervisor, for example, may be expected to assume a rather direct responsibility for training employees to do their jobs. In order to function as an effective trainer, he may be required to possess comprehensive knowledge about a variety of specific tasks at a practical "how to do it" level. This kind of task knowledge is less often expected or required of middle management and top management. The latter groups are expected to be particularly conversant

320

with the problems and considerations bearing upon high-level policy decisions.

In spite of certain differences in leadership functions related to the leader's setting and level, certain broad expectations are appropriate in varying degrees to virtually all leadership. The behaviors expected of leaders have been identified as: executive, planner, policy maker, expert, external group representative, controller of internal relationships, purveyor of rewards and punishments, arbitrator and mediator, and examplar.[1]

It is considerably easier to describe the ways in which leaders can function than it is to define the personal requirements for effective leadership, or to conceptualize the process of "leading." Investigations in the general area of leadership have pointed to the necessity for differentiating between leadership and status, and abandoning the rather prevalently held "great man" theory of leadership.

Leadership versus Status

We have already said that effective leaders are status figures; they occupy a position of esteem and wield power. The converse of this statement, however, need not be true. Persons may have considerable status and power without being effective leaders. This well-recognized fact has led to an important distinction between "headship" and "leadership."[2]

Headship. Headship, or assigned leadership, is imposed upon the group. The person occupying a position of headship has been appointed or assigned to this position by his superordinates. His status is generally reinforced by a title and salary sufficient to differentiate between himself and the members of the group he is assigned to head.

The heads of groups occupy a position of *nominal* leadership by virtue of their appointment to a status position. If they possess sufficient status and have sufficient power, such assigned leaders can command obedience. Whether or not they can function as effective leaders, however, is an entirely different matter.

Leadership. A person cannot really be regarded as a leader unless he has willing followers. Workers who voluntarily accept their

---

[1] D. Krech and R. S. Crutchfield, *Theory and Problems of Social Psychology* (New York: McGraw-Hill Book Co., Inc., 1948), p. 417.

[2] E. L. Hartley and R. E. Hartley, *Fundamentals of Social Psychology* (New York: Alfred A. Knopf, Inc., 1952), pp. 605–6.

supervisor and willingly implement his plans, behave and feel quite differently from those who are compelled to do so unwillingly or involuntarily. The leader who is elected by the group is, by virtue of his election, in a position to evoke a high level of effort and morale. His leadership is predicated upon a feeling of group solidarity, giving him a powerful edge over a titular head.

The distinction between headship and leadership is perhaps most apparent in the military services. Virtually all enlisted men are obedient when an officer issues commands. Such obedience results from the threat of dire consequences for insubordination. However, the officer who can command on the basis of willing followership, whose men respect his superior knowledge and ability, and feel that they are part of a cohesive group pursuing common goals, is in an enviable position indeed. Unpleasant tasks are performed more willingly by the group members, and the general level of performance and personal feelings of satisfaction are considerably heightened under such circumstances.

It is impossible, of course, to eliminate the appointment of nominal heads in either the military services or in large industry. The distinction between headship and leadership, nevertheless, is useful because it alerts us to certain potential difficulties entailed in the imposition of leadership. In order for an appointed leader to function with maximum effectiveness, he must be the sort of person who would have been elected by the group itself if it had been given the opportunity. We have noted previously (Chapter 12) that the existence in a group of a sociometric star is evidence for an elected leader. If the person thus chosen by the group is not also the one who is the appointed leader, the latter's effectiveness is diminished.

Theories of Leadership

The foregoing discussion of the difference between headship and leadership emphasizes the importance of selecting and training appointed leaders with the utmost of care if they are to function effectively. The factors responsible for effective leadership have been approached from two general theoretical positions.

Trait Theories. This approach to leadership maintains that effective leaders possess a unique combination of specific personal characteristics or leadership traits. It is a "great man" concept of leadership: that is, there are some men who are so outstanding, by virtue of their possession of particular traits or trait combinations, that they are "natural" leaders. Other men, according to this theory, are attracted by this generalized leadership quality, and willingly follow its possessor regardless of the particular circumstances under which it is displayed. The personal characteristics usually associated with this general leadership quality include such things as aggressiveness, intelligence, and tact.

Trait theories of leadership are now quite generally regarded by psychologists as sterile because they make little contribution to our understanding of the leadership process.[3] The traits explanation of leadership leads to the expectation that persons who are effective leaders in one situation will tend also to be effective leaders in other situations. This kind of generality of effective leadership is, however, open to serious question. It has been estimated that the correlation between leadership ability in *different* situations would not exceed 0.35.[4] The correlations between several measures of leadership ability in a *given* situation, on the other hand, are considerably higher.

Thus, it is apparent that leadership is somehow a function of the particular situation in which it is displayed. Persons who are effective leaders in one group often are ineffective leaders in another group. The finding that leadership is not a generalizable characteristic has led to the more recent emphasis upon situational rather than trait factors in explaining effective leadership.

Situational Theories. This approach to leadership perceives the leader and followers as engaging in a continual and dynamic personal interaction. Hence, a particular person emerges as the leader in response to the particular combination of individuals in the group, and to the particular problem that serves as the focus of group activity.

The predictions that follow from the situational and the trait approaches to leadership are quite different. The expectations stemming from the trait approach are static: that is, it is anticipated that the person who possesses leadership traits will emerge as the leader and continue to occupy this position as long as the group exists. The situational approach has a much more dynamic flavor since it anticipates that the leadership of a group will change as the needs of

---

[3] R. M. Stogdill, "Personal Factors Associated with Leadership: A Survey of the Literature," *Journal of Psychology*, Vol. XXV (1948), pp. 35–71.

[4] J. Matthews, "Research in the Development of Valid Situational Tests, I: Survey of the Literature" (Pittsburgh: American Institute for Research, 1951).

the group members and the problem orientation of the entire group is changed.

The situational explanation of leadership is substantiated by the finding that the group members' attitudes toward the leader are variable rather than constant. Enlisted men, for example, held much less favorable attitudes toward their officers near the end of World War II than at the beginning of the war, even when the matters of longevity and rank were controlled.[5] The particular task orientation of enlisted men during the early phases of the war made military headship quite acceptable to them. As the war neared its conclusion, however, this focusing orientation disappeared, and authoritarian leadership was much less acceptable to the followers.

The work of the Office of Strategic Services also provides evidence for the fact that leadership is a transitory rather than a permanent phenomenon. Groups of men were presented with a complex task and permitted to elect their own leaders. The person originally elected as the leader was retained in this capacity only so long as he was able to meet the demands of the problem. The group replaced him with another leader whenever it became apparent that this would facilitate progress toward the solution of the problem.[6]

The person chosen by the group as its leader has generally given the group some evidence of his superior general or technical competence and knowledge relative to the group's problem or activity.[7] It is interesting to note that the person who emerges as a leader is not necessarily the one who is best liked by the other group members.[8] Rather, he is the person the other members perceive as the best qualified to deal with the particular situation in question.

One of the fundamental differences between the trait and situational theories of leadership is that the latter stresses the trainability of leader behavior. The ensuing discussion of the effectiveness of various types of leader behavior will lay the foundation for our later consideration of the procedures for identifying and training potential leaders.

---

[5] S. A. Stouffer, et al, The American Soldier (Princeton, N.J.: Princeton University Press, Vol. I, 1949).

[6] OSS Assessment Staff, Assessment of Men (New York: Holt, Rinehart & Winston, Inc., 1948).

[7] W. O. Jenkins, "A Review of Leadership Studies with Particular Reference to Military Problems," Psychological Bulletin, Vol. XVIV (1947), pp. 54–79.

[8] H. H. Jennings, Leadership and Isolation (New York: Longmans, Green & Co., Inc., 1950).

TYPES OF LEADERSHIP

The behavior of leaders is often classified along a continuum ranging from *authoritarian* leadership at one pole to *democratic* leadership at the other. Although the distinction between authoritarian and democratic leadership is a convenient one, it is apparent that these two types rarely exist in a pure form. It is generally recognized also that classification of leadership solely on this dimension does not do justice to multidimensional nature of leadership climates.

Authoritarian Leadership

A group operating under authoritarian leadership is wholly dependent upon the leader for a determination of policies and goals. The authoritarian leader wields absolute power and is the sole unifying factor within the group. Thus, a sociometric pattern for a group operating under such leadership would evidence a well-defined "star" (the leader) and a minimum of choices given or interactions between the group members themselves.

The authoritarian leader is the only person within the group who knows the overall plan of activity. He alone has the responsibility for assigning tasks to individual members. The morale and productivity of the group deteriorates rapidly when such a leader is temporarily absent because the followers have become wholly dependent upon his direction.

Democratic Leadership

The democratic leader is an agent of the group. He facilitates and encourages the members' involvement and participation in achieving the group's goals and, whenever possible, in actually forming its objectives. Thus, the democratic leader encourages a maximum amount of group solidarity founded upon a network of strong interpersonal relationships between the group members.

The sociometric pattern of democratically led groups identifies the leader as a "star" but also displays a pattern of interrelations between the other group members. Since each of the members is an active and informed participant in the group's activity, democratically led groups tend to perform quite effectively even during periods when the leader is temporarily absent.

Studies of Authoritarian versus Democratic Leadership

The most extensive studies concerning the relative effectiveness of authoritarian and democratic leadership were conducted by Lewin, Lippitt, and White.[9] The groups in which these investigations were conducted each consisted of five boys who were 10 years old. These were extracurricular hobby groups and were led by adults primed to exercise three different kinds of leadership behavior: authoritarian, democratic, and laissez-faire. The behavior of the leaders in their attempt to establish each of these three group "atmospheres" is described in Table 15–1.

The experimental design required that the adult leader be changed periodically in order to expose each hobby group to all three types of leadership. The order of leadership was *rotated:* that is, the sequence for one group was democratic, authoritarian, and laissez-faire leadership; for another it was authoritarian, democratic, and laissez-faire, and so on.

In general, the results indicated that democratic leadership is superior for the purpose of evoking creative behavior and cooperativeness. Productivity and member satisfaction was poorest in the laissez-faire situation. It is important to note, however, that there were exceptions to the generalization that democratic leadership was responsible for the highest level of morale. Some of the youngsters, particularly those from autocratic homes, were perfectly satisfied to take orders from an authoritarian leader.

The study described above has important implications for industrial supervision. We must recognize that although democratic leadership is generally the most effective form of supervision *in our society,* there are certain circumstances in which authoritarian leadership may be superior to democratic supervision. Persons who are unprepared for democratic group action, because of lack of prior exposure to and training for such leadership, may feel relatively insecure unless provided with the kind of direction afforded by an authoritarian leader. Thus, the "best" kind of leadership is a func-

---

[9] K. Lewin, R. Lippitt, and R. K. White, "Patterns of Aggressive Behavior in Experimentally Created Social Climates," *Journal of Social Psychology*, Vol. X (1939), pp. 271–301.

R. Lippitt, "An Experimental Study of the Effect of Democratic and Authoritarian Group Atmospheres," *University of Iowa Studies*, Vol. XVI, No. 3 (1940), pp. 43–198.

TABLE 15–1

THREE TYPES OF LEADERSHIP

Variable	Leader's Behavior		
	Democratic	Authoritarian	Laissez-Faire
1. Control over policy formulation.	All policies a matter of group discussion and decision, encouraged and assisted by the leader.	All determination of policy by the leader.	Complete freedom for group or individual decision with a minimum of leader participation.
2. Control over member's activities.	Activity perspective gained during discussion period. General steps to group goal sketched and, when technical advice was needed, leader suggested two or more alternative procedures from which a choice could be made.	Techniques and activity steps dictated by the authority, one at a time, so that future steps were always uncertain to a large degree.	Various materials supplied by the leader who made it clear that he would supply information when asked to do so. He took no other part in the discussion.
3. Control over working associates.	The members were free to work with whomever they chose, and the division of tasks was left to the group.	The leader usually dictated the particular work task and work companion of each member.	Complete nonparticipation of the leader.
4. Dispensation of praise and criticism.	The leader was "objective" or "fact-minded" in his praise or criticism.	The dominator tended to be "personal" in his praise or criticism of each member.	No attempt to appraise or regulate the course of events.
5. Participation by leader.	Leader tried to be a regular group member in spirit without doing too much of the work.	Leader remained aloof from active group participation except when demonstrating.	Infrequent spontaneous comments about members' activities.

Source: R. K. White and R. Lippitt, "Leader Behavior and Member Reaction in Three 'Social Climates,'" in D. Cartwright and A. Zander (eds.), *Group Dynamics* (Evanston, Ill.: Row, Peterson & Co., 1960), p. 528.

tion of such situational factors as the constituency of the particular group and the specific type of problem with which it is confronted.

EFFECTIVE INDUSTRIAL SUPERVISION

A considerable amount of research has been directed specifically to the problem of leadership in industry in an attempt to identify the skills and attitudes underlying effective supervision. Much of this research has centered about two factors, "consideration" and initiating structure," identified as important dimensions of leader behavior. *Consideration* requires awareness by the leader of his subordinates' feelings. It comes closest to the "human relations" aspect of leadership. *Initiating structure* is supervisory behavior facilitating group interaction directed toward goal attainment. The supervisor may accomplish this by organizing, planning, and scheduling the work or by other direct intervention in the group's goal-directed activities.[10]

Although we will discuss each of these leadership dimensions in turn, the relationship between them is of considerable interest. Contrary to what we might expect, these factors are independent of one another. Very considerate supervisors may or may not avoid initiating structure. However, a general pattern of leader behavior is associated with supervisory level. Persons at the upper supervisory echelons demonstrate less consideration and more initiation of structure than those at the lower supervisory levels.[11]

Consideration

The effective supervisor tends to regard his subordinates as individuals, each with his own motives, feelings, and goals. He recognizes that the motives, feelings, and goals of his subordinates are likely to be quite different from those held by himself.[12] An attitude of consideration in dealing with subordinates has been found to

---

[10] E. A. Fleishman, "Leadership Climate, Human Relations Training, and Supervisory Behavior," *Personnel Psychology*, Vol. VI (1955), pp. 205–22.

[11] E. A. Fleishman, "The Description of Supervisory Behavior," *Journal of Applied Psychology*, Vol. XXXVIII (1953), pp. 1–6.

[12] H. H. Meyer, "Factors Related to Success in the Human Relations Aspect of Work Group Leadership," *Psychological Monograph*, Vol. LXV, No. 3 (1951), 29 pp.

correlate positively both with ratings of supervisory effectiveness [13] and productivity of the work group.[14]

This respect for the individuality of each subordinate probably underlies certain specific behaviors that have been found to differentiate between effective and ineffective supervisors. The former (1) evidence trust in the worker's ability to handle the task by not supervising too closely, (2) communicate effectively, and (3) delegate job tasks and provide the delegated persons with sufficient authority to carry out the tasks with which they are charged.[15]

Initiating Structure

We have already emphasized the importance, at least in cultures like ours, of democratic leadership and employee participation. It would be incorrect to assume from this that effective supervisors ought always avoid initiating structure toward goal attainment. Since effective leadership is a situational phenomenon, we should instead expect the optimal combination of "consideration" and "initiating structure" to be dependent upon conditions surrounding the group's activity and structural properties of the group itself.

The dependence of the optimal kind of leadership upon situational factors has been substantiated by investigating the relationship between the flavor of management policy and the attitudes of supervisors. Two companies, one with democratic management and one with authoritarian management, were compared. The results of this comparison suggest that a company can offer authoritarian leadership and still show consideration for the individual worker. The investigator concluded that the success of a democratic approach to leadership rests upon the employees' readiness to accept responsibility, and the possession by them of sufficient experience and knowledge to deal with their work problems. If these conditions do not exist, authoritarian leadership proves to be superior to democratic leadership.[16]

[13] B. M. Bass, "Leadership Opinions as Forecasts of Supervisory Success: A Replication," *Personnel Psychology*, Vol. XI (1958), pp. 515–18.

[14] R. Likert, Measuring Organizational Performance, *Harvard Business Review*, Vol. XXXVI (1958), pp. 41–50.

[15] R. L. Kahn and D. Katz, "Leadership Practices in Relation to Productivity and Morale," in Cartwright and Zander (eds.), *Group Dynamics* (Evanston, Ill.: Row, Peterson and Co., 1953), pp. 612–27.

[16] E. S. Stanton, "Company Policies and Supervisors' Attitudes toward Supervision," *Journal of Applied Psychology*, Vol. XLIV (1960), pp. 22–26.

One of the important determinants of the effectiveness of employee participation is the legitimacy of such participation as perceived by the workers themselves. Worker attitudes are positively influenced by participating in situations in which they regard it as right and proper for them to engage in the decision-making process.[17] However, there are a variety of situations in which the workers regard such participation as inappropriate, and look toward the supervisor for concrete action of a structure-initiating nature.

The tolerance of workers for supervisors who exercise power depends also upon the perceived personal characteristics of the supervisor himself and the psychological needs of each of the subordinates. Workers may express satisfaction with a relatively powerful and directive supervisor who does not encourage much participation, provided such a supervisor is perceived by them as considerate of his men.[18] Furthermore, there are individual differences among workers in their desire for, and hence satisfactions derived from, participation in decision making. Persons who have strong needs for independence react more favorably to participation than do persons with weak independence needs.[19]

Finally, even within a single industrial organization attitudes toward directive and participative supervision may vary because of differences in the structure of various work groups. Large groups characterized by little personal interaction among the workers and between workers and their supervisor were found to favor authoritarian leadership. Conversely, workers within small, highly interactive groups had more positive attitudes toward equalitarian leaders.[20]

It is evident from the foregoing that it is impossible to make blanket generalizations about the most effective supervisory styles. Effective leadership behavior in certain situations may prove relatively ineffective in others because of interactions between variables within the work group. Among others, these include the personal

---

[17] J. R. P. French, J. Israel, and D. Ås, "An Experiment on Participation in a Norwegian Factory: Interpersonal Dimensions of Decision-Making," *Human Relations,* Vol. XIII (1960), pp. 3–19.

[18] F. C. Mann and L. R. Hoffman, *Automation and the Worker: A Study of Social Change in Power Plants* (New York: Henry Holt & Co., 1960).

[19] V. H. Vroom, "Some Personality Determinants of the Effects of Participation," *Journal of Abnormal and Social Psychology,* Vol. LIX (1959), pp. 322–27.

[20] V. H. Vroom and F. C. Mann, "Leader Authoritarianism and Employee Attitudes," *Personnel Psychology,* Vol. XIII (1960), pp. 125–40.

needs of the group members, the tasks in which they are engaged, their perceptions about the legitimacy of participating in decision making, and the structure of the group. These worker and work-group variables are further compounded by the personal characteristics, including the needs, attitudes, and perceptions, of the supervisor himself.

IDENTIFYING POTENTIAL LEADERS

Most industrial supervisors are appointed leaders. Since industrial situations generally preclude the election of a leader by the group itself, it is particularly critical that appointed group heads function so effectively as leaders that they are acceptable to the group. The problem of promoting effective supervision requires that management pursue an active policy of (1) identifying potential leaders within the work force and (2) training these persons in the effective exercise of supervision.

The identification of any ability prior to its emergence or development is, of course, a prediction problem. Thus, the identification of persons who are likely to be effective leaders involves procedures quite similar in nature to those we encountered earlier in our discussion of personnel selection and placement. Nevertheless, certain rather unique problems are encountered in attempts to predict leadership ability. It is virtually impossible, in the first place, to arrive at a uniformly applicable definition of "effective" leadership; hence, predictors of such behavior that are valid in one setting may be quite invalid in some other setting. Secondly, the criteria for "effective" or "ineffective" leader behavior are generally developed from ratings made by subordinates and superordinates. Such subjective criteria are exceedingly unreliable and therefore cannot be predicted very successfully.

The situational explanation of leadership discourages attempts to search for particular traits associated with effective leadership. It suggests, instead, that we must search for persons who demonstrate that they can or do actually emerge as leaders when the circumstances permit for the display of leadership ability. The situational behavior of persons can be studied in its "natural state," that is, as it occurs in real-life situations, or in circumstances deliberately contrived for this purpose.

Buddy Ratings

The existing work group is a real-life situation. Presumably, the members of such a group have had an ample opportunity to observe each other's behavior under a variety of circumstances. Therefore, they should be in an excellent position to evaluate one another's potential for leadership. Such evaluations are most often made in the form of sociometric ("buddy") ratings. Buddy ratings can, of course, be supplemented by ratings made by the supervisor.

Behavioral Tests

The approach to predicting leadership behavior from contrived situations is an extremely interesting one. Persons may be exposed to actual test situations demanding a display of leadership (that is, *behavioral tests*), or they may be required to respond to a paper-and-pencil inventory posing unique leadership problems. Some indication of the kinds of behavioral predictors that have been explored is provided by the following five measures used in an attempt to differentiate between effective and ineffective civilian supervisors at military depots.[21]

1. A standardized panel interview: The candidate was interviewed informally by three interviewers. Topics and questions related to supervisory performance and attitudes were introduced into the discussion and the candidate's responses were evaluated independently by each interviewer.

2. A standardized individual interview: The candidate was interviewed by just one interviewer.

3. A group discussion problem: Four of the candidates were constituted as a committee with instructions to develop recommendations on a particular aspect of plant management. The quality of the contributions made to this discussion by each candidate was rated by the examiner.

4. A role playing situation: The candidate was required to deal with a "staged" personnel problem. An assistant examiner acted the role of the subordinate and the examiner recorded specific aspects of the candidate's performance.

5. A small job management problem: The candidate was required to demonstrate supervisory ability in a miniature work situation. An observer scored the quality of his supervisory behavior and his actual work output.

---

[21] R. Glaser, P. A. Schwarz, and J. C. Flanagan, "The Contribution of Interview and Situational Performance Procedures to the Selection of Supervisory Personnel," *Journal of Applied Psychology*, Vol. XLII (1958), pp. 69–73.

When these five behavioral test situations were compared, it was found that the group discussion problem was the most efficient predictor of effective leadership while the small job management problem was the least efficient predictor.

Paper-and-Pencil Tests

Contrived situations involving supervisory leadership have been presented in paper-and-pencil form in a test of "social attitudes." [22] Each item in this test describes a simple social situation, and the multiple-choice alternatives state various courses of action that might be followed in this situation, or feelings about it. The respondent is asked to mark the alternative stating the course of action or attitude he feels is appropriate. The following items about "Harry," a senior accountant, illustrate the content of this test:

29. Harry's supervisor is near the retirement age. Most of the men will be glad when he retires because he is so grouchy. How would you expect Harry to feel toward him?
    a) He probably agrees with the rest of the men.
    b) He probably feels that he might be grouchy, too, if he were as old as the boss.
    c) He probably tries to avoid the boss.
    d) He probably feels that something must be troubling the boss.
36. The group leader who is in charge in the supervisor's absence, is a young, college-trained man with less experience than Harry and some of the others. When the man was appointed group leader, Harry thought to himself,
    a) "I hope he makes out all right."
    b) "The boss is making a mistake in not appointing a senior man."
    c) "That fellow isn't qualified for the job of group leader."
    d) "I like to see a young fellow get ahead."

Encouraging results have been reported for this approach to identifying leadership ability. Scores on the test were found to correlate positively with criterion ratings of leadership ability. One of the very interesting findings of this study was that the test of "social attitudes" was a much more efficient predictor of leadership ability than was a test of knowledge about supervisory skills. Thus, it appears that leadership training might better concentrate on changing the social attitudes of new supervisors than upon teaching specific leadership skills or techniques.

---

[22] H. H. Meyer, *op. cit.*

TRAINING SUPERVISORS

We may anticipate that as the techniques for identifying potential leaders become more refined, they will play an increasingly prominent role as determinants of promotion from the line. At the present time, however, job experience and proficiency are regarded as the primary prerequisites for such promotion. Although it is desirable for a supervisor to possess the requisite job knowledge and skill, the mere possession of such knowledge is itself no guarantee of leadership ability or supervisory know-how. The supervisor must spend most of his time in activities broadly classified as human relations; he must deal with people rather than with machinery or equipment.

Thus, the transition from a producing role to a supervisory role requires a certain amount of leadership training. Such training must be directed toward developing appropriate supervisory attitudes and a level of facility and skill in dealing with people.

Some of the procedures used for supervisory training include: (1) role playing, (2) case studies, (3) lectures, (4) assigned readings, (5) conferences, (6) formal courses in public speaking, human relations, and so on, (7) personal counseling, (8) job rotation designed to provide an overview of company operations, (9) "sensitivity training" whereby the attempt is made to increase the trainee's awareness of group member's needs and his impact upon their behavior and attitudes.

One of the major problems in leadership training is the distinction made within many companies between supervisory behavior as it is taught in theory or in the classroom and as it is actually practiced in the plant. An excellent training program may be utterly ineffective whenever higher management provides an example of leadership contradicting what the supervisors have been taught in their training classes. It is futile, for example, to attempt to train foremen in techniques of democratic leadership if, when they return to the plant, they are exposed to autocratic leadership from their superordinates. Thus, it is not surprising to find that some leadership training courses are relatively ineffective; that is, they produce no noticeable changes in foremen's attitudes or behaviors when they return to the plant.[23] One of the implications of a negative evalua-

---

[23] E. A. Fleishman, *Leadership Climate and Supervisory Behavior* (Columbus, Ohio: Personnel Research Board, Ohio State University, 1951).

tion of supervisory·training programs is simply that such training cannot be effective if it is conducted solely at the level of the line supervisor. Middle and top management can benefit also from participation in leadership training programs.

INDUSTRIAL RELATIONS

The preceding discussion has been concerned with effective leadership as a factor responsible for improved industrial efficiency. When leadership at all levels of the industrial hierarchy is articulated to permit management and the workers to pursue common goals and share common interests, the members of the industrial organization develop a sense of unity of purpose and identify with the company. This sense of membership in and allegience to the company-group is characteristic of situations in which industrial harmony prevails.

The members of the company-group are, however, also members of many other groups both within and outside of the company itself. Two of these subgroups within industry are particularly pertinent to the present discussion: management and labor. Even when the internal relations within the company are harmonious, the membership of the overall company-group tends to identify with one or the other of these subgroups. The members of management and labor subgroups have certain needs and vested interests that are unique to the subgroup and affect its perceptions. Furthermore, there are superordinate organizations of management and labor that transcend a particular company and may define conflicting goals for their members.

Strikes or lockouts cannot be explained on purely rational grounds. The "reasons" given by the warring factions do not often stand the test of rational consistency. The assumption, for example, that workers strike primarily to earn more money is an obvious oversimplification. The actual cost to the worker of a lengthy strike may offset his financial gain from the strike for a considerable period of time. Similarly, management may suffer a considerable financial loss far exceeding workers' salary demands during a period of industrial warfare.

Thus, the ensuing discussion of industrial conflict is cast in the light of the subjective or human factors operative as determinants of such conflict.

Sources of Industrial Conflict

We can best approach an understanding of industrial conflict by considering some of the differences in needs and perceptions of the two groups involved in the conflict. This focus upon groups rather than upon individuals does not negate the importance of the individual as a determinant of group action. The leader in particular, can exert a powerful influence upon the group members and is, in turn, responsive to the needs of the individuals constituting the group.

Worker Needs. Labor unions develop and grow because their members perceive them as being the only effective satisfiers of some of their needs. The union can operate as effective need-satisfiers in at least two dimensions: (1) It is a liaison between management and labor, providing the worker with a voice that is heard even by top management. (2) The union is itself a structured group and therefore can provide certain gratifications to its members based upon such internal factors as participation in group activities and personal recognition. We will examine each of these functions of labor unions in more detail.

Employees join labor unions partly because of the external representation made to management by such unions. Such representation satisfies many different needs, two of which are highly important. First, the worker needs to feel that he has a voice in decisions that may affect him. The union provides him with a channel of communication with management, and presents his grievances and desires for him. Thus, instead of being subjected solely to downward communication from various levels of the management hierarchy, the union member is enabled also to communicate upward through the management hierarchy. Secondly, the union is perceived by its members as a power-equalizer. The availability of upward communication is of rather dubious value if the communicating voice is a weak one. Thus, although many employees feel that as individuals they are in a disadvantageous power position relative to management, their membership in a union strengthens their voice and puts them in an effective bargaining position.

These needs for representation and power in dealing with management are extremely important. It would be a gross oversimplification, however, to attempt to explain union membership solely on the basis of such needs. The internal dynamics of the union group also satisfy member needs in another direction. The union often provides the worker with a group of his own in which his participation and expression is welcomed; he can speak up without fear of reprisal. In addition, the union provides the member with some status. An employee is a first-rate citizen in his union even though he may feel that he is a second-rate citizen in his company. Unlike the work environment, in which the employee is not consulted on matters of policy, the union *does* consult its members on union-related issues. Union members are provided with avenues for personal recognition, leadership, and authority within the labor organization itself.[24] Finally, the union member feels that he has an organization that is really interested in his feelings and thus provides him with emotional outlets that are impossible for him to attain from either disinterested or overly paternalistic employers.[25]

Management Needs. Unlike the union member who perceives the labor organization as equalizing the balance of power, management may perceive the union as disrupting the balance of power by tipping the scale in favor of the workers. Union demands are often interpreted by management as an encroachment upon its right to run the company. Thus, employers may affiliate with management organizations in order to restore what they perceive to be their rightful prerogatives in the management of the company.

The Power Struggle. If we had to select a dominant thread running through the fabric of industrial conflict, it would be the power struggle between labor and management. This is rooted in emotions and feelings rather than in reason. Unions develop and thrive because they are perceived by their members as removing the power differential between the boss and the worker. Management's antipathy to the union is largely founded upon the belief that its own position of power is weakened by the labor organization.

Although this power struggle between opposing factions has been emphasized, it would be erroneous to regard this as an ever-present feature of industrial relations. The case for a power struggle has been drawn and emphasized because of our present concern with industrial *conflict*. Such conflict in industry is not inevitable. Furthermore, many of the participants in a strike probably do not feel

---

[24] G. Watson, "Labor Unions and Morale," in G. Watson (ed.), *Civilian Morale* (Boston: Houghton Mifflin Co., 1942).

[25] T. Burling, "Disruptive and Cohesive Forces in Job Situations," in G. W. Hartmann and T. Newcomb (eds.), *Industrial Conflict* (New York: Cordon Co., 1939).

any personal involvement in the matter of making a show of strength. They strike simply because they are told to do so by the union and are compelled to do so by the social pressures exerted by co-workers.

Resolving Industrial Conflicts

If we stand apart from the struggle for power between management and the workers, and view it in perspective rather than from management's side or labor's side, one rather obvious fact becomes apparent: the fundamental interests of labor and management are highly interdependent. Management has nothing to offer to potential consumers if it does not have an efficiently functioning work force. Similarly, labor's sole means to product and service consumption is provided by management in the form of opportunities to work.

The fate of both management and labor is tied to the fate of their company, and hence to the fate of one another. Thus, the prevention of industrial conflict and the resolution of such conflict once it occurs is a joint responsibility. Neither side can expect the other to make all necessary concessions.

Collective Bargaining. Collective bargaining is a rather formal arrangement for negotiating labor-management agreements. The purpose of such bargaining between union and management representatives is to permit them to work out peaceful solutions to their mutual problems, and to formalize their agreements by contractual arrangement. Collective bargaining can succeed only when the participants maintain a balance of power and enter into the discussions with a sincere desire to discover mutually acceptable solutions without threat of coercion.

Labor-Management Committees. Labor and management should have further contact continuing beyond that experienced at the bargaining table. Even the best drawn agreements resulting from collective bargaining may be subject to a certain amount of misunderstanding and misinterpretation. If the prevailing atmosphere between management and labor is one of good faith, it is perfectly feasible to discuss and resolve these issues as they arise and in the relatively informal atmosphere of a labor-management committee.

The necessity for such less formal and more frequent contacts between labor and management than that provided by collective bargaining is evident from a study of the dimensions of union-management relations.[26] Union officers were found to seek satisfactions in two dimensions. These were identified as: (1) satisfactions related to contractual accomplishments, and (2) satisfaction with the daily interactions with management. Although successful collective bargaining may contribute positively to the former, it alone is not sufficient to reinforce the feeling of a day-to-day partnership between labor and management.

Grievances of virtually all kinds, including such matters as pay, working conditions, and company policy, may be presented for consideration to the labor-management committee. The success of committees established to discuss and resolve such grievances is dependent upon the underlying attitudes of the committee members. If committee discussion and action is predicated upon feelings of mutual trust between labor's representatives and management's representatives, and if each party appreciates the other's stake in the company's policies and actions, open conflict will most often be averted.

SUMMARY

The specific functions of the leader vary with the setting in which he must operate and his relative position in the hierarchical structure. Employees expect that top management, for example, will assume primary responsibility for the "big company picture" while the line supervisor will assume direct responsibility for day-to-day operations. These differences in expectation about leader behavior are differences of degree rather than kind. Virtually all leaders behave, to varying degrees, as executives, planners, policy makers, experts, and so on.

The essence of effective leadership is a willing group of followers. This fact is recognized in the distinction sometimes made between "headship" and "leadership." An individual may be invested with power by virtue of his appointment to a status position. Unless his subordinates willingly follow him, however, such a person is merely a titular head. He may, to be sure, issue orders and command obedience. But high morale and the maximum expenditure of effort by individuals to achieve the group's goals are beyond the realm of command.

The fact that persons serving as nominal heads may be relatively ineffective as leaders poses a particularly significant problem for industry. The organizational structure of most companies requires that certain in-

[26] R. Stagner, M. Derber and W. E. Chalmers, "The Dimensionality of Union-Management Relations at the Local Level," *Journal of Applied Psychology*, Vol. XLIII (1959), pp. 1–7.

dividuals be appointed to positions of authority. In order for these nominal heads to function as *effective* leaders, they must be carefully selected and trained. Seniority within the company is itself no guarantee of ability or desire to lead. Thus, two questions of fundamental importance in the area of industrial supervision are: (1) On what basis can potentially effective leaders be identified? (2) How can these persons, once identified, be trained in the skills and attitudes underlying effective leadership?

Many different techniques have been developed as aids to management for identifying potentially effective supervisors. The most successful of these techniques are based upon a situational theory of leadership: that is, the successful leader emerges in response to the demands and needs of the particular group in which he holds membership. Since leadership is thus a dynamic rather than a static function, potential leaders must be identified on the basis of their behavior in dynamic interpersonal situations. The search for traits, like intelligence or aggressiveness, predisposing their possessor to leadership in virtually all kinds of situations has generally been abandoned as sterile. The trait approach has been replaced by predictive devices permitting an evaluation of the leadership ability actually demonstrated in a variety of real-life or especially contrived situations.

There is, of course, an important difference between potential and actual effectiveness as a leader. We realize our potential in any area only when we are afforded appropriate opportunities for training. Potentially effective supervisors must learn to exercise certain skills in directing human activities. More important, perhaps, is the fact that they must learn to develop a respect for the individuality of every subordinate.

Effective leadership at all levels of the company hierarchy is a requirement for industrial harmony, but does not in itself guarantee such harmony. Every company is segmented, to some degree, into labor and management subgroups. These subgroups each have certain needs and vested interests that may, on occasion, be in essential conflict. Unions develop and thrive because they are perceived by their members as removing the power differential between the boss and the worker. Management's antipathy to the union is largely grounded in the belief that its own position of power is weakened by the labor organization. More than anything else, then, industrial conflict represents a power struggle between labor and management.

Such conflicts can be prevented or resolved only when the parties to the conflict become fully aware of the interdependence of their fundamental interests. The fate of both management and labor is tied to the fate of the company, and hence they are tied to one another. They are jointly responsible for producing whatever conflict exists, and must act jointly, through collective bargaining and labor-management committees, to resolve their differences.

V.

Consumer Behavior

We have thus far focused our attention upon two of the three groups of persons involved in any industrial enterprise: employees and management. A smoothly functioning business organization is one in which the efficiency of each of these groups is maximized. Under such circumstances intracompany tensions are reduced, employee and employer satisfactions are heightened, and both the quality and quantity, of output may be improved. The economic justification for the existence of a company is, however, ultimately dependent upon the behavior of a third group of persons—the consumers.

You will recall our earlier mention of the fact that psychologists study behavior with a view toward understanding, predicting, and controlling or changing it. The application of these objectives in the realm of consumer behavior is immediately apparent. The purpose of advertising and selling programs is to control or change consumer behavior. The producer, distributor, and advertiser often wish also to predict the way in which potential consumers will respond to various appeals, products, and packages.

The psychological methods and

16. *Consumer Research*

17. *Advertising*

18. *Selling*

principles appropriate to consumer behavior are discussed in Part V. It will be necessary for us to consider such recently well-publicized notions as "motivation research," "images," and "subliminal advertising" as well as the more traditional concepts in advertising and selling.

Consumer Research

16 Two fundamental problems for the producer are: bringing the product to the attention of potential consumers, and influencing them to purchase it. Purchase by the consumer involves an element of decision making. The prospective customer must decide, on occasion, whether or not to buy a product or utilize a service without regard for competing brands. Should he, for example, buy a new car? A new refrigerator? A new coat? He must decide further which of several competing brands or options he ought to select. If he is going to buy a new car, will it be a Falcon, Corvair, or Valiant?

Decisions of this kind are not always predicated upon careful consideration of all alternatives. "Impulse buying" results from decisions made precipitously, without much forethought, and in response to factors about which the buyer himself may be quite unaware. Even decisions considered by the consumer to be highly rational may really be based upon irrational factors and unconscious processes.

The complex area of consumer behavior does not fall exclusively within the province of psychology. A comprehensive understanding of consumer behavior must include contributions from such disciplines as sociology and economics. One of the unique contributions made by the psychologist, however, is the application of rigorous scientific method to consumer research. Psychological methods of inquiry make it possible to replace speculation about consumer behavior with valid and useful information for producers, distributors, and advertisers.

SCOPE OF CONSUMER RESEARCH

There is a fairly prevalent tendency to regard the results of consumer studies with a high degree of suspicion, particularly when such results are incorporated into an advertising campaign. We have all seen "proof" of product superiority presented as part of a TV commercial or in a full-page magazine spread. This kind of "study" does not fall legitimately within the province of consumer research. It often is loaded, either deliberately or unwittingly, in the direction of supporting a predetermined conclusion indicating superiority of the particular product under consideration. By passing out free samples, it would be a simple matter to arrange for nine out of 10 women on the campus to own a bottle of STINKO perfume. However, an advertising campaign based upon the statement that "90 percent of women in a typical Midwestern college use STINKO" would hardly be using the results of a scientifically conducted investigation.

This kind of unethical practice should not be construed as a condemnation either of advertisers or of consumer research. Although many advertising agencies do, in fact, employ psychologists to study consumer behavior, the objectives of their investigations are to test hypotheses and answer questions. It is perfectly possible to be as objective in making inquiries about consumer behavior as in studying the behavior of any other group of persons. In addition to advertising agencies, sound studies of consumer behavior are sponsored by certain manufacturing companies, publishers, federal departments, and universities. Other organizations not maintaining a consumer-research unit may avail themselves of the services of market research companies or consultants who specialize in this area of investigation.

The legitimate areas of inquiry into consumer behavior are tremendously diverse. The following discussion is intended to be illustrative of activity in this field rather than comprehensive. For convenience, we have grouped consumer studies into three classifications or areas of application: (1) delineating, defining, and describing the market; (2) reaching the market; (3) maintaining and expanding the market.

Delineating the Market

Delineation of the market is of particular interest to manufacturers, distributors, and advertisers as they attempt to forecast the sales potential of a product. Furthermore, the characteristics of the persons within this market will, in large measure, determine the way in which the product can be most effectively packaged, displayed, advertised, and sold.

The Short-Term Market. Information about the relative strength of the market over a relatively brief period of time may be critical to maintaining satisfactory production schedules, arranging distribution facilities, and timing advertising campaigns. This is particularly apparent in the case of certain products, like pleasure boats, having a seasonal appeal.

Other characteristics of the product may lead to relatively high saturation of the market over the short-term, and consequent resistance to buying. The consumer is not likely to replace durable goods unless the industry succeeds in convincing him that last year's model is out of date, inferior, or unfashionable. This approach to stimulating short-term markets is obviously successful in the case of the automotive, appliance, and apparel industries.

The Long-Term Market. The fact that an excellent market for a product exists at the present time is no assurance that it will persist in the future. Technological advances may completely outmode a product or heighten the demand for it. If there is evidence for the former, the manufacturer must prepare for economic survival by diversification. Otherwise, he will share the fate of the once prosperous buggy-whip manufacturer who refused to adjust to changing modes of transportation.

The possibility of heightened demand over the long-term must similarly be anticipated. A manufacturer who is unable to fill his orders because he underestimated the demand, issues an open invitation to competitors. Persistently increasing consumer demand is dramatically apparent in the case of equipment, gadgets, clothing, and other paraphernalia in the "sports" and "leisure time" classifications. Increased demand for other products like children's clothing and school equipment can be anticipated on the basis of projected population growth.

The Potential Consumer. Although projections about the short- and long-term markets establish the number of potential consumers, they do not clarify the characteristics of these persons. It is important to supplement information about *how many* persons will buy the product with information about *who* will buy the product, if it is to be effectively advertised and promoted.

Virtually all products are limited in appeal to certain groups. The limiting factors may include such variables as age, sex, occupation, geographic location, socioeconomic level, educational background, and marital status, to name just a few. Studies of these limiting factors often assist companies in selecting appropriate advertising media, appeals, and distribution facilities. There is not much point, after all, to attempting to sell lawnmowers to apartment-dwellers, or horses to Venetians!

Reaching the Market

Once a manufacturer has ascertained the strength of the market and has learned about its composition, he can take steps appropriate to placing the product before the potential consumers. The two primary areas of investigation relative to this problem include studies of advertising and of distribution channels.

Advertising. The ultimate objectives of advertising are to increase consumer awareness of the product, and to impel potential consumers to become actual consumers. The various advertising media are not equally effective for all markets. Thus, comparative studies of the relative effectiveness of advertising media (for example, television versus magazines), and between vehicles within a particular medium (for example, *The New Yorker* versus *The Saturday Evening Post*) may provide valuable clues to the most efficient placement of the advertising dollar.

It is important also to study differences in the relative efficiency of various kinds of advertising copy and appeals. The level of vocabulary utilized and the validity of the appeal for the potential consumer are but two of the vital issues in this regard. One could hardly expect 10-year-old youngsters to be effectively reached by an advertisement for a "prestidigitation kit designed to confound your peers." And an advertisement for an expensive encyclopedia had better not begin, "Boy, oh, boy, Mom, every kid in the neighborhood will want to do his homework at your house when you own this set of books!"

Distribution Channels. The development of appropriate channels for distributing the product must parallel effective advertising. Products with a wide potential market should be made widely available; products with a restricted appeal can best be handled by restricted and carefully selected distribution facilities.

Many of the decisions about channels for distribution can be made without recourse to systematic investigation. However, intuition about appropriate distribution facilities may prove to be misleading either because the product is placed before an inappropriate market, or because the market once served by a channel has changed. Not long ago the consumer went to a drug store to buy pharmaceuticals, and to a hardware store to buy small appliances and housewares. Now, however, many drug stores have become extremely efficient channels for distributing not only pharmaceuticals and small electrical appliances, but a potpourri of other products including such unlikely items as lawn furniture, furnace filters, and potato peelers.

Maintaining and Expanding the Market

A vigorous company cannot afford to maintain an air of complacency about its sales. A once burgeoning market may become progressively diminished by technological advances and products introduced by competitors. Consumer research can profitably be directed toward matters related to the maintenance and expansion of the present market.

Product Testing. The manufacturer is understandably concerned about the public's reactions to his product. If the product is a new one, he may find it worthwhile to subject it to a consumer appraisal before it is released for distribution to the public. It may be initially distributed in trial areas only, or submitted to consumer tests either in the laboratory or the field. Product features that are clearly satisfactory or appealing to consumers during these trials may be exploited in the subsequently developed advertising campaign. The discovery of unsatisfactory features may indicate a need for modification of the product prior to its release or, in extreme cases, to its withdrawal from the market.

The utility of product testing is, of course, not limited to new products. Studies of consumer reaction to a well-established product are vital to the maintenance and expansion of the market. A product once regarded by consumers as outstanding may lose ground rapidly in the face of competition. What was good enough 10 years ago, or even last year, may not be good enough for the present market. Consumer's expectations and standards change. It is imperative that the manufacturer be sensitive to these changes.

Consumer Motivation. The matter of sales cannot be reduced simply to considerations of product excellence, and appropriateness of advertising media and distribution channels. Human behavior is much more complicated than this. Consumers perceive particular products either as being appropriate or inappropriate to their needs; they purchase need-satisfying products and reject the others.

Studies of the complexities involved in consumer motivation are often subsumed under the heading "motivation research." The intent of such investigation is to discover patterns of underlying consumer needs, both at the conscious and unconscious levels. Such information can provide the manufacturer and advertiser with extremely powerful ammunition for effecting brand changes and reinforcing brand loyalties.

AN OVERVIEW OF METHODS

The remainder of this chapter is devoted to a discussion of three approaches to consumer research. It will be helpful for you to know something about the unique purposes of each of these approaches in advance of the more detailed presentation.

Consumer Surveys

A questionnaire or interview survey is conducted for the purpose of ascertaining consumer opinions and attitudes. It often is desirable to find out how consumers feel about the product, the way in which it is advertised, distributed, and serviced, and the company that manufactures it. Survey findings may indicate, for example, that the product is perceived as one of shoddy construction and poor durability; that the service organization is viewed as unequal to the task of repairing the product and obtaining necessary replacement parts speedily and cheerfully; or that there is considerable consumer resistance to purchasing a product made by a company with a widely publicized history of unsatisfactory labor practices. The identification of such unfavorable attitudes can be an important first step in increasing sales.

Depth Procedures

Survey methods sometimes are criticized on the ground that they treat verbalized attitudes and opinions at face value. This argument against the validity of survey findings stems from a distinction between "verbalized" feelings and "real" or underlying feelings. Depth procedures, including projective techniques and probing interviews, are presumed to reveal the core of feeling behind the veneer of verbalized expression.

Behavioral Studies

Opinion surveys and depth studies are alike in that both are concerned with intermediate variables, that is, opinions, attitudes, drives, motives, and so on. The results from such studies contribute to our understanding of consumer behavior and, to a certain extent, permit us to make certain predictions about the behavior. However, since the ultimate focus of consumer research is upon behavior rather than upon these intervening variables, there is some merit to making direct studies of the behavior itself.

SURVEYING CONSUMER OPINION

One of the assumptions underlying survey procedures is that consumers can verbalize at least some of their attitudes and opinions. Thus, if we wish to discover these feelings, we need only ask respondents to reply to questions contained in some kind of opinionnaire.

The conduct of a consumer survey, however, is not as simple as it may appear at first glance. First, it usually is infeasible to administer a questionnaire to all consumers or potential consumers (the universe). This kind of blanket administration generally proves to be too time-consuming and expensive. Instead, the questionnaire is administered to a sample of consumers. The way in which this sample is drawn is of critical importance because we are not, after all, interested only in the opinions of the specific group of persons included within the sample. Since the survey findings must be generalized from the sample to the universe, the ultimate utility of a survey rests heavily upon the adequacy of its underlying sampling procedures.

A second factor affecting the validity of survey findings is the format and method of administration of the questionnaire. The way in which the questions are worded may have serious effects upon the replies. Furthermore, if the questionnaire is to be administered by means of a personal interview, many of the biasing factors discussed in Chapter 4 may act to distort the findings.

Sampling

Suppose we wished to survey the opinions about fluoridation of the water supply held by eligible voters in a particular Midwestern community. The universe with which we are concerned (that is, all eligible voters in this community) would be quite large. It would probably be so large, in fact, as to preclude surveying the opinions of everyone in it because of the time and expense involved in such a comprehensive survey.

Rather than solicit expressions of feeling held by all eligible voters, the decision would probably be made to survey the opinions held by a sample of such voters. We would hope to be able to generalize from the opinions expressed by persons in the sample to the opinions held by the universe. This intent to generalize from sample results places a very important restriction upon the nature of the sample and hence upon the way in which it is drawn: that is, the persons included within the sample must represent the persons in the universe.

The distinction has been made between three fundamental techniques for drawing samples: (1) accidental sampling, (2) random sampling, and (3) stratified sampling.[1] We will discuss each of these procedures, in turn, and evaluate the extent to which they provide representative samples.

Accidental Sampling. This is a relatively simple and inexpensive method for obtaining survey respondents. Once the universe has been defined (for example, eligible voters in a midwestern city), and the questions about the critical issue (for example, fluoridation) have been phrased, the interviewers are turned loose with instructions to question 5, 25, or 100 persons from within the universe. Since specific interviewees are not designated, the interviewer uses his own discretion in selecting respondents. The structure of the sample of persons surveyed is beyond the control of the survey director.

It is obvious that accidental sampling provides none of the safeguards required to insure representativeness of the sample. Attempts to generalize from the responses of interviewees to opinions of the universe are thus on very tenuous ground. The sole value of discussing this procedure is to hold it up to scrutiny as a horrible example of some of the kinds of errors that may creep into a sample and destroy its value for consumer research.

Since the interviewer is not told specifically whom he is to interview, he interviews persons who are readily accessible and with whom he can establish rapport rather easily. This means, in effect, that the respondents included within an accidental sample are very much like the interviewers in such personal characteristics as age,

---

[1] F. Stanton, "Problems of Sampling in Market Research," *Journal of Consulting Psychology*, Vol. V (1941), pp. 154–63.

sex, and socioeconomic level. If the fluoridation survey were conducted by college student interviewers, the results would probably reflect the opinions of a special group of eligible voters: that is, persons who are rather young, reasonably well-educated, and above average in financial means. The sample would probably not include a sufficient representation of persons from socially underprivileged or minority subgroups, of low educational attainment, and earning meager incomes.

Thus, the primary source of bias in the accidentally drawn sample is introduced by the interviewers. They tend to "load" the sample with persons who are like themselves. It might be possible, of course, to compensate for this deficiency of accidental sampling by selecting *interviewers* with extreme care. If the interviewers are themselves representative of the universe, the persons they choose to interview will probably constitute a sample generating more valid findings than if the interviewers are not so selected. There are, however, better and easier methods for obtaining representative samples.

Random Sampling. The selection of respondents by some random procedure overcomes the biases introduced into the sample by the interviewers. The fundamental prerequisite for random sampling is that every member of the universe must have an equal opportunity to be included within the sample. Determination of the particular persons selected from the universe for inclusion within the sample is made in a totally unbiased fashion.

Random sampling begins with a complete listing of every member of the universe. This list must not be arranged or ordered according to such potentially biasing classifications as income level, job status, educational level, or area of residence. The sample is randomly drawn from this complete list by selecting every tenth, twentieth or fiftieth name, depending upon how many persons are desired.

The rationale behind random sampling is a sound one. If the universe is completely listed without biasing subclassifications, if every person randomly selected for inclusion in the sample is actually surveyed, and if a large enough number of names is drawn, the sample should be representative of the total population listed. These three "ifs" are important ones. Failure to comply with any one of these requirements will introduce bias into the sample. Satisfaction of these requirements is not, however, always a simple matter.

Consider the requirement of availability of a complete and unclassified listing of the persons in the universe. Some populations are unlisted. To use a somewhat far-fetched example, how would one go about obtaining a complete list of producers of "home brew" even for survey purposes? Or, to be more realistic, how could a comprehensive list of all persons owning a piano be compiled in advance of conducting a survey?

The second requirement for representativeness of the random sample is that every person selected for inclusion in the sample actually be surveyed. If the survey is conducted by interviewers who canvass during weekdays, they will undoubtedly find that they have much better luck contacting the women than the men assigned for interview. Furthermore, the interviewers will find that it is relatively impossible even to contact some of the women during the day. Some may be away from home because they have jobs, others may be out playing bridge, and a few may be on an extended vacation in the Caribbean. The women who are at home and are willing to answer the interviewer's questions probably represent quite a different social and economic segment of the female population than those who either are away from home or are unwilling to cooperate with the surveyor.

The third prerequisite of adequate sampling (random or otherwise) is sufficient sample size. The size of the sample and its representativeness determine the accuracy with which results obtained from the sample can be generalized to the population. These two factors, size and representativeness, are independent of each other. It is perfectly possible to have a large but unrepresentative sample. It is also possible to draw a representative sample that is, however, too small to permit accurate generalizations to the universe.

There is no simple answer to the question, "How big must the sample be before it is sufficiently large?" Both statistical and economic considerations are involved in the determination of optimal sample size. Although generalizations based upon large representative samples are less subject to statistical error than those based upon small representative samples, the relationship between sample size and statistical error is not an arithmetic one. Improvements in accuracy obtained by increasing the size of the sample reach a point of diminishing returns. Thus, the increased accuracy gained by surveying a larger sample must be weighed against the additional expense entailed by virtue of the increase. Rather accurate nationwide political polls are conducted with 7,500 respondents or less!

Stratified Sampling. We anticipate that a sample drawn by random procedures will be representative because of the lack of systematic bias in identifying the persons to be surveyed. The representativeness of randomly drawn samples is left to "chance." Stratified sampling procedures, however, insure the representativeness of the sample, at least with respect to the characteristics regarded as salient to the investigation. The stratified sample is deliberately structured as a miniature representation of the population with respect to these characteristics.

The population can be stratified, or divided into subgroups, on the basis of such characteristics as geographic distribution, sex, age, educational background, economic level, religion, and so on. Although it is not necessary to stratify the population on all conceivable variables, it is of the utmost importance to stratify on those variables that may be presumed to bear upon the attitudes and opinions under investigation. Population data for many of these variables are available from the U.S. Census Bureau.

Once the significant variables for stratification have been identified, the percentage of the total population within each stratum is determined. These population percentages are used to set sample quotas for each of the strata. The percentages of respondents by sex, age, socioeconomic level and other salient variables included within the sample duplicates the population percentages.

Stratified sampling must ultimately be combined either with random or accidental procedures. To illustrate, suppose we have stratified a university population on just two variables: sex, and fraternity or sorority affiliation. We will assume that 60 percent of the population is male and 40 percent is female; 30 percent belong to a fraternity or sorority and 70 percent is independent. Assuming that each interviewer is assigned to obtain data from 20 students, he must be instructed to select his interviewees so that 12 are men and eight are women; six are fraternity or sorority members and 14 are independents. If, as is often done, the interviewer is permitted to choose his own subjects with the sole restriction that his subsample conform to these stratification requirements, he engages in a kind of accidental sampling. Adherence to the stratification requirements assures representativeness of the sample on the two characteristics

under consideration in spite of the fact that the interviewer ultimately determines which persons to survey.

When stratified and accidental sampling procedures are combined in this fashion, there is the danger that bias will be introduced
into the sample because of critical variables not anticipated in the
original stratification. This danger may be considerably reduced
by combining stratified with random sampling techniques. Let us
again consider the hypothetical survey of university students stratified on two dimensions. After the population characteristics for
each stratum have been determined, the interviewers can be directed to survey specific persons randomly selected from alphabeti-
cal lists of male fraternity members, male independents, female
sorority members, and female independents. The characteristics of
the sample thus constituted would be deliberately controlled on the
two variables known to be critical, and free from interviewer bias
on other variables that may or may not be critical.

Conducting the Survey

The purposes and techniques of consumer surveys are essentially
similar to those of political polls. The basic difference between them
is that in the former we are generally interested in opinions about
products or competing brands, while in the latter we are interested
in opinions about political parties or competing candidates.

Assuming that arrangements have been made for obtaining survey responses from a sufficiently large and representative sample,
there are yet two factors that may exert a considerable influence
upon the survey findings: the structure of the questionnaire (including the way in which questions are phrased, and the format),
and the method by which it is distributed and administered.

Phrasing the Questions.   A questionnaire is a sort of self-descrip-
tive inventory. The respondent may be asked to reveal his past behavior ("What brand of bread did you buy most recently?"), his
intentions regarding future behavior ("Do you expect to buy a new
car this year?"), and his feelings or opinions about something ("Do
you prefer to write with a ball-point pen or one that uses ink?"). The
phraseology of the questions must meet some of the requirements
established for adequate test items: they must be unambiguous, appropriate to the overall purpose of the questionnaire, and free from
internal cues that may influence the nature of the reply. The four
major bugaboos of effective survey-question writing are (1) am-

biguous, (2) nonspecific, (3) leading, and (4) restrictive phraseology.

An *ambiguous* question is interpreted differently by various respondents, hence precluding the combination of replies for summary purposes. Ambiguities may be introduced into a question by using words that vary in meaning (like "usually" and "sometimes"), or that have essentially no meaning for the respondent either because they are overly technical or require an unduly high vocabulary level.

Questions that lack sufficient *specificity* are unnecessarily difficult and do not yield useful information. There is no point, for example, to asking a housewife how many hours she spent washing dishes during the past year. It should be possible, instead, to select a representative and more limited time interval current in the respondent's memory. Housewives can probably estimate dishwashing time with a fair degree of accuracy for an interval like "last week" or "yesterday."

The "why" question tends also to be nonspecific and therefore less than maximally productive, even though it often is used. Since a variety of factors, both conscious and unconscious, generally underlie consumer decisions it is doubtful that a respondent could give all of his reasons for doing something even if he wanted to be cooperative. Furthermore, the reasons cited in response to a "why" question often lack comparability. One respondent may fixate upon considerations of economy, another upon style, another upon durability, and so on. In truth, most respondents may have based their decisions upon all of these factors, but may mention only one or two in a survey in order to get it over with as quickly as possible.

The *leading question* is the most insidious defect in consumer opinionnaires. Its phraseology distorts the response by cueing the reply desired by the interviewer, indicating the answer given by the majority of respondents, or by being emotionally loaded. Few people indeed could be expected to reply truthfully to leading questions like the following:

"You are interested in reading good literature, aren't you?"
"We have found that people tend to spend less and less time watching TV and more time reading. How much time did you devote to TV viewing yesterday?"
"Do you prefer to buy clothes in the 'shocking' colors and patterns, or do you tend to restrict your clothing purchases to the more refined colors and patterns?"

Restrictive wording prevents the respondent from considering all of the possible alternatives. How can the person who intends to buy a cartridge pen cope with the question, "On your next purchase will you buy a ball-point pen or a filler pen?" If the questionnaire is administered by interview, the respondent may protest the inadequacy of a restrictive question. If it is included in a mail survey, the respondent may be tempted either to omit the question or, in disgust, to file the entire questionnaire in the trash can.

It should be apparent, from the preceding discussion, that there are elements of both art and skill involved in writing questions for a consumer survey. One cannot merely write a series of adequate items "off the top of his head." The preliminary versions of the questions must undergo a process of continual refinement based upon pretests and revisions before the questionnaire is structured in its final form.

Format. The organization, arrangement, and mode of presentation of survey questions have been found to exert some influence upon the nature of the elicited responses. The order in which questions are asked may be such that a particular question "sets up" the reply to the next one. You would probably be inclined, for example, to respond more favorably to a question concerning your feelings about the present administrative restrictions upon student behavior if it were preceded by a question suggesting the possibility that such restrictions might be tightened.

A highly structured format providing multiple-choice alternatives for each question may be quite satisfactory for some purposes and misleading for others. If a detergent manufacturer distributes free samples of *Sudsy* to housewives and then asks them to complete an anonymous questionnaire, he might inquire:

How does *Sudsy* compare with the detergent you habitually use?
    a) I haven't tried *Sudsy.*
    b) It is superior to my usual brand.
    c) It is about as good as my usual brand.
    d) It is inferior to my usual brand.

It may appear that all possible opinions are encompassed in the alternatives provided for this question. These alternatives will prove inadequate, however, for a housewife who feels that *Sudsy* is superior for use in her washing machine but not for hand-washable fabrics, or for one who has found that she must use more *Sudsy* to obtain results as good as those obtained with her usual brand.

Some attention has been given to the matter of verbal as opposed to pictorial presentations of questions. A comparison between questionnaires concerning consumer preferences in stove design revealed that the indicated preferences varied with the way in which the questions were presented. The verbal questionnaire consisted of nine items like: "Do you prefer a hinged door or a drawer type storage area?" The pictorial version required the identical discriminations except that the alternatives were presented as drawings rather than verbally. The discrepant results obtained when these two forms of the questionnaire were administered to equated groups of housewives indicated that the two formats under consideration actually yielded statistically different distributions of preference for eight of the nine items. Although the investigation did not demonstrate which of the two versions was more valid for the purpose of actually predicting stove-buying behavior, it provides a convincing demonstration of the potential effects of questionnaire format upon survey responses.[2]

Administering the Questionnaire. Once the questionnaire has been structured in its final form, it may be administered to a sample of consumers in one of three ways: by mail, telephone interview, or personal interview.

The primary advantages of *mail* surveys are simplicity and economy of administration. It is possible, using a mailed questionnaire, economically to survey the opinions of persons in widely separated geographical locations. In addition, the mail survey eliminates one of the potential sources of bias inherent in the other two methods, that is, the interviewer himself.

In spite of these advantages, most mail surveys are inadequate because of the large proportion of persons in the original mailing who fail to return completed questionnaires. Serious errors can be introduced into the study when generalizations are made from the opinions of the persons who *did* reply to the opinions of those who *did not* reply, and thence to the larger population from which the original sample was drawn. There is evidence that respondents to mail questionnaires differ from nonrespondents both in interest in the topic under consideration and in educational level.[3] There is

---

[2] J. Weitz, "Verbal and Pictorial Questionnaires in Market Research," *Journal of Applied Psychology,* Vol. XXXIV (1950), pp. 363–66.

[3] R. Franzen and P. L. Lazarsfeld, "Mail Questionnaire as a Research Problem," *Journal of Psychology,* Vol. XX (1945), pp. 293–310.

some evidence, furthermore, for the conclusion that persons who willingly cooperate with a survey tend to have less traditional or conventional value-orientations than do noncooperative persons.[4] Thus, it is unsafe to generalize from mail surveys unless the returns approach 100 percent of the original sample.

Surveys conducted by *telephone* rarely need be contaminated by nonrespondents. Perseverance in placing telephone calls to persons in the original sample will usually be rewarded by establishing contacts with almost everyone selected for the survey. There is, however, a rather obvious source of bias in telephone surveys. The sample thus contacted does not include an adequate representation of the population segment in the lower socioeconomic levels. Such persons usually are not telephone subscribers.

Because of the deficiencies inherent in mail and telephone surveys, we must conclude that the well-conducted *personal interview* survey tends to produce the most valid findings. It must be remembered, however, that the mere fact that personal interviews have been conducted for survey purposes assures neither representativeness of the sample interviewed nor freedom of the replies from bias. For such a survey to succeed, the interviewers must be carefully trained in the techniques of interviewing and in the requirements of representative sampling.

DEPTH PROCEDURES

The primary value of survey procedures is the accumulation of "head counting" data and expressions of superficial attitudes and feelings. Survey findings tell us *who* bought a product or intends to buy a product. Such data help clarify the present and anticipated market. Depth procedures, on the other hand, are oriented more toward the *why* of consumer behavior. Hence, the application of depth procedures to consumer studies is sometimes referred to as "motivation research."

Motivation research seeks to probe beneath the surface of consumer attitudes and to reveal the underlying values, images, and unconscious or "hidden" feelings influencing consumer behavior. In essence, the approach of the motivation researcher has much in common with that of the clinical psychologist. His tools frequently are similar to those used for clinical diagnosis; they in-

---

[4] L. G. Burchinal, "Personality Characteristics and Sample Bias," *Journal of Applied Psychology*, Vol. XLIV (1960), pp. 172–74.

clude depth interviews, projective techniques of various kinds, and personality inventories. The fundamental difference between the application of these tools in clinical and consumer psychology is in the intent or objective of the study. The clinical psychologist is patient-oriented; his sole concern is with the patient's welfare. The motivation researcher may be similarly consumer-oriented, but the producer or advertising agency paying for the research has just one fundamental objective: that is, selling more goods to more people.

Some Illustrative Studies

The difference between results obtained from surveys and depth procedures is illustrated by a report of the reasons for reading *Time* magazine. Questionnaire responses indicated that *Time* was read for reasons like "It condenses the news for me" or "It is written in brilliant style." When the matter was investigated in greater depth, however, *Time* was found to provide its readers with certain "ego benefits." It conveyed to its readers the feeling that they were busy executives who needed to be well-informed. As one reader said in the course of depth study, "When I read *Time* I like myself."[5]

Another illustration of the power of motivation research to reveal hidden and sometimes highly significant factors affecting consumer behavior is apparent in an ingenious study of attitudes toward instant coffee. Instant coffee was available in the stores for a long time before it was accepted by housewives. Women generally indicated on a questionnaire that they did not like its flavor. The investigator decided to use a projective device in order to discover whether some more basic factor might be responsible for unfavorable attitudes toward instant coffee. He devised two shopping lists, identical in all respects except for the fifth item:

List A	List B
1½ lb. hamburger	1½ lb. hamburger
2 loaves Wonder bread	2 loaves Wonder bread
Bunch of carrots	Bunch of carrots
1 can Rumford's baking powder	1 can Rumford's baking powder
Nescafe instant coffee	Maxwell House coffee, drip grind
2 cans Del Monte peaches	2 cans Del Monte peaches
5 lb. potatoes	5 lb. potatoes

Samples of housewives were asked to characterize the women who would go to the store with one or the other of these shopping

---

[5] E. Dichter, "Psychology in Market Research," *Harvard Business Review*, Vol. XXV (1947), pp. 432–43.

lists. Almost half of the respondents to the list containing *Nescafe* characterized the shopper as lazy and a poor planner, 12 percent indicated that she was a spendthrift, and 16 percent said she was a poor wife. The responses to the *Maxwell House* list were quite different: only 16 percent mentioned laziness or bad planning and none characterized the shopper as a spendthrift or poor wife.[6]

Evaluation of Motivation Research

There is obvious merit to considering motivation when seeking to explain behavior. Furthermore, there is ample evidence for the fact that much human motivation is unconscious. The utilization of depth procedures for discovering such hidden determinants of consumer behavior, and the subsequent application of these findings to advertising and selling does, however, raise two important questions. One of these concerns the validity of the findings uncovered by the motivation researcher; the other concerns the ethics of motivation research.

Validity. Since the procedures employed in motivation research are somewhat similar to those used for clinical purposes, they are open to the same criticisms relative to validity. An essential difference between the application of depth procedures in consumer and clinical studies, however, is that the former usually involves a relatively brief time span (for example, a two-hour "depth" interview or the administration of a single projective instrument) while clinical diagnoses are based upon long-term studies and administration of batteries of instruments.

The effect of misusing instruments that are less than maximally valid to begin with may, on occasion, lead to distorted or misleading findings. This point is effectively made in an article intriguingly subtitled *Is the Prune a Witch?*[7] The author refers in it to a study, made by Dichter, for the California Prune Advisory Board. This study reported that prunes are symbols of old age, a scapegoat food, and that the prune is a witch. In order to sell more prunes, Dichter advised advertisers to make the pitch that prunes are the black diamonds of the fruit family. Furthermore, he suggested that

---

[6] M. Haire, "Projective Techniques in Market Research," *Journal of Marketing*, Vol. XIV (1950), p. 649.

[7] A. Graham, "Adman's Nightmare: Is the Prune a Witch?" *Reporter*, Vol. XII (1953), pp. 27–31. Reported in M. L. Blum, *Industrial Psychology and Its Social Foundations* (New York: Harper & Bros., 1956), p. 519.

women be reassured that it is perfectly acceptable to serve prunes, and that they ought not be ashamed because prunes have a cathartic effect. We must agree that there is much about unconscious motivation that is as yet unknown. However, it would seem that characterizing the prune as a witch is carrying things just a bit too far. We cannot dispute the advertiser's right to combat this witch, if he so chooses; he has paid for it! He should, however, exercise a certain amount of judgment in differentiating between witches or windmills and proper targets for combat.

Ethics. It sometimes is argued that motivation research invades the privacy of our thoughts and leads to insidious marketing and advertising practices against which the consumer has no real defense. This argument has been eloquently carried to the public by authors like Vance Packard.[8]

On the other side of the coin, the suggestion has been made that motivation research applied to consumer behavior may be merely another manifestation of the "genius of our economy." Industrial survival depends upon giving the people what they want, and motivation research may sometimes be necessary to enable industry to discover these wants.[9]

The ethical controversy over motivation research inevitably involves a certain amount of moral judgment. Investigators in this area point out that their subjects are not coerced into cooperating with them, that consumers are not compelled to make a purchase or succumb to an advertising appeal, and that competitive manufacturers are using the methodology of motivation research anyway. The first of these arguments makes sense, but the second begs the question because it is precisely the matter of susceptibility to advertising appeals to unconscious needs that is in question. Ethical justification for motivation research on the ground that competitors are using it is, of course, specious.

Assuming the validity of the information uncovered by depth studies of consumer motivation, what is the investigator's responsibility to the consumer? Is there some point at which he should refuse to undertake studies designed to facilitate manipulation of the public by the advertiser or to reveal motives which the consumer

---

[8] *The Hidden Persuaders* (New York: David McKay Co., Inc., 1957). *The Waste Makers* (New York: David McKay Co., Inc., 1960).

[9] A. W. Rose, "Motivation Research and Subliminal Advertising," *Social Research,* Vol. XXV (1958), pp. 271–84.

himself would rather retain within the privacy of his own being? Ethical guidelines for the psychologist engaged in any endeavor are spelled out rather clearly in the American Psychological Association's publication *Ethical Standards of Psychologists*. Principle 1.12–1 of this publication begins:

> The psychologist's ultimate allegiance is to society, and his professional behavior should demonstrate an awareness of his social responsibilities. The welfare of the profession and of the individual psychologist are clearly subordinate to the welfare of the public. . . .

This principle is particularly pertinent to the matter of motivation research. At any time it is apparent that the object of such research runs counter to the public welfare, the psychologist is ethically bound to dissociate himself from the project.

BEHAVIORAL STUDIES

We might anticipate a high degree of relationship between what consumers *say* they will do and what they *actually* do. However, there is conflicting evidence regarding this relationship. In one instance, a relatively high level of agreement was found between consumers' reports of the brands of certain products last purchased and sales-slip records of the brands actually purchased.[10] There are many other studies, however, that do not support such a relationship. Behavior and verbal expressions were compared for women who had a choice of two rooms in which to wait before a lecture. One was decorated in functional modern; the other in ornate traditional. Although the room furnished in modern decor filled first, 84 percent of the women chose the traditional room in response to the question, "Which room do you like better?"[11]

This type of discrepancy between verbalized preferences and actual behavior points up the fact that people do not always do what they say they will do, and do not always feel the way they say they feel. Some of this discrepancy is undoubtedly deliberate; much of it is not. In either case, the surest way to gage consumer behavior is to make controlled observations of the behavior itself. Records of ac-

---

[10] J. G. Jenkins and H. H. Corbin, Jr., "Dependability of Psychological Brand Barometers, II: The Problem of Validity," *Journal of Applied Psychology*, Vol. XXII (1938), pp. 252–60.

[11] V. Packard, *The Hidden Persuaders, op. cit.* p. 15.

tual purchases and of consumer brand preferences have been used as criteria for such behavioral studies.

Consumer Purchases

Field studies of consumer purchases rarely are productive from a research standpoint. Too many uncontrolled factors may influence the behavior of potential purchasers as they go into a store or market. The sales record may reflect the combined influence of such diverse and relatively inseparable factors as amount and type of advertising, pressures exerted by salesmen and clerks, the relative amount of display space allotted to the product, bonuses or premium stamps offered for the purchase of particular products, and the relative size and attractiveness of the package in which the product is presented.

Even if the effects of such factors could be separated, it is doubtful that the kind of sales records maintained by many stores can serve as adequate criteria for consumer research. Difficulty in this regard was experienced in an aborted attempt (later completed) to validate consumers' verbalized brand preferences against actual buying behavior in a particular store. In the authors' words:

> The bookkeeping system of this particular store exhibited a curious lack of objectivity. An entry reading simply "corn flakes," we were told, always meant X-Brand Corn Flakes. This notation was followed, we found, except in the case of certain regular customers, for whom it meant the brand habitually purchased, which might be A-, B-, or Z-Brand. The clerks expressed surprise, indeed, that anyone should question the comprehensibility of such a system.[12]

We will consider one relatively simple study in some detail in order to indicate the kinds of controls that must be exerted when actual buying behavior is under investigation. The purpose of this study was to determine the effect of shelf display width upon the sales of soap in a self-service market.[13]

Two soap products (A and B) were selected and the shelf arrangements of these products were varied in three ways: three facings of A and one facing of B; two facings of A and two facings of B; one facing of A and three facings of B. The display situations

---

[12] Jenkins and Corbin, op. cit., 1938, p. 254.

[13] D. H. Harris, "The Effect of Display Width in Merchandising Soap," *Journal of Applied Psychology*, Vol. XLII (1958), pp. 283–84.

were changed in each store after a total of 10 boxes of both products had been sold.

The following factors had to be controlled in this study:

1. Location of the stores. (Three stores were selected on the basis of the prevailing socioeconomic level of the residents of the area.)
2. Packaging. (Both products A and B were packaged in identically sized boxes, primarily blue in color.)
3. Pricing. (The selling price was identical for both products.)
4. Product classification. (Both products were classified as "all-purpose" detergents.)
5. Promotion. (Neither product was tied in with a sales promotion gimmick at the time of the study.)
6. Location of the displays. (The two products were located side by side toward the middle of the soap section.)
7. Starting time for the study. (Wednesday afternoon for all three stores.)

The results of this study indicated that increases in the relative display width of these products did not increase their sales. This is an interesting finding because it contraindicates the usual practice of increasing shelf display width to "move" slow selling merchandise. The investigator suggests that the value of this procedure for stimulating sales may be limited to infrequently advertised products. In such instances, there is no established feeling of brand loyalty to deter impulse buying.

Brand Identification and Preferences

Studies of consumer behavior are considerably simplified when the criterion is accuracy of brand identification or expressed preferences for particular brands rather than actual purchases. Criterion data of the former type can be accumulated with a greater degree of accuracy than usually is permitted by sales slips and inventory records.

The results of this kind of study most often indicate that consumers experience considerable difficulty in correctly identifying brands and in expressing consistent preferences for one brand over another. A series of studies with cola drinks, for example, demonstrated that (1) respondents could not distinguish between the best-known brands of these beverages solely on the basis of taste, and (2) cola beverages, regardless of brand, were always identified as either

Coca-Cola, Pepsi-Cola, or Royal Crown Cola.[14] Similarly negative findings have been reported for perfumes, cigarettes, and other products. In contrast, studies with some products, like beer,[15] have indicated that taste and smell panels can indeed express consistent preferences for particular brands.

When consistent preferences are expressed for certain brands by a consumer jury, one may have reason to wonder about the bases upon which such discriminations are made. A certain amount of accumulated evidence seems to indicate that these discriminations are sometimes based upon rather irrelevant considerations. We can assume, for example, that given a choice, consumers would select fresh bread over stale bread. But when loaves of equally fresh bread were wrapped differently for experimental purposes, panels of judges claimed to perceive differences in freshness. Celophane-wrapped bread felt fresher than bread encased in a wax wrapper.[16]

SUMMARY

All parties to the manufacture, distribution, and sale of products have a vital interest in understanding, predicting, and controlling consumer behavior. One of the unique contributions of the psychologist in this general area in his application of rigorous scientific methods of inquiry. The scope of consumer research utilizing psychological methodology is exceedingly broad. It may include studies of the size and constituency of markets, the effectiveness of advertising campaigns and distribution facilities, consumer reactions to the product and the company that manufactures it, and the needs and motives underlying consumer behavior. Data for such studies are obtained by (1) surveying consumer opinions, (2) applying depth procedures, and (3) observing consumer behavior.

One of the assumptions underlying *survey* procedures is that people can verbalize many of their attitudes and opinions on a questionnaire. In the interest of economy and ease of administration, the survey is generally conducted with a sample of respondents rather than with the en-

---

[14] N. H. Pronko and J. W. Bowles, Jr., "Identification of Cola Beverages, I," *Journal of Applied Psychology*, Vol. XXXII (1948), pp. 304–12.

N. H. Pronko and J. W. Bowles, Jr., "Identification of Cola Beverages, II," *Journal of Applied Psychology*, Vol. XXXII (1948), pp. 559–64.

N. H. Pronko and J. H. Bowles, Jr., "Identification of Cola Beverages, III," *Journal of Applied Psychology*, Vol. XXXIII (1949), pp. 605–8.

[15] E. A. Fleishman, "An Experimental Consumer Panel Technique," *Journal of Applied Psychology*, Vol. XXXV (1951), pp. 133–35.

[16] R. L. Brown, "Wrapper Influence on the Perception of Freshness in Bread," *Journal of Applied Psychology*, Vol. XLII (1958), pp. 257–60.

tire population or universe. However, since the survey findings must ultimately be generalized to the larger population, the method whereby the
sample is drawn is of considerable importance. The sample must be large
enough to insure a high level of statistical accuracy, and sufficiently representative of the strata or subgroups within the population to permit for
such generalizations. The specific sampling procedures discussed in this
chapter include accidental, random, and stratified sampling.

Adequate sampling is, however, no guarantee of the validity of survey
findings. Survey responses may be affected by the wording of specific
questions, the format of the questionnaire, and the way in which it is
administered. It is imperative that the entire questionnaire be structured
to insure clarity of the questions and freedom from potential sources of
internal bias (like cues to "desired" replies, or restriction of the range of
possible responses). In addition, the survey must be administered in a
way calculated to insure maximal cooperation from all respondents in the
sample.

Depth procedures, including probing interviews and projective techniques, are sometimes used to study the underlying values, images, and
unconscious feelings affecting consumer behavior. The conduct of such
studies and the subsequent application of the findings from "motivation
research" raises both technical and ethical issues. The misuse of clinical
instruments by some motivation researchers may produce findings of
dubious validity. Even when validity of studies of the drives underlying
consumer behavior can be assumed, the ethics of the approach are open
to question. The psychologist participating in such studies must, of
course, heed his paramount responsibility to the welfare of society rather
than of particular vested interest groups.

Behavioral studies often involve an analysis of actual sales records.
Although buying behavior may be regarded as the ultimate criterion in
consumer research, it must be recognized that sales records sometimes
are inaccurately kept and reflect the combined influence of a variety of
uncontrolled factors. In order to circumvent these difficulties, many behavioral studies forego analysis of sales records in favor of controlled investigations of such criteria as accuracy of brand identification and expressed brand preferences.

Advertising

17

Advertisements make a one-sided pitch in behalf of a particular product, company, or industry. They are disseminated for the express purpose of persuading persons to behave in accord with the desires of a vested interest group. Viewed in this way, the functions and techniques of advertising are similar in many respects to those of propaganda. It is not our purpose, in this Chapter, to add further to the controversy over the broad social implications of advertising. We will be concerned, instead, with the psychological principles underlying effective advertising.

WHY ADVERTISE?

Most potential consumers have a limited amount of money to spend. It has been suggested that consumers seek to spend whatever money is available to them for commodities they value highly.[1] According to this model of consumer behavior, it should be possible to predict actual purchases from knowledge of (1) the prices of various commodities, and (2) the relative preference values attached to these commodities. A preliminary test of this concept led to predictions of restaurant food purchases with a mean error of only six cents.

To the extent that consumers actually do seek to balance available money against commodity preferences, there are two ways in which sales may be increased: either the cost can be reduced, or the preference value attached to a product may be heightened. Advertising seeks to accomplish the latter objective.

Competing Brands

A feature of our economy is the availability of many different brands of the same product all priced competitively. There is little difference indeed between the price of various brands of cigarettes,

---

[1] P. H. Benson, "A Model for the Analysis of Consumer Preferences and an Exploratory Test," *Journal of Applied Psychology*, Vol. XXXIX (1955), pp. 375–81.

detergents, beer, or gasoline. Hence, the consumer's decision about particular brand purchases probably reflects greater discrepancies in perceived preference values than in actual cost.

Much advertising is specifically devoted to manipulating subjective preferences for one brand over competitive brands. The impression is conveyed that standardized pricing among competitors does not assure standardization of the satisfactions derived from purchasing competing products. In essence, the consumer is encouraged to prefer the advertised brand to all others within the same product classification.

This may be accomplished in a variety of ways. The advertiser may appeal to rational considerations of product superiority like "safety" or "durability." He may, on the other hand, attempt to reinforce preferences by manipulating feeling tone. The advertisement may suggest that purchase and/or use of the particular brand will make the consumer feel good, like himself better, or be better liked by others. Thus, advertising slogans proclaim *Satisfy Yourself, Feel Really Clean,* and *Be Sociable.*

Competing Products

The consumer's choice between competing brands is often preceded by a choice between products. He must decide, for example, to buy a car rather than a boat before he is ready to select from among the automobiles offered within a price bracket by various manufacturers.

Here again, advertising seeks to strengthen preference values in relation to cost. The general approach underlying product advertising is that "you will derive the greatest satisfaction from using your money to buy what we have to sell." On occasion, product advertising (and to a certain extent, brand advertising) is directed toward strengthening relatively weak drives and awakening relatively passive ones. This is particularly true when the market is highly saturated. In order to maintain a high volume of automotive sales, the second car must be regarded as a necessity instead of a luxury.

Although it may not be correct to characterize us as a nation of persons primarily concerned with body odor, our flourishing deodorant industry is some kind of tribute to highly effective advertising. As Americans, we seem to be peculiarly preoccupied with product ownership as symbolic of economic, social, and sexual status. This kind of personalization of the products we own is a reflection of the interactive and mutually enhancing effects of our expanding economy, increased leisure time, and vulnerability to advertising appeals. The latter is not simply a fortuitous circumstance. The effectiveness of advertising is the subject of voluminous research.

ADVERTISING RESEARCH

Market research of the type outlined in Chapter 16 often provides clues helpful to the advertiser. However, in view of the staggering amount of money spent each year for advertising, it is not surprising that clients demand some more direct kind of reassurance that their money is being well spent. Such reassurance can only be provided by studies of the effectiveness of the message and the medium conveying it.

The Message

Every advertisement attempts to tell us something. This *message* may be relatively obvious, as in the case of a simple declaration of product superiority. It may, however, be quite subtle, suggesting that our virility, status, or likeability will be enhanced by using the product in question. Regardless of the nature of the message, it must attract and maintain our attention, and ultimately get us to do something or experience particular feelings.

Attentiveness. Recall and recognition tests of various kinds are particularly appropriate for assessing attentiveness to advertisements in the printed media. Subscribers to a particular magazine may be asked to recall as many advertisements as they can from a recent issue or to select from a scrapbook (that is, recognize) those advertisements that have actually appeared in the magazine. An interesting finding with reference to the scrapbook technique is that a correction must be made for persons claiming to "recognize" advertisements that have not yet appeared in print! The percentage of such false identifications was found, in one study, to be as high as 15–20 percent.[2]

Effectiveness. It is exceedingly difficult to gage the effectiveness of the message utilizing sales as the criterion. Many advertisements

---

[2] E. B. Lucas and M. J. Murphy, "Faults of Identification of Advertisements in Recognition Tests," *Journal of Applied Psychology*, Vol. XXIII (1939), pp. 264–69.

have delayed or cumulative effects not reflected in sales records for the period immediately following the advertisement. Furthermore, seasonal, economic, and other factors extraneous to the advertisement itself may contaminate an advertising criterion based upon sales.

One type of behavioral criterion that has been extensively used in advertising research is coupon returns and contest entries. Two or more versions of the same basic advertisement are run in alternate copies of a particular publication (*split-run*). Although the contents of these versions are different, all forms of the advertisement contain a coupon to be sent to the company or taken to the dealer, or a suggestion that the reader telephone or write regarding the product. The relative effectiveness of the several versions of the advertisement is determined by comparing the rate of consumer replies evoked by each one.

Audience reaction to TV and radio programs and commercials is automatically recorded by a mechanical device called the *Program Analyzer* developed by Stanton and Lazarsfeld.[3] This device is used exclusively by the Columbia Broadcasting System and the McCann-Erickson advertising agency.[4] During a test session, members of the audience react to various portions of the program by pressing "like" or "dislike" buttons. Their responses are recorded and supplemented by replies to questionnaires and interviews.

Another approach to both program and commercial testing is that employed by the Schwerin Research Corporation. The Schwerin system exposes a preselected test audience to the program under study and each member of the audience records his reaction on a three-point scale (*interesting, mildly interesting, not interesting*) at selected points in the program. Tabulations and summaries of these reactions are used to construct a "profile" of audience reaction during the program. Recall data and changes in preference for particular products are used also to evaluate the effectiveness of the commercials.

A rather interesting approach to assessing the impact of a message capitalizes upon the fact that the autonomic nervous system responds to stimuli generating feelings or tension. The effects of

---

[3] P. F. Lazarsfeld and F. N. Stanton, *Radio Research* (New York: Duell, Sloan & Pearce, Inc., 1944).

[4] G. F. Seehafer and J. W. Laemmar, *Successful Television and Radio Advertising* (New York: McGraw-Hill Book Co., Inc, 1959).

autonomic nervous system activity are reflected in a variety of physiological changes, some of which are recorded by "lie detectors." One such effect is a change in the electrical resistance of the skin (that is, *galvanic skin response* or, more simply, *GSR*) measured by a device called a *psychogalvanometer*. In one study, the recorded *GSR*'s as a panel of women examined advertisements for pancake flour correlated with the sales effectiveness of these advertisements in field tests.[5] Changes in *GSR* were found to be sensitive also to differences in advertising layout.[6]

A limitation of this method is the fact that although change in *GSR* correlates with the existence of feeling tone, it provides no indication of the direction of the feeling. Thus, psychogalvanometric responses indicate that a person is "aroused" but provide no basis for differentiating between favorable or pleasant arousal and unfavorable or unpleasant arousal.

The Medium

Estimating the size and characteristics of the audience exposed to the advertiser's message is a fundamental problem requiring media research. This problem can be attacked somewhat more easily for the printed media than for the broadcast media because the number of issues of a particular magazine or newspaper sold can be determined with a fair degree of accuracy.

However, even in the case of printed media, there are certain difficulties in estimating the size of the audience reached by an advertisement. The fact that a particular magazine is purchased does not mean that it is read; conversely, a substantial number of persons read magazines they do not actually purchase. Estimates of audience exposure to printed media are further complicated by the fact that there is a certain amount of duplication between the readership of various magazines carrying the same advertisement. It is likely that simple consideration of the circulation of a particular publication without regard for overlapping publications carrying the same advertisement leads to an overestimate of the size of the advertiser's audience.

---

[5] G. Eckstand and A. R. Gilliland, "The Psychogalvanometric Method for Measuring the Effectiveness of Advertising," *Journal of Applied Psychology*, Vol. XXXII (1948), pp. 415–25.

[6] E. Golin and S. B. Lyerly, "The Galvanic Skin Response as a Test of Advertising Impact," *Journal of Applied Psychology*, Vol. XXXIV (1950), pp. 440–43.

The audience reached by the broadcast media (radio and TV) is even more difficult to estimate. The program rating services gather their information in a variety of ways, each with unique shortcomings. The A. C. Nielson Company, for example, compiles its basic data for program ratings from mechanical recorders attached to radio and TV receivers. This device maintains a continuous record of set usage throughout the day for a sample of homes. However, the fact that a receiver is tuned to a particular program is itself no assurance that anyone in the home is actually viewing or listening to the program and its accompanying commercials.

Hooper ratings for radio and Trendex ratings for TV are based upon the "coincidental telephone" survey. Telephone interviews are conducted with a sample of persons while the program under consideration is in progress. In addition to sample bias introduced by limiting the rating to results obtained from telephone-owning homes, this procedure cannot be used for early morning or late evening programs. One just doesn't place telephone calls at 6:00 A.M. or midnight to randomly selected persons inquiring whether they have their TV receiver on and, if so, which program they are watching.

Other rating services conduct coincidental personal (rather than telephone) interviews and use the diary method. In the latter procedure, a sample of respondents is requested to keep a log of all viewing or listening activities. The effect of keeping such a diary upon program selection, and the accuracy of the logs themselves, are both open questions.

FORMAT AND STRUCTURE OF ADVERTISEMENTS

The foregoing discussion has been concerned with techniques for appraising the effectiveness of advertisements and the vehicles by which they are transmitted rather than with the structure of the advertisements themselves. It is appropriate now to examine the format of advertising from a psychological vantage point. In so doing, however, we must be aware that psychologists are not advertising men either by training or, for the most part, by inclination. Developing a good advertisement requires the skills of a number of specialists, including copywriters, artists, layout specialists, and others. The unique contributions of psychologists stem from their fundamental concern with human behavior and familiarity with techniques for investigating changes in behavior.

Advertisements are structured in a manner calculated to attract and maintain attention, spotlight the salient aspects of the message, and encourage retention of the message as well as subsequent action in accord with it. We will briefly review some evidence concerning the effects of several format variables upon the realization of these objectives.

Color

The legibility of colored lettering is less dependent upon the specific colors used than upon the brightness differential between the colored letter and the background. In general, the most satisfactory background for colored lettering is grey, and dark colors on a light background are most legible in daylight.[7]

The value of color in advertising for attracting and maintaining interest is somewhat obscured by such other considerations as the skill with which the color is used, its appropriateness to the product being advertised, and the fundamental purpose of the advertisement. In the latter regard, it has been suggested that color is maximally valuable for advertising an established brand, and not much superior to black-and-white advertising for promoting a new brand.[8]

Movement

The fact that a moving object attracts more attention than a stationary one is well-known. Youngsters playing hide-and-seek remain as motionless as possible in their hiding place in order to avoid detection. The student who wants desperately to be recognized by his instructor does not merely raise his arm; he often waves his hand rather frantically.

The primary applications of the principle of movement in advertising occur in television and in the outdoor spectacular signs showing bread being sliced, bottles pouring liquid, and water cascading over a dam. In most TV advertising, the movement is "real." The viewer watches a skin diver plunging under water to shave, or observes the needle pointer swing revealing the deodorizing power of

---

[7] E. H. Jones and F. C. Sumner, "Relation of Brightness Differences of Colors to Their Apparent Distances," *Journal of Applied Psychology,* Vol. XXVI (1948), pp. 25–29.

[8] L. Warner and R. Franzen, "Value of Color in Advertising," *Journal of Applied Psychology,* Vol. XXXI (1947), pp. 260–70.

a mouthwash. The outdoor spectacular signs make use of "apparent" movement created by lights successively illuminated in sequence with a brief time interval between them. It makes no difference to the observer whether the movement is real or apparent. Movement attracts attention.

Repetition

Much advertising is repetitive in nature. The slogan, jingle, or catchy tune repeated over and over again capitalizes upon certain well established psychological principles. Frequency of presentation both attracts attention and leads to overlearning. Thus, if you let your thoughts wander during a TV commercial, an insistent chant like "Double the flavor, double the fun, with Doublemint, Doublemint, Doublemint gum" is bound to part your intellectual curtain and bring you back to the realities of the world of commercialism. Similarly, after years of exposure to the contest between little hard-working Aspirins and Bufferins fighting their way out of the human stomach, it is unlikely that there are very many persons who are still doubtful about the outcome.

Novelty

Things that appear to be new and different contrast markedly with the old and familiar, and hence stand out in bold relief. The extent to which product novelty is stressed in magazine advertising is evident from the frequent use of words and phrases like "New!" "No more (messy hands, and so on)" "Revolutionary," "Now! At Last!" "Never before!"[9]

In addition to showing that they have a product that is "new" or "different," many advertisers attempt to advertise in novel ways. There is, after all, something rather compelling about seeing a miniature butler dispensing paper napkins or omnipotent Mr. Clean springing to life.

The Illustration

The total advertisement, words (or text) and illustration, conveys an overall impression and generates a complex of feeling. In addition to demonstrating an increased use of illustration, in general, during the years 1900 to 1940, one investigator found a

---

[9] W. H. Whyte, Jr., "The Language of Advertising," *Fortune,* September, 1952, p. 99.

parallel change in the nature of the illustrations: that is, an increasingly prevalent tendency to show pictures of people actually relevant to the use of the product.[10]

The nature of the relationship between person and product shown in the illustration varies considerably in different advertisements. Some use eye-catching illustrations in which this relationship, if it exists at all, is exceedingly obscure. Others structure illustrations to permit facile identification between the consumer and the persons depicted in the advertisement. An attempt to order person-product relationships in illustrations as attention-getters and -holders led to the conclusion that illustrations showing the effects of *not using* the product were much more effective than those showing the effects of *using* the product.[11] Concretely, advertisements for a hair tonic ought to show the full transformation from dry, dandruffy, weather-worn hair to the conventional stereotype of well-groomed hair.

THE APPEAL

Even attractively structured and effectively presented advertisements are relatively powerless unless they make an appropriate appeal. In order to stimulate purchase of a particular product, the advertiser must either promise to satisfy some already existent needs or strengthen weak ones to the point where the promise of need satisfaction assumes real importance to the consumer. This point is made rather succinctly by Dichter as follows:

No item of merchandise is ever sold unless a psychological need exists which it satisfies. In other words, the actual merchandise is secondary. Advertising's goal has to be the mobilization and manipulation of human needs as they exist in the customer.[12]

For a number of years advertisers sought some kind of magic key to successful appeals by consulting presumably exhaustive compilations of motives, wants, and needs. This tack proved to be relatively fruitless. Human motivation is exceedingly complex and therefore defies neat classification and categorization. Even a fundamentally

---

[10] O. E. Klapp, "Imitation Value in Advertising," *Journal of Applied Psychology* Vol. XXV (1941), pp. 243–50.

[11] H. J. Rudolph, *Attention and Interest Factors in Advertising*, Printers' Ink Business Bookshelf (New York: Printers' Ink Publishing Co., Inc., 1947), pp. 68 ff.

[12] E. Dichter, "A Psychological View of Advertising Effectiveness," *Journal of Marketing* (national quarterly publication of the American Marketing Association), Vol. XIV (1949), pp. 61–66.

biological drive like hunger, for example, becomes rapidly over-laid with learned preferences and feelings. The food advertiser can-not make a successful appeal to the "need for food." He must ap-peal, instead, to needs for particular kinds of foods, appetizing in appearance, attractively served, and appropriate to particular cir-cumstances which we have learned to associate with them. Thus, margarine manufacturers learned that they could not compete ef-fectively with butter by emphasizing only the economy and nutri-tive value of their product. People are reluctant to accept something they can justify solely on the grounds that it is an effective substi-tute.

Product Images

We are sometimes led by advertising to invest products and com-panies with particular "personalities," and to formulate an image of the kind of person for whom the product is appropriate. If we can project ourselves into the advertisement, perceiving ourselves as users of the product, the advertiser has come a long way toward in-ducing us to make the purchase.

The image of the appropriate purchaser of a particular product is conveyed by the dominant verbal and pictorial aspects of its under-lying advertising appeal. Pepsi-Cola has never tried to capture the old age retirement market! It has a well-established, youthful, light-hearted, gay, "sociable" image. Similarly, Chrysler Corporation au-tomobiles were perceived, for many years, as sound, conservative investments in transportation. Prior to the radical change in styling and advertising for the 1957 model, the image of the Plymouth buyer was expressed by such adjectives as "quiet," "careful," "slow," "silent," "moral," "fat," "gentle," and "calm."[13]

Product images, once well-established, tend to be quite resistant to change. A recent illustration of a successful change in the product image is the case of Marlboro cigarettes which overcame its feminine association by virtue of outdoor he-man-type-complete-with-tatoo advertising. A somewhat similar change is currently being at-tempted by the tea industry.

The pre-1957 image for Plymouth automobiles has changed rather markedly also. In that year, styling changes were accompanied by

---

[13] W. D. Wells, F. J. Andriuli, F. J. Goi, and S. Seader, "An Adjective Checklist for the Study of 'Product Personality,'" *Journal of Applied Psychology*, Vol. XLI (1957), pp. 317–19.

advertisements peppered with references to *The Forward Look,* *Three Years Ahead, Flight Sweep Styling,* and the *Fabulous Fury 301 V-8 Engine.* The effectiveness of this campaign is evident from the findings, in a follow-up study, that the Plymouth buyer was subsequently characterized by adjectives like "high-class," "important," "rich," "different," and "particular."[14]

Institutional Advertising

A considerable amount of advertising is devoted to establishing a favorable attitude toward a company and investing the company with a "personality." This advertising approach is particularly useful when the company's products are sold to producers rather than individual consumers (for example, steel, rubber, oil) or when the advertiser sells services like insurance, communications, or travel.

Corporate Images. Advertising to develop a corporate image aims to convince the public that although the company exists for monetary reasons, its concerns extend considerably beyond the balance sheet and the ledger. The company is personalized and humanized. It is transformed by institutional advertising from a huge, impersonal organization controlling the lives of its employees and the tastes of the public to an organization in which employees are partners in an enterprise providing consumers with beneficial goods and services.

Some of the dominant themes of such advertising have been identified as:

1. Elaboration of latent consequences: The company's activities benefit you or some group in which you have a direct and vital interest.
2. Humanization: The company is a warm, friendly, hard-working "individual."
3. Denial and Conversion: Odious charges about big business are either denied or converted to have socially acceptable implications.
4. Sympathy or Ego-Involvement: Since you have a vital stake in the company, it is in your interest to understand and be sympathetic to the company's problems and to appreciate its solutions.[15]

Some of these appeals are illustrated in Figure 17–1.

Public Service. Quite often, institutional advertising takes a less direct approach to developing favorable attitudes. Rather than

---

[14] W. D. Wells, F. J. Goi, and S. Seader, "A Change in a Product Image," *Journal of Applied Psychology,* Vol. XLII (1958), pp. 120–21.

[15] L. I. Pearlin and M. Rosenberg, "Propaganda Techniques in Institutional Advertising," *Public Opinion Quarterly,* Vol. XVI (1952), pp. 5–26.

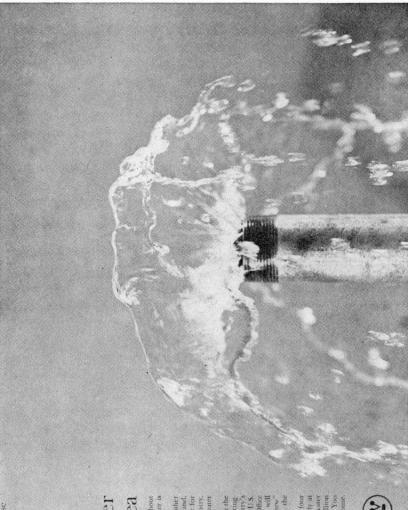

New from Westinghouse

Fresh water
from the sea

Today, in many places throughout
the world, the shortage of water is
a critical problem.

By 1975, there will be another
billion people in the world . . . and,
unless we find "new" water for
drinking, irrigation and industry,
there won't be enough fresh water
for them all.

We are starting to find it in the
salt sea. At San Diego, Westinghouse is building the country's
largest seawater plant for the U.S.
Department of the Interior's Office
of Saline Water. This plant will
provide 7,000,000 gallons of "new"
drinking water a week from the
Pacific Ocean.

In the desert of Kuwait, four
Westinghouse units are already at
work taking in Persian Gulf water
and pouring out nearly 17 million
gallons of fresh water a week. You
can be sure . . . if it's Westinghouse.

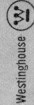 **Westinghouse**

FIGURE 17–1. Corporate Image Advertising.

Curator of the mind's riches

No bank holds riches such as this—the great legacy of learning in our libraries. Here every man may maintain an account. Here all may borrow, in any amount, from the endless assets of the mind.

The men and women who create and keep our libraries perform far more than an essential service—they guard a priceless trust. It is to their greater credit that our country's librarians accept their charge as a

labor of love as well as a great responsibility. To them a nation is grateful.

Among the books in today's libraries are many published by Rand McNally, or printed and bound by us for other American publishers. Even above our pride in more than a century of fine craftsmanship, we hold this privilege of contributing tangibly to our libraries' inestimable wealth.

RAND McNALLY

PUBLISHERS • PRINTERS • MAP MAKERS • ESTABLISHED 1856 • CHICAGO • NEW YORK • NASHVILLE • SAN FRANCISCO • WASHINGTON

TIME, APRIL 21, 1961   103

Courtesy: Rand McNally

FIGURE 17–1.   (*Continued.*)

*JAMES LIND—Conqueror of Scurvy—reproduced here is one of a series
of original oil paintings commissioned by Parke-Davis.*

Great Moments in Medicine

James Lind, a British Naval Surgeon, in 1747 proved experimentally the value of a treatment for a disease that had incapacitated more seamen than all other diseases, naval engagements, marine mishaps, shipwrecks, and accidents combined. The disease was scurvy . . . , a severe vitamin deficiency resulting from sailors' unvaried diet of salt meat and sea biscuits.

Lind's recommendation was the addition of fresh limes, other citrus fruits, and their juices to diets of seamen. Though not adopted generally by the British Navy until after his death, this diet saved countless lives. British seamen, thereafter called "Limeys," were the first men to receive prophylactic vitamin therapy.

Although some vitamin deficiencies in man cannot be prevented or corrected as dramatically and as simply as scurvy, modern medical research is constantly giving physicians better and more effective weapons for use in the fight for better health for people world wide.

Original research, conducted at Parke-Davis laboratories into causes and control of disease, has made significant contributions to world health. These medicines, prescribed by physicians and dispensed by pharmacists, help you to enjoy a healthier, longer life.

PARKE-DAVIS

Pioneers in better medicines

Courtesy: Parke, Davis & Co.

FIGURE 17–1. *(Continued.)*

stressing the company's contribution to your welfare, public service advertising seeks to clarify the company's stake in our society and its role as a "good citizen." The distinction between direct attempts to create a corporate image and the public service approach is a rather fine one. In the latter, the advertisement seeks to establish a rapprochement between the broader interests and welfare of society on the one hand, and the company on the other. It attempts to capitalize upon what has been termed "significant involvement"[16] serving the private interests of the advertiser, the personal interest of the consumer, and the public interest of the nation.

An illustration of public service advertising is shown in Figure 17–2. This advertisement was judged by *Saturday Review's* Ninth Annual Advertising Awards Committee to be one of the most distinguished public service advertisements of 1960.

The New York Life Insurance Company is undoubtedly interested in establishing rapport with parents interested in insuring their children's education. However, the advertisement also serves the public interest. Its appeal extends beyond a mere justification of the company's products or services.

SUBLIMINAL ADVERTISING

Quite a furor developed a few years ago when an apparently successful attempt to capitalize upon subliminal perception for advertising purposes was reported by Vicary.[17] The procedure consisted of flashing the phrases "Eat Popcorn" and "Drink Coca-Cola" at 0.003 second on a movie screen during the showing of a film. According to the report, Coca-Cola sales increased 18 percent and popcorn sales increased 57 percent although the audience did not suspect they were participating in a deliberate attempt to influence their behavior. Thus, the application of subliminal perception in advertising has been aptly termed "the little ad that isn't there."[18]

Vicary's procedure and findings were never reported in any professional publication. Hence, it is impossible to evaluate the validity

---

[16] W. D. Patterson, "The Power of Significant Involvement," *Saturday Review*, April 22, 1961, pp. 41–46.

[17] Results obtained by James M. Vicary and reported in a memorandum from Subliminal Projection Co., Inc. to the Federal Communications Commission, January 13, 1958. Cited by R. Wilhelm, "Are Subliminal Commercials Bad?" *Michigan Business Review*, January, 1958, p. 26.

[18] J. Brooks, *Consumer Reports*, Vol. XXIII, No. 1 (1958), pp. 7–10.

FIGURE 17–2. Public Service Advertising.

of his results. The implications of this technique for presenting advertisements would, if it worked, be at once startling and frightening. It is repugnant enough to some people to be bombarded by advertisements they can see and hear. But to be victimized by advertising below the threshold of awareness raises such serious moral concerns that it has been banned from both TV and radio, and the FCC has thus far granted no patent for its use.

Subliminal perception is a well-established psychological phenomenon. The brain can receive sensations from briefly presented stimuli below the threshold of awareness. In the tradition of experimental psychology, the *limen,* or threshold of awareness, is defined as a stimulus intensity perceived exactly half the time.

Research Findings

The available evidence concerning subliminal stimulation in situations similar to those that might be employed for advertising is quite conflictual. Negative findings were reported, for example, in one study in which subjects had to choose between pairs of circles projected on a screen. One circle of each pair was designated by the experimenter as "correct" and the answer was flashed on the screen for a brief interval (systematically varied between 0.01 second and 0.03 second). The subjects were unable to identify the "correct" circles with greater than chance accuracy.[19] Negative findings were reported also in an attempt to develop an association between a stimulus slide showing a spoon of rice and the subliminally presented "brand name" *Wonder Rice.*[20]

On the positive side, students taking a test projected item-by-item on a screen with the right answer superimposed subliminally made significantly greater improvement over their pretest scores (that is, without superimposed answers) than did a control group.[21]

One additional investigation, also producing positive results, is of particular interest because it attempted to do something like Vicary's "popcorn, Coca-Cola" study under carefully controlled conditions. Two groups of students in a freshman psychology course watched a 16-minute movie related to the course. During the show-

[19] A. D. Calvin and K. S. Dollenmayer, "Subliminal Perception: Some Negative Findings," *Journal of Applied Psychology,* Vol. XLIII (1959), pp. 187–88.

[20] J. M. Champion and W. W. Turner, "An Experimental Investigation of Subliminal Perception," *Journal of Applied Psychology,* Vol. XLIII (1959), pp. 382–84.

[21] H. C. Sharp, "Effect of Subliminal Cues on Test Results," *Journal of Applied Psychology,* Vol. XLIII (1959), pp. 369–71.

ing to the experimental group, the word "beef" was briefly flashed on the screen every seven seconds. The control group saw the movie without the subliminally presented stimulus. Following the movie, both groups completed a "health inventory" asking them to (1) rate their hunger and (2) indicate their sandwich preferences. The members of the experimental group rated themselves as hungrier than the members of the control group, and the difference between ratings was statistically significant. Furthermore, although not statistically significant, the experimental group tended more often than the control group to indicate a preference for beef over other kinds of sandwiches.[22]

Evaluation

It is apparent, from the foregoing, that definitive answers to the feasibility and effectiveness of subliminal advertising are not yet available. The lack of consistency in the variously reported findings raises a number of questions related both to the technology and effects of commercial applications.[23]

On the technological side, even if subliminal advertising were effective, and this is still a big *if*, commercial applications would be premature. We lack sufficient information about such things as the optimal frequency of stimulus presentation, size of the stimulus, length of the message, and possibility of satiation (diminished receptivity to the stimulus). However, technical roadblocks like these probably will not be difficult to remove if commercial applications of subliminal perception are clearly shown to be effective.

About all that can be said, at present, concerning the effectiveness of subliminal advertising is that we are unsure of the power of this technique. Some as yet unanswered questions are: (1) Can such advertising actually create new needs, or does it merely raise the level of awareness of an existent but weak need? (2) Can subliminal advertising alter long-established behavior patterns, or will it simply affect a choice between equally desirable and familiar alternatives? (3) Is it possible, as suggested by the hunger-inducing study cited earlier,[24] that subliminal advertising may lead to drive arousal

---

[22] D. Byrne, "The Effect of a Subliminal Food Stimulus on Verbal Responses," *Journal of Applied Psychology* Vol. XLIII (1959), pp. 249–52.

[23] J. V. McConnell, R. L. Cutler, and E. B. McNeil, "Subliminal Stimulation: An Overview," *American Psychologist*, Vol. XIII (1958), pp. 229–43.

[24] D. Byrne, *op. cit.*

(for example, experiencing hunger) without fixating it on a particular objective (for example, beef)?

The answers to such questions will probably be forthcoming before long. For the present, most psychologists are skeptical about commercial applications of subliminal perception, and the networks' ban on its use indicates that they are taking no chances. There is undoubtedly an "inescapable implication of deviousness in the use of such a technique."[25] And, as we pointed out in the earlier discussion of motivation research, the psychologist is obligated to disassociate himself from any intended use of subliminal perception which is not in the public interest.

SUMMARY

Advertising is a form of propaganda seeking to heighten subjective preferences for particular products. These preferences may be predicated upon such rational appeals as durability and economy, or emotional appeals as status and social acceptance.

Advertising research is directed toward evaluation of the effectiveness of the message and the medium by which it is conveyed. The advertiser sponsoring such research wishes to know whether (1) his message is reaching the intended audience, (2) this audience actually attends to the message, (3) the message is understood, and (4) the advertisement has the desired impact upon feeling tone and purchasing behavior.

Although psychologists are not advertising specialists, they have a fundamental interest in virtually any attempt to influence human behavior. Successful advertisements capitalize upon certain psychological principles related to attentiveness. Beyond this, the successful advertisement makes an appeal to human needs and motives. If we can project ourselves into the advertisement and perceive ourselves as users of the product, the advertiser has come a long way toward inducing us to make the purchase.

Considerable attention has recently been focused upon the possibility of subliminally presented advertising. The fact that persons can actually perceive stimuli below the threshold of awareness is well-established in the psychological literature. The utility of subliminal perception in advertising is, however, quite another matter. The available evidence on this point is conflictual.

At present, most psychologists are skeptical about commercial applications of subliminal perception. The limits of utility of the technique, if indeed it has any utility at all, are ill-defined. Subliminal advertising has been banned from both radio and television. Psychologists are, of course, ethically bound to disassociate themselves from any intended use of subliminal perception not in the public interest.

---

[25] McConnell, Cutler, and McNeil, *op. cit.*, p. 239.

Selling

18 We have attempted throughout all of the preceding chapters to develop a feeling for psychology as a science. Psychologist's conclusions about human behavior are based upon careful investigation under controlled circumstances. Casual observation, armchair speculation, and hunches "off the top of the head" may occasionally serve as a starting point for subsequent investigation. They do not, however, constitute a reasonable basis for scientific conclusions without empirical verification. A "psychology" of anything lacking an experimental literature reflecting a history of careful investigation is not psychology at all; it is common sense. And the wisdom of common sense often is open to question.

A designation like "the psychology of selling" exemplifies a tendency to confuse common sense analyses of human behavior with a rigorous scientific approach to inquiry. For the present, salesmanship must be regarded pretty much as an art to which psychologists have devoted relatively little attention. The effectiveness of various sales approaches has been demonstrated in the past by experience rather than controlled investigation. This is an area in which there is a serious need for scientific study.

ADVERTISING AND SELLING

Viewed in terms of the end result desired, advertising and selling have an identical objective. They both aim to persuade potential buyers to purchase products or avail themselves of services.

The fundamental difference between advertising and selling inheres in the personal component of the latter. The salesman does not make a blanket appeal to a mass audience. He seeks, instead, to discover the individual buyer's needs and emphasizes particular product features appropriate to these needs in order to close the sale.

Thus, advertising is a form of preselling. It informs large segments of the buying public about the existence and unique or special features of a product or service. The salesman for a well-advertised product does not have to approach his prospect "cold." To the extent that the advertising has been successful, the prospective buyer has some prior knowledge about the product. What is required of the salesman under these circumstances is to individualize the strengths of the product so the prospect sees it as one that will benefit *him*.

WHAT IS SALESMANSHIP?

One approach to selling is based upon the view that the salesman and prospective purchaser are antagonists in a struggle. The salesman is seen as attempting, by virtually any means, to persuade a reluctant prospect to make the purchase. Salesmanship seen in this way involves high pressure tactics and even devious or deceitful practices, when necessary to force a sale. It likens the prospect to an almost inanimate and unresponsive recipient of the sales "pitch." He remains, in this view, relatively passive while something is done to him.

The characterization above is generally odious to both buyers and sellers. Most companies and sales managers prefer to think of their salesmen as filling quite a different role. Instead of an active seller and passive prospect with persuasive communication flowing from the former to the latter, the selling-buying relationship is viewed as an interactive process. The effective salesman cannot rely solely upon a "canned" presentation. Instead he must continually tailor and modify his presentation in terms of the response it is evoking from the prospect. Rather than *selling* the buyer in spite of his reservations or misgivings, the effective salesman must be prepared and willing to confront objections and resolve them openly and honestly. Only in this way can the relationship between buyer and seller be mutually advantageous over a long term.

These contrasting views of salesmanship are reflected in two fundamental approaches to selling: (1) selling formulas, and (2) need-satisfaction.

Selling Formulas

Selling by formula is predicated upon the assumption of buyer passivity during the sales interaction. If selling consists primarily of doing something *to* the buyer, then it should be possible to produce the desired outcome by leading the prospect through a sequence of steps terminating in his purchase.

A-I-D-A. Common sense dictates that the first step in salesmanship must be to *attract attention*. Once the salesman has the prospect's attention, he makes a pitch calculated to maintain *interest* and to create a *desire* for the product or service. Finally, he must close the sale or get *action*. These four steps—Attention, Interest, Desire, Action—constitute the A-I-D-A selling formula originally proposed before the turn of the century.

This formula assumes that all prospects think alike, and that the nature of this stream of thought proceeds in orderly fashion through the four stages embodied in the formula. It disregards such important considerations as: the buyer's perceived need for the product (we desire many things we do not buy because we do not need them); his ability to make a purchase (including his authority to buy and the availability of sufficient funds); counterpressures upon him *not* to buy the product in spite of his desire and need for it (including his reactions to the salesperson); conflicting desires for several purchases all of which cannot be simultaneously gratified, and so on. It is naive to assume that the thinking process can be reduced to the uniformly applicable sequential stream hypothesized by the A-I-D-A formula.

Want-Solution-Action-Satisfaction. This is another, slightly more sophisticated selling formula proposed about 35 years ago.[1] The added sophistication of this formula is derived from the fact that it embodies the notion of *homeostasis* or equilibrium as a nonmotivated condition. A hypothetical organism in a complete state of satisfaction experiences no needs or wants and therefore is not impelled toward any kind of action. Thus, the first step postulated by this formula involves either discovery of a state of disequilibrium in the prospect (that is, a want) or, failing this, to create such a state. The salesman proposes his product or service as the solution promising to restore equilibrium, and encourages the prospect to act favorably upon this solution. Once action is taken it is reinforced by satisfaction of the prospect's want, and equilibrium with respect to this want is restored.

Although this prescription for salesmanship is an improvement upon the A-I-D-A formula, it suffers from the deficiencies inherent in any attempt to routinize selling. We pointed out earlier that recognition of the complexity of consumer's wants, needs, and strivings

[1] E. K. Strong, Jr., *Psychology of Advertising and Selling* (New York: McGraw-Hill Book Co., Inc., 1925), chap. xxii.

was responsible for the development of "motivation research." Such research consistently finds that the real mainsprings to action often are quite different from those verbalized by the consumer.

Suppose a prospect maintains that she needs a new refrigerator with increased storage capacity. She may really mean quite a variety of things not verbalized in her original statement, including: (1) Although her present refrigerator is serviceable, she is embarrassed for her Koffee Klatch Kronies to see the older model in her kitchen. (2) She wants a new refrigerator in contemporary style regardless of its capacity, provided that it costs no more than $250. (3) She will buy from a salesman who can help her rationalize the purchase on the grounds of "economy," "improved vitamin content of stored foods," and so on. The salesman who accepts her verbalized want for a larger refrigerator at face value and attempts merely to present solutions to this want will probably not succeed in making the sale.

Need Satisfaction

Salesmanship viewed as a process of need-satisfaction focuses more upon the buying process than the selling process. This approach to salesmanship rejects selling formulas as stilted, oversimplified, and unduly concerned with the actions of the seller.

A need-satisfaction point of view is accepted by virtually all sound recent writers on salesmanship. As one author states, salesmanship is ". . . the process whereby the seller ascertains and activates the needs or wants of the buyer and satisfies these needs or wants to the mutual, continuous advantage of both the buyer and the seller."[2] Thus, the buyer's needs are regarded as central to the selling process; the salesman's behavior assumes importance only as a vehicle for promising and providing need satisfaction.

There are a number of practical implications of the need-satisfaction approach to salesmanship. Since every prospective buyer is a unique individual with unique needs and perceptions, every sales presentation must be somewhat different. A particular prospect may need assurance that he is getting maximum value for his money; another may need to derive feelings of heightened status by virtue of his dealings with the salesman; yet another may be particularly concerned about the reliability of the company with respect to cus-

---

[2] C. A. Pederson and M. D. Wright, *Salesmanship: Principles and Methods* (3d ed.; Homewood, Ill.: Richard D. Irwin, Inc., 1961), pp. 45–46.

tomer-service or its reputation for prompt delivery. The salesman's initial endeavor must be in the direction of discovering the prospect's needs and/or stimulating needs appropriate to whatever he is selling.

Both need-discovery and need-stimulation require a high degree of sensitivity. The salesman must be a careful listener and an astute observer of the prospect's behavior.

Once the particular buyer's needs are evident, the salesman is in a position to demonstrate and discuss his product or service as a need-satisfier. He must be exceedingly flexible, realizing that whatever he is selling can be presented from numerous aspects, each satisfying to particular needs. The salesman attempts to stress those particular satisfactions appropriate to the buyer's needs.

Assuming that the product or service is properly presented, the prospect will want it. He has not been hoodwinked, high-pressured, or embarrassed into making the purchase; he has been convinced that he will benefit from it. It is not surprising, then, that the most effective salesmen tend themselves to be convinced of the value of whatever it is they are selling. A study of variables contributing to success of life insurance salesmen, for example, determined that the amount of life insurance owned by the agent (indicating belief in the value of his product) correlated more significantly with a composite criterion of selling effectiveness than several other factors, including product knowledge and length of service.[3]

Finally, the salesman's responsibility extends beyond closing the sale to assuring customer satisfaction with his purchase. This is particularly important when repeat sales are desired. Satisfied customers tend to make additional purchases of the product perceived as satisfying. Further, since such customers are favorably disposed to the salesman and the organization he represents, they are an excellent form of word-of-mouth advertising.

The importance of buyer satisfaction was illustrated in an analysis of recordings of the actual selling behavior of expert department store sales personnel. Personal selling of the department store variety is, very often, a rather routine affair. The customer sees what she likes on the rack, the clerk proffers it for her inspection, shows variations in color, style, and so on, upon request, and ultimately either wraps it and accepts the cash, or replaces it on the rack.

---

[3] D. E. Baier and R. D. Dugan, "Factors in Sales Success," *Journal of Applied Psychology,* Vol. XLI (1957), pp. 37–40.

Analysis of the recordings of expert salespersons, however, indicated that the most effective personal selling goes an important step beyond facilitating the customer's purchase. The ingredient added by these salespersons is that they help the customer obtain maximum personal satisfaction for the money she spends.[4]

THE SELLING-BUYING PROCESS

We have already indicated that a need-satisfactions approach to salesmanship leads necessarily to a flexible view of selling. Each sales appeal must be individually tailored to the needs of individual prospects. In this section, we will examine the diversity of reasons for buying and describe the interaction between buyer and seller.

Why People Buy

Here again there is considerable conflict between a common sense analysis and a psychological analysis of human behavior. It seems just plain good common sense that people buy food to prepare for hunger, new appliances to replace ones that are worn out or defective, and bigger houses to accommodate larger families. Further, assuming the decision has been made, for example, to buy a refrigerator, it is common sense to buy the make and model offering maximum value for the money. Such factors as initial cost, reputation of the manufacturer and retail outlet, and availability of servicing ought to be critical to such a purchase.

Common sense assumes a highly rational basis for buying behavior. However, the point was made in Chapter 16 that buyers often behave rather irrationally by external standards. The reasons given for making a purchase may not be the really operative reasons at all. Thus, although unverbalized as needs, the purchaser may seek to identify with persons whom he respects by buying products endorsed by them. He may seek social approval by purchasing in conformance with certain stereotypes of the "well-groomed" or "masculine" man; heightened status by buying expensive or "exclusive" items; or simply a "bargain." Derived (learned) needs for social approval and status rarely are verbalized. Instead, the purchaser prefers to think he is a highly rational buyer basing his decisions upon a careful consideration of the available alternatives.

---

[4] W. M. Thompson, "How Expert Salespeople Sell," *Journal of Retailing*, 1955, p. 150.

Thus, the salesman must often provide the customer with such *rationalizations* (acceptable "reasons") as "economy," "low upkeep," and "once-in-a-lifetime value," if he is to close the sale successfully.

Making the Sale

Much more research has been devoted to selecting and training salesmen than to the sales presentation itself. The relative lack of research activity in the latter area is attributable to a number of factors. Laboratory studies of the sales interview suffer rather seriously from a sense of artificiality. Field studies, on the other hand, are difficult to conduct because of the enormous range of variation in prospect needs and personalities necessitating a high degree of flexibility in sales presentations. Such flexibility probably increases the number of sales closed, but precludes the kinds of control necessary to conduct satisfactory investigations.

Occasionally the sales presentation is atomized for the purpose of study. One investigator, for example, found that department store sales were increased when clerks kept their voices up on the last syllable of the "Good Morning" greeting.[5] Another found that superior and inferior sales clerks could be differentiated on the basis of ratings of voice transcriptions. The recordings of voices of superior clerks were rated higher by a group of college students on "enthusiasm," "convincingness," and "sales ability."[6]

Studies like these barely scratch the surface of the sales presentation. At the present time, effective salesmanship must be regarded as an art refined by experience rather than by experimentation, and heavily dependent upon general skills in human relations.

Starting the Sale.   The conversation between salesman and prospect generally begins with some kind of overture by the salesman. Most sales training programs place considerable emphasis upon the initial few seconds of the sales interview. As is true of all interpersonal relationships, impressions formulated early in the interview tend to persist. The salesman wishes to create a highly favorable first impression. He wants a positive halo effect to generalize from him to the product he is selling.

---

[5] J. N. Bauman, "How the Professional Salesman Makes his Approach," *Sales Management,* June 15, 1955, p. 58.

[6] E. J. Fay and W. C. Middleton, "Relationship between Sales Ability and Rating of Transcribed Voices of Salesmen," *Journal of Applied Psychology,* Vol. XXVI (1942), pp. 499–509.

The usual advice when starting the sale is to be friendly and interested in the customer. Such "friendly interest" can be communicated in a number of ways. In addition to the words spoken, the prospect reacts to the salesman's tone of voice, gestures and facial expression, the way he is dressed, the firmness of his handshake, and so on.

During this initial period the salesman should be customer-oriented. His focus is less upon what he wants to sell than upon the customer's characteristics and expressions of needs and interests. The prospect's manner of dress and speech often cues the salesman to the appropriate price range and style. Careful appraisal of the prospect's behavior may lead to an assessment of his readiness to buy and cue the sales approach most likely to be successful with him.

The Sales Presentation. If the prospect appears to be seriously considering a purchase the salesman begins his sales presentation. Some salesmen rely heavily upon a memorized or "canned" presentation. This is a particularly useful crutch for inexperienced and insecure salesmen, and is advocated also by certain companies even for experienced salesmen. If well prepared, this type of presentation assures narration of the complete sales story in a logical and systematic sequence. The danger in memorized sales presentations is that they too often sound stilted, and portions may actually be inappropriate to the prospect's needs or concerns. Thus, in order to be successfully used, it is imperative that the memorized presentations be skillfully presented and modified as necessary in individual instances.

The alternative to a canned talk is the carefully preplanned un-memorized presentation. The salesman using this approach must be thoroughly familiar with his product and those offered by competitors. Since the purpose of the sales presentation is to make the customer aware of the unique benefits he will derive from the product's particular features, the salesman must be "tuned to the prospect's wave length." He must discover the kinds of satisfactions the prospect is seeking and be able to show how his product will provide precisely these satisfactions.

Quite often it is desirable to supplement the verbal portion of the presentation with some kind of dramatization of product superiority. Testimonials, samples, films, photos, and so on all have some utility in this regard. Perhaps the most dramatically useful adjunct to the verbal presentation is an actual demonstration of product features. Car salesmen generally encourage the prospect to take a test drive. Similarly, vacuum sweeper salesmen usually demonstrate the superior suction and dirt-sweeping capability of the model they are selling.

Answering Objections. The prospect who does not voice objections during the sales presentation is rare indeed. Such objections may be raised throughout the sales interview: during the approach, the presentation, and after the presentation when the salesman attempts to close.

Part of the salesman's skill involves differentiating between valid and invalid objections. If, for example, the prospect maintains that the product or service is too expensive for him, or that he has no need for it, he may be raising a valid objection which the salesman would do well to heed. However, these same objections often are raised by prospects in an attempt to dodge the salesman or because the sales presentation has had insufficient impact. "I don't have the money for this" may mean, "I'm too busy to listen now" or "I don't see why I should spend more for your product than the one sold by your competitor." Similarly, "I don't need what you are selling" may mean, "I don't like your approach" or, "I'm accustomed to buying X-brand and don't see why I should change."

The salesman's best defenses against objections are (1) to anticipate and plan for them, (2) to answer directly and factually without either belittling the prospect or attempting to prove him wrong. The argumentative approach to countering objections is not conducive to making sales. Much better is an approach like, "You've raised a good point there. Our research department was concerned with this same problem, so they ran a comparison wherein, . . . and so on." If objections center about cost, the salesman might say something like, "The initial cost *does* seem a little high, but look at these upkeep figures compiled in plants very similar to yours. They show a net saving at the end of the first year of . . . and so on."

Closing the Sale. This is the ultimate test of the effectiveness of the sales presentation. Somewhere along the line the prospect is encouraged to place an order.

The importance of the "psychological moment" for closing the sale often receives considerable attention in discussions of salesmanship. If by this is meant a moment in which the prospect is worn down by the salesman and can be high-pressured into signing on the dotted line, the salesman would do well *not* to attempt to close. Such high pressure closings often lead to subsequent cancellations or, if the order is not canceled, a feeling by the buyer that he has been pushed into making a purchase. Such a feeling does not generally lead to repeat orders.

There are, however, several moments during the presentation in which the prospect gives subtle bodily or verbal cues indicating that he may be willing to buy. Such cues might involve toying with the sample, or asking again about the delivery date. Salesmen use a variety of closing techniques to help the prospect make the decision to buy.

Some salesmen build gradually toward the final decision by a series of smaller *minor decisions*. The customer may be asked to express his preferences for style, color, delivery date, and so on. As the number of minor decisions accumulates, the close becomes merely an extension of the decisions preceding it.

It is possible also to lead to a successful close by stressing some *impending event* making the present a particularly propitious time to buy. Anticipated price increases, changing weather conditions, improving property values, and model changes are but a few of the conditions that may induce a prospect to buy *now*. Stress upon *limited supplies* is a variation of the impending event technique. This is a legitimate closing approach when the item is in such heavy demand that supplies are low or when it is a floor sample or one-of-a-kind. The "get-it-now-it-won't-be-here-later" close is sometimes irritating if it is evident that the salesman is working from an inventory sufficiently deep to cover all foreseeable sales for the next several months! Furthermore, some buyers react negatively to this type of close because of its urgency. They do not like to feel pressured into making a speedy decision. Thus, this approach should be used sparingly and only when, in fact, supplies are limited.

SELECTING SALESMEN

Three general approaches to selecting personnel, including salesmen, were described in earlier chapters: weighted application blanks, standardized interviews, and psychological tests of various kinds. Rather than review these selection procedures, we will direct our attention to some of the special problems indigenous to selecting salesmen.

Kinds of Salesmen

Salesmanship is not a homogeneous activity. The available classifications of sales occupations generally reflect either the nature of the goods and services sold or the type of employer the salesman represents. Although we need not be concerned with particular classificatory schemes, certain distinctions have important implications for selection.

Manufacturer's salesmen represent the manufacturer to wholesalers, retailers, and others who sell to the ultimate consumer. The manufacturer may be represented in a variety of ways: sales engineers generally assist with improving factory operations; merchandising salesmen engage in sales promotion encouraging greater efforts in selling the company's goods; and so on. *Retail salesmen* sell to customers who come into a store generally committed to the purchase of a product. The retail salesman's primary function is to help the customer make the purchase. The skills and requirements for retail salesmen vary considerably from one store to another. In some, he is essentially a purchase-wrapper and change-maker. In others, particularly where a significant amount of brand competition exists, he must engage in a high level of salesmanship.

These differences in function between salesmen servicing industry and those serving retail customers are reinforced by the self-perceptions of salesmen in these two classifications. Industrial salesmen see their job as placing a heavy emphasis upon ingenuity and inventiveness. Retail salesmen see, as prime requirements for success in their job: planning, hard work, and persuading people to their point of view or way of doing things.[7]

Interesting differences between specialty salesmen, route salesmen, and sales engineers emerged from a comparison of Strong Vocational Interest Blank scores earned by representatives of these three groups. The route salesmen tended to display greater interest than either of the other groups in "business details"; the sales engineers tended to be less interested than either of the other groups in "salesmanship" as measured by two subscales of this inventory.[8]

---

[7] M. D. Dunnette and W. K. Kirchner, "Psychological Test Differences between Industrial Salesmen and Retail Salesmen," *Journal of Applied Psychology*, Vol. XLIV (1960), pp. 121–25.

[8] A. A. Witkin, "Differential Interest Patterns in Salesmen," *Journal of Applied Psychology*, Vol. XL (1956), pp. 338–40.

The latter finding is understandable when we recall that sales engineers are technically trained manufacturer's representatives rather than salesmen in the traditional sense.

Results like these support a trend away from the concept of salesmen as a general occupational category and toward the concept of special, more homogeneous, sales occupational groups. In view of the functional differences between various kinds of salesmen, it is unreasonable to expect a single predictor or combination of predictors to be universally applicable for selecting salesmen. Selection procedures must be tailored to the specific requirements and activities of particular sales positions.

Criteria

As of 1945 it was concluded by one reviewer that, all claims to the contrary, no one selection technique had emerged as clearly superior to all others.[9] The emphasis in predicting sales personnel success has shifted somewhat during the past 20 years, with considerable attention devoted recently to biographical inventories and personal history blanks. Newer tests, like those measuring Sales Comprehension and Sales Motivation, have also been proposed.[10] However, to the author's knowledge, the conclusion of 1945 is still applicable today.

Why is it that no one outstanding type of predictor of sales success has been discovered? Part of the answer has already been given in the previous discussion of the heterogeneous nature of positions designated "salesman." A related factor is the problem of identifying a satisfactory criterion of job performance for salesmen.

The criterion problem does not seem especially formidable at first glance. If we want to evaluate the effectiveness of a particular salesman in comparison with others in a comparable position, we might consider using a measure of his productivity: that is, gross sales per unit of time.

Such data usually are readily available but must be corrected for a number of factors in order to make them meaningful as criteria. One such factor is job experience. Salesmen with some experience

---

[9] E. A. Cleveland, "Sales Personnel Research, 1935–1945: A Review," *Personnel Psychology,* Vol. I (1948), pp. 211–55.

[10] M. M. Bruce, "A Sales Comprehension Test," *Journal of Applied Psychology,* Vol. XXXVIII (1954), pp. 302–4.

M. M. Bruce, *Examiner's Manual, Sales Motivation Inventory* (New Rochelle, N.Y.: Author, 1953).

tend to make more sales per unit of time than inexperienced sales-men, other things being equal. Secondly, it would be necessary to adjust for the potential of the sales territory or outlet. Certain geo-graphical areas, cities, and neighborhoods are more likely to be pro-ductive for the salesman than others both because of population density and receptivity to the particular commodity being sold. Third, a correction must be applied for orders that are later re-scinded or upon which payment is defaulted. It would probably be wise also to adjust gross sales per unit of time for such factors as repeat orders subsequently placed, and the productivity of a par-ticular territory prior to the time the salesman in question ac-quired it.

Assuming that a reasonably adequate correction could be devised and applied to a record of gross sales, there is yet the issue of ap-propriateness of such a criterion. Adjusted sales is only a partial in-dex of success because, when considered alone, it neglects the im-portant factor of termination/survival. The effective salesman, defined by adjusted gross sales, who remains with the company for a long period of time is a greater asset to that company than the equally effective salesman who terminates his employment after relatively brief tenure. Predictors of adjusted gross sales may be relatively ineffective for a termination/survival criterion and vice versa.

It is obvious that as the time interval between initial selection and measurement of a performance criterion increases, the criterion itself becomes increasingly contaminated by the factor of voluntary job termination. It has been hypothesized that for studies involving a relatively brief time interval between selection and criterion measurement (that is, when voluntary termination is not a signifi-cant factor) successful prediction will depend much more upon measures of *ability* than interest. Conversely, predictions made against a delayed criterion will depend more upon *interest* than ability since the former reflects a desire to stay with a particular company or in a particular position.[12] Regardless of the merits of this suggestion for improving the accuracy of selecting salesmen, it calls attention to the issue of criterion contamination and the con-sequence of such contamination for reducing predictive efficiency.

---

[12] L. W. Ferguson, "Ability, Interest and Aptitude," *Journal of Applied Psychology*, Vol. XLIV (1960), pp. 126–31.

SUMMARY

To the present, psychologists have devoted relatively little attention to a study of salesmanship *per se*. Whatever research has been done in this general area has been directed almost exclusively to the matters of selecting and training salesmen. Current thinking about the conduct of sales interviews and the effectiveness of various kinds of sales presentations is based more upon experience than upon the results of carefully controlled investigation.

Advertising and selling are closely related in that both aim to persuade potential buyers to purchase products or avail themselves of services. However, while advertising appeals to the mass market, selling appeals to the individual consumer. Thus, advertising is a form of preselling whereby the buying public is informed about the existence and special features of a product or service. The salesman attempts to personalize the strengths of the product or service so it is perceived as beneficial by individual consumers.

Early approaches to salesmanship capitalized upon the use of selling formulas. These formulas assumed that buyers are relatively passive and that their thinking proceeded in a uniform and predictable stream through several rather distinct stages.

More recently this rather naive approach to salesmanship has been replaced by one capitalizing upon need-satisfaction. The buyer's needs are regarded as central to the selling process. The salesman's behavior assumes importance only as a vehicle for promising and providing need-satisfaction. The fundamental implication of this approach to salesmanship is that since every prospect is a unique individual with unique needs, every sales presentation must be custom-tailored to him.

Effective salesmanship is heavily dependent upon general skills in human relations. The salesman must express friendly interest in the prospect when starting the sale. His presentation should be carefully preplanned to spotlight unique product strengths and suited to the needs of individual prospects. He should be skilled in differentiating between valid and invalid objections, accepting the former and dealing with the latter without belittling the prospect. Finally, he must be able to close the sale without high pressuring the customer.

Two problems of particular significance to selecting effective salesmen are (1) the diversity of duties of and requirements for different kinds of salesmen, and (2) the inadequacies of various criteria of selling "success." Thus, it is unreasonable to expect a single predictor or combination of predictors to be universally applicable for selecting salesmen. Selection procedures must be tailored to the specific requirements of particular sales positions.

Indexes

Name Index

403

Subject Index

407

This book has been set in 11 on 13 and 10 on 11 Caledonia. Part titles are 24 point Goudy Handtooled; chapter titles are 24 point Goudy Old Style. The size of the type page is 27 by 45½ picas.